VIOLENCE AND RELIGION
Cross-Cultural Opinions and Consequences

About the Author

Ralph Tanner has a B.Sc. and Diploma in Social Anthropology from Oxford University and a D Phil in Law from Stockholm University. He has done fieldwork in Thailand, the Philippines, Guyana, Zambia, Zimbabwe, Tanzania, Uganda and Kenya as well as in Britain and Eire. He was Chairman of the East African Institute of Social Research and Lecturer in Comparative Religion in the University of London. He has published books on Murder in Uganda, Witchcraft killings and religious change in Tanzania, modern religions and successful change and a cross cultural study of the Roman Catholic Mass. He has co-authored books on the social ecology of religion, the recreation of tribal identity and religious change and on religion and the environment. He has written numerous articles on the social aspects of religious change, translation and language use in religion, as well as on behavioural theories in the Journal of Modern African Studies, Africa, Journal of the Social Sciences, Nordic Journal of African Studies, Anthropos, Studia Missionalia and others. He has just completed a study of the issues involved in social science fieldwork in developing countries by nationals and in on-nationals and is currently working on a cross cultural study of spirituality, well being and health.

VIOLENCE AND RELIGION
Cross-Cultural Opinions and Consequences

R.E.S. Tanner

CONCEPT PUBLISHING COMPANY PVT. LTD.
NEW DELHI-110059

ISBN-13: 978-81-8069-376-2

Edition 2017

Published and Printed by

Concept
Since 1974

Concept Publishing Company Pvt. Ltd.
A/15-16, Commercial Block, Mohan Garden
New Delhi-110059 (India)
T: 25351460, 25351794, *F*: 091-11-25357109
E: publishing@conceptpub.com, W: www.conceptpub.com
Editorial Office: H-13, Bali Nagar, New Delhi-110 015, India.

Cataloging in Publication Data--Courtesy: D.K. Agencies (P) Ltd. <docinfo@dkagencies.com>

Tanner, R. E. S. (Ralph E. S.), 1921-
Violence and religion : cross-cultural opinions and consequences / R.E.S. Tanner.
p. cm.
Includes bibliographical references (p.)
Includes index.
ISBN 9788180693762

1. Violence—Religious aspects—Cross-cultural studies. 2. Religion and sociology—Cross-cultural studies. I. Title.

DDC 306.6 22

For
Amoret

Preface

The reasons for writing a book even if it is the culmination of research remain obscure. My reason for examining the connections between religion and violence come from my experiences before I entered university life which had a lasting effect.

In the highlands of Myanmar I remember Protestant Kachins explaining that they had killed Buddhist Shans, my Urdu 'munshi' telling me that I should keep my copy of the Koran properly and respectfully covered when it was not being used, a Sukuma pastor quietening a potential riot by praying for reconciliation, a Hindu showing me his personal picture of Krishna but which because of pollution I was not allowed to touch and the Roman Catholic priest who was killed by guerrillas in Rhodesia and another who was tortured by the Japanese Kempitai, and the screaming of Muslim children as they were being circumcised in coastal Tanzania. Finally, the fact that the five million Sukuma who were not particularly interested in becoming either Christians or Muslims despite a century of exposure to these religious alternatives.

So long before the destruction of the World Trade Centre by Muslim terrorists or seekers for entry to Paradise, I was personally aware that religions could be dangerous not only because of their violence but because of their self-defined exclusivities. There were either/or binary states of mind in which I myself was involved while there were whole cultures with dominating religious ideas did not seem to need to be violent with others of different beliefs, although within their own faiths they were quite violent. It was stimulating to be exposed to such over-demanding paradoxes.

I also became aware that despite the amount of contemporary violence which had some relationship to religion, it was not acceptable to most Western thinkers to make any such connection. It was much the same with the biological rather than psychological influences of religion on which I have also written. It was regrettably acceptable and understandable to fight over economic, social and political issues, but to fight over religious issues were often passed over and despite Northern Ireland and Kossovo, and perhaps were often thought of only in the African and Asian contexts of economically underdeveloped societies.

So this study approaches violence and religion with an acceptance that they have been and are connected and their correlations should be examined without any particular religious, cultural or ethnic considerations and more particularly to avoid seeing this matter as largely an historical issue. Violence connected with religion is a major feature of contemporary societies from which few if any are exempt.

R.E.S. Tanner

Acknowledgements

My thanks are due to the Librarians of Trinity College, University of Oxford, the Institute of Social Anthropology, University of Oxford and the Tadley branch of the Hampshire County Library.

My thanks are also due to my memories of the formative help which I received from Sao Hkun Hkio of Mongmit, Dashi Yaw of the Kodaung, Myanmar and from Juma Ndamulo, Nfumo Kabadi and Ntemi Kapongo of the Sukuma,Tanzania and above all to the artist, poet and author Poppy Dell who enabled my work to develop over the years.

Contents

PART B
VIOLENCE AND FEAR WITHIN RELIGIONS

PART D
COMPARATIVE FACTORS IN CONSIDERING RELIGIOUS VIOLENCE

1

Introduction

The combination of religion and violence in a single phrase is an unhappy one and religious thinkers spend much of their time avoiding this conjunction and in suggesting that it is only valid in certain circumstances which are invariably one sided. Many who have no particular religious beliefs would even suggest that violence is a consequence of being religious in the first place and that the irrationality of such beliefs makes violence if not inevitable at least likely.

Up to recently most Westerners if they considered religious violence at all would have seen it as something which had occurred in western history and out of which they had intellectually and politically grown. Furthermore this was the type of behaviour to be expected in ethnically different less economically and politically developed cultures elsewhere in the world.

The British may vaguely remember the Crusades but not the barbarous behaviour of the Christians and the more restrained Muslim response under such leaders as Saladin. The French with their greater historical sense may remember the Roman Catholic killing of Protestants on St Bartholomew's Day in AD1572 but not the Roman Catholic Breton rebellions against the First Republic. For the Spanish the throwing off of the Muslim occupation of the south after several centuries of intermittent warfare may well be a part of folk memory enshrined in the song of Roland and Oliver which enlarged a minor skirmish into heroism.

Even those Westerners with some memories of their own domestic religious violence know nothing of Tamurlane, the 'earth shaker' who destroyed the agricultural civilisations of Central Asia for religious reasons or the Taiping rebellion 1851-64 in China under a religious leader who considered himself to be the brother of Jesus Christ which resulted in an estimated 20 million dead. We forget that the Partition of India led to murderous religious violence on a massive scale between Hindus, Muslims and Sikhs and that this has occurred much more recently on a smaller but still horrendous scale in Bosnia, Croatia and Serbia which are European countries. We also forget that in a mainly Roman Catholic Ruanda Christians organised and at best just participated in widespread massacres leaving some one million dead and millions more homeless.

Perhaps the Western approach to and understanding of religion comes from the European Enlightenment of the 18th century which requires definitions of what is believed in and if it could not be defined it was just superstition. This pattern of thinking sees religious activities and beliefs as behaviour on the fringes of necessity and religious practices as more or less deviant at best if not downright abnormal, reflecting psychological weaknesses and an overall sign of traditional backwardness.

While the Western world has continued to see religious violence as particularly Asian and at best endemic in the Indian subcontinent, it has failed to accept that it has occurred and persisted in contemporary Europe. In the last hundred years there have been pogroms against Jews in Russia and Poland, the Holocaust German killing of the Jews, half a century of violence in Palestine between Jews and Muslims initiated by Western colonists, a religious civil war in the Lebanon and something approaching this in Northern Ireland which has lasted even longer as well as the division of Greece, Crete and Cyprus on religious lines typified by the desecration of Christian cemeteries. The break-up of Yugoslavia along religious lines so that even bus drivers going through the road blocks of the United Nations Peace Keeping Force refer to the demarcation lines as the boundary between East and West. A retired United States professional diplomat commented that 'conflict along the fault line between Western and Islamic civilizations.... as the flash points for crises and bloodshed has been going on for 1300 years...this military interaction is unlikely to decline' (Huntington, 1993: 29). Lastly, the terrorist attacks in the United States, Russia and Israel are greeted there with some incredulity that in this day and age religious beliefs should be held so strongly that young Muslims could kill and be killed for such irrational ends.

Social scientists, economists and political analysts have generally forecast that with economic development based on pragmatism and widespread secularised education, religion would become a private matter and wherever it appeared in public, it would have the appearance of deviance and abnormality. It was certainly not to be seen as a major problem equalling the ideological and material schisms of the long Cold War.

It is not only Islamic nationalism in the Middle East, Eastern Europe and in the break-up of the Soviet Union that religion is becoming prominent and violent but also in the Philippines, Indonesia, Kashmir and the Sudan, and there is also the growth of aggressive Hindu and Buddhist nationalism in India and Sri Lanka against Muslim and Hindu minorities respectively.

The Understanding of Religion and the Problem of Definitions

The initial difficulty in connecting violence to religious ideas and practices is that both these key words seem clear enough to common-sense understandings; everyone knows what they mean, but this clarity is far from simple and varies with almost every category employed. The passivity of the supposed sayings of the Buddha written down three centuries after his death and the violence of the Words of God in the Koran as well as the range of violence from blood shedding to bullying, all have to be considered.

There is also the simple fact that any monotheistic administration of a religious definition beyond the purely personal, divides those 'within' from those 'without'. Christians have never had any difficulty in killing large numbers of unbelievers and large numbers of outsiders as well which was once less common with Muslims. The Eastern religions with their absence of definitions appear less likely to be involved in religiously motivated violence.

The Understanding of Religion

In thinking about religion, the ideas and practices of the Great Traditions (Redfield, 1956) dominate. Around the ideas and practices of the Lord Buddha, Jesus Christ the Son of God, the Prophet Mohammad the Messenger of Allah and the sacred books of Judaism and Hinduism, there has grown up theological and philosophical thought and an establishment of thinkers and practitioners of a single religion who sincerely believe in the rectitude of one religious foundation. Further it is believed that the followers of these faiths should model their lives on these ideas as recorded in writing and this in turn frequently becomes a source of stress and violence.

The difficulty here is that while most believers accept that their faith is based on a Great Tradition, a long term vision of what they should do to have any hope of supernatural fulfilment, it is not of much help in their immediate lives. Thus it is for most if not all believers that the Little Tradition takes over and provides for their immediate religious needs. A comprehensive range of practices, decried or tolerated by the administrators of the Great Tradition religions which fulfil the needs of millions of believers whether in Beijing, Banaras, Benin or Birmingham. They want supernatural help to ameliorate if not to change their individual, familial or communal misfortunes or the major difficulties affecting them from outside in the forms of famine and war.

This leads to a further problem in that the differences between the Great and Little Traditions coalesce around the terms 'religion' and 'magic'. Both relate to the supernatural and are thus beyond pragmatic analysis. It may well be that this difference is not only beyond any satisfactory analytical distinction but comes down to a question of status. Magic is inferior to religion and that its practitioners are assumed to be less intellectually developed. What then is the status of petitionary prayer at Lourdes (Harris, R., 1999) and Medjugorje (Bax., 1995) or while bathing in the Ganges during the Kumba Mela on a particular lunar date? Whether anyone sees these practices as devotions within the highest ideals of the Great Traditions or merely giving way to the irrational fears related to personal anxieties organised within the Little Traditions, depends now as it has always done on personal understandings and situational factors which may well vary from day to day.

However even for those steeped in the ideas or practices of either of these traditions as part of their on-going social as much as religious lives, there is an awareness of the other one and most believers fluctuate between the two. The regularities of religious practices in church, mosque, synagogue or temple are in terms of the Great Tradition while the personal prayers and practices impelled by personal difficulties are those of the Little Tradition.

These popular and regular practices may provide the cementing incentives for these faiths within both Traditions in which the Great has little connection with what goes on. The seasonal parades of Hindus and Muslims in India and of Protestants in Northern Ireland are the dyadic occasions for violence and not demonstrations of the personal self-abnegation required by their faiths.

There is, therefore, the analytical problem of activities which are labelled religious but which have little beyond this attribution to connect what is going on with the officially defined supernatural aspects of their faiths. The pagoda festivals in Myanmar have gambling as a popular feature for which the rights are auctioned.

The least economically developed societies which have no long or widespread connection with literacy, may not have a word for 'religion' and if asked what is their religion, using an imported word, they give an ethnic answer. In their intellectualising of the relationships with the supernatural, they will see religious activities as part of social life and only isolatable if an outsider wants to classify it as such. A sacrifice to an ancestor, prayers for aid to a Sufi Saint or the carrying of a sacred statue are related to social standing and other factors. Their thinking can be on the basis of a cost-benefit analysis as to what they might get out of it and as much the basis for violence as any other social activity; the non-literate subsistence farmers and casual workers are pragmatists.

Of course, there are situations in which the Great Tradition predominates as in the formal prayers inside a dedicated building or at a shrine, but even here secular factors creep in over how much time can be spent doing 'nothing' and noisy interruptions from outside can lead to violence.

In the possible relationships with violence, religions must surely be classified without differentiating between magical and religious practices which is usually an intellectualised definition made by outside non-believers and to accept that the Great and Little Traditions mingle with personal needs and fluctuate almost on an hourly basis. Furthermore that always in the context of violence, religious ideas and practices cannot be analytically separated from economic, political and environmental aspects.

The Meaning of Violence

The definition of violence in the Oxford English Dictionary (OED., 1956, 2359) goes far beyond pain and the shedding of blood. It is firstly the exercise of physical force so as to damage persons or property, but more importantly for our purposes the forcible interference with personal freedom, violent or passionate conduct or language; finally, passion or fury.

So clearly religious violence cannot just be seen in its more obvious sense of killing or wounding and destroying property for religious reasons. More importantly for our needs is the use of the abstract word 'freedom' in these definitions, so threatening others for a religious purpose must be part of our discussion on religious violence.

In considering religious violence, self-expression on one side of a religious divide, can be seen and experienced as violence by those on the other side. Newspaper comments on the Miss World competition in Nigeria linking the occasion with the Prophet Mohammad led to the burning of its offices in a northern state by Islamic fundamentalists. So into this perspective comes journalism, satire, graffiti, posters, cinema and theatre performances, religiously justified domestic abuse and books even those of academic analysis and sport where the teams are known to have specific religious affiliations as the long rivalry between Roman Catholic Celtic and Protestant Rangers football teams in Scotland which often led to rioting.

The more obvious aspects of religious violence which are associated with individual self-imposed martyrdoms and massacres for religious reasons have been a constant feature of known history. Very much in the public mind is active suicide in which an individual kills himself in New York or Israel as they kill others and this has a long history. There is also passive suicide to avoid religious debasement as in the mass suicide of the Jewish defenders of Masada (Yadin, 1970), and death in a religious war by which those killed gain supernatural benefits as in the recent Iraq-Iran war came under both categories and is similarly common enough.

Any definition has also to cover body mutilations required by religious practices such as the acts of Shia Moslems in commemoration of the martyrdom of Ali, Christians copying of the crucifixion, the circumcision of Muslim women and Jewish and Muslim men and the amputation of the hands of thieves under Islamic laws. There is also physical mortification for the sake of personal religion; self-denial through private pain which is common in both Christianity and Hinduism.

There is also indirect killing where religious warfare destroys an environment and many more die from starvation and disease than from the sword and gun as in the Christian siege of Damietta in AD 1219 when almost all the Muslim population died of hunger (Oliver, 1894), paralleled by the current situation in the southern Sudan. A parallel example would be the Xhosa killing of their cattle and refusing to cultivate in the late 1850s on the advice of a prophetess which led to a marked population loss.

There is also the violence to animals in the obligatory killing of enormous numbers by pilgrims on the Hajj which for a century or more has been far in excess of any possible local consumption by the needy. There is also the killing by special methods enjoined by both Judaism and Islam which involves morally questionable violence to animals.

There is also the massive destruction of property which might cover the use of trees to make paper for religious publications as well as its direct use in hostilities such as has been seen recently with the public burning of copies of Rushdie's '*Satanic Verses*'. The destruction of property and people because of their religious significance such as the current burning of mosques and churches in Nigeria and Indonesia and the wholesale wastage of the environment as in the Lebanese civil war has far exceeded the human and material losses of the destruction of the World Trade Centre in 2001.

Much more subtle and difficult to define is verbal violence for religious reasons. Violent words in the mass media are perhaps now a common place feature of Islamic broadcasts and are just as common in areas of inter-religious tension as in the abuse of Roman Catholic children going to school through a Protestant area of Belfast, the principle city in Northern Ireland. More obliquely Israeli television crews having to stop work because of the muezzins' calls to prayer through loud-speakers (Armstrong, 1992: 533). On another level the ability to be verbally abusive for religious reasons may be an aspect of the restricted linguistic code identified in English (Bernstein, 1975), which must be a feature of other languages as it is common enough in the verbal abuse of contemporary Muslim and Hindu crowds in religiously motivated demonstrations in contemporary India.

Definitions and Typologies of Religion and Violence

So we see that the joining together of religion and violence in a single all-embracing phrase involves the need for wide ranging rather than confining definitions. We take religion to involve any beliefs or practices for which there are no pragmatic foundations other than belief although there may be basic historical facts behind some activities. Such a definition would cover not only the heavily institutionalised religions supported by theological and philosophical reasoning which have often been involved in violent confrontations in Israel, Sri Lanka, the Philippines, Sudan, Afghanistan and the USA, as well as beliefs which have resulted in such events as the recent mass killings of witches in Tanzania and the spirit cult civil war in northern Uganda.

Violence is even more difficult to define because it has to cover both words and actions causing both physical and psychological damage to both people, property, animals and the environment. Violence against the person as in suicide abetted or encouraged by a religion as in the mass Jonestown suicides of 1978 (Lasaga, 1980) as well as self-mutilation for religious purposes and sacrifices of both people and animals. There are also various forms of direct and indirect violence based on religious differences as well as violence to the already dead in cemeteries and numerous forms of curses by the dead and the living on their descendents and against those against whom they have grudges.

Outside scientific classifications and perhaps even within them, there are inevitable problems over typologies covering human behaviour. Any religious activity fits clearly into a classification only at the centre of its range and at each end it inevitably elides into the adjoining categories. Martyrdom may seem to a clear enough category but there are difficulties over degrees of premeditation and circumstantial pressures as well as psychological predispositions as in the recent re-evaluation that most Hindu widows who committed suicide on the funeral pyres of their husbands were forced to do so (Mani, 1992).

An individual may be destroying property or killing individuals of another religion for reasons which they themselves state to be religious or that these actions have nothing to do with religion which were just coincidental or based on personal grudges related to business. Apart from whether these statements are believable in a particular social environment, there are usually a range of non-religious connecting, correlating or causal factors in which the time scale may involve everything from immediacy to centuries old remembered tensions.

Thus there is the almost insuperable problem of classification when a human act which appears to have religious elements is on the margin between sub-categories which already involve macro-distinctions over these same boundaries. An assumption of intellectual probity in making such distinctions is no guarantee of accuracy and may indeed be no more than an act of faith within an academic environment. When indeed and to what extent is religious violence a facet of economics, politics, personal hostility and psychopathology?

The Division between Eastern and Western Religious Understandings

The differences between East and West in their understandings of religious violence is usually shown in the fact that it is only noted when it comes into prominence; some unusual event such as the destruction of the World Trade Centre by Islamic suicide pilots or in the context of unusual religious activities which are usually defined as deviancy. The visibly distinctive Amish and the Nation of Islam believers are examples of behaviour which is deviant from the normalities of Americanism, but which in terms of their own religious ideas is totally rational from its religious bases and that other Americans are regrettably too blind to realise their deprivations as they are outsiders to the Truth.

Although most Western societies, if pushed, would describe themselves if not exactly as Christian at least as inheritors of a Christian tradition but which is no longer a prominent part of public life and thinking, religious affiliation is not the first thing that comes to mind in the context of Swedish, Canadian or British cultures. Such people are more inclined to describe their societies as multi-cultural or multi-ethnic rather than multi-religious and such events as the My-Lai massacre of Vietnamese civilians by American soldiers did not involve religious issues (Kelman & Hamilton, 1989). This study of obedience did not contain any reference to Islam and Islamic States in which religion is a dominant issue for a very wide range of public and private behaviour and in which Muslims are required to be obedient to the interpreted requirements of Allah recorded by the Prophet Mohammad in the Koran.

It is hard to see religious motivations as dominating the behaviour of many Western people except in the case of conscientious objectors in World Wars First and Second. Indeed it is quite exceptional for communities rather than individuals to put themselves in danger to protect others for religious reasons as with Le Chambon the village in southern France that hid many non-French Jews during the Nazi occupation and the Vichy years (Hallie, 1979). Any study of religious violence has to consider not only those that carry out violence but also those who fail to make any effort to stop it which enables violence to continue.

The Great Tradition in the Eastern religions retain their ambiguous and amorphous nature combining authority from those who choose to expound it and who are accepted as charismatic interpreters with the accepted ability of individuals to mingle this with their own understandings without being restricted by orthodoxy. The Western monotheistic religions do not have this plasticity as they are either/or religions in what they believe and in what believers are required to do.

In the Christian West the rationalization of religion in modern societies combined literacy and professional organisations, but the preoccupation of theologians with logical consistency antedates the Enlightenment by several centuries in the fundamental works writings of Saint Thomas Aquinas in which conclusions came from the data presented. There had to be a right answer to any problem and thus religion situated on the edges of rationalism came to be based on specialised theological and philosophical understandings and the European Enlightenment. The effect of this in religious thinking in the Christian West tended to confine its appeal to the upper echelons of society protected by wealth, education and employment from the more immediate strains of living.

Divine intervention came to be relegated to the popular religious practices of individuals and fringe groups away from the clear cut boundaries of defined faiths in which believers were either 'in' or 'out', either a Baptist or a Roman Catholic, whereas in the eastern religions there are numerous examples of individuals belonging to different faiths at the same time.

The distinctions between the Great and Little Traditions apply just as much in Western societies as elsewhere. This upper status faith and practice is differentiated from the rituals and beliefs of the mass of the population. It is a specialised and specialising faith which is little concerned with or have impact upon either the routine activities of day-to-day life or the grand projects of political leadership (Giddens. 1985: 71-73).

Orthodox Judaism with its obsessive ritualism based on their Holy books and a professional quasi-priesthood has cut itself off from being attractive to a wider population. Islam on the other hand makes fewer obligatory and sanctified demands on their faithful except where it is the State religion committed to following and administering

Islamic law as developed by its theological lawyers interpreting the Koran after the death of the Prophet Mohammad.

The Eastern religions have not been affected by rationalization and the evolution of restricting and excluding definitions and have remained far more usable to be picked up when needed and at least historically not so involved in religiously related violence. The Hindus see their cosmologies as a kind of see-saw movement in which mutations arise due to the magnetic influence of great personalities giving new directions (Aiyappan, 1968: 46-48). Their Great Traditions remain as a backdrop of accepted and acceptable religious specialisation not overtly separated from their Little Traditions by definitions and bounded institutions.

It may be prudent to see definitions more narrowly in the context of the authority with which they are made and their applicability. Definitions never sit in a society as abstractions since they have none of the qualities of inorganic chemistry. Whether a definition is seen as applicable to religion and to violence, depends on the personal and social situations of those who are using them and for what purposes. A definition is for the use of the definers and not in the first instance for those whose activities are being defined. Any coincidence between definitions and behaviour in the enormous spread of possible and actual variations of behaviour to which it is being applied is more often than not accidental.

Therefore, it is prudent to see the correlations of religions to violence not in the simplicities of East-West dichotomies, and ethnicities, levels of education and economic and political development but in four broad types of societies types; polytheistic oriental, monotheistic western, polytheistic Indian and African traditional societies with their concern for sorcery (Hsu, 1972).

George Kennan, the retired ambassador of the United States to Stalinist Russia who became an active scholar commented (Kennan, 2000: 98) that the Holocaust had brought home to a great many that in a large proportion of humanity if some of the cultural restraints and civilising customs are put to too great a test, there prove to be resources of unmitigated cruelty and evil in most human psyches. He concluded that the bestial potentialities of the human psyche are probably almost everywhere inexistence.

This study endeavours to explore not only the extent of obvious religious violence including the relative simplicities of terrorism but its widespread social and political potential and presence among believers in every faith. It has to cover the extent to which religion restricts alternatives and while it has often been involved in violence, there is also its failure to prevent violence despite the wide ranging contemporary theological and philosophical insistence on the essentially peaceful nature of all faiths, has also to be examined.

PART A

Background Considerations for Assessing Religious Violence

Violence is an obvious form of behaviour which is often defined as an unpleasant aspect of human behaviour in general and certainly in the circumstances in which it is seemingly related to religion. We need to know what, if any, is the relationship of violence to human nature; what part is nature and what part is attributable to nurture. Are there biological predispositions which are genetic or at least ethologically explicable and to what extent does psychology explain this form of behaviour? Is there any information to be gained from the behaviour of the higher primates which might make humans predisposed to violence both within and without their own social groups? Does psychology provide information on how the mind creates the need for or triggers off violence in otherwise normally quiet individuals and how might this affect group behaviour?

Then there are problems of meaning which would seem easy enough to solve when every dictionary will define both religion and violence, but this becomes much more complicated on examination. We find that meanings adapt to circumstances and experience, as well as metaphysical interventions, and are divided between those applicable to communities and individuals, the tensions of conscience, semantic codifications and the difficulties of translations. Religion and violence in one language do not have the same meanings in another.

Finally, it is necessary to look at religious morality and how these may correlate to the possibilities and realities of violence with which they may be directly or indirectly involved. Thus, it divides between the Great and Little Traditions in the main religions, Buddhism, Hinduism, Taoism, Christianity and Islam as well as the undercurrents which may have come from the unrecorded past in current traditional and covert personal faiths.

2

The Human Background to Religious Violence

Religious practices and ideas are to be seen and understood in their human form regardless of what theologians state to be their divine origin. This is not to deny the reality of these beliefs which may indeed be true but how these systems of understanding operate with humans means that we have first to investigate how they may develop in humans biologically, environmentally and psychologically. These practices cannot be evaluated independently of what humans may or may not be capable of doing or thinking as there are always limiting and enabling boundaries.

The Biological Disposition to be Violent

The physical ability to be violent would be a necessary prerequisite for religious violence; to think violently is not enough and it has to be put into bodily form. Abuse has to be vocalised and some part of the body has to be involved. Thus even the mentally and physically handicapped are capable of violence for a religious issue about which they may or may not have any understandings.

There are two aspects in which human biology might be correlated to religious violence; changes or states originating within the body and having effects on its functions and changes or states caused by the ingestion of outside substances.

The functions of the endocrine system vary with sex and stress. Testosterone is associated with aggressiveness in the male and oestrogen in the female which can turn to aggression in defence of their young or in situations in which their status is ambivalent. This is all very general and perhaps tied closely to the oestrous cycle. In humans the non-seasonal menstrual cycle may or may not lead to any seasonal endocrine enhancing tensions.

Stress does cause rises in the testosterone levels and this is as likely as any other social situation to be associated with religion as when individuals feel that their status after their deaths is being threatened by non-believers or others and in material senses when the believers in one religion invade the social spaces of another faith.

Interpreted or experienced stress which can turn to aggressiveness (Wilson, 1975: 244) can be based on encounters with outsiders to the group, territorial intruders such as intrusive religious processions of one faith through the area psychologically or socially owned by another faith. We know from ethnology that no group is happy with intruders and prefers its own company and in that sense the Christian ecumenical movement except as a moral imperative is unlikely to attract.

Aggressiveness over food supplies is not likely to involve religion directly if it is just a survival requirement but in some New Guinea societies in which pigs are accumulated for communal sacrifices and feasting, it might well be a source of violence or when food is stored by the members of one faith and not shared with others in times of difficulty.

Overcrowding which is biologically experienced but psychologically interpreted can turn to aggressiveness but not inevitably; Tokyo is densely populated with a low rate of violence while Calcutta is the reverse. Separating groups of people who see their hostilities in religious terms as in Belfast with fences dividing Protestant from Roman Catholic areas may reduce some forms of violence but not the effects of such inter-religious stress on the endocrine system because social life cannot be kept entirely within such boundaries.

Lastly, there is the seasonality of violence which cannot in humans be correlated to breeding tensions but group and individual aggressiveness does tend to be seasonal. In Christian societies Christmas tends to have higher levels of violence as people come together who do not normally associate and systems of control are then less efficient, particularly as higher intakes of alcohol are involved.

Seasonality is certainly involved in aggressiveness in which biology and social behaviour combine. Extreme climatic conditions may prevent violence and religious fighting is less likely to take place in the monsoon, with snow on the ground or in extreme heat. Since these conditions have existed climatically for a very long time, there might well be some genetic correlations with the presence or absence of religious aggressiveness. This is certainly one of the factors by which public order authorities rate their need for preparedness. In Northern Ireland where there is what the police refer to as 'the marching season' when the annual Protestant processions of the Orange Order are certain to provoke Roman Catholics and much the same will apply to the Indian Police when the year comes round to the annual religious festival processions of Hindus and Muslims through the cities in which these communities are intermingled and have been so for centuries.

If animals can be trained to be aggressive, then certainly it is just as likely and indeed more so for humans who have the ability to organise for any religious or secular purpose. Humans alone have the ability to adapt immediately to stress but the effect of stress on the endocrine system is likely to be highly variable. Stress itself is variable as the social conditions in which it appears and the humans experiencing stress do not have the uniformities assessable in less complicated species. What one person might assess as a religious disagreement verging on violence could be seen by others as a well argued difference of opinion, and in another situation the riot was not seen as inter-religious at all but a creation of the police for their own purposes.

The endocrine system itself as it relates to aggressiveness is an adaptive one which is going to change between states of preparedness of indeterminate length, the quick responsiveness to an emergency and the consequences of active or passive aggressiveness. Individuals may learn to cope with both types of aggressive experience through meditation and this would cause endocrine changes.

The ambivalence of relating stress to endocrine change is shown in a group of white American women in Boston in 1975 kneeling in the street to protest against the busing of children from one part of the city to another in order to have a more racially integrated education. Even allowing for individual variations, the stressful effects may well have cancelled each other out; prayer pulling one way, anger against the authorities another, the comfort of solidarity and conflict with those whose street they were blocking apart from the physical strain of kneeling on the ground (Broom and Selznick, 1977: 11).

We can conclude that while endocrine changes can be correlated to individual aggressiveness but with a large number of influences increasing or inhibiting its expression, it is hard to see it having any group correlations so that a large number of men should have similar increases in testosterone and that this alone would led to group violence in a religious situation.

The second factor is the possibility of outside chemicals influencing behaviour in both individuals and groups in a religious situations. Of course there are cases in which individual violence appears to have been initiated by drug taking but as with most examples of extreme behaviour it is very much a biased assessment working backwards from violence and without any possibility of any control group of people being subject to the same predisposing conditions.

Most drug taking for religious purposes induces passivity as in the use of 'peyote' cactus seeds by American Indians in long night sessions and in more westernised social environments where hallucinogenic drugs are used in the search for personal enlightenment. Even the use of drugs for enabling killings by the mediaeval Muslim Assassins involved individuals rather than groups. Excessive eating of meat by the cattle herding Maasai men is associated with outbreaks of hysteric religious behaviour, the leaping up and down and becoming possessed but the same meat-eating behaviour by Americans and Argentines is likely to induce lethargy.

Alcohol is certainly a factor in some inter-religious rioting but this is more likely to be the result of breaking into liquor stores rather than as a collective act prior to religious violence. The action of any chemical on bodily functions does not necessarily commit those individuals to either aggressiveness or passivity and for such ingestion to have an effect on groups of individuals to make them aggressive would certainly require a promoting social environment.

If we look at bodily formation and what it is capable of doing, it is obviously highly adaptive and successfully so in the survival and development of the human species. Of course, the body is adapted to being both violent and reacting to violence, but nothing biological can be so narrowly specific as to tie the human being to being naturally and inevitably aggressive. Throwing a cricket ball in a game and a stone in a religious protest demonstration are similar actions just as are hitting a ball and beating a drum to drown out the sounds of a rival religious group.

It is safe to conclude that biological characteristics allow humans to be aggressive for religious or any other reasons should they wish and the circumstances permit, but it has no genetically controlled inevitability.

Ethology and Religious Violence

The question has to be asked as to whether humans are genetically programmed for violence as a whole or is it a characteristic of the species only or does it occur in certain situations for which there are structural/functional explanations (Eibl-Eibesfeldt, 1975).

It is certainly an attractive theory that humans and the higher primates have certain behavioural features in common, but there are numerous snags to any such assumption when one accepts that even bacteria have differences between them in the situations in which they are presumed to be passively involved but to which they react.

It is easy enough to find some parallels between the behaviour of higher primates and humans but any such comparison is not just between species in which for comparative terms it is assumed that all chimpanzees are the same and similarly that humans are biologically a single species. Once one leaves the concept of the animal as a single species and the humans as another, there are problems over comparison going further than the characteristics detailed in theoretical biology which outline the physical differences (Hinde, 1987).

Human behaviour cannot be explained in terms of ideal situations in which anyone questioned will detail what they think they should do as a result of socialisation when it has to be accepted that evasions of what is required by society, even when codified in law and custom, are likely to be far commoner than compliance. We cannot use data from observing primate behaviour as if they were forms of comparable data.

There are differences in the cognitive abilities within the higher primates. Just as much as there are in humans; hyper-intelligent chimpanzees and humans and ones in each category who are less than bright and it can perhaps be assumed that this intelligence is a composition of both innate and socialised abilities (Reynolds, 1986).

Secondly, there is the factor of culture in which humans have developed in a great variety of social situations, so much so that Papuans, Paraguayans, and Pathans would have trouble in understanding what each might be doing if only because they do not speak the same language. A primate may have a very limited vocabulary of sounds with social meanings, whereas an educated Chinese may have seventeen different ways of expressing the concept of 'happiness' (Bauer, 1976: 9). Humans live in widely different social and geographical habitats. The serious practitioners of one faith involved in religious violence often do not accept that their opponents are entitled to the same social and religious considerations.

Of course, primates live in what they experience as a single environment which includes seasonal changes and adaptations to this, but this is severely limited and does not compare in any way to humans living in an urban slum, commuting to work and going on holiday to the seaside or on a pilgrimage with millions of others.

Lorenz puts the possibility of innate violence to account for human aggressiveness too dogmatically when he maintains that 'human behaviour and particularly human social behaviour far from being determined by reason and cultural tradition alone is still subject to all the laws prevailing in all phylogenetically adapted instinctive behaviour' (Lorenz, 1966: 209).

The existence of aggression in any species is never free and unlimited as there are mechanisms which have evolved to restrict the situations in which intra-specific violence can occur and thus to limit its effects. There is the possibility that the forms of known social life are dependent on this same seemingly controlled aggressiveness.

Overt fighting among species in the wild is rare and an important aspect of mammal behaviour is that it is so dangerous to intra-specific survival that it is minimised by rituals of display, threat and submission or appeasement so that fights are generally no more than trials of strength followed by disengagement and rapid withdrawal by the weaker (Eibl-Eibesfeldt, 1975: 339). It is of course impossible to tell whether aggression predates forms of social control in evolutionary time, but it certainly appears very early in pre-mammalian species.

'The idea of a tendency to fight which must be constantly held in and restrained by social controls is something of an artefact. On the one hand, we have the aggressive tendency contributing to a total social structure, which in turn governs behaviour in such a way as to minimize violence among animals of the same species. On the other hand most animal fights are themselves highly controlled affairs, control being exercised through ritualised components at almost every point in the fighting sequence' (Callan, 1970: 85).

Can human aggressiveness be taken for granted as so commonplace and acceptable that it can be expected to appear in religious and other social situations as a matter of course as Lorenz would have us believe?

Firstly, violence is as conceptually varied as eating; abusing someone, smacking a child, stabbing and murdering an adult and the group killings of Palestinians in Gaza by an Israeli aircraft or by a suicide bomber in Tel Aviv. These commonplace events cannot be considered as similar enough to be genetically determined and indeed it is possible that some individuals go through their lives without any overt aggression at all.

Not all violence is directly aggressive as in judicial executions and head-hunting and serve far wider ends than inter-personal fighting. 'Konyak Nagas were certainly not inspired by any ill-feeling against the slaves they bought in order to obtain heads without running the risk of raiding, and I remember well how an elderly Konyak expressed pity for a boy he and his fellow-clansmen had bought with the express purpose of cutting off his head... In these cases killing is an action undertaken to achieve specific results but not motivated by fury or personal feelings of hatred' (Haimendorf, 1967: 113-4). These are parallel situations to Serb-Croat and Hindu-Muslim violence in which none of those involved may have any specific reasons to be violent to anyone in the defined opposition apart from the human tendency to fight and kill other people with whom they have no social relationships at all.

Then there are the diversities of primate behaviour which is not overtly complex with a limited range of facial expressions and bodily movements. In comparison the human repertoire is extremely diverse with ranges of physical expertise which cannot be entirely attributed to innate aptitudes. The fact that some primates can do what researchers see as quite remarkable quasi-human actions such as making up words from cards or painting is not really a basis for comparison of species with species.

Finally, in any comparison between primate and human behaviour what is the unit of analysis. Certainly it can be as it were person to person, but most social life is not spent in isolation so if a large number is taken into consideration there is an immediate problem because primate groups are perhaps numbered in tens for most of their social lives whereas humans spend any day in groups which vary by the hour from two in a double bed to thousands when going to work in Calcutta or London or in a crowd at a church, mosque or temple.

Aggressive behaviour in primates and humans can be broadly categorised in terms of tensions over territory, food, protection of their young and over sexual access to another but beyond these, there are more exacting requirements for any acceptable comparison. What are the soliciting and motivating situations which bring about aggression since a quarrel about food depends on a particular individual being there in confrontation, when there may be similar food nearby or alternatives for sexual matings; there are no inevitabilities here which can be attributed to genetic restrictions. The motor patterns used even in primates when one individual can use some twenty body movements in an enormous range of permutations and a human has to all intents and purposes an unlimited range of alternative combinations (Moyer, 1968).

Among children there may be four types of aggressive behaviour; instrumental directed towards securing some object or status, hostile or teasing aggression, defensive aggression reacting to an attack and games aggression developing from rough and tumble play (Feshback, 1970).

However among adults there are many more (Tinklenberg & Ochberg, 1981) but group aggression among primates is extremely rare (Goodall, 1986). While violence is certainly the most obvious form of aggression among humans who kill each other publicly for religious and other reasons, most violent quarrelling occurs in private. This human violence can only be very distantly related to life goals or the motivations of individuals; a religiously motivated riot is difficult if not impossible to correlate to any primate activity. Violence between persons cannot be classified as the same as regular intra-specific killing in wars and civil disturbances in which religious differences are important factors.

Then there is the problem of aggressive activities which are divorced from any interpersonal element such as those involved in the slaughter of animals, the demolition of buildings, the cutting down of trees and the cutting up of vegetables with a knife before they are cooked or eaten; all of these activities can be correlated to religious occasions.

There is the fact that intra-specific violence with stone tools going back several million years may have had genetic correlations. However very recently in evolutionary time humans have developed the means to kill and damage at a distance; there are no personal connections and the violence is very random. Much of it is so detached that it cannot be classified as part of any human aggressiveness as a genetic component in the human social make-up. This type of killing and damage does not involve anxieties about revenge and 'the natural propensities of man do not account for the systematic killing in which mankind indulges, because this practice is at variance with what goes on among other mammals' (Andreski, 1964), and it is without the ritualisations which are commonplace in animal fighting. Animal ritualised fighting is only occasionally lethal while human violence in many of its modern aspects divorces aggression from fighting altogether.

There is a third factor in that the gene cannot distinguish between the actions with a spade to turn the soil which might in Jain thinking involve violence to worms and an axe to kill animals or humans and certainly would not cover the Tibetan Buddhist anxiety over disinfectants killing microbes.

If there is an ethological background to human behaviour in religious violence it would seem to be towards the avoidance of being involved in anything like aggressiveness. Any human aggressive tendencies are constrained by many ritualised elements which contribute to the internal motivational structure and to an external social one and the stress here must be on contributing to rather than being a dominant element. 'It would be an error to mark off a set of human activities and say, this much we biologically inherit, the rest is culture' (Callan, 1970: 93).

Is it possible to suggest that violence in fact cannot be limited and that animal species have not so much recognised this but have in evolutionary terms been biased in favour of communities/species which do not get involved and damaged by violence. It seems that there are evolutionary advantages in submission to a powerful and protective individual as it aids group cohesion; an accident from the varying natures of the higher mammal personality.

If there is unlimited violence, the social grouping cannot survive and its members would presumably be picked off by predatory outsiders. This would appear to be a modern development where violence becomes depersonalised and not limited by ritualisations which at least leave the community intact. In Columbia the Roman Catholic Church which had consistently supported the right and the rebels the left have both come to recognise that the unlimited and limitless nature of free-form violence in this political civil war, which had killed thousands over 20 years, would ultimately destroy their own shared society (Levine, 1981: 192).

There are two additional factors which come from knowledge of non-human primate behaviour and are relevant to religious violence.

There is the preference for small group life probably related to the nature of food availability which in humans has developed into being emotionally important; an inward looking dominance.

Secondly, the hostility to out-groups even of their own species which is usually in nature provided by distance keeping; the space which allows for manoeuvring. The example of the Chenchu hunter gatherers in southern India who led peaceable lives but who were moved into villages for the social advantages which the government had thought would come to them automatically from closer settlement and which resulted in higher rates of murder, rape and assault. 'Chenchu society adjusted to lessen and remove friction by placing social distance between opponents, and had no other machinery to restrain violence, and (in the new settlements) as men who had quarrelled or were rivals were prevented from getting out of each other's way, the traditional means of avoiding clashes could not operate' (Haimendorf, 1967: 22).

It would seem therefore that there are ethological grounds for seeing religious preference for small groups isolated from outsiders to have some quasi-natural support. Also that there is some potential hostility built into relationships with outsider groups even of the same religion and very much more so for those who are assessed as different on any range of observable or rumoured characteristics including that of religion.

We can conclude that there is little genetically which can account for religious violence since violence and aggressiveness have no finite identifiable characteristics but that mammalian and more particularly hominid preference for small groups, ritualised hostilities and avoidance does have some significance for our understandings of religious violence. However, the whole issue of ethnology is perhaps outdated by the human development of weapons which allow for depersonalised violence. 'The eschatological teachings of the Sermon on the Mount and their culmination in the non-violence of the Cross cannot be converted directly into norms of human conduct for complex situations' (Levine, 1981: 113) and this applies as much to all other faiths which reach out and involve more than small largely self-governing communities.

The Psychological Predisposition to Religious Violence

In crude terms the assumed functions of the mind and of the body are accessible to different standards of scientific acceptability; the former largely requires and depends on the mind's possessor cooperating and the latter does not necessarily require a person's cooperation.

We know from long ago that 'when a native is asked what he would do in such-and-such a case, he answers what he should do; he lays down the pattern of best possible conduct. When he acts as an informant...it costs him nothing to retail the ideal of the law. His sentiments, his propensities, his bias, his self-indulgences as well as the tolerance of other's lapses, he reserves for his behaviour in real life' (Malinowski, 1926: 120-121). This applies in much the same way to the theologian's explanations of religious behaviour. This is the basic problem of assessing mental behaviour whether in the Trobriand Islands or Trichinopolly; what people say they do and think is not too closely related to what they actually do, even if we had some scientifically acceptable method of overseeing anyone's personal behaviour for a long period of time.

How much more important for finding the connections between the workings of the individual mind and religious violence, must be the differences between how people express themselves, indeed their ability and wish to do so and what we can presuppose as the actual complicated workings of any mind. Further there is no reason to suppose except by the exclusion of bias, that these workings are likely to be any less complicated in the cognitive and other processes of subsistence farmers and social scientists. So that in working with what must always be inadequate data apart from lapses in coherence and reasoning, interpretations must be a very personal matter for even the most sophisticated of psychologists.

A personal opinion given by an individual in response to questioning about why they behave in a particular way is likely to be a contrived answer and even more so when the matter is religious since these are questions which few people ask themselves. It seems likely that the answers will be along the lines that this is what we have always done in our particular socio-religious environment; how else could they answer when most rites of the major religions come from the repetition of organisationally approved rituals. Their answers are likely to change according to the environment of the questioning, the questioner, the time since particular events occurred or their regularity and the changing personal background of the person being questioned which must be varying all the time even if we are dealing with 'flash-back' memories. Of course, there are those who have given much careful thought to their own behaviour and its supportive religious reasonings but the 'ordinary' Hindu worshipping Ganesh or Hanuman and the 'ordinary' Christian singing hymns in a German church, are not likely to provide anything more than stereotyped answers to intrusive questionings paralleling those of an African or Chinese propitiating their ancestors.

As in all individual actions, there may be social and psychological reasons and those related to the mind may well go back as far as the framework of analysis is designed to go. What is near in time may be remembered and articulated well but what has gone on before may be equally if not more important such as traumatic events in childhood involving a religiously motivated killing.

The social sciences have known for a long time that religious violence has occurred repetitively in history and perhaps now reluctantly accept that it is a contemporary issue. Further that it is not just something that can be related to the extremely deviant when others considering the same facts consider these people to be unusually holy. Similarly it is not something which has faded away or is in the process of doing so with widening education and social change.

Psychology preoccupies itself very much with the behaviour of individuals and has much to say about these personal aspects whether it is altruism, meditation or self-mutilation. Freud would appear to belittle religious behaviour and while Jung is more sympathetic towards those involved in religious beliefs and practices, but it is still seen as partial reactions to stress which cannot be coped with as effectively by any other means This is still a functionalist approach and there are no means of knowing the extent and value of archetypes.

Religious violence in its wide variety of forms is usually a group activity in which the individualism of psychology must by definition have little to say except possibly about the influence of charismatic religious figures. The individual who in isolation kills for a religious reason must be rare indeed but those that do so today as part of groups are a commonplace even though the charismatic initiator remains an historical figure or is alive but does not participate himself. The reasons which an individual may give for their own activities, will often minimize their group involvements in religious violence of which they may well be ashamed.

Aggressiveness in a religious context relates very much to intention and aggressive behaviour in a religious riot may be clear enough to the observer but the person waving the sword and shrieking abuse at those of another faith may be doing so because of the anticipated social consequences of staying at home. Serbian killers of Albanian and other Muslims stated that they felt no personal animosity at all particularly as they had never met any. It is quite possible in Northern Ireland today to find members of one faith who have had no conscious social dealings with those of the other faith to which they are hostile.

It seems altogether more likely that the psychological explanations for religious violence are likely to be more tenuous than those that can be deduced from their common foundation of observation and even in that we should remember Kuhn's hypothesis about fashions in science rather than imagine that there are incontrovertible facts (Kuhn, 1982).

3

Theoretical Issues in Religious Violence

Since religions are based on ideas of relationships with some form of the divine, social scientists have problems from their need to define and the difficulties which come from trying to understand social behaviour which in the opinion of those involved is beyond human comprehension. It would appear, therefore, that much understanding and the form which this takes will depend upon the approach which is made; for this there is possibly the difficulty that such researchers comes out at the door through which they first entered.

Levels of Meaning

It seems obvious that there are different meanings of both religion and violence and the half-way concept of magic in the languages and understandings of different cultures. In fact this is so obvious that it tends to obscure and avoid the differences in the use of these words both within and between cultures. Further there never has been in any culture or the social situations within it, single understandings much less definitions of these emotive words. Single definitions may well be the spin-offs from the pragmatic sciences and the existence of a class of literate specialised thinkers who do not physically have to work for their own survival. Let us then look at both religion and violence to examine the different levels of alternative meanings.

An important aspect of meaning is the fact that most people accept whatever they do in religion as having meaning without detailing for themselves what that meaning actually is; defining is not a natural method of thinking. Researchers asking questions about the meaning of religious activities whether in Benin or Banaras will usually get the answer that this is what they have always done, while the local experts will give more detailed and varied explanations more often than not provoked by the questioning. It seems likely that the average person in Bhopal or Berlin would give much the same answers; it is not a question that any person anywhere expects to be asked for which they have answers and which are part of their ready-to-hand cultural repertoire.

On the other hand it is part of the professional's job specification to ask such questions. Few find getting explanations of what is done ritually easy. 'Indians (in Fiji) do not ordinarily provide or perform exegesis on their rituals. The ritual specialists are notably mute when it comes to explanations of the ceremony' (Brown, 1984: 276-777). Malaysian Hindus on being asked why they pierce their bodies, explain that they were fulfilling a vow and usually recount the initiating problem that has led them to ask for the help of Murugan. 'But why do you pierce your tongue, they were puzzled and could not answer my questions... I was referred to someone whom they thought of as an authority in religious matters usually a priest' (Collins, 1997: 87).

In answer to all questions related to religion, there is a tendency to emphasize the importance of proper ritual performance, while remaining unable to articulate the meaning of the ritual is almost a general characteristic of ritual performance. Bourdieu (1990) described the importance of proper ritual performance as 'embodied' understandings of the relations of humans to the divine as 'doxa', as activities which contrasted with both orthodoxy and heterodoxy; the unarticulated understandings by which most people carry on with or carry out their religious lives.

So we have a situation in which the majority of those involved in religion and connected violence certainly give little attention to the meanings of what they do ; such questions and answers are an outsider imposition on their usual behaviour. In the same vein it is probably considered a silly question rather like asking walkers why they are walking, building or eating a particular food; the hostility of Arabs for Jews or Hindus for Muslims does not require explanation.

There is in all activities whether they are pragmatic or metaphysical, an element of unthinking social or psychological conformity. Very few think in terms of meanings before they act or are acted upon and even fewer think of ritual acts as involving alternative courses of action beyond the simplest one of doing or not doing and that probably does not involve meaning. This leaves the analysis and interpretation of religion and correlated violence very much in the hands of intellectualised outsiders who see these personal activities from a professionally impersonal viewpoint; they were never there in any personal sense and if they were, they would have been unlikely to see these events in such an impersonal way.

Meaning as Adaptation

The consideration of meaning is an unsettling process when most people in terms of Merton's typology of adaptation either consciously conform, repetitively ritualise or psychologically retreat into some alternative such as drugs or devotion. Only initiating revolution and reorganisation require thought and these are alternatives chosen by individuals and initially the small minorities which they can influence and as such are more likely to be the objects of personalised contacts by researchers.

To be asked why one does something as personally important as religion and more specifically asked in the context of violence, involves thinking up answers which are not part of the process itself, since an answer would be to some extent a justification. Such questioning however tactfully done immediately puts people on the defensive towards an intrusive individual from whom they are socially distant by almost any social category that comes to mind.

Why think up a special and personalised answer when it seems obvious that this is just what they do or have done for a long time, particularly when there are experts whose job it is to answer such questions; this applies as much to people in New York as it would be to those living in the New Hebrides. The obvious answers are blanket coverages within the general assumption that thinking and speaking about it is a specialised activity which few want to be involved in with strangers.

There are a few examples in which close personal relationships between a researcher and single and perhaps singular individuals go beyond stand-off answers to intrusive questioning on matters to which there are perhaps no answers that can be encapsulated in a sentence or two. The philosophy of an elderly Navaho which led to a complete book (Ladd, 1957) and Turner's relationship with the Ndembu ritual specialist, Muchona the Hornet (Turner, V., 1967: 131-150), which was certainly experienced by both these men as both exceptional and personal.

At whatever level of enquiry there are likely to be a high proportion of stand-off answers or evasions. In questioning Roman Catholic priests in Zambia and Zimbabwe about what they did–just the one question–led to replies differing from a twenty minute stand-off to fourteen hours from a more reflective one. This range is always likely to be towards the stand-off end of the scale for those who have never been required to specifically think about religion and violence and indeed to produce answers in what they would experience at best as a mildly hostile social environment. Answers to questioning in such potentially sensitive matters as religion is likely to be adaptation to a form of stress.

Thus we have to look for the meanings of religion to people whose actions are being examined and indeed the extent of correlated violence in ways that do not rely upon their answers in what they may experience as confrontational experiences.

Meaning and Typified Experience

The meaning of the words commonly understood as 'religion' and 'violence' may be obvious enough to outsiders in their own languages and if such words exist their meanings will lie in what is done rather than what is thought about them. Beyond these meanings, motives and origins are unknown because that is not the way that commonplace semantics operate. In any culture the phrase or the framework of thinking 'what do you mean by these words or actions' is rare indeed and probably commonest in Western legal systems but not generally in most contemporary societies.

Most people in their religious activities are in practice ritualists whether in Nijmegan, Naini Tal or Nairobi in which something is done regularly or in response to personal or communal emergencies and in this violence may be commonplace not only in the sense of hostility to those of other faiths but in the sacrifices of animals and in bodily mutilations such as circumcision.

'Culture appears as an enormous repertoire of typified experience, glossed together as 'normal events' (Diehl, 1956: 222). It is normal to accompany rites of passage with rituals which are always in the process of change and perhaps are usually thought to be traditional at least over proximate generations; it is normal in religious matters to copy what others do or wear; it is normal to slap one's wife or children in some societies because it is written in a holy book that it is a man's right to do so. Overall all people in all cultures are copy-cats and the range of choices is always limited both subjectively and objectively.

The menu of meaning is always restricted and in addition what is on offer is always syncretic; there probably never has been and certainly is not now any religion which in its rituals is not affected by the religious behaviour of other cultures. The Sukuma diviner who introduced fire-walking as part of his ancestor propitiation repertoire may be a social mutation or had he seen a picture ? (Tanner. 1997). What is considered normal is always personally experienced and understood. Variations are always provided by outsiders increasing with social distance starting with partners and ending with others defined as different and within these categories there are considerable semantic differences. The real meaning is taken for granted so that everything that people do in connection with religion and correlated violence is normal and consequently bestowed with the moral feelings associated with normality.

The trance of a Tamil Hindu priest in southern India is understood as a dramatic manifestation of divine power intruding into the social world. 'His body becomes stiff and he would have fallen if people did not support him, his eyes have a fixed stare and suddenly he becomes violent... he soon calms down and now people will ask him questions... This is in plain words what people see happens and their explanation is obvious 'a God has descended on him' (Diehl, 1956: 222).

Meaning and the Pragmatic Motive

The everyday world which uses the words religion and correlated violence is oriented towards action rather than reflection and for most people their meanings lie in their uses and it is moreover true if it is workable and works; a form of secularised pragmatism. It has worked before for those involved, for their nearest and dearest or because of the performer's reputation for success. Abstract thought is a luxury which few can afford to practice.

People have lived meanings of these words in the coming together of an accumulated history of experiences which mould into a stock of typical behaviour based on precedents which are tacked onto actual experience. Into this can be injected relatively recent pragmatism; the Muslim suicide bombers in Israel consider that their actions will bring immediate results in furthering the Palestinian cause as well as getting themselves admitted to Paradise which is detailed in the Koran, the Words of God; it is a logical whole.

The meaning of religious rules lies in the expected results whether this is for a particular need or the religious advantages which come from repetition; they are done for a purpose even if it is a subconscious one. An act of violence connected to religion has a purpose even if it lies in the realms of psychopathology. For most cases of violence, whether it is individually or communally perpetrated, the primary correlation is likely to be as it has always been for most people, a bottom-up activation, however imported observers may consider the top-down religious justification. It is always necessary to tick off the pragmatic objectives and options that are available to the users of religion and violence either together or separately, even allowing for the possibility of social mutations. We may have to accept that the background to religious practices is as personally pragmatic as any other activity.

Meanings at the Level of Metaphysical Intervention

In the practising of a religious faith there may be little difference between the technical and what might be called the magical procedures. The singing of hymns whether by Christians or Hindus or the recitation of ritual prayers by Muslims and Buddhists are technical processes; each can be equally obvious and equally mysterious. We have already suggested that religious action is largely based on the pragmatic principle that it works. However, how it works is not known but accepted so that for many belief is a form of pragmatism.

A distinction between the known fact that prayers should be said in a particular way and what is by definition unknowable as the ways that the spirits, Saints, God or the ancestors react to the technical performances addressed to them, is rarely made because it requires a particular mind-set of detachment; for those praying it would be rather like pulling the carpet out from under their own feet. In traditional sacrifices required by the ancestor spirits, the killing of goats at the Goddess Kali's temples in India and the hundreds of thousands of animals killed by pilgrims on the Hajj to Mecca, a metaphysical idea becomes the basis for religious actions and their explanation. It was not so long ago that the British in India in recognition of the signing of the Treaty of Amiens carried out a military parade with bands to the Temple of the Goddess Kali in Calcutta (Morris, J., 1973: 75).

The completion of the Hajj pilgrimage for all its physical obviousness to the non-Muslim is a religious experience for most of kthose involved today much as it was in the past despite the enormous numbers who are now able to complete it due to the ease of modern transportation (Long, 1979; Wolfe, 1994).

On this level in Islam there is prescriptive violence towards animals and indeed to non-believers written into the Koran, just as passivity is written into the Dialogues of the Buddha but how each came to be there is an unknown reality. Almost all of those involved do not ask themselves for any proofs of metaphysical intervention as they know that at some level it works. The Malaysian Hindu running his own body through with metal spikes knows that he has made a promise to the God Murugan to do this if his child was made well and the God did so; only to outsiders does he appear to be torturing himself but for him it is a logical and necessary pay-off. It seems that at the personal level in all religions most prayers are interpreted as having worked.

Meaning at the Level of the Whole

Cultural understandings are not just discernible units of existing meanings and their functions in the lives of their users from which individuals pick and choose what is relevant to what they do in what appears to be religiously motivated violence; their understandings of their own lives are a constantly changing sense of wholeness. These individual perceptions parallel the instant acceptance of what is in a picture. Of course, the individual is changing and is exposed to innumerable new situations but the whole time there is this sense of completeness rather than picking and choosing their understandings.

No person who considers that they are religious or who follows a particular religion considers that they are practising magic as little can be proved scientifically nor indeed is there any wish for such proofs. In the same way that people who are violent in some aspects of their lives do not consider that they are violent. There is always the experiential indivisibility in individual perceptions.

The words used in spoken or unspoken prayers are 'clearly modelled, fashioned and construed in relation to other cultural units. (There are) underlying images and metonymical elaborations moulding the cultural unit on what is not. Meaning is no longer solely apperceptual. It is not only a self. It becomes an index. No abstract ideas underlie these absorbed socialized understandings; they are concrete tangible images imploding into one' (Bekaert, 1997: 141).

Meaning at the Level of Explicit Metaphors

In their understandings of religion and its connection with violence, people make explicit and elaborate metaphors and they do this with considerable ease; to what phrases are they linked and to what other processes are they metaphorically allied? There is an apparent incapacity of people to see these metaphors as important explanations of how these actions are viewed. It seems unlikely that Christians who hear the hymn 'fight the good fight' and who know about the Salvation Army and its good social service record, think of the words 'fight' and 'army' as having the meanings with which dictionaries associate them.

At a more complex level the sacred literature of the Eastern religions are full of metaphors in dead languages which have to be explained to them by the learned using more commonplace ones. Semantic understandings are linked to metaphors linking religion and its violence with everyday events.

Sometimes they see a metaphorical explanation in the use by the Sukuma of Tanzania of black clothes and the sacrifice of a black animal in the rituals of rain-making but their accompanying invocations are linguistically complex and provide few metaphors. On the other hand few if any Western Roman Catholics see their use of the word 'sacrifice' as paralleling the killings of animals during the Hajj. Eastern believers may have few difficulties over the use of the word in environments which have commonplace blood sacrifices in traditional faiths and of course in sacrifices to the Hindu Goddess Kali.

Meaning at the Level of Codified Oppositions

Every single element in the individual's understandings of religion and violence derive their meanings from its relationship to other cultural and religious elements but these connections are not simple. At this level of cultural signification, meaning is diacritical, codified, oppositional and relational. These cultural units derive their meaning through opposition with one another; it is as much what they are supposed to mean as what they are not.

These are structural relationships with a single articulation. A double articulation presupposes that cultural units are constituted from smaller units that relate logically but this is probably an illusion created by analysis. These smaller units might bear semantic contents 'male/ female, strong/weak but they can also be same/different and competitive/complementary' (Bekaert, 1997: 146). The outsider may see meaning in terms of categories which they have imputed to the language and its usages, but speakers in their understandings of their faiths may well see their practices has having meanings in oppositional terms.

Meaning and the Tensions of Consciousness

All the different levels at which people perceive and interpret religion and violence are true (Schutz, 1962: 207-259). They are all empirical in the sense that they are all at work in the individual's interpretative procedures in the ongoing construction of cultural meanings. We do not have to discard these repertoires to finally come to the hidden system nor do we have to see the code as 'building up' member's experience nor do we have to completely accept member's rationalisations and do away with the systematic as anthropological fictions.

In some societies at a particular intellectual level there is a move from the pre-reflective to the more reflective, from the familiar and commonplace to the more detached, from the level of experience to the thinking about the event and from the experience of religion and violence to the search for those things which have some coherence and link them to a larger logic.

This is rare in any society, certainly there are reflective individuals in pre-industrial traditional societies such as Victor Turner's Muchona and in more developed societies there are whole classes of professional detachers of thought from experience. It is often difficult to explain to those who are in effect subsistence cultivators or casual workers in any modern society that there are possible realities which do not relate to the immediate conditions in which they live.

There are multiple realities and every individual lives in multiple worlds of understandings between which they move with lightening speed as the situation requires without being aware of these changes as each situation has an immediate wholeness.

A prayer is different in dreams, pre-reflection, reflection, necessity and in routine because the paradigm of personalised meanings allows for these changes. Different worlds have different tensions of consciousness, a different suspension of doubt or beliefs, different forms of spontaneity and endlessly different social environments and above all different time perspectives according to the frame in which they are thinking. The relevance structure of religion and connected violence is always changing; any unitary conceptions are the consequences of abstraction.

The Meanings of Key Words: Religion and Violence

So there are major difficulties in correlating religion to violence even in contemporary monotheistic faiths with their insistence on absoluteness and definitions enabled if not promoted by literacy. This is combined with the inevitability that these logically constructed definitions do not to any great extent coincide with the practicalities and experiences of social life. Meaning is not a quality but a function of a term and a function is a pattern viewed with reference to one specific term round which it centres (Langer, 1951: 56).

The meaning of words as they relate to religious practices including violence cannot lie in such definitions however carefully constructed, and must lie in the situations of their use. Since few words are representational, they illustrate a symbolic world subject to constant adjustments to the situations met by people and as such are largely personal however collectively they may occasionally be expressed. There is no knowing at all that the meanings attributed to their faiths by any two Buddhists, Christians, Hindus and Muslims and of course traditional faiths, are ever the same even if they say and indeed write that they are. There are always the factors of translation between the ideas of the donors and recipients as well as between the promoters and users of the Great and Little Traditions with the inevitable variations which have nothing directly related to religion.

There are also the differences between the original sacred spoken words with their written forms varying over the years and their translation into new languages. While there may be equivalents for a limited number of nouns, abstract words are to all intents and purposes untranslatable; the translators interpret and they are creatures of their own cultures and natal languages. The semantically constructed morality of one culture cannot transfer to another without considerable conscious and unconscious alteration.

If we take the wide-ranging East African language kiSwahili words for religion, magic and violence, the dictionaries do not provide explicit meanings and for each there are a variety of terms which depend as always upon the semantics involved. Comparing the two currently available kiSwahili dictionaries published thirty years apart of which the first was largely composed by Europeans with two African contributors listed last and the latter with a totally African authorship.

In the older dictionary (Johnson, F., 1950) of which there are English into Swahili and Swahili into English volumes, there are many words stated to relate to religion; creed or worship, divine or regular service, habit or characteristic, faith, trust, confidence, honesty, God, a god, providence, luck, accident, unaccountable and a pious life or staying in the house and seclusion. There are clearly secular elements here which would appear to have nothing to do with religion as understood in the formalities of monotheistic faiths.

The modern dictionary (Kamusi, 1981) which uses no English. so that Swahili words are given Swahili explanations describes the words listed in the first older dictionary as matters affecting the relationship of the soul between God and man, matters relating to worshipping God, matters treated as true by anyone to which they give honour in particular in religion, considerations of the heart which men consider to be important, the state of being in a religious life and avoiding earthly disturbances, the creator of the world and everything in it and anything arranged in religious affairs.

So we can see that the understanding of what is religion in kiSwahili, a language both widely spoken with a long literary tradition behind its contemporary use written in both Roman and Arabic scripts, is confusing and in some cases tautological. More particularly these definitions exclude a wide range of African and Asian belief systems which involve ancestors, spirits and a lesser god(s) which are less than supreme in what affects these people directly.

The definitions of magic are similarly wideranging involving doctoring, healing, charms, surgical aid, sorcery, enchantment, witchcraft, involving meanings excluding the use of the word in association with religion but involving a widerange of benign pragmatic and non-pragmatic activities as well as evil ones.

The word violence has eight words in both dictionaries with an equally widerange of meanings. In the earlier dictionary force, strength, power, authority, compulsion, acid test, keenness, bravery, cruelty, effort, exertion, strain, ardour, zeal, act characterised by suddenness, outrage, brutality, assault, injustice, oppression, anger, energy, insistence, fearlessness, tyranny and roughness. In the latter dictionary these same words have the meanings of the ability to do something and force as the state of not being peaceful, state of being bitter, going beyond what is customarily considered to be proper behaviour, effort, sound of fighting, knowing what is going on, pushing something and to hit each other. Thus we see that the meanings of these three words are extremely wideranging and do not translate easily into and indeed only partially into English; there are no one-to-one meanings.

The search for definitions controlling or covering meaning has been the cause of much dissension particularly in Christianity and to a lesser extent in Islam and there has been an overspill into cultures in which missionary Christianity has continually searched for an equality of words between those needed to explain that faith and the pre-existing faiths of the cultures to which they are newcomers.

It seems certain that similar differences will occur between all languages which are not at least part of the same language group and that they run parallel to differences between cultures which have either monotheistic or polytheistic religions and belief in diffused disembodied spirit forces or just benign or malignant spirits.

The Christians have a God and they wanted to find in Africa and indeed everywhere the existence of a similar concept and a term which they could then use in missionary work (Worger, 2001). The Sukuma of Tanzania have different words for different spirits in different areas and the same word having different attributes in different places; a minor inland spirit associated with seasonal springs and near to the enormous lake Victoria a force which has some aspects of suzerainty.

They have no word for religion and use the Swahili word 'dini' which itself comes from the Arabic. It seems reasonable to conclude that this tribal group of five millions has no concept paralleling the Christian and indeed Muslim God and semantically have never seen the need to develop such an idea.

There can never be exactness between the words used in different languages but that has never restrained religious people from quarrelling about definitions rather than to respect the separating genius of all the languages involved in religious discourse (Nida & Taber, 1974; Nida & Reyburn, 1981). Once literacy appears and people become committed to the possibility of narrowed certainties in religion, then we have a contributory basis for dispute. It appears moreover that this type of intellectual violence correlates with monotheism which causes a certain narrowness of concepts capable of definition and dispute. This is made even more difficult by constant attempts to use everyday language and a multiplicity of translations between and within language groups. It is logical, therefore, to accept that it is not possible to start from any wide ranging definitions of these key words much less their semantic understandings.

Violence and Morality: General and Specific Issues

The approach to the analysis of religion is almost inevitably from the top down; the Great Traditions dominate with their theologies and philosophies and their relationship to everyday social life is not overwhelmingly obvious. Certainly within these basic ideas there are intentions which individuals and institutions aim to follow but it is the Little Traditions within and outside these lines of thought occurring within individual and communal practices which dominate behaviour. It would be more reasonable to look at what people do within their particular religious viewpoints, the powerful forces of their Little Traditions. These practices show that while they accept the overall directions of their Great Traditions because of social and environmental factors, it is the latter which dominate religious activities; they accept that they should not kill but in these particular circumstances, they feel justified to kill.

At the individual level religious ideas and practices are always syncretistic and despite a label of belonging to a certain Great Tradition, the Little Traditions whether in Berlin, Bamako or Banaras are always a mixture of personal choices from within the mind and from social contacts which cannot be restrained or restricted by even the most thoroughly supervised religious community or sect. We have to examine these Great Traditions and see the extent to which these classical doctrines have enabled or restrained violence and further the extent to which the Little Traditions have created local pockets of social and religious activities which have only nominal connections with the Great Traditions within which they may think they are operating.

If we look at Thomas Muntzer's 1525 call to battle during the German Peasant's War 'For the godless the time is up…have you no concern for their misery; they will be you, they will whine and cry like children. Do not show any mercy. Strike, strike while the fire's hot…. Have no fear, God is on your side'(Blickle. 1981) and then at the mediaeval theologian Victoria's reasoning for widespread violence in war 'sometimes it is lawful and expedient to kill all the guilty. The proof is that war is waged in order to get peace and security. But there are times when security cannot be got except by destroying all one's enemies and this is especially the case against unbelievers from whom it is useless ever to hope for a just peace on any terms' (Victoria. 1934, 48: lxvi). Although these words date from centuries ago they are reminiscent of contemporary Islamic fundamentalist reasoning in support of attacks on American lives and property.

Morality and the Social Practicalities of Religious Violence

The religious morality as a background to violence has two polarities; the universality of a particular view that some behaviour is justified and some is not and that there are exceptional situations leading to violence in which little attention is paid to abstract morality.

The universality of a particular moral view may be one that accords with the generally held views of a particular society which dovetails into the religious morality of the dominant religion and their traditional practices. At the other extreme there may be theological and philosophical rulings made by experts who have no situational responsibility for the violence which may be occurring; abstractions from the situations in which believers find themselves.

Thus the moralities of the Great Traditions in which individuals are placed in relation to violence, have a certain detachment from the social realities in which individuals are placed. The choice of being violent or not may not be an option because they are members of communities already acting in a certain way or are being the recipients of violence; it may be more difficult to abstain from violence than to participate. In any case feelings of guilt or responsibility are diffused.

For those who were involved in inter-religious violence in Bosnia and Croatia, the justifications were communal, a predisposition to hostility to those of another religion which was above both individual and village concern. Any individual refusing to participate would be excluding themselves from communal membership and it would probably mean that they would have to emigrate. Killing or attempting to kill outsiders and destroying their property or religious buildings, is a short-term circumscribed event in comparison to the long-term involvement of the individual in a community containing both their relatives and their livelihoods

Moral issues are not involved and they could be seen as ideological luxuries requiring a considerable amount of practical detachment. The Serbian sniper did not see his activities as involving any moral issues and even to elevate his work as the banality of evil is perhaps not justified. He was acting as a detached individual in a situation combining his personal aptitudes within a frame of animosities into which he had been socialised from birth.

Such situations of inter-religious violence whatever their political and economic backgrounds would have involved communities rather than organisations. They do not seem to require the provision of moral justifications other than the dehumanisation of the 'other' in the crudities of their everyday language which occurred in the appalling planned violence of the Khmer Rouge in Cambodia (Hinton, 1996).

The Moralities of the Great and Little Traditions

There may well be similarities in the abstract moralities of the Great Traditions (Zaehner, 1970). Virtually every person of any faith would agree that it is wrong to kill humans, steal, murder, commit incest and to reject their parents and that these ideas are consistent with the religions in which they believe.

The learned people in traditional societies will assist in producing codes of customary law which detail offences and their penalties. But when it comes to applying these abstract moral laws to actual situations, these same leaders will state that in this or that situation these moral abstractions do not apply quite so neatly. Social circumstances surrounding these situations mean different solutions.

Much the same applies to the religious laws of the Great Traditions for which their theologians and philosophers have reached institutionalised agreements. In their actual application there are detailed and narrowly argued variations related to social and psychological circumstances; nothing is as simple as these abstract moral generalities would suggest. The Great Traditions provide guide lines but in most cases do not and indeed cannot control their application in particular and varied circumstances.

In this respect they are no different to the legal systems of secular states in which a whole profession devotes itself to circumstantial interpretations in which their processes of thought are similar to those of theologians. Of course, most religious thinkers will state that violence against or for a religion and its beliefs is obviously wrong but then come the complications of violence in war, the use of human bodies after death, assisted suicide, the elements which constitute informed consent, parental powers and so on. A list of issues which involve some aspect of physical and psychological violence on which the Great Traditions have institutionalised opinions is long and wide-ranging.

So in theory the Great Traditions have specific moral doctrines based as far as possible on their written sacred texts which vary from the abstract and mythological in Hinduism to the more practical and specific requirements of Islam. In virtually every case the Great Traditions are broken down into the practices rather more than the thought processes of the Little Traditions whether in Patna, Peshawar or Paris. Alternatively they remain intact as far as possible in small deliberately isolated religious institutions such as Buddhist and Christian monasteries and in the Christian isolated communities of the Amish and the Hutterites. However, even in these specialised social circumstances there are Little Tradition modifications.

It would seem likely except in the case of Islam, that violence correlated to religion or in which religion is a component comes more often than not from the Little Traditions in environmental circumstances which are both concrete and local. Overall moralities are usually seen as abstractions from what people feel they need to do or actually do in specific circumstances.

Buddhism

It is necessary to recognise that to follow the Buddhist path is to all intents and purposes an impossibility because it is a doctrine of progressive detachment from all social involvements. 'Full of hindrances is household life, a path for the dust of passions. Free as the air is the life of him who has renounced all worldly things' (Dialogues of the Buddha, 1: 78). Freedom can only be achieved by a total and radical rejection of the world in all its aspects.

Buddhism is 'the most radical form of salvation striving conceivable' (Weber, 1958: 206), but its goals and methods are too hard, too distant and indeed impossible. Most people, even the most observant of the Buddha's requirements, would not be attracted to a form of salvation which is just oblivion and in which failure to achieve detachment results in long if not endless periods in a variety of hot and cold hells. It is not surprising therefore that most nominal Buddhists have developed a system of religion which has very little to do with the teachings of the Gautama Buddha and indeed that subsequent to his death, no comparable figure has appeared to alter his doctrines.

'The complex and incomprehensible nature of Buddhist doctrine, very likely the most aridly convoluted theology of any major religion, persuaded many clerics and laymen that their only hope rested in salvation by faith in the saving powers of Buddha' (Moore, 2000: 111), the Boddhisattvas of northern Mahayana Buddhism and the spirits, the 'nats' of Myanmar.

The Five Precepts include the prohibition of all killing including insects and indeed microbes (Winnington, 1957: 181-84), so that doctors using Western scientific medicine have to be circumspect in explaining the actions of antiseptics and butchers in Tibet are considered to be professional sinners (Ekvall, 1964: 76); even eating honey causes moral problems as dead bees are often found in it. In Myanmar butchering is usually done by Muslims who are similarly despised.

So it requires casuistry to get round this wholesale prohibition; the use of DDT kills mosquitoes but it is their choice to use that water just as it is the choice of dogs to eat poisoned meat intended to reduce the numbers infesting towns because they may be carrying rabies. In their moral thinking there are clearly grades of killing but Buddhist Cambodians reputedly a gentle people, were the instruments through which Pol Pot regime carried out genocide. To be Burmese is to be Buddhist and the others such as the Karen Christians are outsiders which may account in part for their resistance to and violence by the Burmese military rule.

Most Buddhists do not think about the millions of rebirths necessary to attain the required detachment of which only the Buddha himself achieved and the Bodhisattvas delayed achieving in order to help suffering mankind. They think and act in terms of a more immediate proximate salvation combined with many forms of magical protection and metaphysical accountancy so that they have a favourable balance of merit at any one time. There are also chiliastic cults aiming at immediate salvation such as the 1930-32 Saya San rebellion in Burma in which he provided his followers with magic protection against bullets (Spiro, 1971: 172).

Buddhism did not develop any system of moral purity within binary oppositions. Since its main objective was to escape from worldly life rather than to reorder life in this world, there is no part of its Great Tradition which could be used to justify violence although there have been periods in both China and Myanmar in which monks were involved in violent politics or as communities of warriors. Also it is part of its Great Tradition that the individual personality is constantly changing and there is no such thing as a soul. So Buddhists are not actively involved in violence and their preoccupations are more associated with its avoidance in a wider field than humanity.

Hinduism

Down the centuries Hinduism has been a tolerant religion of which the Indian ruler Asoka was a prominent example (Sen, 1956) though perhaps not in the sense of charity towards the sinner because it has no such classification. Its Great Tradition revolves round purity and impurity, which was institutionalised by keeping those involved in disgusting activities as socially distant as possible by creating the religiously based hierarchy of caste and the category of outcaste. This religion perhaps because it has no founder, has no dogma or core of central beliefs in which all Hindus are expected to believe (Savarkar, 1964) and which they could be expected to defend by force. Now as much as in the past new ideas and new rituals become the bases for thousands of new sub-castes.

This tolerance is not just a moral kindness to deviants from some idealised state of good behaviour similar to that of Christian social concern, but extends to sanctifying many forms of deviant and indeed criminal behaviour. In the 19th century the Thugs killed hundreds of travellers by strangulation in order to make offerings of their property to the Goddess Kali and their killings were so widespread that its suppression required enormous British secular efforts. There are allegedly criminal sub-castes whose hereditary occupations are crime and who offer prayers to their special divinities before setting out on expeditions to rob and murder. These Hindus believed that their crimes were carried out under divine favour and failure to practice made them liable to divine anger (O'Malley, L.S.S., 1935: 79).

This tolerance did nothing to stop wars among Hindus but not over religious issues until the Muslim conquest which were then stopped by the British. It seems reasonably clear that Hindus learnt religious hatred as a result of this imposition of Muslim rule over northern India in the 16th century.

The current political development of Hinduism as part of a national patriotic movement may have come as part of a reaction to the failure of Nehru's post-independence secularising quasi-socialism which failed to produce the expected benefits from the departure of the British and which in the opinion of caste Hindus had led to legal biases in favour of the enormous Islamic minority and an equally large number of Untouchables. This militancy augmented and capitalised on the Great Tradition ideas of disgust with impurity which is made all the more difficult and likely since Hinduism mingles human and divine qualities in a much more specific way than any other religions.

Taoism and Other Chinese Religions

With Chinese religions it is impossible to keep Buddhism, Confucianism and Taoism separate since the Chinese have always syncretised their religious practices. A visit to the Jade Buddha temple in contemporary Shanghai shows the relative simplicity of the statue of the Buddha and the symbolic complexities of the other images which come from a range of religious sources. A religious banner may contain twenty or more figures to be worshipped.

Taoism in its Great Tradition is a religious system of philosophical complexity which would seem to have little practical relevance to the everyday life of Chinese subsistence farmers. It suggests that from knowledge come definitions and it is these objectifications which separate men from each other. It is uncompromisingly anti-intellectual by which knowledge, reason and the acts of civilisation are assessed as decadence (Zaehner, 1970: 216).

Indeed Lao-Tzu's plea for no government (Lao-Tzu, 1934: 57), 'The adherence of all under heaven can only be won by letting alone. How do I know this is so? The more prohibitions there are, the more ritual avoidances, the poorer people will be...The more laws are promulgated, the more thieves and bandits there will be...Therefore a sage has said 'So long as I do nothing the people will of themselves be transformed... So long as I practice only by inactivity, the people will be themselves become prosperous'. This is echoed by 'Be benign and impartial like the god of the soil at the sacrifice–he grants no private blessing. Be broad and expansive like the endlessness of the four directions-they have nothing which bounds or hedges them. Embrace the ten thousand things universally—how could there be one you should give special support to' (Chuang-Tzu, 1964: 17, 6). Whatever these expositions may intend and achieve, their idealised attractions are certainly not the bases for aggressive behaviour.

Christianity

There would seem to be very little in the Christian Great Tradition which could be easily translated into violence; it is not only a message of peace in Christ's saying that 'Peace I bequeath to you, my own peace I give you, a peace the world cannot give, this is my gift to you (John, 14: 27). But it is one which very specifically separates itself from being involved in government. On the other hand it was Christ who is recorded as having said 'Do not suppose that I have come to bring peace to the earth; it is not peace I have come to bring but a sword. For I have come to set a man against his father, a daughter against her mother, a daughter-in-law against her mother-in-law. A man's enemies will be those of his own household' (Matthew, 11: 34-6) and in this was seen the justification for persecution. But Christ did violently throw the money changers and traders out of the Temple. An ambivalent message which seems to suggest that peace can only be obtained in spiritual attainments in a world which is irredeemably violent.

Islam

The Great Tradition of Islam is the latest of the great religions to emerge and the clearest because the contemporary foundations on which it was based are known from history with some clarity. Thus it is much more difficult for Muslims to change a message which is historically clear and which might well seem to be inappropriate in a global society which owes no contemporary affiliation to what the inspired Prophet Mohammad recorded as the words of Allah. It would seem then that Islam has not become aggressive in pursuit so much of its religious aims but that its periodic violence in certain societies would seem to come from what their religious leaders assess as a failure to follow its divinely inspired requirements.

At the beginning of his religious calling when his position was insecure and nothing more than his secular rectitude was accepted, the message was that Allah was prepared to leave unbelievers to their own devises 'Say; O ye that reject Faith, I worship not what ye worship, nor will ye worship that which I worship.... To you be your way, and to me mine' (Koran, 109).

Latter as his position became secure and he had assumed the combined roles of religious leader and secular ruler, the message was conversion or total submission. 'Fight those who do not believe in Allah nor in the last Day, nor hold that forbidden which hath been forbidden by Allah and His Prophet, nor acknowledge the religion of Truth, until they pay the tribute willingly, and feel themselves subdued' (Koran, 9: 29) and 'Fight with them until there is no more tumult or oppression, and there prevail justice and faith in Allah altogether and everywhere.' (Koran, 8: 39).

Other verses are equally specific: 'Against them make ready your strength to the utmost of your power, including the steeds of war, to strike terror into the hearts of the enemies of Allah and your enemies, and others besides, whom ye may not know, but whom Allah doth know. Whatever ye shall spend in the cause of Allah, shall be repaid unto you, and ye shall not be treated unjustly (Koran, 8: 60). Even more specific instructions relate to property gained by these wars 'And know that out of the booty that ye may acquire in war, a fifth share is assigned to Allah – and to the Messenger, and to near relatives, orphans, the needy and the wayfarer' (Koran: 8: 41). Even this chapter is entitled 'The spoils of war'.

These are not the words of a Buddha who withdrew from much human contact or those of Christ as a little known unsuccessful leader of a new sect in Palestine and who was soon to be executed, but a successful war leader who had been wounded in furthering his new religious message.

It is not the legitimacy but rather the sanctity of warfare which is typical of the whole Koranic outlook. As in the Old Testament, so in Islam, fighting is God's favourite way of achieving His ends. Whatever Islamic modernists may say, war is the normal and moral state of affairs enshrined in the Koran between the Muslim community and their surrounding infidels; it is the Muslim's duty in the long run to subdue the whole world to believe in Allah and in not so doing he is betraying his God (Zaehner, 1970: 373).

There is also the fact that the inspired Koran is to be believed in its entirety and contains specific instructions for the behaviour of those who believe in Allah and his Prophet. There is no distinction between the secular and the religious or between Church and State. The fact that affairs went wrong with the violent death of Ali, the fourth successor of the Prophet so that disunity appeared and there was no longer a single leader of the Faith, is not the only difficulty in modernisation. The divine nature of the original message cannot be obliterated as it is a fundamental article of Faith and thus there is an either/or nature of its instructions. Both give now as much as then the substantive divine grounds for violence and indeed for the persecution of non-believers. Its development into unjustifiable terrorism as seen from the perspectives of outsider non-believers is for Islamic fundamentalists just specious dialectics.

Comparative Religious Attitudes to War and Violence

There is always a basic division between religions as to how subsequent generations of theologians explain the words in their sacred literature and the actions of their founders. This is no problem with Hinduism which has no founding figure and less of a problem for Buddhism of which little is known of the life of the Buddha as his sayings were recorded for the first time some three hundred years after his death. In both these religions this allows a certain latitude in interpretation. Within these Eastern religions any concept of orthodoxy must be highly contentious for which there can never be any validity.

Islam and Christianity are quite separate. With the former faith the Koran is the Word of God and as such beyond argument as to its authenticity and with the latter what Christ may have said is significantly less recognised and accepted in the same literal sense with which the Muslims treat the Koran. The Bible is not treated with the physical reverence which is accorded the Koran.

Islamic theologians are dealing with the written down Word of God which certainly restricts interpretations in dealing with situations which could not have occurred in the lifetime of the Prophet Mohammad. They are faced with the Word of God in the original language in which it was recorded and this certainly inhibits what theologians can say about it and restricts the possibilities of any updating of the message except in retrogressive thinking. Muslim theologians cannot say that the requirements written into the Koran were progressive ideas at that time but are not easily accepted as such in the contemporary world of individualism and equality.

In eastern Africa where the main language is kiSwahili, there have been on-going attempts to propagate Islam without converts having to both learn and use classical Arabic which would lead to irreversible changes similar to the changing of the Roman Catholic liturgy from Latin to local languages. Since translation is always a dialectical process particularly across a linguistic group divide, it would provide for some updating of Islamic thought as well as shaking off the yoke of religious colonialism (Balda, 1993). But the violent hostility in Pakistan to the more modernistic Ahmaddiya movement in Islam restricts this possible avenue of progressive change.

The alleged words of Christ even accepting his stature as the Son of God, provide theologians with quite different opportunities. Christ wrote nothing during his lifetime and we are left with recorded statements not made at the time in the sense of what newspaper reporters might have written down with appropriated supporting information. The Gospels have none of the definitional sanctity given to the Koran. This allows their theologians far greater automatic latitude than could be the case with Muslim ones and this applies particularly to the relationship of their faith to religious violence.

Muslim theological leaders are basically lawyers and speak with the accepted and acquired skills which come from study and it is only with Shia leaders to whom quasi-divine status is attributed that calls for violence often come. It is the relationship of their pronouncements to the one sacred text which gives power to their statements.

The Christian Church which in fact is always Christian Churches even in their most institutional forms such as the official theological statements of the Roman Catholic Pope do not operate from a single one language divine text. The Bible has gone thought many sequential translations, even before the more than three hundred currently available translations into non-European languages. What the Bible says does not restrict but enable cross-cultural discussions over meanings and their reinterpretations for contemporary use; translation is always a dialectic.

Since in South Africa alone there were over 4000 different independent Christian Churches (Barrett, 1968) there is never likely to be any uniformity there or anywhere else as to what Christians should or should not do concerning violence. Christians can use their Church affiliations as soft walls off which to bounce their own difficulties and convictions. If indeed Christians are thinking about the moral issues in violence, their interpretations are as much likely to be individual as collective; there is no uniform Christian viewpoint.

The attitudes of Christian theologians generally consist of regretting the need for military violence, while at the same time applauding its relationship to a 'just' war and deploring other forms of inter-religious and inter-ethnic violence as regrettable breakdowns in individual and communal morality. In these approaches there is much that parallels Islamic fundamentalist reasoning on the 'justice' of attacks on Americans and Israelis.

There are two aspects to such difficult reasoning, the detached and abstract and the active and involved. As an Australian military chaplain stated that 'if a clergyman felt that he had conscientious objection to fighting, he was of little use in military work of any kind' (Smith, J. nd).

For Christians there is the background of required peacefulness, constantly depicted in the language of violence, fighting the good fight and onward Christian soldiers, the Salvation Army and so on. There is little doubt that Christian clergy who served as chaplains had attitudes that morally justified warfare and the killing involved. The chaplains' duty included inculcating the 'fighting spirit' (Bramwell, 1943: 51) and their duty was to 'spotlight…the conflict of Good and Evil, the opposing standards of Right and Wrong, the just foundations of our cause, the Presence of Christ, the value of prayer, the glory of sacrifice, the gift of eternal life and such things as deepened their sincerity and confidence as soldiers gathered to battle by God' (Anonymous, 1943: 65-66).

Vietnam for American servicemen was totally different to what they had encountered in Second World War in Europe in which 'us' and 'them' were more clearly separated both ideologically and physically. But in their Asian involvements, the 'us' and 'them' simplicities were no more than theoretical divisions. Whereas the German side of World War Second could be classed as ideologically wrong, the main theme against Japan was revenge for the Pearl Harbour attack and their constantly revealed savagery, a much more elemental reaction in which moral issues rarely surfaced.

The 'them' did not conform to definable separateness, they did not give up and in Vietnam did not wear uniforms as with the Irish Republican Army in Northern Ireland who only conformed publicly to the definition of 'them' by wearing symbolic uniforms at funerals. In many cases the absence of separation led to uncontrolled and uncontrollable savagery on both sides escalated by its own momentum and certainly with the Americans in Vietnam, the presence of military chaplains was unsettling as reminding service men of moral issues which their present circumstances made irrelevant. As a military chaplain remarked (Lifton, 1974: 336) 'the men felt that it was one thing to be ordered by command to commit atrocities on an everyday basis in Vietnam but another to have spiritual authorities of one's society rationalize and attempt to justify and legitimise that process. They felt it to be a kind of ultimate corruption of the spirit.'

In the conditions of modern warfare, it may well be that religions can initiate violence but in the conditions of engagement once individuals are committed to violent situations over which they have no control, religion becomes for Christians no more than the subject for after-the-event evaluations.

As conclusion to a chapter on priests and padres (Burke, 2000: 304-5) 'although some religious representatives consistently stood out against shedding human blood and there were pained consciences over the cutting of ties with religious communities in hostile countries, reconciling combat with Christianity was remarkably non-controversial. Indeed in wartime many clergymen longed to take part in the blood letting and, frustrated in their ambition, sanctified the slaughter and surrendered themselves to the cult of arms. It was possible to kill without sin and without guilt, they assured combatants. Spiritual guidance was in perfect harmony with military needs.'

Religious Violence and the Silence of Moral Concern

In considering the relationship to religions to horrific violence such as the Holocaust killing of the Jews by the Germans, there is a necessary distinction in how religions work. A traditional religion with no written beliefs or centralised and centralising institutions would have difficulty in taking a moral view of any issues beyond those of concern to the communities in which the religion was active and in those circumstances there would be thousands upon thousands of different moral views of what should or should not be done in relation to the ancestors and spirits.

Once literacy and institutionalisation come together, then thought and regulations become detached from the immediacies with which traditional religions coped with so adequately and innovatively. Christianity and Judaism have organisations which make statements about moral issues but today the other faiths have no formal centralising institutions which can produce and spread rulings on the moral issues facing mankind. Any Muslim dignitary can make a religious ruling, a '*fatwa*' but it would only be binding on those who accept the authority of the particular person making such a decision.

In the aftermath of the Holocaust there has been considerable interest in the silence of the Roman Catholic Church over the destruction of the European Jews (Kertzer, 2002; Zuccotti, 2002; Sanchez, 2001). While the Roman Catholic Church is certainly a centralised institution in terms of its ideology and theoretical structure, it is not the same as a political and economic one with a controlling bureaucracy within the Weber's definition. It is the morally reprehensible silence whether or not it would have made any difference, is speculative and indeed unlikely to have had any influence at all in view of the Nazi Wannsee conference in January 1942 on how to organise the killing of all possible numbers of Jews (Roseman. 2002).

It may be that the higher up in an organisation decisions are made, whether it is a religious or secular one, it becomes more difficult for those involved to see a situation in moral terms separated from the practical balances among prominent people and their policies which are less accessible to moral reasoning. There is a difficult difference between specific and accountable responsibilities and moral generalities. Pope Pius XI took a strong position to protect the rights of Christian Jews to marry Christian Gentiles for which there were legal grounds for protesting because it was a breach of the Lateran Treaty signed by him and Mussolini in 1929 (Chadwick, 2002: 16).

This moral failure to protest by religious leaders who did not have the economic or political power, much less any military might, to follow up their protests is paralleled by their far more reprehensible failure to protest and indeed to act as would have been possible had they been politicians with moral pretensions and the secular means to back their protests on the ground. The Armenians had no political influence in the United States so despite the fact that the *New York Times* carried 145 stories in 1915 about the Turkish Muslim killings of the Christian Armenians, now classified as genocide, but the American authorities did nothing because those in power could pretend that they did not know.

Even more so with the instant communication of events when the Rwandan Hutu in 1994 could freely, joyfully and systematically slaughter eight thousand Tutsi a day for a hundred days without any foreign interference. This genocide occurred after the Cold War; after the growth of human rights groups; after the advent of technology that allowed for instant communication, and after the erection of the Holocaust Museum in Washington, DC (Power, 2002).

Post Holocaust concern for the Jewish vote in key American cities is a reality to which their politicians have to react, but there was no need to worry about the votes of the very few Americans of Rwandan origin. Politicians in the world of real rather than moral politics often choose to remain 'in the twilight between knowing and not knowing as the General Secretary of the World Council of Churches remarked about his life in Switzerland at the time of the Holocaust (Hooft, 1973: 166).

The Difficulties Over Defining a Religious Culture

Culture is indeed a popular word and as such has proved impossible to define with any degree of satisfaction since it is internalised in different ways by people according to the different roles they have in a society (Shore, 1996; Shweder, 1991). The difficulties are increased when it is linked to religion over which there are similar problems over definitions. The interpretation of culture by a devout Muslim in a university environment is not likely to be shared by an Iranian Shia living on the boundary of Afghanistan or in Baghdad or Basra or by a subsistence Muslim Fulani farmer and cattle herder in northern Nigeria.

It would be correct to identify the Amish culture since their way of life is observably distinct with their special way of dressing, and horse drawn transport and agricultural machinery. Indeed their religious based culture is so distinct that there are serious theological arguments about the circumstances for which community members can use telephones and electrically powered drills for house construction. Much the same would apply to Orthodox Jews and the nuns and monks of any religion who dress distinctively and live separately. In this it is necessary to remember that overt distinctiveness is certainly a factor in provoking or participating in religious violence.

In a general sense to talk of a Christian parish in a Western or Indian city as a Christian community and thus exhibiting a Christian culture, would seem to be illusory because their specifically Christian activities are minimal rarely extending beyond attending the ceremonies of their denomination particularly for rites of passage; they wear no distinctive costume, nor eat any religiously specified food and in the Western case do not marry with any overtly strong attention to the denominational faiths of their particular partners.

The interpretation of a religious culture as being pacific rather than violent is circumstantial and the internalisation of cultural traits will always be a matter of degree related to personality and social circumstances. The motivation to kill for a religious reason as in Islamic based terrorist bomb attacks or to take part in the destruction of another religion's place of worship as in the demolition of the mosque at Ayodha by Hindu zealots, can be explained in part by a variety of cultural paradigms, but for it to become active requires the individual and the circumstances to be filtered through a variety of social and political factors (D'Andrade, 1992).

With culture to be considered as a model for religious behaviour it requires a substantial background understanding of its force in the build-up within the individual and that society for it to be expressed in violence. Neither German nor Russian culture includes any persistent or required expressions of violence except over the defence of territory and yet both nations have successfully bureaucratised violence against their own Jewish and Christian citizens.

It is not only the existence of a cultural model but the extent to which its ingredients are considered to be 'natural' for that particular society irrespective of whether it is seen as such by outsiders. The wholesale slaughter of hundreds of thousands of animals as a religious requirement for pilgrims on the Hajj is a basic Islamic necessity but it might be difficult to define it as an important part of Islamic culture but most contemporary outsiders would consider this event to be both unnecessarily violent and out of date.

Culture is often defined by elites as related to survivable features of their societies such as architecture, art, literature and generally static objects capable of being analysed but at the lower levels of popular living, very little of what has been defined as culturally important is likely to be accepted as more than marginally part of their social understandings and appreciations. Popular religious art is often only peripherally connected to the central tenets of any faith; they can be supportive of violence as in the amulets and tattoos worn by soldiers or have no connection at all as in the fertility promoting figurines on sale in the forecourt of an important Buddhist temple in Bangkok.

An observable tendency to be communally or individually violent in ways that are supported by their religious conceptions as amongst the Papuan Dani can be seen as a cultural trait. But then it is difficult to know for how long this trait has been active as amongst the Brazilian Yanomamo who have been described as a violent people (Chagnon, 1977). It has now been suggested (Tierney, 2000) that this 'cultural' predisposition to violence may at least in part have been initiated by visiting anthropologists who by providing them with agricultural tools as gifts usable as weapons in return for their participation in their investigations, turned the tribe into aggressors and aggressiveness.

Even amongst the Dani who had at least some religious justification for their violence in their need to appease their ancestors, were not violent all the time and no doubt spent most of their time in the perfectly peaceful conduct of their domestic lives; perpetual violence on anything beyond short-term and small scale regularities does not make either biological or social sense since such communities would extinguish themselves quite quickly.

Cultural models may provide patterns to copy but this will be interpreted according to particular situations. The customary law of a tribal society discussed in the abstract and written down by cultural outsiders, will usually provide cognitive models for behaviour which are significantly cross-cultural. 'Thou shall not kill' as phrased would be widely if not universally accepted but when this is subject to a more careful examination of this morally acceptable statement, then there are exceptions; the justified killing of suspected witches, seducers of daughters, cattle thieves and the insulters of a particular faith if the community has become committed believers (Holland & Quinn, 1987). A violent culture just as a pacific one may well be the creation of analysts who abstract certain behavioural traits and situations out of the totality of their experiential lives.

It is better to suggest that in so far as culture forms the background to motivation, it is always subject to situational controls rather more than predispositions and if looked at in the whole there are certainly always going to be clashes, role conflicts between the various aspects of a culture, religious or otherwise. Some of these might be taken out of the range of religiously motivated violence as is the case for making Mecca into an exclusively Muslim area, but that has not prevented extreme deliberate violence there by Muslim religious zealots. Even if the Gulf states are seen as overwhelmingly Muslim in law and practice, they are still forced to accept heterodoxy along with their immigrant workers and in their commercial dealings with the outside world. Saudi Arabia which allows no other faith to have a toe hold within their territory was forced to tacitly accept American and their allies aid against the Iraqi invasion of Kuwait along with their chaplains and female service personnel.

All conurbations are heterodox in practice even if they are orthodox officially and if the followers of a particular religion want to create the illusion as much as the reality of being a special community, then they have to make special provisions for this. The Orthodox Jews in New York whose men live on their fire escapes for a time in commemoration of their desert life while being expelled from their homes in the distant past or to create a religiously legal community according to Jewish law by a single strand of virtually invisible wire round their periphery. These arrangements require the tolerance of the surrounding society which does not extend to ritual animal sacrifices being performed in the suburban gardens of London according to African traditional religious practices.

So the use of the phrase religious culture is a cover for an idea which is not based analytically on any systematic understanding of how that society works on religious lines. Perhaps conceptual consistency is part of the Judaeo-Christian emphasis on intellectualised logic which is not shared by the thinkers in Eastern religions or probably by men and women in the streets or fields anywhere.

An example of the disparate nature of the constituent elements of a culture can be taken from the Yemen (Gilsenan, 1982: 9-10). "It was all an enchantment, a desert, an oasis, a holy town, an age old tradition. The fullness of sanctity and a ritualised sense of gracious order and harmony were added as a young man stopped respectfully to kiss the young sharif's hand (a descendent of the Prophet) as we passed, thus marking his respect and acknowledgement of their position.... The front-door slammed behind us. The spell was broken. Our companion swiftly closed the window shutters so that no one would see us, a tape recorder played Western pop music and strictly forbidden whisky came out of the cupboard. A day latter I met the young man who had kissed their hands 'we kiss their hands now but just wait until tomorrow."

In that narrative we can surely see three quite separate understandings of Islamic culture, not only as not particularly binding on the participants but all in the process of change but even with a suggestion of future revolutionary violence from what were very ordinary Muslims. It would seem, therefore, that culture as having an intrinsic religious quality and moreover as a binding one which may narrowly encourage passivity or violence is probably an illusion (Underwood and Underwood, 1980).

The Types of Religious Violence

The extremes of any type of behaviour are easily located and form the basis of any discussion about that activity, but it is usually only the tip of a behavioural pattern which catches the attention of outsiders. The writers of the United Nations Report on Arab Development listed one of the three main features of Arab backwardness in development was the suppression of women from developing their potentialities and that is an Islamically motivated restriction which global public opinion would class as a form of violence in its religious context has to be seen as more than death and destruction.

The Polarities Related to Religious Violence

It is necessary to see religious violence in terms of a series of polarities. Firstly, there is the polarity between direct violence identifiable by the standards of the criminal and customary laws in the legal systems of particular cultures and indirect violence as forms of incitement difficult to prove and less legally acceptable.

Then there are the polarities which come from various types of precipitating factors; a persŏnal attack for ostensibly religious reasons which from its immediacy does not require much reasoning. At the other extreme there are a wide range of social, political and economic factors which appear to come together and to correlate with religious violence which participants see as contributing to some immediately satisfying solution but which may or may not have any affect on reducing these tensions; rather distant push and pull factors.

There are also the polarities between the doer of religious violence and those to whom it is done. Violence presupposes a dyad even if the violence turns in upon itself in self-mutilation and these dyads vary enormously in terms of social distance. The closeness of religiously different people fighting each other on an almost personal name basis; the internecine violence of the small community. Partially at the other end of the scale are crowd situations in which members of the dyad are only known by their collective names, 'isolated, a person may be a cultivated individual, in a crowd he is a barbarian – that is a creature acting by instinct. He possesses the spontaneity, the violence, the ferocity and also the enthusiasm and heroism of primitive beings' (Le Bon, 1960: 12). In this context it is inevitable that violence will be promoted against people whom one has never seen except on television; the mass hostility of Muslim fundamentalists to Americans in general as unbelievers rather than as Christians or Jews in which neither side has ever seen the other except on television, much less talked to any of them.

Primary Religious Violence

Violence from personal animosity in which it seems likely that religious differences are an adjunct to the actual tensions in a community. The precipitating excuse for a wide variety of religious violence are differences between neighbours over feelings that they have been overcharged, insulted or their women molested, animals straying into fields or being too noisy as in the amplified Islamic calling to prayers which may coincide with Jewish prayers or indeed their sleep.

When there is the killing of someone known to the killer but of a different religion it is probably rare for religious differences to be the reason. Face to face violence between people knowing each other is more likely to be related to jealousy or some long standing quarrel which a permissive environment for violence allows for its expression within a certain amount of anonymity or the breakdown of communally acceptable rituals of conciliation. In south-west Ethiopia among the Suri and Dizi the rituals of conciliation because of the increased external trade in grain and cattle, the rapid adoption of the semi-automatic rifle, the claims of the centralising Ethiopian state, tensions between their gerontocratic traditional system of governance and the overall decline in respect for their traditional religion and its supernatural sanctions, notions and rituals (Abbink, 2000); all these have led to more violence within each community.

One of its commonest examples is the aim to exclude certain people from an area or neighbourhood even though they may have lived there side by side for years as the actions against Sikhs in Delhi after assassination of Indira Gandhi by her Sikh bodyguards or Roman Catholics and Protestants in Northern Ireland when tensions have been initiated by events occurring outside the communities in which violence erupts and even centuries before when Cromwell put down an Irish rebellion in the 17th century. Mixed marriages over religious boundaries have often caused these couples to be killed or have forced them to emigrate to localities where it is not an issue; mixed religion couples in Northern Ireland find it easier to live away from their birthplaces in mainland Britain.

In communities with mixed religions this is more likely to happen on the edges of religiously exclusive localities. It seems likely that primary personal animosity has proportionately little part in religious violence. Where religions and their subdivisions are important, then there is always a certain amount of self-segregation so that personal animosity is reduced by long standing processes of geographical and social distancing. In India there has been a steady moving apart of both Hindus and Muslims who have previously been more closely intermingled as both become aware of the greater relative safety of living surrounded by their co-believers. The behaviour and appearance of Orthodox Jews may offend their non-believing neighbours and a process of division occurs which is not ostensibly anti-Semitic but relates to cultural differences and as a by-product allows them to follow more exactly their specialised ritual requirements.

Secondary Involvements: Part-time Religious Violence

In some communities inter-religious hostility is part of the process of socialisation as in Palestine between Arabs and Jews and in India between Hindus and Muslims. On the other hand it may suddenly erupt in a community because of an event elsewhere such as the demolition of the mosque at Ayodha by a Hindu mob or widespread attacks on Sikhs by Hindus after the assassination of Indira Gandhi. These violent events would not have erupted so quickly and widely without previously existing tensions which made outbreaks of religious violence not only to be expected but quite legitimate in the minds of those involved.

Where there are persistent but irregular hostilities between members of different religions which have been going on for so long that no contemporary generation has known a time free from this covert tension, hostility as well as occasions of periodic overt violence towards members and institutions of another religion are likely to be commonplace.

There are two extremes to these situations. In India where Hindus and Muslims have led economically and socially integrated lives, indeed often participating in each other's festivals and using each other's charismatic persons for healing and advice and who have periodically erupted into mutual violence and indeed have done so for centuries.

In these circumstances the community leaders of these polarised religions know that they cannot stop these eruptions of violence, but they know as do the participants that there are necessary boundaries to this violence. In riots in Hyderabad it was acceptable that shops should be burnt but rape was unacceptable (Kakar. 1995: 110). When it has died down the two communities will still be interdependent since neither is economically complete. Their leaders may well be able to negotiate potential difficulties and arrange compromises as they know that these outbreaks are bad for business. In Hyderabad the Hindu leader Mangal Singh remarked a few days after a riot that whatever the bitterness in their hearts and however cold our voices are initially, the Moslem leader Akbar Pelwan still has to call me and say 'brother Mangal, what do we do about that disputed land at Begumpet and I still have to answer, brother Akbar, let's get together on that and solve the problem peacefully'.

At the other extreme there was the Partition of India into two states in which there were horrendous outbreaks of killing, rape, abduction and migration over the newly created boundaries which gave Muslims exclusive control over East and West Pakistan mirroring the Prophet Mohammad's original control of Arabia by largely violent means so that it became a unified socio-religious state.

In between were the riots against Sikhs after the assassination of Indira Gandhi in which the men were attacked but not their women in an endeavour to move them out of Hindu neighbourhoods. Eviction in order to establish ghettoes since there can have been no anticipation that urban commercial Sikhs would migrate to their agricultural communities in the Punjab with which they may not have any renewable connections. Similarly force created Protestant and Roman Catholic ghettoes in contemporary Belfast.

In all these outbreaks there seems to have been little overt encouragement to violence but covert support in order that communal-cum-political leaders would retain their pre-eminence. The direct initiators of periodic inter-religious violence are likely to have been those aspiring to leadership and to take these opportunities to achieve local prominence.

On the other hand these lesser outbreaks may be no more than the working out publicly of a paradigm of hostility to out groups for which almost any cause might have been sufficient. But what is striking in India is that those involved are interconnected and have a broadly similar socio-economic level; a paradigm of hostility between people who are broadly similar but different in appearance.

There are however mutually hostile groups whose religious differences are made worse by a combination of factors of which the most obvious is a difference in standards of living. Apart from the political issue of the eviction of Muslims in Palestine from their hereditary land, the Jews for whatever reason have a much higher standard of living than the Muslims surrounding them. The Jewish settlements have good housing and clean water and the Muslims do not have such state supported benefits. Thus onto an accumulation of grievances into which every Muslim child is socialised to accept as a fact of life, comes the visual incitement of these disparities. It would seem that in these visual circumstances acclimatisation to periodic inter-religious violence is added to their socialisation to hostility.

In these situations the profit on periodic active hostility, the crowd factor, is likely to be much more psychologically and socially valuable than considering the extent of interconnectedness, the usefulness of a shop or the provision of a service and the absence of alternatives. Situations in tandem might develop into active hostility; its imposition on the individual by forces outside their control of such power that it overrides personal disinclinations to participate in violence and this combines with the opportunities which such violence provides for personal social and psychological advantages.

For many of those involved in these periodic outbreaks of inter-religious violence, it cannot be assumed that they are highly committed and involved members of their particular religions since the unemployed and younger men figure prominently in such events. Just as with the violence their religious commitments are touch-and-go ones involving participation in religious festivals and rites of passage rituals; an age group activity in which younger males may not always predominate. Older males may participate as part reaction to their decline in status from ageing and because they may be more affected than younger ones by economic and social changes.

Tertiary Religious Violence: Non-violent Initiators

While there have been historical figures who have preached religious hatred and who physically led attacks on the people and property of another religion, modern scientific developments in communications technology have made their physical presence often unnecessary. Terrorists-cum-religious leaders can remain physically isolated but yet able to promote violence and to organise cells without any expectation that they themselves will be in physical danger of which Osma bin Laden is an example.

This man has risen to prominence as the leader of an extremist Muslim movement by a combination of wealth and charisma. There is nothing to suggest that his private and familial life has been anything other than conforming to orthodox Sunni Moslem standards nor is there any currently available evidence that he has ever been personally violent. However, in a 1998 interview for Al-Jazeera television (Laden, 1998), he stated that 'every grown up Muslim hates American Jews and Christians. It is our belief and religion. Since I was a boy I have been at work with and harbouring hatred towards the American'. In a February 1998 '*fatwa*' he stated that 'we with God's help, call upon every Muslim who believes in God and wishes to be rewarded, to comply with God's order to kill Americans and plunder their money whenever and wherever they find it.'

It may be that inter-religious violence has never been the working out of some primordial need to be violent. It would seem that in numerous cases the cultural paradigm of dislike for those of a different religion, particularly those who look and who behave differently to themselves, can be activated by political and social processes initiated but perhaps then not controllable by those who started these sequences. A recent example of such initiation must be the visit to the Temple Mount in Jerusalem by Aaron Sharon, before he was elected Prime Minister, knowing full well that it would provoke Palestinian violence.

In December 1992 at Ayodhya Lal Krishan Advani, the leader of the Hindu fundamentalist Bharatiya Janata party distanced himself from the demolition of the mosque there by a Hindu mob. Nevertheless he had made this almost inevitable by representing himself at public meetings as a personification of Rama and the consequences were widespread inter-religious rioting in which over a thousand Muslims were killed with the active support of the police in Bombay and elsewhere.

He also started ritual processions criss-crossing India carrying symbolic bricks for the construction of a new temple there to Rama in combination with the Vishva Hindu Parishad, stating that the original temple at Ayodhya marked the actual birthplace of Rama which had been demolished by Muslims and replaced by the mosque there (Bakker, 1986).

In both these cases there is a direct link between the actions of leaders and the ensuing violence in which the appeal to those who reacted violently could have been anticipated as almost inevitable because of the commonplaceness of similar reactions in the past.

A clearer connection is that of command responsibility defined in cases before the International Criminal Tribunal in regard to Bosnia as 'responsibility for the criminal actions of a subordinate when he knew or had reason to know that the subordinate was about to commit such acts or had done so and the superior had failed to take the necessary and responsible measures to prevent such acts and pursue the perpetrator (International Criminal Tribunal, 1996).

However, there are various aspects of command responsibility even in centralised religions such as Roman Catholicism and in armies acting on behalf of political-cum-religious interests. The connection between individuals acting as such and their connection with what subordinates may be doing when it involves thousands of individuals outside the boundaries of direct control makes responsibility hard to establish.

In all situations of mass inter-religious violence there is a background readiness coming from long-running and widespread hostility and the development of situations which are so widespread as to make restraint and control impossible if it does not come from the consciences of the individuals concerned.

This is considered to apply more strongly when individuals are within a chain of command in which they are ordered to behave in a violent way and have ordered others to do so. When the German Police Battalion 101 was told to kill Polish Jews *en masse* and their commander told those men who felt unable to do so to let him know only 12 out of 450 did so and no discriminatory action was taken against them (Goldhagen, 1996: 181-263). In terms parallel to that of the Cambodian genocide, the Jews had already been dehumanised in a long-running socio-political process.

It would seem that little inter-religious violence is the work of full-time professionals and that most is done by part-timers, while the principal influence to violence rather than in restraining it lies with inciters to violence who are able to do so by a combination of charisma, favourable backgrounds combined with circumstances favourable for violence and modern communication methods.

The Triple Viewpoint and Hostility

Perhaps rather more than any other human activity, violence correlated with religious beliefs and practices is associated with moral issues. The conflicts between religious precepts and practices and what is considered justifiable and the whole issue of socialisation into particular practices.

This goes beyond the possibility of triple vision (Armstrong, 1992: xi) in considering the Christians, Jews and Muslims in the ongoing Palestine conflict. In violence associated with religion, there may be a victimless aspect as in the thousands of Japanese suicides on the Saipan and Okinawa islands in 1945 (Toland, 1971) and to a lesser extent in the sacrificing of first-born children in Carthage in the 4th century BC (Weyl, 1968).

In most cases there tends to be a concentration on the immediacy of violence almost in terms of newspaper headlines, the victims and those who have made them victims as if such cases of brutality could be isolated in time. Religious violence should not be considered as social mutations but springs out of centuries of actual and latent violence dating back to the Ottoman suzerainty of the Balkans, Cromwell's actions in Ireland, the Crusades, Muslim expansion into Europe and Central Asia, the Moghul conquest of northern India and anti-Semitism in Europe.

In all these cases and in many others the moral guilt swings backwards and forwards, the pendulum of justification goes from one extreme to the other. Almost every issue is clouded by reciprocal brutality over a social time span of many generations. Fear of the 'other' is outside any considered moral justification because it has not only been socialised into the people involved into these specific scenarios but in the general human framework of their social thinking.

We are left with the numerical knowledge of lives and environments which have been destroyed or mutilated and the justifications and attributions of blame by contemporary survivors and observers which contribute little to any detached assessment.

Many can understand violence in fighting over territory, resources, cattle or indeed women and that the attainment and retention of power is worth fighting for. But violence for religious reasons is in a class by itself because the God(s), spirits or whatever are silent and can only be known from the affirmations of those who state that they have heard from these silent realities. Thomas Hobbes stated in 1651 that anyone assuring others that God spoke to him in a dream, only says that he dreamed that God spoke to him. To go beyond that requires a personality and a cogency which leads to the needs of others and these are few and far between.

In such situations any neutrality of assessment is virtually impossible since if some violence is justified as the will of God or whatever, to take up a detached viewpoint as if it could be somewhere between 'yes' and 'no' is probably impossible or at best just insulting to those involved. They would see this neutrality as either hostile or benign; but not that there is scientific isolation against which their activities and values could be weighed.

Theories of Religious Influence

The influence on and interrelationships between religion and social behaviour and in particular concerning violence appear to rest on two theoretical approaches. The one in which social needs are expressed in part by religious behaviour and beliefs and the other in which religious beliefs initiate social behaviour. Whichever of these theoretical viewpoints are consciously or unconsciously retained, it is almost inevitable that certain supporting evidence and results will be produced, but it is not just that religious and irreligious mindedness produce results which can be correlated to these frameworks of thinking.

In contradistinction to this approach there is the hypothesis that whatever the basis for beliefs, they do have a direct effect on and promote certain patterns of thought and behaviour which are augmented if not aided by social conditions. Max Weber (1958) wrote "it is not our thesis that the specific nature of a religion is a simple 'function' of the social situation or the stratum which appears as its characteristic bearer, or that it represents the stratum's ideology or that it is a 'reflection' of a stratum's material or ideal interest-situation."

To state that religion and by analogy all the imaginative influences of artists, poets and writers just as much as prophets, are no more than functional reactions to social situations, is to diminish the exceptional characteristics of human beings, even if it does correlate to violence in the situations and events which this study endeavours to cover.

The first approach does not attribute to religious beliefs any existence as an independent variable and is the theoretical stance of many social scientists that religion is a by-product of particular social environments and thus does not merit any particular serious and separate attention.

If beliefs including religious ones are created by social conditions, then they can only be secondary factors in the polarisation of societies which has already existed which have no intrinsic connection with religion. It is these later connections which dominate their lives and motivate the hostility which turns to violence (Hickey, 1984: 58-62).

Earlier studies of belief have stated that polarisation comes from social conditions or dominating personal initiatives and that they persist because groups become committed to it and seek validation for these hostilities in religious beliefs (Borhek & Curtis, 1975: 132-33). People work backwards from their existing social positions; because I dislike these people of another religion for reasons that are social, economic and political, then I am happier if religious reasons can be found for this.

The weakness of this theoretical approach is that many of the social, economic and political conditions which correlate to religious beliefs also correlate to behaviour which has no religious connections. Although it could be pointed out that some form of religious belief and practice is universal if its 'magical' aspect is included, difficult living conditions are often correlated to violence which has no religious aspects. Possibly a better approach would be to recognise that holding particular beliefs in common with others in ways that have become institutionalised, must channel thinking and behaviour into certain patterns.

It would seem to be a distortion of reality to suggest that the persistence of Hindu-Muslim violence in India over several centuries has been a reflection of social, political and economic differences and not in part a development of patterns of behaviour and thinking which are based on the dichotomies of monotheism-polytheism and a single life *versus* transmigration of souls. Such beliefs are deeply imbedded and to think otherwise would be to trivialise the importance of these differences. In a sense all religious believers and practitioners are lapsed from the requirements of the Great Traditions to which they belong and their minds and actions are always likely to be merged with their personal, familial and communal Little Traditions. Let us now look at circumstantial factors in religious violence.

4

Circumstantial Factors in Religious Violence

We have seen that categorizations in definitional and circumstantial terms may provide no more than a broad framework of correlations between religion and violence. These might be of value within a single identifiable culture with its own language but not otherwise. There can only be weak links between Buddhist, Christian, Hindu, and Muslim and traditional religious practices as within these Great and Little Traditions there are many different groupings.

Above all each incident of violence is always going to be quite individual and although there may be some shared characteristics and their accumulation into seemingly major trends may suggest essential correlations, it may obscure other factors which may not have any observable relevancy. This is a process of elimination in which some factors in some incidents are defined as inconsequential and others as being of sufficient importance to become notice by media agencies external to the communities involved. It is not that the selection of factors is arbitrary but that it is inherently biased.

How does it come about that certain people come to be violent for ostensibly religious reasons and is there a process of social learning which overrides the social need to have predominantly passive interrelationships? Outside Islam how do groups of religiously motivated people come to see violence as a way of solving their problems when it seems obvious that it will not bring about what they want.

What are the objectives of religious violence when a high proportion of religious practices are private rather than public and only some people choose to look different in ways that correlate with their religion. For ideas to become visible and thus potentially involved in violence, require social pressures which may have little to do with religion.

How do some religions but not others reach rulings which for some justify violence? To what extent are the founders of faiths models for passive or violent behaviour. Few contemporary Christians model themselves on Christ while it is common enough for Muslims to see the Prophet Mohammad as a model for their contemporary behaviour.

Many justify contemporary religious violence in terms of past events when that is always a reconstruction of what may or may not have happened. A detached impersonal view of what occurred in the past is rarely popular and acceptable to a wider public who have other reasons for remembering special versions of their religious history. Past brutalities are remembered for just that and their context may be telescoped to fit in with their contemporary needs.

The mass media can certainly be influential in religious matters but there may be little correlation between the intentions of its authors and how their productions are interpreted. Furthermore, the assessments of influence are always problematic and relate to the persistence and simplicity of a theme as well as its appropriateness and generality.

The Models for Religious Violence

Are there paradigms which might account for the believers in particular religions becoming violent on occasions and are these just ideas or are they ideas modelled on some historical figure. The Lord Buddha in so far as he is thought to have preached a specific doctrine, preached progressive non-involvement in mundane activities if not the total avoidance of all earthly activities. There can be nothing in Buddhist doctrine or in the way that Buddhists have organised their monastic lives to promote violence; detachment and violence cannot easily be bound up into a socially active and popular whole. What might be called the expressionless face of a meditating man and the monk wandering the streets with his begging bowl are not models for any type of external violence.

Hinduism has mythological figures correlated to violence with Vishnu becoming incarnate as Krishna to restore among other things the duty of the warrior caste to kill and be killed and the *Mahabharata* with its bitter feud between the Pandavas and the Kauravas clans (Zaehner, 1970: 176). These are not models for contemporary behaviour; there is no paradigm of secular involvement in which violence is an obvious and continuing element; it is perhaps episodic and infrequent and more than anything else very obviously mythological Hinduism has a clear difference between religious and secular preoccupations. The models for Hindu behaviour are more modern figures such as Mahatma Gandhi with his active forms of passivity in his 'Non-Violent' political campaigns against British authority and the many thousands of wandering *saddhus* who exhibit forms of retreatism rather than violence.

With Christianity the message and practices are ambiguous. Christ threw the money changers out of the Temple and latter died violently perhaps as a potential focus of opposition to Roman suzerainty in an already volatile Palestine. Although the New Testament showed his frequent involvement in secular activities, he never took on what would now be described as secular leadership. Whatever the ambiguities of the Christian message Christ said 'Render unto Caesar that which is Caesar's and unto God that which is God's'. He was not speaking as a potential ruler and theology has been preoccupied ever since with this division and the elaborations of influence. Modern popular models for Christian behaviour are Mother Teresa and such lesser known figures as Dietrich Bonhoeffer who was killed by the Nazis, are not models for violence. The violent Christian has no place in their modern ideology even for fundamentalist sects.

For Muslims on the other hand the model for them is that of a man, the Prophet Mohammad who almost as soon as he was sure of his divine mission, was involved in running a small state. In this work there was an undivided life in which there was no evasion of violence if it served a religious-cum-secular purpose as a necessary part of following the instructions of Allah.

His biography was written in some detail within the lifetime of his associates and much more is known about him than has ever been discovered about Christ who has no place in history outside the Gospels and non-religious writings except for a passing reference in Josephus' history (Josephus, 1890). His life clearly shows that he was directly involved in what he saw as necessary violence. He operated on a wide screen around Mecca and Medina and there is not only an exact model for Muslims in his behaviour but a much narrower range of possible alternative explanations.

The biographies of Mohammad (Ibn Hisham, 1859-60; Al Waqidi, 1882) detail him as the leader of some 25 raids, battles and sieges out of some eighty in which the new Muslims were engaged in the course of which he was wounded; he had a satirical poet executed and he ordered the killing off of the Qurayzaha Jewish community which was opposed to him and his religious message which included political domination and the enslavement of their women and children. It would seem, therefore, that the theology and peacefulness created out of this personal history and the Koran is one within an Islamic totality; it is not a peace which permits a variety of faiths except for the subordination within Islam of the people of the book, *Jews and Christians*.

The Prophet Mohammad as a role model is thus based on a considerable amount of accurate historical data over which there can be little argument despite doubts about some of the recorded memories, the *Hadith* of what he may have said with their detailed pedigrees of attribution.

In comparison, Christ's known life is full of gaps and suppositions and it is thus easier for the Christian theoreticians to elaborate his life in non-violent terms as a necessity of life in those times. He lived in a Roman world in which religiously motivated rebellion was always a possibility to which the Romans had already reacted with violence. Had the Prophet Mohammad attempted to spread his message in either Baghdad or Byzantium, he might well have met a violent end; he survived with his Divine message on the edge of this civilised world in a political vacuum. His message was not impeded by any external political powers. In this there are parallels to Brigham Young moving the Latter Day Saints, the Mormons, into unadministered and inhospitable Utah where his inspired religious message could be put into secular practice.

As a model for the behaviour of Muslims, the inspired behaviour of the Messenger of God, the Prophet Mohammad has to be accepted as firstly as a response to the conditions in which he was trying to establish his religious and political suzerainty for the new faith. Secondly, that this Messenger of God in whatever he did became and continues to be the model for Muslim behaviour in a modern world which has nothing at all in common with 8th century Arabia.

Thus it is not a question of whether such behaviour is justifiable in terms of the then Arab morality or how he saw his political and religious status at that time (Watt, 1956: 192-220) but these events are the model for contemporary Muslim behaviour. It would seem that according to this example Muslims are justified in killing those who deny the religious and political suzerainty of Islam.

It seems clear, therefore, that the role models for the believers in Buddhism, Christianity, Hinduism and Taoism are peaceful and popularised ones which give no support to violence. It is only in Islam that the role model centring on the Prophet Mohammad is one in which violence has a prominent place as a religious necessity and neo-fundamentalism has him as the model for all behaviour. Let us now look at religious symbols as to their correlation to religious violence.

Religious Symbols and the Depiction of Violence

Whereas a television programme or film provides a long series of images, religious symbols are isolated and static; they have none of the many opportunities for the sequential interpretations of a film. A picture and a statue are static and their effects on their viewers will be an ever varying mixture of cultural-cum-religious paradigms and personal social and psychological needs. Popular religious art and indeed all art is what people read into it not just what is supposed to be pushed into their understandings by the particular religious message of the artist.

What the painter or sculptor intended to depict may well be known but not necessarily something that can be deduced from what the viewers see and interpret within their own individual minds. Although all believers have experienced violence, seen it on television or know of it from the history of their religion or state, Islam alone has a form of art from which little or no violence can be elicited.

Art in Islam is designed without personifications and mainly calligraphic. The Taj Mahal tomb in India has quotations from the Koran round its walls. There are no pictures of the Prophet Mohammad except in some North African popular religious postcards and if he is represented at all in Moghul art his face is veiled. So while there is some Islamic art with figures particularly from the Mughal era in India, it is not popular iconography depicting violent scenes from history connected with Islam which could have had any effect on popular understandings of how Muslims should behave violently or otherwise.

So it is in other faiths that active or passive violence is on popular view and may have an effect on religious understandings and behaviour. In this there are difficulties over what is being represented and what is being taken into the mind; after all there just are no elephants that look like Ganesh the Hindu God nor people with multiple arms like the Goddess Kali, nor indeed people whose skin is naturally blue. These may be extreme examples which Westerners pick up but the representations of Christian art are just as improbable as Graham Sutherland's tapestry of Christ in Coventry cathedral and the enormous painting in a Southall church in London by Annigoni of the Virgin Mary treading on a snake.

The Hindu temple at Khajuraho, Madhya Pradesh, India dating from the 14th century is covered externally with explicit pictures of exotic sexual activity displaying a calculated and languid eroticism (Rowland, 1954: 164). Indeed these sculptures go far further than what can be seen in western pornography. There is little if any data to suggest that locally or indeed in the Hindu population at large that such depictions have had specific effects. Any more than the writings on such themes in the '*Kama Sutra*' (Burton and Arbuthnot, 1963) and for Muslims 'The *Perfumed Garden of Shaykh Nefzawi*' (Burton, 1963) have had any known effects on commonplace sexual behaviour. However, there must be a difference between books which require the effort of reading before any interpretation is possible and the seeing and believing of the instant appreciation of a religious images.

Christian Depictions of Violence

Modern Christian popular and intellectual art may not be a stimulus to or depict violence except in the most abstract terms. Contemporary prayer cards do not depict martyrdoms modern or otherwise and are stylised to fit into either older styles such as the use of iconic presentations or modern forms avoiding reality. Since the majority of Christians are not Caucasian, the depiction of Christ and his family as Asian is rarely attempted although common in Ethiopean traditional paintings. Even local pictures of the Ugandan Christian martyrs and Greek Orthodox depictions of martyrdoms and miraculous healings are not too evocative of violence.

In general historical Christian art depicts Christians as being the victims of violence rather than as lauding those who are violent for ostensible Christian ends. Indeed the agony of those killed as Christians is rarely depicted with any great attention to reality; Christ on the cross often has a detached appearance rather than one of his intense physical pain. Modern Christian art is usually abstract and as such may only be able to stimulate those who are intellectually prepared for that type of representation. However, the recent American film '*The Passion*' directed by Mel Gibson, a traditional Roman Catholic, in which the final hours of Christ are depicted with extreme violence, has explicitly overturned the pietistic conventions of the Crucifixion; in ecumenical terms it is a documentary of religiously motivated horror.

Buddhist Depiction of Violence

An analytical difficulty in evaluating Buddhism and its art is that few practising Buddhists are attempting to follow the Buddha's precepts of detachment. In Spiro's ground-breaking study of Burmese Buddhism (Spiro, 1971), he divides their practices into four ideological systems of which only its nibbanic form based on the doctrine of *nirvana*, a religion of radical salvation, could be described as Buddhist.

Its artistic form which predominates in popular Buddhism is of a seated figure with a facial expression of detachment and only variations in the hands symbolising various stages of meditation. Those depicted as being in the presence of the Buddha are often shown to be more like popular film stars than known religious practitioners.

It is on the fringes of northern Hinayana Buddhism rather than in its southern Mahayana form that violence is depicted. In this system there are various depictions of the various hells and their guardians through which pass those who fail to attain detachment. But the violence shown is seen as self-inflicted rather than what they do to others.

The pictures of spirits, 'nats' in Burmese, and their preoccupation with human affairs would parallel in many ways the Christian saints and for the northern Buddhists the Bodhisattvas who have delayed entering into the total detachment of *nirvana*, in order to help others to achieve the same state, do not suggest violence.

Thus we see in Buddhist art vivid representations of the violence to themselves which individuals can avoid by progressive detachment and this would include participation in violence to both man and beast. There is nothing there which could be correlated to instigating violence to others or indeed to themselves since self-torture and asceticism would be seen as forms of personal attachment from which humans should be freeing themselves.

Hindu Depictions of Violence

In Hindu historical art and its modern iconographic representations in popular form and on television presentations of Hindu writings such as the *Mahabharata*, violence is a constant mythological theme. In this we are up against the rationalist assumptions underwriting any form of analysis and the plain fact that modern Hindus as much as their ancestors, find little irrelevance in the physical improbabilities of Krishna's multiple sexual achievements and the humanised activities of the monkey God Hanuman and the elephant God Ganesh.

Violence is present in most Hindu historical monuments and numerous paintings involve fighting, murder, poisoning and fire ordeals whether in the museum collections of 18th century Kangra works or in popular religious posters. There is always the figure of black faced Goddess Kali with her necklace of skulls (Moorkerjee and Khanna, 1977: 84). So clearly Hindu popular art is full of violence and its printings are now commercially important as a growth industry but popular as it is, it runs counter to the passivity of working towards personal detachment and the peaceful nature of Hindu role models. Supernatural imagery and its depictions of improbable violence has perhaps always been part of the Hindu understandings of life but its correlations to actual violence may well be illusory.

In all religions artists have striven to depict the objects of faith on stone, canvas, vellum and paper and these have been used by millions of believers as objects of and aids to personal devotion. But they are seen and experienced in the first instance on an individual basis and may stimulate people to torture themselves. For violence to others as coming from this art is a doubtful leap of understanding and we must look for more likely correlations in the ways that societies function.

Religious Violence as a Resource

Reaching the Decision to be Violent for a Religious End

We have established that there is little evidence that humans are biologically programmed for inevitable violence although it is clear that they have the physical and indeed linguistic ability to be violent should the circumstances and personal characteristics encourage such behaviour.

The evidence for a psychological disposition to violence independent of social circumstances continues to be thin because experiments cannot include actual violence in its social environment; a riot for an ostensible religious reason cannot be created experimentally. Working backwards from actual events involving violence by individuals over a religious issue must remain suspect for providing definitive evidence.

However, ethological data does suggest that social and individual behaviour will always tend towards supporting any group in which individuals are situated and which they consider to be important and that there is always general hostility to outsiders varying in intensity with social distance as in the sentence 'I may not steal from close relatives but I can borrow and not return from more distant ones and I can steal whenever possible from outsiders'. From what sources do individuals learn to be violent for religious purposes?

Social Learning and Religious Violence

There are three major sources of violent behaviour which can influence the behaviour of individuals over issues which they feel to contain an important religious element (Bandura, 1973). Firstly, violence modelled and reinforced by family members. While there is much evidence that domestic violence continues over generations, there does seem some likelihood of violence for a political-cum-religious cause would be transmitted within a family whether or not it has any communal support, if the father or mother is committed to such a cause. Mrs. Pankhurst's devotion to women's rights led her family into a commitment to that cause including public violence and extreme Irish Republican violence seems to run in families.

Then there is the sub-culture in which an individual resides and in which they grow up with a particular attitude to violence. It is tempting to see Palestinian young men as an unusual and regrettable example of the ways in which particular circumstances have led them and the whole society in which they live to see violence as the only way to further their political and religious ends. But cultures have always had an attitude which predisposes or dissuades individuals to or from violent solutions to their personal and social problems. The American ideal which is passed to their children of standing up for themselves, is not an attitude of mind which favours negotiation particularly in the south and west of that country (Cohen *et al.*, 1998). There are many examples of societies which have had well developed socializing processes which make their children see certain behaviours as desirable.

The Duoum Dani of New Guinea (Gardner and Heider, 1969) were described as a warrior society in which inter-tribal warfare was their most valued activity and they fought intermittently for social and religious purposes but not for land, food resources or the conquest of opponents. Fighting was instigated and perpetuated by fear of the ghosts of dead warriors' spirits who had the power to cause misfortunes to living relatives until they were avenged. Perhaps it is valid to remember that the American war against the Japanese was based partly on revenge for the dead killed in the Pearl Harbour attack and that this is probably just as much in their minds over the dead killed in the attacks on the World Trade Centre and Pentagon; a national reaction to underhand violence who killed while disguised as peaceful guests in their country.

On the other hand the Tahitians (Levy, R., 1969) devalued physical aggression and the ancestral spirits served as punishers rather than inciters of aggression and since they were omnipresent, they served as a more generalized source of control over aggression than parents or peers. So we see from such examples that a society can have a code of conduct into which its children are socialized for or against violence and more importantly the ancestor spirits back up these attitudes. The highest rates of aggressive behaviour are found in social environments where there are plenty of aggressive models and where aggression is regarded as a highly valued personal attribute such as Afghanistan and possibly in parts of contemporary America and Sicily.

Lastly, symbolic models for or against violence which are provided by the mass media. As far back as we have recorded history there have been depictions by societies which suggest their approach to violence. Statues of the Buddha and pictures of Christ illustrate passivity and we have none from Islam which prohibits depictions of the human face and certainly few which might have given them ideas of the appearance of the Prophet Mohammad. Hinduism provides an enormous range of statuary illustrating every conceivable human emotion and posture but it seems doubtful whether violence comes from or is initiated into thinking by seeing such often inhuman illustrations of what their Gods and Goddesses look like and how they behave.

But with printing and then television the range of symbolic forms available to each and everyone in a society, makes the mass media an important influence since what is seen and heard is dictated more by economics than by concern for moral values. Television provides unlimited amounts of violence and ways of dealing with it and which are seen mostly in the comfort of the viewers' homes. We also know that televised mediated learning is usually as effective as that achieved by actual face to face class-room teaching.

It is safe to conclude that television and its depiction of violence does have an effect but the amount of resulting influence and the circumstances in which it occurs are highly variable and in effect impossible to quantify. Television demands attention and cannot be ignored if the set is switched on and usually presents its material in short sequences in which problems are depicted and solved often by violence.

However, even the 'simplest' of presentations is in fact complex in which the viewer's mind picks and chooses; they are far less likely to be influenced by fantasy as the depiction of actual events. It is one thing to quantify the gross totals of murders and assaults which the average viewer will see in a year and another thing to suggest that it inhibits passivity and increases violence. What one sees and stores in the mind are subject to a large number of variables (Singer and Singer, 1984: 24). This is well illustrated by televised pictures of the World Trade Centre's destruction in which American men and women weep and Palestinian women wave their arms with jubilation. Much lies in the social and religious programming of the viewers and listeners.

Violence as a Religious Resource

Violence is a very human response to any stressful situation whether it means violence against others or against oneself in compulsive fasting or whipping or the carrying of thorns in bundles on Good Friday in imitation of Christ's suffering. It is a very efficacious activity since it fulfils both instrumental and expressive functions at the same time. In the context of religion it can certainly be manipulated by religions in the context of conflict and contention since it requires remarkably little specific resources or knowledge. The kitchen of every household contains many weapons which could be used aggressively and many public places are full of stones.

It was noted in the Colombian 'violence' between Communists and Christians which had go on for decades with an enormous loss of life and livelihoods, that it was an easy option to initiate but it was much more difficult to stop or to keep it within acceptable boundaries (Levine, 1981: 192).

Systems of belief involve threats and promises which are closely related and the withdrawal of a promise is a threat whether made institutionally or subjectively assessed and their reality correlates to the depth of belief which in turn correlates to their social and biological environment.

To convert threats into actual violence again is the result of socio-religious factors in reacting to real or imaginary violence and the compulsion to act comes from the intensity and conviction of rightness and of course to the instant satisfactions which might come from violence.

To deliberately invoke violence in a religious context requires the build-up of a considerable supportive background which most religions are reluctant to give but it can flow freely enough from no more than accidental flash-points which have initiated religious riots often enough in India and Egypt.

As we have shown it is hard outside Islam to find any specific injunctions to violence as a religious obligation, but there are frequent analogies to violence in religious myths, songs and prayers, even the titles of religious dignitaries. Violence in a religious contexts should be seen as something which has evolved for situations which are rarely primarily religious. Western religions find difficulty in coming to terms with violence of any type, and avoid as far as possible the tedious equivocations of any moral rulings by concentrating their support instead for those involved in opposing violence.

Then there are always different levels of understanding violence connected with religion. The Holy Spirit Movement which erupted in northern Uganda challenging the quasi-legitimate government can be explained with difficulty as there may have been at least five such movements operating in the 1980s with similar names. A possible reaction to the tribal biases of Idi Amin who placed members of his own tribe in many positions of authority; not so much ethnic as not that particular ethnicity. The fact that he was actively Muslim in a predominantly Christian society was an important indicator of how his actions would be interpreted. There were other factors involved such as a generational conflict between the Acholi gerontocratic establishment and the ex-soldiers who had been removed from the army after Amin's defeat. This movement provided opportunities to regain status for both men and women since there were many widows as a result of the prolonged civil war and there were no longer brothers-in-law to inherit them as a family responsibility (Brett. 1996: 291).

In addition it was a movement to purge society of witches and wizards paralleling the mass killings in Usukuma to the south in Tanzania. As well as being a movement which involved possession by foreign spirits from China, Zaire and the United States and the assurance that the dead would be resurrected and given cows and houses and of course, the use of magical potions to prevent the power of bullets (Behrend, 1991: 162-9. 1997). In this amalgam of causes and consequences undefined religious needs provided the means for their attempted satisfaction. It is not too difficult to transpose this complexity into any situation in which religion and violence seem to have come together. In Uganda it may have been relatively easy to see the advantages which individuals may have gained from this resort to religious violence and the fact that it is more difficult to find its significance in supposedly more complex societies and situations, cannot mean that the similar substrata are not also in existence there.

The Selection of Objectives for Religious Violence

On occasions discovering the objectives of religious violence may require analyses of some subtlety if the aims are intellectual rather than emotional although it may often seem mindless or irrational to outside observers, but in published inter-religious issues this is not likely to be a dominating factor.

The dominant public opinions of particular societies may draw lines of legitimacy and this may change from day-to-day. The border line over which violence becomes likely is always a variable one. Unacceptable behaviour relating to religion varies with public opinion. The national climate of opinion may provide a legal entitlement of which the local elite do not approve and in which the public authorities are disinterested. This may mean that Hindu Untouchables may be attacked because they are overstepping this local power-structured border line of acceptable behaviour. Although the regulations of the Northern Ireland Police may have stated that recruitment was open to Roman Catholics, it remained for decades a Protestant enclave maintained by the persistent in-group hostility of the police themselves to these outsiders and they would socially and professionally try to freeze them out.

Unacceptable religious behaviour in a small community in which the religious status of individuals is public knowledge and Hindus of one caste would find it difficult to enter the temples of another, would pass unnoticed in a city. Untouchables in a city can go freely in to Hindu temples there because their caste status would not be known and their offerings are as acceptable as those of any other person. Anonymity in terms of animosities is a neutral condition unless individuals choose to be recognizable by appearance, costume, occupation or neighbourhood.

Then there are the differences between a reaction to a situation in personal terms and one in which a person of some prominence in a family, lineage, clan or community voices an opinion to which their social subordinates react; strong opinions are likely to be more pervasive than less firmly expressed ones.

There is also the availability of support. The high caste militant Hindus in an Indian city made a particular point of recruiting the unemployed because they would always be available for demonstrations as the employed would be less likely to come to demonstrations of which their employers might disapprove. This form of aggression meant that the Untouchables as Buddhists had to confine their religious activities to inside the temples which they had made for themselves (Contursi, 1989). This form of implicit and potential violence is common enough.

So the division between the expected if not predictable violence and the unexpected relates to the degree of planning. Protestant or Hindu processions in Northern Ireland or urban India in which the planned route goes through or near to Roman Catholic or Muslim areas can be expected to provoke automatic reactions. Even if these parades are monitored by stewards and the police, nothing can be done about spontaneous abuse and little about the use of loudspeakers. Groups can perhaps be regimented but individuals are much more difficult to control when inter-religious resentments have been consistently maintained over generations.

Since the specific objectives of any religion can only be assessed through personal statements, they tend to be judged by observable behaviour, so it is often on religious sites that violence tends to be concentrated. It would seem therefore that sites which are isolated from the worshippers of other faiths might well be free from violence but their very existence is sometimes seen as provocation. Mecca is a prohibited area for non-Muslims but the Great Mosque was invaded by Muslim dissidents in the mid 70s which involved prolonged violence and a large number of deaths. Similar events have occurred in Northern Ireland in the destruction of churches in areas segregated by religion.

So the possibility of religious violence is not necessarily solved by legislated isolation of places of worship and the intermingling of faiths and their places of worship is a feature of every city. Coptic churches in Egypt and Jewish synagogues elsewhere have been consistently the objects of deliberate desecration. However, in Israel they do not seem to have been the objects of Muslim violence possibly because the Jews rather than the Israelis are acceptable by Muslims as 'people of the book'.

It is when religions share a city as Jerusalem and more specifically the Temple Mount that the situation becomes beyond negotiation since it is based on emotion (Pollock, 1950). Goldstein the killer of 29 unarmed praying Muslims in that most holy of mosques second only to that of Mecca itself, is treated as a saint by extremist Jews who have built a monument to his memory and as a mass-murderer by Palestinians so that it has to be guarded. We can conclude that this area as historically part of ancient Jewish history and with an important mosque there for over a millennia, it is not a negotiable situation without prolonged and amicable changes in the surrounding dichotomised societies (Friedland and Hecht, 1991).

Hostility over Muslim and Hindu places of worship can at least be minimised since everyone knows when religious festivals with their parades are going to occur and it is probably only in the interests of fundamentally antagonised believers and politicians who hope to benefit with votes from such riots to encourage the possibility of violence. But there are always flash-points in which individuals react violently even when they know that it may well catch on. Long standing predispositions to inter-religious antagonisms do not require very much to turn them into public violence.

The Availability of Binding Religious Rulings

Religiously motivated people often require or are provided with reasons for their actions which are the result of their leaders putting their rulings into print. These religious rulings vary in importance with their structures and the degrees in which they might be acceptable and thus of influence. Their availability varies between those which have a recognised and sanctified corpus of sacred writings of which the Torah and the Koran are examples to Hinduism which has doctrines in many documents which have wide ranging potential applications which make rulings of little immediate social utility.

All Christian denominations, sects and cults are organisationally centralised of which the Roman Catholic Church and the Church of the Latter Day Saints, the Mormons, are examples. The former has divine support for its rulings when the Pope speaks officially as head of the Roman Catholic Church and the later has a structure by which various branches support each other through centralised contributions and funding. The differences between these types of Christian rulings and the Islamic '*fatwa*' and the Judaic '*proposa*' are the long-standing organisational structures of which they are a part.

Both Islam and Judaism have systems of rulings related to specific situations paralleling the case stated system of Western legal practice but which are not part of a hierarchical structure in which a ruling is binding on all subordinate parts of the same system. Rabbis and imams may be asked for opinions on matters put before them, but both are in effect professional religious lawyers relating the details recorded in sacred or sacralised literature to some particular situation. They are not pinnacle executives in a recognised official religious structure.

The issue here is twofold; firstly, the acknowledgement that they have the religious learning sufficient to make such rulings and secondly, of course, this applies to the rulings of all religious bodies and their executives, whether they get the support of public opinion.

Of course, some interpreters hold positions of religious authority such as the Rector of the prestigious Al-Azhar University in Cairo or the Chief Rabbi of Israel but the former would have little relevance to Shia Moslems and the latter for the more extreme Orthodox or Reformist Jews in Israel and indeed not those elsewhere. To a large measure these men could be classed as either self-employed or employees of particular communities. There is a need for them to make acceptable rulings which must be correlated to their incomes and status, and this which may well make their rulings rather local in their significance. Then there are political rather than religious leaders such as bin Laden who issue '*fatwas*' in support of the quasi-underground violent movement which they have founded through their own charisma and funding.

However carefully thought out such rulings may be, they have to be somewhat ambiguous to involve large number of people in a range of situations or very narrow and thus of limited use. Any Muslim who for one reason or another, is considered or considers himself to be an authority, may issue a ruling, a '*fatwa*' on any point which he considers to be important. Whether or not such rulings are obeyed depends on the numbers who consider them relevant and of course there would always be the factor of his personal charisma. A '*fatwa*' requiring violent action against America as the Great Satan ignores the fact that religion in this issue is entangled with every other aspect of human social, political and economic relationships; much the same applies to religious support for violence against Israel. Religion has been mixed into secular factors as far back as recorded history is available.

It seems likely that when opinions are asked for about matters which are not personal and which are relevant to some aspects of public opinion such as might be provided by a Shia Ayatollah, those asking for a ruling will usually be looking for support for a viewpoint on which they have already made up their minds; thus the requests for religious opinions are often made to authorities who are known to support an existing viewpoint.

Those expressing hostility to America and Israel are well known but Jewish ones against Arabs are less so and equally virulent as incitements to or in support of violence. A statement in Israeli papers by fifteen prominent rabbis that there was a Torah prohibition against the evacuation of any Israeli army posts and their replacement by Gentiles (Yediot Asharonot, 1995) and Rabbi Ginsberg's ruling on the virtuous aspects of Goldstein's killing of 29 Muslims while they were praying in 1994 (Ginsberg, 1995: 20) as embodying sanctification of the name of God, saving the lives of Jews, revenge against Palestinians, cleansing evil and the struggle for the Kingdom of Israel.

It would seem that in the context of violence these religious rulings have been used rather more to justify violence than to restrain it and that rulings on general moral issues end up with so many qualifications that they defeat the original moral intention. The concept of the just war is indeed a laudable one over which there is never likely to be agreement as between Muslims and Jews just as much as between Christians, Hindus and Muslims in current inter-religious violence.

A centralised religious organisation will usually provide rulings on matters of concern to its believers or indeed avoid doing so when any such ruling would span cultures which have little in common other than membership of a particular faith, which itself would be divided by many different styles of living and thinking.

The smaller the religious group, the more detailed can be such rulings and the greater their binding nature. The Amish Christian communities in the eastern United States have always been extraordinarily peaceful in how they organise themselves internally and how they relate to the outside world in refusing any type of military service even to the extent of some dying from mistreatment in first World War. A similar small sect the Doukhobors in Canada while no doubt peaceful internally, were violent externally by blowing up Canadian government property and when prosecuted demonstrating their disapproval by talking off their clothes in court to the great embarrassment of the judiciary (Holt, 1964).

Many in the larger religious groupings would consider its institutional rulings to be statements of the ideals of which they approve, particularly as they may not be considered relevant to anything that they do or are likely to do and that the ideal is so far separated from social reality that it is in practice ignored. The prohibitions of Eastern religions against killing is only followed by extremely orthodox Jains, but in modern life such a prohibition comes up against tinned food and public restaurants where the conditions under which food is prepared cannot be known.

We can perhaps conclude that religious rulings may be binding, particularly as they concern violence in particular circumstances and for limited number of people who consider themselves bound by their provisions for any number of religious and secular reasons.

The Past and Religious Violence

The Importance of the Past to Present Religious Violence

In a society which has suffered extensive violence and in which religion has been a known factor, the imposition of peace by internal exhaustion, negotiation or by external sanctions, will not create peace in the mind. It might take two full generations for such violence to cease to be of contemporary importance and all along fluctuating memory will be augmenting realities. The past is something that once existed but what is thought to have happened then are not necessarily facts. 'The past is a foreign country, they do things differently there' (Hartley, 1953).

Reactions to Religious Persecutions

It is not only violence but the potentiality to be the victims of violence that makes the religious and social practices of any religiously motivated group adjust as a necessity for their own survival. Some indeed will conform to the dominant religion or at least conform to overt rituals. Muslims who converted to Christianity in Spain to avoid being expelled, were always suspect and in the Roman persecutions of Christians many converted to the state religion of emperor worship to save their lives and then recanted. There is always the factor of the embedded nature of faith and persecuted Japanese Christians after a time remembered only that they should not marry their cousins which gave them a distinctive biological profile different to the others on their island (Schull *et al.* 1953).

In such situations of persecution the Orthodox, Maronite and Roman Catholic Churches are at a marked disadvantage since they are all centred on ordained priests as intermediaries with the Divine and more specifically require a designated place of worship. Other religions which centre themselves on a book which can be easily hidden if only by changing the cover and on private worship such as the Christian Baptists and the Muslims are easier to survive persecution. Judaism as well does have collective worship and prayer leaders but these are not essential to retaining their personal identities as Jews. Thus any decentralised religion is at a marked advantage in being able to retain their religious identities under conditions of persecution or even plain unpopularity.

The extreme persecutions of the Stalinist, Khruschev and Cultural Revolution periods of Communist states do not seem to have permanently damaged the major faiths from recovery despite their experiences. Of course religious tourism can be misinterpreted but it is unusual to see platoons of Chinese soldiers in a functioning Buddhist temple in Wuhang and the number of young people praying in the Jade Buddha temple in Shanghai apart from the thousands there on a major feast day. The prayer group in the Shanghai Roman Catholic cathedral on a weekday seemed no different to a similar group in a European church. A weekday late evening queue in St Petersburg three deep and over half a mile long outside an Orthodox cathedral to see and perhaps kiss an icon on a short loan from the USA testifies to this resilience.

It might be that persecution as a reality modifying religious behaviour in practical terms may fade quite quickly from memory if there is no current value in keeping it alive and more cogent reasons for getting on with their own private personal religious practices. In a sense the Israeli and Pakistani politicians see many advantages in keeping alive the memories of past horrors which in the latter case are regularly refreshed by fighting in Kashmir and inter-religious rioting in India. The British remember the hundreds of thousands who died in the two World Wars but it required the small numbers who have died in subsequent skirmishes to make the annual ceremonies of remembrance of importance to the current political life of the country. There is no social or political 'statute of limitations' on the practical religious value of historical persecution.

The Chinese authorities may not have felt any need to persecute the Muslims because they were without centralised religious authorities which could have challenged their secular authority. In Tibet the Dalai Lama as the political and religious head of the state made the persecution of Buddhist institutions almost inevitable and this is a current issue in Tibetan thinking as it is kept alive by the Chinese dominance of Tibetan social, economic and political life.

The Chinese Communist Government has always seen Christianity as an imported religion with no automatic Asian status so that their persecution of Roman Catholics came as much as anything from the Roman connection and it has continued to function as a national Catholic Church with the current government objecting to the appointment of a Chinese priest to the College of Cardinals without receiving their prior agreement after consultation.

In Indonesia the official policy required that every citizen had to belong to one of the major religions, the Great Traditions which was written on their identity card without which they could not vote in official elections. This led to substantial increases in the number of Christians and gave them an established position as an official recognised religious minority but this has not prevented a marked increase in violence between Christians and Muslims which was not ignited by memories of past persecutions and the Christian colonial government.

However the attitudes of centralised governments with authoritarian tendencies is not of much concern to established and well-known faiths as they have rather similar ways of maintaining themselves. All governments keep a wary eye on new cults and their practices which are actively if not potentially violent or at least disruptive of established political structures. The Chinese Government's hostility to the Falun Gong as a sect able to organise embarrassing protests electronically in support of its individualities in ways that injured the dignity of national leaders.

The Legacy of Brutality in Memory and Reality

The position of the Jews with the Holocaust fading into history as survivors die out, is perhaps unique since the creation of Israel and the immigration there of a majority of European Jews which has meant that they are no longer confronted across the street so to speak with the very people who sent their friends and relatives to wholesale destruction. Life in the new country allowed the Holocaust as one particular form of religious violence to fade from immediate refreshment but for the fact that they have come to occupy the land of the Palestinians by force and thus they face a crescendo of new forms of violence and a border ringed with latently hostile states. Just as the Holocaust may fade as a reality after two generations, the arrival of any form of peace in Israel may similarly take another two generations to become a reality.

Thus there are two forms of violence which leave a legacy of hate and fear. One is religious violence fixed in time and which can be brought up to date as the political and social situation may require and secondly, situations of religious violence in which the protagonists are across the road or just around the corner and does not need the reinvention of historical memories to keep hostility going; the protagonists are constantly seeing the 'enemy'.

The Partition of India into two states occasioned widespread killing and the abduction of women so that each side has missing members who are either dead or abducted and thus unrecoverable in terms of the customs of their natal communities (Butallia, 1993). In Pakistan there are now so few Hindus that Muslims who fled from India are not being constantly confronted with the people whose relatives caused their flight and the loss of all their property.

On the Indian side more than a hundred million Muslims exist dispersed in every town and in many villages in the country, thus most Hindus have no chance to forget the dismemberment of their country and Muslim brutality even if it was not constantly refreshed by contemporary events both within and without their country.

The Sikhs in India who were made the victims of mob violence after the assassination of Indira Gandhi by members of her Sikh bodyguard, often moved into areas where there were other Sikhs but the alternative of moving to the Punjab as farmers was not a possibility for most of these urban families. They are now left with the real likelihood of coming across their attackers since they still live in the same towns. Much the same applies to Belfast in Northern Ireland in which the Roman Catholics and Protestants have been separated by barricades and live in segregated housing, but they can still see their enemies and might well meet them shopping and in government offices (Boal, 1982).

So there are also many situations in which the past is brought in to support contemporary antagonisms. The Palestinians see the arrival of the Israelis as yet another invasion by Europeans just like the Crusades. The significance of the Crusades for Westerners is as a little known part of history which has no correlation at all with any of their contemporary political, economic or social concerns. Whereas for the Arabs, they now have a significance comparable to that of the Holocaust for Jews in the creation of Israel; more specifically they are part of the background thinking of every Palestinian today (Armstrong, 1992: 123).

Within the Islamic empire there was no particular pressure to convert Jews and Christians who paid a special tax from which Muslims were exempt and they were tolerated and accept as believers in inferior faiths which had been superseded by Islam; there were no particular persecutions organised and supported by the state.

As the Arabs see it in retrospect the Christians of Europe declared war on Muslim Palestine in order to occupy Jerusalem as the centre of Christianity which the Muslims had respected; they massacred Muslims and in some cases Jews as well, defiled Islamic holy places and drove Muslims from their homes. For them it is now the ex-Western Jews who are behaving like the Christians in the Crusades in the territorial expansion of Zionism at the expense of Asian Arabs.

For Roman Catholics in Northern Ireland the distant past is a present reality and see Cromwell's suppression of the Irish in the 17th century and the failure of the British to bring relief for the potato blight famine of 1846 as relevant to the present disturbances. No matter how long they have lived there, the Protestants are still invaders foisted on the Irish. British commentators would consider these past events as not worth much more than a passing reference.

The expulsion of the Orthodox Christian Greeks from Turkey after the failed Greek military invasion in the early 1920s and the reciprocal exclusion of Muslims from Greece is still a factor in the present relationships between the two countries, brought up to date by the divisions of Cyprus into two religion based countries with very few Christians in the north or Muslims in the south, perhaps made worse by the Muslim defiling of Christian cemeteries.

It seems likely that a situation of religious violence will develop in Spain which now has large numbers of legal and illegal Moroccan migrants. Southern Spain was ruled for some centuries by Muslims and after three centuries of intermittent fighting, they were expelled in large numbers to Morocco. Morocco certainly benefited from the arrival of so many hard working Spaniards just as Spain lost economically but in present terms, the history of these prolonged religious wars may well be brought up to date in popular violence against these useful but socially unwanted immigrants.

There is little doubt that the history of religious tensions is not just of interest to educators and researchers but is fuel to contemporary difficulties for which it may have no direct relevance except as an adjusting and adjustable folk memory.

The Historical Present and Religious Violence

The fact that religious violence may be part of a community's history and seemingly should only be of interest to historians does not necessarily mean that it is forgotten. In Crete Turkish molestation of Christian women during their suzerainty tends now to be elided into German atrocities during their occupation 1941-45 in which the misuse of women had no part.

Western analysis of Islamic hostility to the United States and Europe would think of the Crusades as an interesting example of Christian ideology without seeing it as bigotry and the oppression of Muslims. Any examination of history will show that Christianity or at least ostensibly Christian societies have been persistently violent in every century and the Muslims less so but still significantly violent.

Such examination will show that the Eastern religions also have had violent episodes such as the Sufi saints as the leaders of military bands of their disciples constantly engaged in violence with non-Muslims and the fighting monks of Chinese Buddhism opposing the state religion (Veer, 1994: 34, 93). The conclusion must be that

Christianity and Islam have historically predominated in ostensibly religious based violence.

History is continually rewritten into the memories of people to suit the political and social needs of the present. Certainly historical facts are readily available for those who wish to find them and have the time and incentive to do so. But this is a specialised exercise and few events are free from the historian's own viewpoint and cultural biases.

While the Holocaust may be accepted as a regrettable but possibly exaggerated fact by the Palestinian negotiators, it is not likely to be in the forefront of their minds which it will certainly be for the Israelis at all levels. To the Palestinians in the occupied West Bank who were born after the creation of the State of Israel, this is an irrelevance in assessing the presence of Israeli tanks on their streets and their helicopter gun-ships overhead. The historical present for them would be classed more specifically as religiously motivated colonialism.

Memory can be both updated and altered in a contemporary religious as much as in any social context and for a wide range of what might be called quite understandable and circumstantially acceptable social and psychological reasons.

The Media and Religious Violence

One can speculate that in the historic past with its absence of widespread literacy, the precipitating factors initiating violence would have involved more direct structural ones as well as along lines of rumour and gossip with a limited contribution by individuals outside their own personal ranges of influence.

In contemporary social environments there is the factor of widespread literacy which may not be quite so influential as it is estimated since reading up to a standard which may influence behaviour requires a combination of intellectual skill and the using up of time.

Wireless requires only the ability to hear and because of this is more popular than reading since it has parallels with conversation. Almost certainly television is becoming if it has not already become the most influential of all forms of media. It requires no additional skills for an appreciation of what is being viewed ; nothing more than an individual's self-understood intellectual level and a social environment which provides the opportunity to view. What is viewed is always appreciated before it is interpreted and this personal interpretation is immediate. There is in reading perhaps always the feeling that one may have missed something; that one has to measure up to what the writing is trying to say. It is almost an adversarial situation but this is not so with television viewing.

It seems obvious that if Western people from highly literate cultures are moved to tears or joy by depictions which they know to be created by authors, actors and actresses who are known to be equally proficient in other roles producing alternative expressions of joy and tears, then it is likely to be just as influential in less literate cultures and that information is as likely to be just as influential. Further that imagination everywhere and in every culture and may initiate religious emotions leading to violence.

There is, of course, the possibility that a high proportion of individuals in a society under certain conditions are more emotionally sensitive as in the reactions of teenagers to pop-stars and people attending services at a religious shrine. It seems certain that illusions provided by television as well as its depictions of actual events however edited by the camera crews, which may be filtered through religious understandings, are likely to be influential in any culture.

Few people see religious events in the context of real or anticipated violence and in the past have reacted quickly enough to rumour, but now with television, even allowing for a saturation of channels, it seems likely that most individuals will have seen many more incidents related to religion and violence than ever before. What is seen on television is both clear and near, much more so than for persons attending a public meeting or religious ceremony who will be on the fringes of what is happening at the centre, and all that is likely to be missed is the emotionally loaded atmosphere. It seems unusually short-sighted to suggest that the immediate as much as the indirect influence of television on human behaviour has yet to be proved. In the context of religious violence it would be more prudent to suggest that there is a correlation and that in some circumstances the social and psychological connection is close.

The Media and Correlations to Violence

If those in intellectual and political positions to influence others are reluctant to accept that there is a connection between the media and human behaviour because they want the proofs parallel to those of hard science, then they will never find it in the variability of human behaviour both individually and environmentally.

No doubt they have their reasons for being so publicly cautious but they still act on the assumption that there are such connections and the latter spend large sums of money on public opinion surveys to further their own political progress. Whether they are parents or not, few adults are comfortable with the exposure of children to violence on television and every producer of consumer products advertises to increase sales. There would be no point in political speeches being reported in the press and being broadcast if they were not felt to influence viewers and listeners. In the same vein there are large numbers of religious broadcasts by independent stations in Western states and even more in Islamic countries where broadcasting stations are either directly controlled by the state which defines itself as Islamic or keeps closely to an Islamic line out of political and religious prudence.

On these bases it would be safer to assume that there are correlations between what is broadcast and printed and attitudes of mind and social behaviour and moreover in situations combining the media, religion and violence, such influences are likely to be strong.

However an equally important point is not so much that religiously inflammatory broadcasts or at least ones that seem so to outsiders, are made but that they are listened to in ways that seem to correlate to some degree of understanding of the message. Egyptians in a café in which a Friday sermon is being given on the radio, were not listening at all and their only reaction was perhaps to talk louder; it was the done thing to have the radio on all the time just as it was the done thing not to pay specific attention to the programme except as background noise.

Television as a Purveyor of Violence

Certainly in the Western world many are concerned that there is a close correlation between the constant depiction of violence on television despite its three-way mixture of fantasy, fantasy-cum-reality and reality Whether a depicted event comes into one or another of these categories is very much a personal assessment and may have little to do with any independent assessment of its reality. Terrorist or freedom fighter, suicide bomber or martyr are words whose meanings vary between those using them and the situations in which they are used.

Any evaluation to be valid would have to involve and reach agreement on at least five variables; the context in which it was used, what they in fact watch in the varying images that appear on the screen as a mixture of sight and sound, the ways in which individuals watch and for how long varying from full attention to background similar to seeing pictures on the wall, the meanings that they find in it and lastly the people's experience of the world and of television as a medium for expressing this (Josephson, 1995).

These are all variables in which there may be significant differences in the context of religion and violence between those who see violence in someway through the cultural view point of its relationship to religion 'defending the faith' and those who see it as at least partially understandable in terms of social and psychological abnormality. Many Middle Eastern broadcasts would fall clearly into the first category, just as their Western explainers and commentators see it in terms of the latter.

The Possibility of Viewpoints Biasing Assessments of Media Influence

The influence of the written, aural and visual television media is an important part of any understanding of violence and religion but they are dependent variables. An essential precondition to any such appreciation must be the semantic framework within which it is approached and the possible ways in which this diminishes the basic individualism of violence.

It is individuals who read, listen and watch and the phrase 'mass media' can be understood as a pejorative term; a similar offering which is often assumed to have similar influences on a large number of people who are considered to be similar in their basic behavioural patterns. What individuals get out of this exposure which is often expressed in the numbers who view a certain programme or have a certain newspaper in their possession is obviously variable. Only in some extreme situations can observers conclude that there are short-term similarities in consequential behaviour which probably depend as much on a range of other factors. So it seems likely that mass similarities in reactions to media exposure come from the restricted range of factors used in the analysis as the social sciences have yet to develop a methodology which can cope with a multiplicity of coinciding factors. There is also the partial assumption in this that those who are so influenced are lacking in the intellectual or social capacity to think and act independently.

There are other pejorative words used in the understandings of media influence which coalesce round an assumption that many rather stupid people are influenced by such illusions. Researchers tend to observe if not to think in terms of some ideal world of rationality and that much of the influence of the media is pushing irrational illusions onto an otherwise natural predisposition to logic. Of course, all people are logical in a small proportion of their activities but for most of the time they act on illusions of facts; some are generally true but rarely so and most facts are thought to be true for small numbers of people for socially restricted events.

Rationality in human understandings is not some universal and impersonal standard extending from science into social behaviour and social choice. Certainly there is the capacity to be logical and pre-industrial subsistence farmers have worked out much of what they have done for generations by logical thought and it seems likely that the modern urban industrial worker has less need for logic for their own survival than traditional farmers.

What is offered in the media may be either an accidental or deliberate illusion as in a television serial, popular novel or concentrated documentary but in the reactions of individuals there is a self-created and self-understood rationality. They 'know' it to be true and they react accordingly. Individuals are moved to outrage and then violence by some published illusion and are acting rationally according to their understandings at that time, however much the researchers according to their understandings see such behaviour as irrational.

Perhaps it is even erroneous to use non-rational or indeed irrationality as descriptive terms and that there are multi-levels and multi-layers of rationality within which the correlations of religious violence and media influence should be approached. There are four factors which are correlated to the possibilities of religious violence which should be considered; the persistence of a theme, the simplicity, appropriateness and generality of the message.

The Persistence of a Theme

The history of Islam in comparison to Christianity shows a continuing overwhelming majority retaining in both belief and practice the simplicity of the original message. There has only been the Shia-Sunni split over the possibility of continuing divine inspiration which occurred early on and has subsequently centred on the particular social and historical environment of Iran and the various Mahdi movements in Africa. In the 19th century there was the breakaway Ahmaddiya sect in India which has attracted only small numbers of cross-converts and is perhaps best known for its translations of the Koran out of the original classical Arabic.

The Shia and Sunni have fought periodically such as the recent Iran-Iraq war for which there was a dominant religious theme on the Iranian side and in the current civil war in Iraq. There are also the four schools of law with different interpretations of the Sharia and Sufi devotional groups based on hereditary themes, but none question the basic unity of Islamic belief and practice. The Islamic media message over the centuries has been of a single faith rather than the well publicized Christian denominational differences with their somewhat unconvincing unity.

The media message of Christianity has been the reverse and from the earliest times that its beliefs were written down there has been an inability to agree on virtually anything in either beliefs or practices. This quarrelsomeness has been shown in a long history of Christian internal and external violence currently occurring in northern Ireland and recently in the dismemberment of Yugoslavia.

These differences from the early days of Byzantine theological disputes which excited the man in the street almost as much as circus entertainment (Runciman, 1957: 16) have been enhanced and supported by denominational media and numbers of professional denominational differentiators who run separate schools, hospitals and training establishments. The persistent media message of Christianity is one of disagreement at best and violence on occasions.

The persistent theme of Buddhism is one of inactivity and passivity and its rules and beliefs written in an archaic language are themselves so complicated that the Buddha himself is alleged to have said that discussions over doctrine never had an end and that monasteries should split rather than continue them in arguments.

The other Eastern religions with their multitude of mythical deities have no persistent themes except that of existential differences and the ephemeral nature of all religious groupings. It could even be said that religious affiliations are no more than the acceptance of a personal label as much for social as religious reasons. The media can propagate a message but the themes are more socio-political interpretations of temporary expediency.

The overall background themes from religiously motivated media presentations are of Christian disunity disguised by affluence contrasting with a very obvious Islamic unity, while the Eastern religions have no beliefs or structures enabling persistent themes.

However, the persistence of a media presented theme in the context of religions and violence need not be a specifically religious one as it may relate to historical events as amalgams of remembered history culturally retained and reinterpreted for reasons that are not entirely religious. The memories of the Irish on both sides of the denominational divide as well as that of the Palestinians and Indians go back to events which often do not have much relevance to contemporary events except to make feelings worse.

It may be that economically developed societies with well organised social support systems, do not need a socially modified cultural history to explain and support their current lives and more specifically not one which focuses on hostility to people with whom they are in close contact. They find it difficult to understand why other peoples cannot forget the past or rather cannot leave alone events far back beyond anything more than media presented and interpreted historical memories.

Other societies in which substantial numbers lead economically, socially and politically disadvantaged lives, the past is reinterpreted as a useful and indeed popular support explaining their current difficulties and in this religious issues constantly appear. What may or may not have happened in the past as professionally interpreted by historians may have little relationship to what the media may persistently repeat to be appreciated by their readers, listeners and viewers.

There are persisting themes of inter-religious significance in many areas originating in ancient events updated for contemporary relevance; these ghastly events certainly happened but the past is not left alone as beyond any living memories and it is interpreted in terms supporting contemporary hostilities. The Irish famine 1845-49, the Crusades, the Partition of India, the Israeli destruction of Palestine, Christian-Hindu-Muslim massacres are all kept alive as persistent themes and in many cases the presentation in the media is horrifyingly repetitive.

The Simplicity of the Message

The Islamic message is particularly suited to media transmission. It has been suggested that the Prophet Mohammad relayed his inspired message in as simple a form as possible as he did not think that the Bedu at whom it was directed, would have been attracted to or indeed have understood a more complicated new religious message. It was also possible that he did not himself understand the complexities of the Christian message and that he knew about the quarrels over meanings which had led to violence in Byzantium.

'The strength of Islam lay in its simplicity. There was one God in heaven, one Commander of the Faithful to rule on earth and one law, the Koran by which he would rule. Unlike Christianity which preached a peace that it never achieved, Islam unashamedly came with a sword' (Runciman, 1957: 1, 15). Any partially knowledgeable Muslim knows that the Prophet Mohammad had been a successful war leader and that this faith had been spread by war as much as by conviction.

The Five Pillars of Islam are not ambiguous and the basic message reiterated from every mosque before prayer and in every prayer, is not only clear but it does not involve the intermediation of priest or pastor. The media message is the inclusiveness of this single phrase which does not require long explanations or the long permutations of pre-baptism learning. For most of the Islamic world, this simple message of the power of God is spread through the language in which Allah gave it to the Prophet Mohammad originally.

What can media presentations do for the believers of other religions. The Christian message is seemingly clear enough but their meanings require personal interpretations as they are more in the nature of an invitation to construct social systems of morality. The Christian creed involves not only complex ideas such as the Trinity which the Prophet Mohammad misunderstood as including the Virgin Mary but also a series of statements requiring belief, whereas the Islamic one is encapsulated in a single phrase. Even in its fundamentalist forms of belief in the Bible there is an absence of simplicity and the inevitable consequences of having to pick and choose what to believe in and practice from a translated book.

The Eastern religions do not attempt to provide dogma and their complex ideas allow almost as many interpretations as there are believers. The possibilities of religious violence with and between faiths does not come through as clearly as it does from the Islamic message. The seeming peacefulness of the Buddhist, Hindu and Taoist messages come as much as anything from the absence of any felt need for creedal uniformity as a necessary part of those religions in the contexts of those societies.

The Generality of the Media Provided Message

The more specific the media message the narrower will be the range of people who will feel that it can apply or be of use to them. A message propagated through the media has to have as wide an appeal as possible if it is to catch on. The ambiguities of the Christian message make it appealing and individually interpretable but the Muslim message is not only unambiguous but leaves man's destiny in the hands of Allah tied to a few simple rules. The media tells the faithful that the message applies to every situation while the message itself is not overburdened with the problems of interpretation and conscience.

The message in the form of the Five Pillars of the Faith have only one item of belief, the basic dogma of a single God and Mohammad as his Prophet and four requirements of individual practice independent of any institutional intervention; prayers that can be said anywhere and are not particularly clock related, charity on Fridays, fasting during daylight hours for one lunar month per year and the pilgrimage to Mecca once in a lifetime. This is a message to individuals that has no particular difficulties over its implementation and it has a general appeal which has not developed into sectarian interpretations and moreover it has always been tied historically to political success and wide ranging suzerainty over Christian and Jewish communities.

When the Christian denominational message is specific, it can have no general appeal or application except when taken up by separatist sects which have isolated themselves as much as possible from their surrounding society. It would seem that a general message with its ambiguities allows it to be used as much for violence as for peaceful purposes. A leaflet handed out at a 1995 meeting in Portadown, Northern Ireland showed the British Prime Minister Blair with a Roman Catholic priest after his church had been fire bombed by Protestants. This had biblical texts above and below the picture, 'But thus shall ye deal with them; ye shall destroy their altars, and break down their images, and cut down their groves and burn their graven images with fire' (Deuteronomy, 7: 5), and 'And the kings of the earth, who have committed fornication and lived deliciously with her, shall bewail her, and lament for her, when they shall see the smoke of her burning' (Revelation: 18, 9). In huge print at the bottom 'and again, they said, Alleluia. And her smoke rose up for ever and ever' (Revelation, 19: 3; McKay. 1995: 175).

In addition there is the selective reading of the media which certainly correlates at best to bias and more importantly to violence.

The following example from a novel concerned with the protracted inter-religious violence in northern Ireland could apply equally well to Muslims, Hindus and Jews wherever they are in conflict. '(He) read the newspaper as other men play cards, shuffling through a page of stories until he found one to confirm him in his prejudice. A Jewish name discovered in an account of a financial transaction, a Franco victory over the godless Reds, a hint of British perfidy in international affairs, an Irish triumph on the sports field, an evidence of Protestant bigotry, a discovery of Ulster governmental corruption; these were his reading goals, (Moore, 1965: 29).

So we can see that the generalities in a wide-ranging religious message would, of course, allow specifically religious ideas to be spread under the guidance of religious administrators and theologians who may wish that it spread to a wider audience than their immediate clientele including such messages as peace. Pictures of armed Shia divines in Iran and Iraq and Maronite priests in Lebanon dispute the peacefulness of their faiths. The appeal of universal aims will usually be to those with no immediate proximate difficulties correlated to their religion; a very small minority of religious activists.

In the use of the media, whether people are religiously motivated or not, some degree of self-interest must always predominate. Watching, listening or reading takes up time and money so few are going to do this if it involves something they do not like. Hindus and Jews are not likely to read Muslim newspapers and broadsheets anymore than Protestants in Northern Ireland are likely to reads Roman Catholic literature. It requires a very detached intellectualism to read the media which gives viewpoints of which they disapprove and indeed which they may consider threatening to their own survival.

The use of the media is not a search for truth but a search for support for opinions which people consider that they have held all along. The general applicability of a religious message closely correlates to the uses which people wish to make of it. To the outsider much of this is no more than bigotry but to those actually involved in religious violence either as givers or receivers there is a need to find in the media some religious confirmation of their own positions.

The Appropriateness of the Media Carried Message

We can see that virtually any Christian or Islamic text can be taken out of its historical context and used in support of contemporary violence and that this is a particular feature of monotheistic faiths which have the words of God in print. The Eastern faiths have no such certainties and for this reason are reluctant to use religious texts, even those pronounced by transitory charismatic leaders as having divine authenticity.

Thus the connections between monotheism and activism is closer because of the divine origins of its message however interpreted and this interpretation is probably likely to be more active in its popular appeal rather than in intellectual reflection and less immediate reactions.

There is a balancing act in the minds of Christian believers between the message in the media and the appropriateness of its particularities; to Protestants in Northern Ireland brought up to avoid and dislike Roman Catholics for a variety of real or imaginary secular and religious reasons. There is an immediate appeal in the verse from Deuteronomy quote above as it fits exactly into a pre-existing mind-set. Perhaps the belligerency of Christians comes in part from the need to defend their choice of belief regardless of its appropriateness.

The appropriateness of the Islamic message is different because the Prophet Mohammad is a firm historical figure about whom much is accurately known (Watt, 1953, 1956) and except for his receipt of divine revelations, he has none of the quasi-mythical nature of the historical Christ. The appropriateness of the Muslim message comes from its generality which individuals and groups can interpret as they wish; it is Allah's will.

The Reading of Violent Words

Even the most passive of religions and their purveyors use violent words for spiritual processes in the war within the bodies and minds of Buddhists, Christians, Hindus or Muslims for the spiritual mastery of their senses. Just as it is certain that the writers in most cases never intended that they should be the cause of violent action and would indeed have been disturbed by any such attribution taken out of its context. Nevertheless St. Bernard in a sermon in praise of the Crusading Templers wrote 'a new sort of army has appeared. It fights a double war; the first against flesh and blood enemies; the second, the war of the spirit against Satan and vice. The soldiers of Christ kills with safety; he dies with more safety still. He serves Christ when he kills, he serves himself when he is killed, (Bernard, 1919, 204-6). This could have been written by a contemporary Muslim about the suicide bombers in Israel and by a Shia divine during the continuing civil war within Iraq. So violent words are common enough in religious documents and broadcasts but it seems unlikely that they ever had any direct and immediate effects creating actual violence.

Words once printed have a life of their own detached from the social ambience in which they were created so that once they have left the printer, they can turn up anywhere. While they may be sold or handed out to those who are actively interested or marginally involved in violence, there is no guarantee that they will be read and even less that they will be read and understood in the ways that the writer intended.

Of course the written media can inspire and provoke their readers into violent reactions but 'the symbolic efficacy of words is exercised only in so far as the person subjected to it recognises the person who exercises it as authorised to do so, or what amounts to the same thing, only in so far as he fails to realize, in submitting to it, he himself has contributed through his recognition, to its establishment' (Bourdieu, 1991: 116).

The power of words must surely relate more to when they are spoken or reproduced electronically than to their appearance in print. Reading only uses a single sense and in so far as it has any immediate or long-lasting effects, it depends very much on a skill which has not existed in human history for very long. It is by no means widespread as a precipitator of violence; at the very least it requires an enabling and indeed a supportive environment.

Is what is written just another religious tract bought out of denominational loyalty and not much looked at beyond the cover or is it something in which the contents are specifically believed in? A very high proportion of Muslims believe in the obligatory truth of the Koran but far fewer believe in the Bible, the Torah or the Hindu *Puranas* in this way. For the Buddhist, Hindu or Taoist, the proportion who have any such sense of narrow religious obligation to a single text, is virtually non-existent because that sort of defined commitment is no part of their religious understandings which are more likely to be passively individual than violent.

Few Christians read the Bible except in translation and their primary understandings are likely to be in the class related, intellectual and time worn linguistic variations from what they speak and read daily. There is no great difficulty for people of average education to interpret and to understand in their own terms what is printed. The parables in the New Testament are not difficult to understand and they are elaborated often enough in sermons for those who go to church or chapel; except for the removal of the money changers from the temple it is not a violent message. The Old Testament is likely to be read as a tribal but violent history. Overall it does not seem that the Biblical wordings and those of the hymns will have any direct influence promoting violence.

With Judaism there is an obligation to read their scriptures in the language of their faith for the Bar Mitzvah ceremony of confirmation as an adult Jew rather than in translation. But these are complex books and Judaism has always stressed the importance of religious scholarship so that this role is performed by their rabbis. There is no violence in the message other than that which evolves from the protection of their landed rights. The role of the rabbi is well illustrated in the series of detective novels about the American rabbi solving crimes by the use of Jewish analytical procedures (Kemelman, 1979). The media message of Judaism is introspection and the applicability of the Torah to social practices.

In Islam a high proportion of Muslims know the Koran by heart or are able to read it in Arabic without necessarily understanding its meanings and this again is performed by scholars so that neither Islam nor Júdaism have priests. So for both Jews and Muslims the meanings of sacred texts are likely to be interpretations by those who are accepted as scholars combined with their communal acceptance of their personal worth and the applicability of their interpretations (Lambek, 1989).

The extent of the influence of such interpretations has been modified by literacy and certainly for Judaism by the difficulty of their application in modern not necessarily Israeli social life. On the other hand with Islam there has been a flood of media interpretations directed at the non-Muslim world and its influences which can be assumed to have contributed to the build-up of hostility to the Western but not necessarily Christian secularising influences.

The situation of the Eastern religions is totally different and more complex since they are written in the classical Pali and Sanskrit languages which have no modern usages outside their related religions which require comprehensive and specialised training of no use outside the religious sphere. In the case of Chinese this requires the learning of a whole new class of ideograms of no secular use at all; a contemporary educated Chinese in Shanghai finds it impossible to interpret the ideograms of a modern religious poster.

The Attractions of Media Promoted Myth

To the outsider the difficulty is in relating these media promoted sacred documents to contemporary violence as the tales they tell appear to have little relevance to the contemporary situations in which believers are likely to find themselves. By and large they are fairy tales, and no doubt of great literary merit to those who can read them in their original languages. Generally they are of more influence as entertainment than as an influence towards violence such as the twenty-six episodes of the Hindu Mahabharata epic on Indian television.

No doubt Max Muller, the noted Indologist went too far in writing about the *Brahmanas* as 'a literature which for pedantry and downright absurdity can hardly be matched anywhere...The general character of these works is marked by a shallow and insipid grandiloquence, by priestly conceit and antiquarian pedantry, (Muller, 1860: 389), in fact he referred to this literature as 'twaddle' several times in the next forty years.

The point must surely be that they have no direct relationship to religious violence and that their value and popularity lies in the public and media supported appreciation of them not as fairy tales but as tales having popular merit which has transferred easily to television and popular poster art. If Hans Anderson or Walt Disney have not been correlated to violence, then it is hard to attribute religious violence to the fairy tale horrors of Hindu mythology. They may carry within them the Great Tradition but in the popular mind, they are part and parcel of popular religiosity.

By any standards of analysis these are violent tales about mythological events and indeed about excesses of behaviour and this is their appeal but it is not an appeal easily transferred to contemporary hostility to Muslims since in their relationship to distant mythological time, no Muslims existed. Media promoted Islamic tales are totally different since they are based however inaccurately on historical events; the mythological input is minimal in comparison.

Aurobindo has denied that these ancient writings have a parallel to modern ideas 'we are told continuously by many authoritative voices that the (*Bhagavad*) *Gita*, opposing in this the ordinary ascetic and quietist tendencies of Indian thought and spirituality, proclaim with no uncertain sound the gospel of human action, the ideal of disinterested performance of social duties, nay, even it would seem the quite modern ideal of social service. To all this I can only reply that very patently and even on the very surface of it the (*Bhagavad*) *Gita* does nothing of this kind' (Aurobindo, 1922: 38) and he goes on to explain that its purpose is to aid detachment not to promote involvement.

Hindu sacred literature is too far beyond rational understandings to form the background for inciting religious violence, although particular parts may appeal and even control the mind to the extent that some might consider to be socially and psychologically unbalanced. These writings and depictions can be socially interpreted but it is difficult to see them as directing group violence; they have none of 'the do this or that' applicability and directness of the Koran and Torah and to a less extent the New Testament.

Two disparate quotations highlight this difficulty 'Indra said to Sumitra, you are good looking, flirt with this long-tongue demoness. Sumitra went to her and said Long Tongue make love with me. She said you have just one penis and I have a vagina in every limb. He went back and told this to Indra who said I will make penises for you on every limb' (Jaiminiya Brahmana, 1954: 1, 1-20; O'Flaherty, 1985). The descriptions of the goddess Kali are even more repulsive to the Western mind 'She is dark as a great cloud, clad in dark clothes. Her tongue is poised as if to lick. She has fearful teeth, sunken eyes and is smiling. She wears a necklace of snakes, the half moon rests on her forehead. She has matted hair and is engaged in licking a corpse. She has corpses for ear ornaments (Brhat Tantrasara, 1934: 1, 326). These quotations and their like are not the backgrounds for violence to other people however widely distributed in print or picture.

The Influence of Violence on Television

It would seem incorrect to suggest that there is no correlation between violence depicted on television and violent behaviour and much of any accepted correlation comes up against the moral and political difficulties of censorship in Western societies with a long standing and well developed tradition of free speech.

There can be little doubt that in Western uncensored or self-censored television programmes there is a very high rate of violence depicted. It has been estimated that in an average hour of United States prime time viewing there are some fifty crimes and twelve murders which would be a thousand times higher than the overall world murder rate (Meier, 1984). But this violence is only related to religion in an historical context such as the Salem witch killings or as the totally mythological stories illustrated as vividly as possible in the Indian Hindu Mahabharata serial.

The depiction principally in news programmes of such events as the September 11th destruction of the World Trade Centre in New York and suicide bombings in Israel are attributed to terrorism and political indoctrination and there would appear to be a reluctance in Western public opinion and political thinking to connect them with the strongly held religious beliefs of the Muslims involved based on verses in the Koran.

However research has shown that children react in the same way to real violence as they do to television violence with little emotion or care. A study of Canadian children watching much television showed that they saw the world as meaner, scarier and more dangerous than it is and that this fear was more likely if what was depicted was seen as possible or in circumstances resembling their own (Josephson, 1995).

Even allowing for all the differences in the factors used in surveys there seems little doubt that persistent watchers of television and the inevitable quantity of real or fictional violence depicted will desensitise them to real life violence (Singer and Singer 1984). But does this apply to non-Western viewers for whom programmes are subject to political control and some form of censorship ?

In those countries there is likely to be severe restrictions on the showing of fictional violence although it is likely to be widely available on videos. What will be shown are pictures of real violence which is considered politically and religiously appropriate for that country which and its public opinion which does not require surveys to disclose. Pakistan television will have shown the results of Indian shelling in Kashmir and Indian stations will have shown the other side in just as much detail. Above all Muslim television will have shown repeatedly Israeli destruction of Palestinian homes and to a major extent laud Palestinian suicide bombings both as retaliation and as an expression of their Islamic ideals supported by hand-bills detailing the martyr of the month. Desensitisation may well occur but in the context of defending not just their religion but their political rights as well.

Television and its legal and illegal video derivatives whatever governments may feel or attempt to control is a growing creator of changing ideas wherever it is available and getting a colour television set is high on almost every peasant's list of priorities and it is watched almost endlessly wherever and whenever there is electric power. Even if it only shows domestic television serials parallel to the Western ones which have run for years with millions of devoted viewers, it brings vivid experiences of the non-local into their homes, particularly giving women, the young and rural villagers; it gives them access to stories of another world from which they are socially distant but nearby. In this it is not the governments which are guiding their peoples through the complexities of modernity but the culture industry's professionals (Abu-Lughod, L., 1993).

The nationalist and often the religious message is broadcast into a complex social space where the very local and the trans-national are both equally powerful pulls Whereas in Western societies television violence is an unequal mixture of predominantly fiction over reality, elsewhere it involves more current religiously connected depictions which are more likely to stimulate and in some cases to promote religious violence rather than to desensitise such viewers to the consequences of violence.

The Importance of Non-literacy in Religious Practice

The basic approach to the study of any major religion is to read its literature and each religion has an enormous mass not only of sacred writings but commentaries and elaborations of their themes. Since all these writings are in print and survive their authors, they are gone over again and again by generations of scholars and theologians. In such circumstances it is easy to forget that alongside this literature are various types of believers and gradations of belief. The literature has in theory passed through the hands and minds of countless generations but the effect it may have had on actual practices is rarely the subject of prolonged theological thought which is not often market orientated.

To read and think about these writings is convenient and makes time and motion economic sense; it is all there in one place under the eyes of the reader. To go and study religious practices is tiring and time consuming and there is always the feeling that it may not be typical, much less an average when the participants are so obviously different one from another and anyway represent no more than a small number of those adhering to the same faith.

The study of any religion is likely to start with their codes of belief of which Christianity is the best example since it is a creedal religion. Each Christian denomination has always wanted their beliefs to be supported by exact statements of their nature and meanings. It is from these creeds that the nature and substance of their religious practices develop, which is particularly clear in Roman Catholicism's creed and even clearer with Islam which has a one sentence creed.

Many religions have no creeds because they are practised in cultures which are non-literate so that belief is not really distinguishable from practice which is a day to day affair. It is understandable enough that non-literate cultures have not produced creeds and Mbiti's seminal study of African religions does not contain the word 'belief' in either the table of contents or the index (Mbiti. 1969).

Of course, both Christian and Muslim believers have read their creeds often enough and probably can recognise the Muslim one written in Arabic, but except in the initial stages of affirmation and conversion, it is recitation which counts. Is literacy an important factor in worship and certainly most Christian denominations see literacy as an essential element in personal religious development, and indeed early catechumens were known as 'readers' in Africa. Most of those believers can recite their creeds so automatically that in practical terms they have the characteristics of *mantras* and it is from their recitation rather than from any understanding that religious values accrue to individuals.

Christianity has always been associated with learning and as printing developed requiring Christians to be able to read the Bible in whatever languages it was printed while Muslims have concentrated on being able to recite and read the Koran in classical Arabic as a certain sign of piety. It seems unlikely that literacy is a major factor in initiating violence unless it is done through easily readable slogans; it is more likely to be a response to the shouted evocations to violence in the name of a faith.

The religions of the East with written legacies which must easily antedate both Christian and Muslim religious writings, have not made reading and learning sacred texts to be an important part of faith. Religious learning is a professional occupation in special languages or vocabularies and there has been little effort to popularise sacred texts, if only because it would have been a long and laborious process with none of the simplicities of the twenty-six letters of the Roman alphabet. There has never been any concerted effort to construct restrictive creeds and many worshippers at temples in China and Japan take away printed literature which can only be of totemic value since they cannot read what they have bought with their multiplicity of specialised ideograms.

It would seem likely that the vast majority of practising believers use what may been written down in their religious books as providing results from the mere recitation of words. It can always be inferred that they have certain beliefs because they do certain rituals; 'I do therefore I believe'. The business suited Chinese man in Beijing holding smouldering incense sticks in his hand and repetitively bowing, while talking into a mobile phone, perhaps typified this approach.

The monotheistic faiths use fixed institutionalised formulas as a sign of commitment would seem to have the opposite approach. 'I believe therefore I do' but it seems unlikely that this is what is actually happening. For most believers religion is a practical process and the grounds for violence are more likely to be in what believers see and hear than in what they read. Public confrontations as in the debates between Buddhist and Christian theologians in Sri Lanka at the end of the 19th century, were intellectual exercises which had no practical relevance to the religious lives of either sets of believers.

This is not to say that the written word is unimportant because it clearly is to the minority of high level literates in any religion who do read and are motivated to some extent by what they read. For the majority of Western Christians the enormous quantities of religious literature which they buy is kept rather than read because it represents some form of protection against misfortune. Taiwanese Chinese go on circular pilgrimages to temples round the island where they do secular and religious shopping including the purchase of unreadable Taoist literature.

In Islam Koranic texts are made into amulets for personal use and also written in charcoal and washed into water which is then drunk, as powerful prophylactics against many misfortunes and the cure of other problems. In Buddhism similarly quotations from the scriptures are used in protective tattoos on the bodies of many Burmese and Shans. The use of writing in religion has to be seen largely as an advanced form of symbolism mainly used for protective purposes.

Overall the practices of religion are mostly mnemonic and even when they are linked to writing, it is unlikely to initiate violence except in exceptional circumstances. Certainly there are inflammatory religious texts which may be used as tools by would-be leaders to initiate violence in others. For an individual to be inflamed to the point of violence as a result of reading a religious text is rare as it requires a high level of literacy and imagination to reach such levels of personal stimulus.

An example of this would be the public demonstrations by outraged Muslims in many countries and the burning of Salmon Rushdie's 'Satanic Verses' by many who had never read the offending book. The 'fatwa' calling for his killing issued by the Ayatollah Khomeini may well have been issued on the bases of outlines provided for him by politically minded clerics who wanted a popular topic in their campaign against Western influence.

While religious writings are clearly important at an intellectual level and to the structure of institutionalised faiths and as a back-up for dogmatic positioning, it seems unlikely to have any primary position as a contemporary instigator of religious violence.

The Participants in Religious Violence

Whatever the situation in which there is collective violence correlating to religion whether it is one which ostensibly peaceful such as the collective circumcision of screaming Muslim children in coastal Tanzania or in the riots related to the Palestinian 'intifada' against the Israeli occupation or specifically inter-religious confrontations in India, there can be no assumption of uniformity among those involved. The rioters may appear at first glance to be a mass of individuals engaged in similar violence but this is not so.

The primary divisions among those involved will always be the usual classifications of social science investigation which destroys the possibility of uniformity. These divisions will be age and sex but if there are any women involved they may be carrying their babies. From where do the participants come since many may have been brought into the area to participate and the converse those in the neighbourhood may be conspicuously absent; they lock up their shops and hide. From what religion do they come as many of those involved stating that they are believers in a particular faith, may not be practising according to its requirements. Whatever classifiers are used the uniformity of the crowd as a single entity except in police reports that a riot occurred somewhere involving an estimated number of people, does not exist.

While the eye tends to concentrate on the stone throwers, there are always large numbers of onlookers on the fringe of the violence watching from doorways, the side streets, windows and roofs. Common sense should have made them realise that they are likely to be hit by gunfire, and tear gas can blow in any direction. We have here something similar to injuries by friendly fire in war. The people are drawn into danger by curiosity and the stimulus this gives to their rather dull lives.

Then there are those who are drawn into mass activity by group loyalty; friends are there and it is difficult for them not to go along with the rest as they would have to explain their absence latter when all their neighbours are out on the streets. But group loyalty verges into the accidents of presence, family visitors and the case of the Burmese traditional leader who had his children join the demonstration against himself as it would turn the protest into a subject of laughter; they thought it was great fun to parade and shout the slogans and to see some bystanders applauding them. In another case in Tanzania a student in sports clothes was drawn into a student demonstration on the way back from a game and he ended up being expelled under the orders of the government. Individual loyalty may and may not coincide in any way with the supposed purposes of the crowd.

Whereas in the Cambodian genocide there can have been little or no opportunity to opt out of involvement in this progressive growth of ideological paranoia, it was not always so in the German situation. There seems to have been a tacit understanding that those who felt unable to fulfil orders to kill, would be given other duties. We have already seen that the German Officer Commanding Police Battalion 112 when detailed to carry out mass killings in Russia allowed some soldiers to opt out and were given other duties without anything detrimental being entered in their military records (Goldhagen, 1996), but this could not have happened within the Pol Pot regime.

Many involved in systematic and horrific violence whether or not they found it initially personally distasteful, will have continued within this bureaucratic structure of violence without any individual sense of cognitive dissonance. The sense of belonging to a military unit with a set of known associates guaranteeing food and order may have been sufficient to overlay any emotional disquiet.

Thirdly, there are those who get particular satisfactions from participation in what turns into inter-religious violence; stone throwing youths are a feature of Palestinian and Northern Ireland demonstrations; they are showing off their virility. The urban unemployed are often conspicuous in Hindu demonstrations as they are the object of deliberate recruitment, possibly not altogether because they have grievances against society or more specifically because they feel that caste reservation laws have deprived them of employment. The local party officials know that they are always available to demonstrate, and the employed would have to be approached in a much more planned way for them to leave offices or shut up their shops.

Even the old might be seen in religiously motivated demonstrations as it would give them a recognisable place in their society once again. Certainly the younger men may often predominate as they want to assert themselves and have no responsibilities which they have to consider before appearing on the streets particularly as in Israel most Arab youths have already been arrested and beaten by the police and thus have nothing much to lose by protesting. For the powerless to participate in crowd ostensibly for religious and political purposes gives them a sense of power and righteousness in collective action.

Fourthly, there are those who have in advance committed themselves to a particular course of action in support of a cause. Sometimes these can make up almost the entire body of the crowd involved as the 30,000 women who held hands in a single line surrounding the Greenham Common United States Air Force Base in Britain supporting the global peace movement and against Cruise Missiles. This also happened in the *Chipko* movement in which women prevented the commercial cutting of trees in the foothills of the Himalayas.

In more violent religious confrontations it seems likely that the committed in advance are relatively few and that the crowds have picked up many others along the way and in the course of the action. But the dividing line between the committed in advance and in the sympathetically inclined is not clear. It can be assumed that religion in Northern Ireland means that most individuals would support one or the other Christian denominations without thinking twice about it and much the same would apply to the generality of Arabs, Muslims and Hindus in their oppositional thinking.

The people in the last category who may be invisible in public confrontations are the organisers of religious demonstrations whose status as leaders of political parties or religious groups depends on the support they get from such disturbances. Such people can remain either passive or silent and have to build up their organisation by recruiting new members. For them the possibility of a religious confrontation is an opportunity to exploit rather than one to diminish; the fact that they have a depersonalised perspective allows them to manipulate individuals for a cause. This is not to denigrate their sense of purpose but only in some circumstances are they themselves in danger as with bin Laden and his promotion of violence based on his understandings of Islam.

There are many other exploiters of religious violence who do not have any religious commitments at all; the range of people who will gain from the settling of personal scores, the occupiers of property when another community is expelled and the looters who will seize the opportunity to steal whatever they can lay their hands on. We can see, therefore, that in any collective violence, the sense of unanimity which the observer might conclude from being a witness, may be an illusion.

Sex and Gender Issues in the Religious Violence

Sex and gender tend to be separated in both the mind and in the categories used in social science analyses as if the former was exact and the latter a social creation. Sexual attributions are not exact and remain associated with external characteristics and perhaps the species specific ability to breed. The religious law records of the monotheistic religions are replete with cases involving issues of ambiguous sexuality. The Eastern religions with their absence of definitions do not seem to be concerned with such issues.

Sex and gender cannot be seen as separate categorisations even before considering homosexual and lesbian cases in which the attributions may be as much physical as psychological. Most societies if they have thought about it at all, apart from creating their own gender roles, have always recognised that there are grades in the sexual attributions of individuals since they often recognise cross-dressing and inter-sexuality. In these matters quasi-Christian and secular

Western governments have become more permissive while newly established Islamic ones such as Malaysia have passed laws forbidding such activities for Muslims (Peletz, 1997: 240).

Gender roles develop and change in the special social and religious conditions of the environments in which they occur and those that are enshrined in the sacred writings of a particular religion should be evaluated in terms of that time and then assessed according to contemporary situations. This is particularly so in the case of Islam which according to some modern commentators gives categorical inferiority to women in their property rights, limits their personal freedoms in marriage and divorce and in the value of their evidence. It seems likely that what are now seen as restrictions were in seventh century Arabia an improvement giving them legal rights in a rapidly changing social environment. What then can be discussed about the violence done to women's rights in modern terms in both traditional and Eastern and monotheistic religions, particularly as women have participated as equals in Islamic violence in both Israel and Indonesia and against the restrictions of Islam in Saudi Arabia.

In traditional non-literate religions there is an absence of impersonal dogma which can be applied to both men and women. Participation in religion and the taking of leading roles by women is either the development of some form of personal charisma or related to their lineal positions. Thus amongst the Sukuma of Tanzania women will be unable to participate in some ancestor or spirit propitiation ceremonies because they are related by marriage to the sufferers, while in others they will be participating as members of the matri- or patri-lineages. In practice gender in relationship to the spirit world has not much to do with excluding or including people because they are men or women; the categories are social rather than sexual.

Sometimes women develop religious systems which are both parallel to the religious systems run by men and also cope with issues for which the male run other system provides limited help. Women in the Sudan and East Africa have created 'zar' spirit possession cults in which men have no roles other than financially supporting the involvement of their wives despite the overall disapproval of the Muslim establishment (Kenyon, 1999). Amongst the Muslim Hausa in Nigeria for centuries there have been women involved in quasi-Islamic practices enabled in part by spirit cults, female titles and the predominance of women in subsistence farming making them much less likely to be influenced by orthodox practices which exclude them (Cooper, 1998).

In contemporary Okinawa women priestesses are pre-eminent in keeping the proper balances between the spirits and the general health of the people coexisting with Chinese ancestor worship, American cinemas and the Japanese educational system. Despite their successive occupation by two foreign powers this professional role for women has probably come about and even increased in viability because of village endogamy, male absence to work away from the island for long periods, the central role of women in subsistence farming and commerce, lack of heritable property, female longevity, weak political structures, aversion to hierarchy and strong social integration among women (Sered, 1999). Given the male propensity to dominance these two examples show that the circumstances are rarely so strongly structured that women cannot develop systems to cope with their needs and in the Okinawa case coping with the welfare needs of both men and women.

No religion can be defined as an equal opportunity religious environment but it is the monotheistic faiths which have sexual restrictions on women written into their sacred writings but only Islam has had this written as divine requirements. In terms of conversion to orthodox Islam, a woman from a traditional social and religious system would immediately be at a disadvantage but this is a hypothetical issue since it is a rare occurrence. But legalistic blocks are invitations to religious ingenuity made within perceptions of religious needs and the ambiguities built into all religious rulings. The restrictions on women may not have been a prominent part of the reasons for the splits in Judaism between the various orthodox sects and the more modern minded reform blocks which in some places now have women rabbis.

Religious restrictions on women can be divided between systems of worship and control of behaviour rulings. Once worship occurs in buildings women can be excluded or shown that they are less than equal in worshipping God there. In orthodox Islam men are required to participate in congregational prayers at the mosque and for women to pray at home; but when they do attend, they are peripheral, separate and invisible. In a Canadian mosque women have to pray in a multi-purpose side-room used for such activities as eating which are prohibited in the more sacred space in which men pray (Marshall, 1994).

But this is not just an Islamic restriction since such restrictions are part of public worship in all the monotheistic religions, but it is only Islam which appears to degrade the public worship of women. In the synagogue women sit separately and in many African and Asian churches women sit on the left and men on the right. This is not a total block in Islam since in Taiwan women worship in the mosque alongside men but separated from them by a green curtain and in mainland China there are women's mosques and women religious leaders (Pillsbury, 1978: 655-66).

However, it is amongst the Shia in Iran that women have been most active in circumventing the apparent restrictions of orthodoxy by creating what is in effect a parallel system of worship which avoids the taint of 'zar' spirit possession in which ostensibly Muslim women are controlled by invading spirits. The number of religious schools for women founded by women have increased dramatically, a new cadre of women religious experts, use of mosques by women for teaching, women reciting the Koran and their voices being taped and sold for public use. It is in shrine visiting that women have developed a pattern of worship as a result of being excluded from mosque worship and its unsatisfactory emotional environment and it is at these shrines that women with only a nominal male presence are able to find spiritual comfort, make and fulfil vows, gain relief from household pressures and of course leisure and recreation (Kamalkani, 1991: 62-3).

In the immigrant Muslim communities of North America in a social and political environment which is openly hostile to such restrictions on women, they have redefined themselves Islamic roles as religious teachers, study group leaders, fund raisers, community leaders, social activists against the domestic abuse of women and active participants in mosque worship (Mazumdar and Mazumdar, 2002).

The Hindu Laws of Manu make all women subordinate in succession to their fathers, husbands and finally their sons. This is seen as a family issue in which the Indian government would not want to be actively involved for fear of antagonising women voters. Much of such Hindu law depends on the religious needs of sub-castes and the availability of socially and economically powerful Brahmins. It would seem more to be an injunction to take care of the less socially powerful than that women should be treated permanently as juveniles, particularly as Hindu women have been prominent in politics and many professions.

In Islam the shrouding of women seems to have been the adoption by well-to-do Muslims of an upper-class Persian practice. It seems likely that where women work in the fields for family survival, such an enforcement would have been ridiculous, so it seems to be a practice among the well-to-do as a sign that their women do not have to work.

However, in these new states it was often seen that the advancement of women not so much in their own rights but seemingly at the expense of their control by their men-folk, they were subject to new legislative diminishment. 'In the 1970s various revivalist groups began to proselytise the modernist 'dakwa' movement inventing practices harking back to a mythic homogeneous Islamic past while rejecting their Malay-Muslim cultural heritage. This Arabization of Malay society depended in large part on implementing a rigid separation between male public and female domestic roles, a separation quite contrary to indigenous arrangements. A new radical separation of Malay men and women, Muslims and non-Muslims was created in public life, primarily by institutionalising this spatialization of power on woman's bodies' (Ong, 1989).

Thus it would seem that only in some states under Muslim control has the social progress of women been impeded for religious reasons rather than implemented for social, economic or political ones and that this violence to their rights is a handicap to overall progress and this has increasingly become a matter of comment and protest.

APPENDIX

Intra- and Inter-religious Tensions in East African Tribal Environments: A Case Study

The East African cultural area is of value for the study of religious violence because of its is relatively recent involvement with the major international religions except for some outside influences along the coast and missionary efforts for just over a century (Tanner, 2001). So traditional non-literate religions have predominated.

The definitions of 'religion' are probably as varied as the numbers of those who attempt to provide them, but most implicitly ally their responses to the four great international religions; Buddhism, Christianity, Hinduism and Islam for which there is substantial theological and social background data in these Great Traditions. Such definitions leave out perhaps the majority of activities involving metaphysics and thus makes much of these into 'magic', the Little Traditions. We have suggested that any such distinction is a socially biased one and does not correspond with social realities.

'Tribe' is another difficulty as historically a tribe may well have been a loose category which varied with the circumstances and had no clearly defined boundaries. The colonial governments with administrative needs, defined tribes as living in specific areas and indeed during the colonial period in Tanzania, the number of tribes recognised for census purposes doubled. The tribal allegiance of any individual may then as now depend on whatever matrilineal, marital or residential connections were advantageous at a particular time.

Since there are no Buddhist or Hindu Africans, it is proposed to treat the practices of the three faiths operating there, the quasi-traditional, Christian and Muslim, without distinguishing or dividing their practices into magical, non-magical or religious categories. This has the advantage of eliminating any definition of religious practices which would automatically relegate most quasi-traditional ones to a position of ideological and social inferiority which their contemporary popularity cannot justify.

'Tribe' has a rural and static flavour to it whereas in practice individuals have always been on the move particularly now between the expanding towns and the rural areas whenever they deem it necessary. Few are so permanently committed to the towns that their tribal ways of thinking and perhaps behaving no longer apply. Certainly some like the pastoral Maasai, Pokot and Karamajong are more committed to a rural way of life but they certainly visit the towns and are aware of what urban life offers. Others such as the Ganda, Kikuyu and Sukuma often commute to towns for work and business living most of their lives beyond the urban fringes. Children may spend their time equally between rural and urban relatives so that their patterns of thought and behaviour will be that of their natal tribes as modified by circumstances beyond their control and according to where the best opportunities for survival are located.

The legal definition of urban areas may well exclude the septic fringe of peri-urban slums which are clearly not rural or in any way connected to subsistence agriculture but substantial amounts of food are grown in these urban areas. In these circumstances there can be no defined dividing line between town and country in either social and religious practices. It is a highly porous situation in which language, histories and identities are constantly subject to mutation (Chambers, 1994: 5).

The East African Religious Paradigm

The history of religion in this region antedates the arrival of Christianity in the late 1800s and Islam by at least the 12th century by many millennia. Its development in antiquity will have correlated with the social and ecological environments which have lasted to a very similar extent to the present-day. Geographically dispersed social systems which only in the colonial period came to have static administrative rather than social characteristics.

Overwhelmingly this must be a picture which has rarely involved anything approaching semi-centralised states except in the 'kingdoms' of Uganda. Without a social structure which would at least in part be maintained by literate administrators, the social and religious structure was and is segmentary with constant adaptations to social, political, economic and ecological circumstances.

The absence of towns except for some clustering round the houses of chiefs, the fortified villages of the Ssonjo near to their irrigated fields, and the villages of the Yao, shows that the social practices of these people, their pattern of living and thinking was centrifugal rather than centripetal. These people lived as they do now in family groups away from rather than near to their neighbours.

Since these people lived dispersed, they did not develop centralised religious institutions. Their religious practices just as much as their social ones will have been developed under these conditions of permanent dispersal. This was not a social environment in which there could be any permanent centralising cults imposing a pattern of religious behaviour on their followers and thus creating minter-cult tensions. The Buchwezi cult exists both north and south of Lake Victoria with virtually nothing in common beyond the similarities of some head-dresses. The initiation ceremonies of a Sukuma Buchwezi group observed over a ten-year gap had almost nothing in common; there could be no question of the cult having a specific ritual, only some possible shared ideas of their spirit origin.

Thus it would seem that religious practices must have had in antiquity characteristics which now form a paradigm of contemporary importance predisposing these people to accept certain religious ideas and practices.

Firstly, religious ideas and practices focus on individuals and their families. The protective activities of individuals shown in the amulets they wear on arms or loins (Tanner, 1975), the domestic cults of family, lineage and clan with identifying taboos and the cults related to various levels of chiefs. Low-key regular practices were not maintained under any overt burden of social or religious sanctions.

Secondly, cyclical and linear rites of passage involving a wider range of people, neighbours as much as relatives but usually of sufficient importance to overcome the centrifugal pattern of their social lives. The main factor will have been a balance between the benefits and the economic costs of such ceremonies.

Finally, there are reactive religious activities, overwhelmingly the most common, in which the numbers involved are related to the importance of the problem experienced. At its minimum the problems of particular individuals or families over illness, infertility and accident involving a few people to the problems of drought in an area for which thousands would attend a rain-making ceremony. Again these would be evaluated on a cost-benefit basis; infertile women may go to many quasi-traditional healers in search of a cure. It is cults reacting to public anxieties which come to public attention with their potentiality for violence typified by the mass killings in which the Movement for the Restoration of the Ten Commandments in western Uganda was involved in March 2000.

The contemporary East African has inherited a highly dispersed pattern of religious behaviour overwhelmingly client and problem oriented (Whyte, 1997). The form that it takes now as it has always done depends on particular personal skills rather than on office holding. It thus has the capacity to expand and contract with the circumstances such as the Holy Spirit Movement in northern Uganda which grew in disruptive strength with widespread popular anxieties among the Acholi tribe, discharged and unemployed soldiers and the easy availability of arms (Behrend, 1997).

This inherited religious and social paradigm into which they have been socialised, would not give them any background for the development of centralising and centralised religions. There is rarely an 'either/or' religious commitment to either an inter-national Great Tradition faith or a quasi-traditional one. Personal religious systems of parallel practices in which individuals keep several options open according to their circumstantial interpretation of their needs based on economic and personal factors, anticipated returns on the performance of a prescribed ritual, the advice of friends and relatives, the propinquity of the suggested quasi-traditional healer and local rather more than a more general public opinion. It is not a paradigm predisposing individuals and groups of varying and variable beliefs to violence.

The Pattern of Segmented Religious Practice

The paradigm of a religious system in which there are great variations in dealing with the spirit world, shows that it can only be described as a single system in very general terms. Ancestors influencing the living, malevolence passing between the dead and the living and between the living as well as the influence on the living of spirits with which they have no lineal connections. Only in this last category is there any corporate activity of individuals not previously connected by blood or marriage.

The fact that anthropological studies have often shown a greater interest in religious than economic matters, does not make it an activity in any way comparable to the observable religious preoccupations of Hindus and the regular devotions of devout Christians and Muslims. East African religion has been a response to demand one, a practical rather than a practising system in which those involved, except for a few popular quasi-traditional healers, are part-time, depending more on their subsistence farming and livestock tending (Platvoet, 1993).

The basis of social segmentation is competition and quasi-traditional healers as much as the Christian leaders of the major and Independent Churches are in covert competition with each other within their ostensible commitment to and involvement in the more general spirit world and spirituality. Thus in what these quasi-traditional healers practise and prescribe for those who consult them, there are idiosyncratic themes, eccentricity and inspiration (Tanner, 1997). In effect it is always competition to draw clients to them and away from their rivals. Numbers mean status as well as economic and social security.

Anthropologists see few ceremonies and may thus tend to assume a pattern of stability in form and practice which is far from being the case. How could it be otherwise when there are no written requirements for rituals, no centralised training schemes and subsequent supervision. It seems certain that almost all religious activities which are not related to infrequent rites of passage, are based entirely on particular situations involving different peoples which invite if not require disparate responses. The five million Sukuma have a traditional system of involvement with their ancestors whom they propitiate in times of difficulty when such causes are diagnosed by diviners. An examination of these propitiation ceremonies show different rituals for what are different situations according to the ideas of the leaders of the rituals and of participants as to what materials are available and what can be afforded; there was no liturgical order for religious observance.

East Africans as they experience the processes of continual and rapid social change, start with the assumption of disparate rather than predefined responses to their problems involving the spirit world. This traditional segmentary religious system and the religious paradigm that sustains it, transfers easily to the growing towns and cities. It is in some respects a religious 'do it yourself' system.

What centripetal socio-religious activities existed in rural areas relating to rites of passage involving larger numbers of people rather than single families, have disappeared in the urban areas with their mixture of tribal cultures and the development of a class structure coming from a combination of literacy, regular employment, corruption and nepotism (Iliffe, 1975).

In the urban areas there is not only a proliferation of quasi-traditional healers relating to the opportunities there and to the larger population. In the early 60s it was estimated that on any one day in Dar Es Salaam, the then capital of Tanzania, there were more people consulting quasi-traditional practitioners than were using all the other official and non-official welfare and medical institutions (Swantz, 1974). There are far fewer in rural areas where the social sanctions on deviant behaviour are operative and the opportunities fewer. These men and women have developed a working relationship with non-ancestral spirits rather than ancestors who are less influentially active on the members of dispersed families, combined with a growing concern over witchcraft.

Since witchcraft is not defined or perhaps definable, it is an explanation for almost any real or imagined unpleasantness. In societies which have undergone many radical changes due in part to factors over which people have little or no control, it is not surprising that this has become a matter of growing popular fear and national concern. Amongst the Sukuma and Nyamwwezi particularly there has been widespread killings of suspected witches. In 1970-84 there have been 3693 known killings amongst the Sukuma alone of whom 62 per cent were of women over 41 years. This shows the cultural clash between the idealized modernization goals of the state and the cosmology of the Sukuma people (Mesaki, 1992). Whatever rapid political and social changes that may occur, the pattern of thinking within their quasi-traditional paradigm is likely to continue relatively unchanged despite the fact that the social institutions with which they were originally correlated have ceased to exist.

Most areas have Christian churches of various denominations with their conspicuous buildings and permanent staffs as well as those of the so-called Independent Churches and similar Muslim institutions and groupings particularly along the coast and in townships.

In economic terms this is a consumer society for religion in which all can choose from goods displayed in the religious market-place in which the Little Traditions predominate in the rural areas and are combined with the Great Traditions in the towns. In this respect there are factors which account for the increased religious tensions in towns where there are people permanently involved in organised religion.

The colonial period with its obvious 'us and them' polarisation came to an end in Eastern Africa in a wave of universal optimism rather than that of violent political tensions. Over the years since then this has been replaced by the severe depression of what almost all the people expected. In addition the end of apartheid in South

Africa meant the loss of an emotional political focus of which everyone even children were aware.

All three countries on gaining political independence ceased to balance their budgets and indulged in wide-ranging policies designed to make up for the years of what the new politicians saw as the minimal and lethargic development programmes of the previous colonial regimes.

This resulted in an expanded civil service which became increasingly underpaid as inflation took hold of the economy. These civil servants had to find alternative ways of maintaining their livelihoods and were less and less able to fulfil the functions for which their posts were designed. No doubt this was caused in part by a widespread feeling that administration was relatively easy leading to many ambitious schemes for which there were not enough competent long-service African civil servants to replace the expatriates whose contracts had terminated with the transfer of sovereignty.

A series of long droughts was bad enough for subsistence farmers but in Tanzania this was aggravated by the Villagisation Policy which uprooted a high proportion of cultivators without providing them with the facilities in the new villages which the government had hoped to provide and which these people considered to have been promised them. The resentment engendered by this mass internal migration carried out with little planning and some force will not only be long lasting, but reduced the capacity of the country to feed itself.

Uganda suffered the inefficiency and brutality of the Idi Amin regime which was overthrown by an invasion from Tanzania which further impoverished the economies of both countries and resulted in a long lasting civil war there, aggravated by the Holy Spirit Movement. The fact that Amin was a Muslim led to Moslem aggression against their Christian neighbours (Whyte, 1997: 53).

Both Tanzania and Uganda abolished their chiefs and their chiefdoms who had both emotional and political functions and these were not replaced in the peoples' hearts by politicians and political parties. Kenya suffered droughts and inter-tribal tensions as well as a lack of economic growth. All three states had serious problems from corruption which led to the increased wariness of international donors supporting inefficient regimes.

Further all three countries suffered border problems and floods of refugees from Zaire, Ruanda, Urundi, Ethiopia, Somalia and the Sudan for which international aid was needed.

The control of mass diseases and some reduction in infant mortality led to an increase in the youthfulness and size of the population rather than any marked lengthening of life. This was balanced by the fear of the AIDS pandemic for which scientific medicines provided no cures.

Overall the people who had expected a marked and early improvement in their standard of living, have in fact suffered a decline and a growth of cynicism over the political process and their politicians in particular; 'a revolution of rising disappointments'(Geertz, 2000: 32) In addition the growth of the tourist industry has meant that more and more poor East Africans have been faced with obviously wealthy foreigners. Possibly a far more invasive 'us and them' emotional rather than ideological situation that existed prior to independence.

People now have a largely recreated traditional religion running parallel to or as an alternative to Christianity and Islam rather than having a religion coinciding with their tribal identity. In this situation practitioners who are able to show that they have some links with what the people see as their traditional beliefs, have great advantages since there are few institutional or ideological barriers to discourage consumer utilisation and personal initiatives in religious matters.

The Latency of Inter-religious Tensions

If East African religions are considered in terms of their three focii, the modernised traditional, Christianity and Islam, there are structural difficulties in comparing them in terms of beliefs and practices. Attendance at Christian ceremonies and Friday prayers in the mosques can be assessed, but beyond that there can be no accurate details of private prayers and none at all on the frequencies of using traditional rituals.

The East African modernised or quasi-traditional religion has no intellectualised core which can be grasped as the model to which there are conformities and deviations. The simplicity of belief in active spirits and the transmittable malevolence of innumerable and unknown ancestors, relatives and outsiders and the many ways in which this can be interpreted by individuals, gives it an immediate adaptability which is institutionally absent from the major Christian Churches and to a lesser extent from Islam which has no parochial supervisory system to insure religious conformity.

Whether this widening faith indicates, correlates to or follows after secular, economic, political and social problems is difficult to evaluate. There are widespread examples of this religion being involved in the expression of social and political unrest in the last century against outsiders. The Nyabingi cult in south-west Uganda (Hopkins, 1970), the 1905 Maji Maji rebellion in German East Africa (Iliffe, 1979), the Mau Mau Kikuyu revolt in Kenya (Nottingham and Rosberg. 1966), millennial cults in Gusii, Kenya (Wipper, 1970), as well as repeated rebellions in Southern Rhodesia (Ranger, 1967). All involved divination and the use of religious protection against gunfire.

We can perhaps see these modernised traditional religious activities which do develop into cults and sects, as having the potential to embody and exemplify difficulties in any society where there are no other ways beyond violence of expressing their misery. It will not take the form of open tension between cults until other factors come into play such as the prolonged civil war in Uganda, where the cultic origins of those acting more or less in the name of the Holy Spirit Movement are obscure.

However there seems little doubt that the increase in personal and collective difficulties has been accompanied by an increased use of what the people themselves consider to be their traditional religions and not just in its violent corporate manifestations. Such tensions as do occur are related to the gossip associated with competition rather than ideological religious rivalry for hearts and minds. People speaking in tongues while possessed can be believed or not but the predisposition is to believe as it is a basic feature of their religious paradigm. Ideological rivalry would be hard to initiate without the prior formulation of beliefs and practices in writing; they cannot rush to the Bible and Koran for support for or against quasi-traditional religious activities.

Any secular evaluation of missionary Christianity in Eastern Africa has to consider rivalry between Churches as important. Colonial administrators were always wary of missionaries who couched their expansionist and rival aims in terms of theological rectitude. The enunciation of the aim of doing God's work invited secular and defensive responses from civil servants trying to prevent possible tensions while promoting the social services which these Churches could provide and for which the governments then as now do not have sufficient funds.

Whether they said as much or not, they were all aiming at area exclusivities in the sitting of their churches, schools and medical centres for which overseas personnel and funds were available. This was known in colonial Tanganyika as 'ecclesiastical chess'. In the 1960s a Roman Catholic bishop in Usukuma thought that the building of a church anywhere would produce 2000 converts, but the Sukuma have never taken to Christianity with any marked enthusiasm. The parish of Bukumbi where there have been resident priests for over a century, does not have a majority of Roman Catholics in its neighbourhood; the majority remain in effect traditional believers.

As these mainstream Churches came under national leadership, the staff to run their institutions has shrunk considerably, so that despite overseas capital to initiate projects, accredited personnel has become the main problem. It has become more a question of servicing their existing followers than in embarking on any obvious rivalry, which the new governments would not have tolerated as in some ways as instigated from abroad and thus a relic of colonialism. Rome is hardly a centre of economic influence but Churches with Scotland and England in their titles raise national issues eyebrows in an ostensibly anti-tribal political set-up.

It is hard to consider that there is any real possibility of tensions between the main Christian denominations at the institutional level. Their leaders are well aware that ecumenism is now not only a part of overall Christian ideology but a political necessity as well.

In Islam the African Sunni majority have had tensions over the Ahmaddiya translation of the Koran into kiSwahili which circulates but is not widely known. Many Indians are Shia, but their internal differences have never spread into the surrounding African Sunni communities from whom they have never sought converts. Sufi prayer groups have in some ways the characteristics of quasi-traditional spirit cults and depend on the personalities of their leaders.

Religious Inspiration and the Formulation of New Cults

Independent Churches have been infrequently conspicuous in the East African religious scene, although they have existed in some distinctive forms (Welbourn, 1961). They do not have sufficient economic support to maintain any large institutional and separate presence, although under the cloak of universality they are in fact tribally based.

There are not as numerically distinctive as they have been in their thousands in South Africa (Barrett. 1968).

However, there is no reason to suppose that Independent Churches do not have the potential to respond collectively to the need for locally based Christian institutions in which people can feel 'at home' in the impersonal wilderness of an increasingly mass society (Welbourn and Ogot, 1966: 144-45).

While many are inclined to see these Independent Churches in derogatory terms as the semi-pathological creations of individuals disrupting the lives of simple peasantry, some have developed impressive support for those in misery. The Legio Maria, a breakaway Church from Roman Catholicism, with its Latin liturgy, ecclesiastical hierarchy, and intense ritualism, provides for the laying on of hands for the cure of illness and misfortune which the main denominations are reluctant to perform. The African Israeli Church Ninevah with its distinctive dress and jogging to services has many social attractions. Overall the major ones in Zambia and Zimbabwe and their quasi-traditional counterparts, have the function of knitting together tribal areas divided by the ecclesiastical boundaries of the main-line Churches (Werbner, 1977).

These Churches are very much the creation of their living originators' inspirations and accordingly have difficulty in maintaining an identity independent of these charismatic figures. As with the leaders of quasi-traditional cults, it is the combination of charisma and ritual exclusivities couched in mainly natal languages which attract and retain supporters.

A recent example was the Lumpa Church of Alice Lenshina in Northern Rhodesia in the 1950-60s (Lehmann, 1961; Roberts, 1970). This was a popular movement originating in her breakaway from the Church of Scotland and it drew members from other Churches as well, opposing the administration instituted by the central government. The emotional intensity shown by its members who were prepared to die in defence of their wish to live in separate communities and its popular approach to salvation and the elimination of witchcraft, is not the framework of thinking in which mutual tolerance develops. In fact they rebelled against the government and were suppressed by force.

That this was likely to be the form of any future religious protest movements was shown in the Holy Spirit Movement in northern Uganda (Behrend, 1991). Alice Lakwena and those who carried on the movement after she went to Kenya, through prophetic and spirit communication were able to create an armed movement which nearly captured Kampala and has been responsible for substantial violence, killings and the continuing abduction of children.

The Rise in Inter-faith Tensions

It has perhaps been one of the axioms of Western thinkers that religion would recede as one of the major confrontational issues in public life and that it would remain as a personal or at the most a small community issue. This has not happened and inter-religious violence has been a major part of political and social life in the Sudan, Ethiopia and Uganda.

East African Muslims have not been isolated from these events and there has been a general rise in Muslim sense of corporate identity aided by Arab oil money to build urban mosques and subsidize a Muslim university in Tanzania in attempting to overcome its muted political voice and its reputation for backwardness. The Zanzibar region of secular Tanzania recently attempted to affiliate itself independently with pan-Islamic Middle-Eastern organisations.

The fundamentalist frame of Muslim thinking as a background for Islamic actions is clear, combined as it is with some religious rigidity as to how to cope with rapid social change. There seem to be parallels here to the much earlier Christian approach to missionary work which was both culturally and theologically aggressive. During this period Islam was not specifically expansionist (Tanner. 1992) except though marriage and trade.

Now Islam in Eastern Africa is becoming much more visible with the building of mosques with oil money and very audible amplified calls to prayer. This is apart from the Yao, Zigua, Digo and the coastal Swahili who are almost all nominal Muslims, while continuing to practise quasi-traditional rituals. There is also the National Bakwata Missionary organisation. There have been some commercialised conversions, the modern equivalent of earlier 'rice' Christians.

Nevertheless Islam still remains handicapped by having its one Holy book written in Arabic, although this always has been used for divination, and its historical association with slavery and with the coastal people's sense of cultural superiority and their economic backwardness. However, it does affiliate easily into the social lives of those who consider their tribal affiliations to be important a Sukuma chief had children in all three religions with perhaps a fine sense of opportunism, and Uganda chiefs who converted to the new faiths on almost a *pro rata* basis, do not seem to have brought many others into their new faiths.

Islam has the advantage of tenets which are easy to learn and to follow in comparison to Christianity, no pre-conversion training and a more institutionally relaxed view of what is religiously permissible, combined with the absence of a supervisory priesthood interested in morals rather than ritual practices (Tanner and Wijsen, 1995). Even senior Muslims are concerned at the activities of their coreligionists in the development of 'zar' spirit possession cults among Muslim women in many communities including Eastern Africa (Boddy, 1989. Kenyon, 1999. Messing, 1958).

Entering the Religious Ambivalence of the Modern World

If the East African could be typified, then it is as a subsistence farmer with a vague tribal paradigm dictating thoughts rather than specific behaviour but with a very clear and calculated idea of how to make the best out of a possibly increasingly difficult life. While not denying those who have religious vocations as such, almost all their religious behaviour has a cost-benefit dimension; an outlay of time and materials against a calculation of the expected returns. Religious rituals are seen in much the same terms as social activities and their agricultural practices.

While it is obvious that almost all those involved in religious activities see themselves as acting for religious rather than secular reasons, it is these secular reasons in a tribal framework of thinking that may dictate membership of a particular Christian denomination and now to a certain extent Islam.

Some of course convert and maintain their commitment for almost exclusively religious reasons, but others convert or maintain membership for more material reasons, some of which involve considerable foresight (Tanner, 1969a).

The main-line Churches have material resources, schools, hospitals, training colleges, educational bursaries and access to funds for charity. In the absence of anything more than minimal welfare provisions by governments, this is bound to be an important factor. Others convert in order to marry or to join new social groupings such as the Legion of Mary (not the Legio Maria) or because membership provides physical and ritual protections (Tanner, 1970).

Islam and the major Christian denominations could have become closely connected to particular tribes by couching their rituals in their languages. Protestantism particularly produced the Bible in a number of tribal languages. Their missionaries as well as the Roman Catholics preached and did their parochial work in them. Both Roman Catholics and Muslims were stuck with canonical languages, Latin and classical Arabic, which were of little pastoral but considerable ritual value.

The Muslims were not in a position to change as the Koran in Arabic was the literal Word of God. The Roman Catholics can and did change after Vatican II to local languages but here there were difficulties. In Tanzania the change was to kiSwahili, the national language from the end of the 19th century, thus tacitly allying itself with national political rather than tribal ambitions. While this may have been justifiable with small tribes for which the expense of translation and publishing would have been out of the question. Its effect on the six million Sukuma and Nyamwezi, who have already been reluctant to become Christians, would have become more marked.

However in Uganda and Kenya there are no such widely acceptable and common-sense use of an agreed national language. Thus the main-line denominations and of course, the Independent Churches have no alternative but to be involved with tribal languages; Roman Catholic dioceses among the Luo and Kikuyu, whatever their views are in practice tribal dioceses and this of course aids the paralleling of religious practices. Their sense of nominal religious identity will be denominational and readily relatable to their tribal paradigms of thought sustained by their languages.

Even with the use of tribal languages there are the persistent problems of translation. The semantic battle between languages which have no common background is complicated by theological abstractions. Whatever words are used for God, including the use of capital letters, spirit, sin and the list is virtually endless, they carry with them a seemingly dominant Western paraphernalia of meaning; ostensibly equivalent words may not mean equivalent popular understandings (Tanner, 1993b). The kiSwahili use of the word 'mungu' for the Christian all-loving God to a Sukuma congregation, will not mean that the word is accepted in this framework of religious thinking however admirable. The tribal linguistic paradigm will always be present in the subconscious if not in the forefront of their minds that their God is a backup figure whom they hope would leave them alone (Tanner, 1956). Tribal languages are more used by women than any national language and thus these traditional patterns of thinking are likely to be stronger with them than men.

There may indeed be cross-conversions between denominations but this will not be towards any greater experience of Christian unity, but towards varying levels of conformity to denominational practices, a periodic lapsing much the same as with Western Christians (Tanner, 1969(b)), and as always a paralleling of religious practices between the ostensibly non-tribal Christianity and Islam of the Great Traditions and the quasi-traditional tribal practicalities of dealing with immediate problems of the Little Traditions (Spyer, 1996).

But it is in quasi-traditional religious practices that there is constant adaptation to the needs of those sharing traditional paradigms. They are up-to-date because the changes that individual practitioners make, which are not related to past texts and resolutions, nor are the changes that occur the result of long and laborious institutional processes. Perhaps they have a feel for what is useful in the beliefs as much as the practices of the main-line Christian denominations. Modern quasi-traditional religions are now making use of non-African spirits as an important part of their help for people adjusting to modern life (Krings, 1999; Masquelier, 1999). The Holy Spirit Movement in Uganda had an Italian spirit guiding their mobile force and a Korean one their weapons and transport (Behrend, 1997).

The picture of a traditional religious system which at one time coincided with the tribe one was probably always an illusion except where uninhabited areas isolated communities. Even then there would have been areas of unconformity and change enabled by non-literacy.

It is possible to identify tribal rural areas as specifically different to urban ones in which a single tribe may be in the majority and urban areas in which there are tribal enclaves. The population is constantly on the move between rural and urban locations for both short and long term reasons. Only the old in the rural areas and a small minority of committed urbanites are excluded from this migratory cross-cultural lifestyle.

It has always been possible for non-literate people to claim a traditional basis for their religious practices which overall enabled them to feel comfortable with what they were doing but this has had the potential to erupt into violence in situations of cumulative distress and the opportunism of religiously inspired charismatic figures. Any memory of the past is always subject to considerable social adjustment as time goes by. So it seems that the religious and social paradigm in which East Africans think is a tribal one adjusted to modern circumstances.

Political and economic circumstances may change in the short-term but the semantic usages of their tribally based languages are always at the back of national-cum-tribal Christian and Muslim practitioners of these Great Traditions and are likely to remain so for many decades to come. Translations of meaning for ambiguous terms allows plenty of areas for private reinterpretations and adjustments.

When it is recognised that there are more Sukuma than Scots and Welsh put together in the United Kingdom and many American Indian tribal groups, it should be accepted that thinking within a tribal paradigm in East Africa is not only acceptable but is to be expected. It is in the private as much as public areas of personal need that the tribal paradigm there fulfils important functions that can only be met by a broad largely non-literate interpretation of religion, the quasi-traditional of the Little Traditions.

It seems likely that tensions with a predisposition to violence will remain between Christians and Muslims at the local level and may well increase for which the rising political and religious expectations of the latter may be responsible. It has certainly occurred in Uganda against Muslims who were considered to have benefited from the Amin regime.

All quasi-traditional religious practitioners and their cults are in covert competition with each other as they have always been. It seems unlikely that this would create tension which would diminish the opportunities for personal service. This is their most popular feature.

Covert competition between the mainline Christian denominations is no longer an obvious issue because the governments are much less tolerant of such manoeuvres. Independent Christian sects are likely to be part of any popular movement encouraged and enabled by civil unrest and particularly when they act in support of the widespread fear of witchcraft. But in the background remains charismatic individuals who can gain contemporary pre-eminence for their ideas from spirit world and these have repeatedly turned to violence.

PART B

Violence and Fear within Religions

5

Fear and Anxieties within a Particular Religion

Physical violence is probably only a small part of the damage which is done to the lives of any involved community's members even if they have not been directly affected. Knowledge that violence has occurred and may occur again is erosive to the peace of mind of everyone who lives on its fringes.

In this there is a scale of anxieties from the whole Palestinian community who have all suffered in some degree from the brutalities of the Israeli occupation, then to the Israelis, worries over the sporadic killings by Muslim suicide bombers and then to Hindus and Muslims in India and Christians and Muslims in Indonesia touched by the real possibilities of inter-communal violence based on religious differences.

All these anxieties will have differential affects within the communities involved in which the young men and women may be openly resentful and the older man and women passively resigned to the probable disruptions and damage to their families and livelihoods. In addition there will be the subconsciously erosive and long lasting damage to children's peace of mind.

In addition there will be the anxieties created in societies in which religious authorities with political power endeavour to impose ways of behaving as religious rules on a society whose members have not actively agreed to their imposition and who think differently as to how their religion should be related to their everyday lives.

States Tied to a Dominant Religion

Any state with a dominant religion tied into their constitutions which is part and parcel of their political ideology and practices and which tries to enforce its code of observable religious practices is inevitably going to create internal tensions. There can never be any such thing as intellectual and social uniformity on any topic much less that of religion in any community.

Thus in such states as Saudi Arabia and Iran there is either a religious establishment in the background dominating the secular political power holders' freedom of action in the former state or as in Iran a theocratic system with clerics directly holding the reins of power. Both states have religious police whose personnel can be presumed to be recruited from the more conservative sections of those societies. Their job is to supervise a dress code almost exclusively aimed at controlling female deviations, fasting during Ramadan etc. In the case of the Afghan Taliban the range of repressive activities went far further and restricted popular male activities over music, television watching and videos (Rashid, 2000).

It is one of the features of economic, social and political development in Western Europe and North America that religion has become both more individualised and more internal, but this does not appear to have happened elsewhere except perhaps among the more intellectualised middle classes. However, there are parallel feelings in these Muslim countries that they are being prevented from enjoying some of the commonplace pleasures which they know are being enjoyed by ordinary people elsewhere. So there are pressures from within these states to alter the restrictive rules which seem to look slightly ridiculous in the contemporary world such as the Saudi prohibition against women driving or against their holding positions of authority when women prime ministers are now quite common in both East and West societies.

At the same time those experiencing these restrictions will have been using their ingenuity to work round them particularly over relationships between men and women which can be circumvented through telephones and computers as well as in the circulation of videos and cassettes. The restrictions on the mixing of the unmarried has been circumvented in Iran by the increased use of the Shia '*mutaa*' practice of short-term contractual marriage for periods from a day to a lifetime, which would appear to undercut the government's social and Islamic aim to confine all such social and sexual activities to family life.

It is symptomatic of the overall backwardness of the Arab world that they have a low computer ownership and use and they are losing by emigration those who feel that they are intellectually and socially stifled by these seemingly outdated social rather than religious restrictions.

Newspapers are important vehicles for the expression of public opinion and public anxieties not only in their investigative journalism but in their correspondence columns in which ordinary people express their local and personal concerns. During the Communist domination of Russia the official press paid systematic attention to these individual complaints and had through these letters an understanding of popular anxieties.

Even when there is no overt censorship, editors know that they can only go so far in printing public concerns about the policies and behaviour of their political power-holders; it is a state of compulsory self-censorship in which fear of being prosecuted, losing their jobs and the owners losing their papers, goes much further than the feeling among editors in Western journalism that certain topics should not be publicised in the public interest and not because of behind the scenes political pressure.

Papers in Saudi Arabia in their blandness will stay well clear of religious controversy and the behaviour of those within the royal establishment and it requires an unusual and horrific event to push these limits aside. In the case of the fire in a Saudi girls school in August 2002 in which fifteen died, it was alleged that the gates were locked and could not be opened by the headmistress without the permission of her male superior and that the religious police would not let the girls out improperly dressed. This received national newspaper coverage after their editors had worried over breaking through this implied wall of obligatory silence. These articles questioned for the first time that the religious police were not answerable to any publicly accountable body.

Extreme Control in the Name of Religion–the Taliban and Iranian Cases

While contemporary systems of justice in the western world may have had their origins in religious thinking but most states have found any connection between their current systems and these religious foundations absurd. There are few criminal and civil cases that can be narrowed to a religiously defined event and modern states contain citizens of many religions which they may or may not practice and consider that what they do or do not do is their private affair unless it affects the public good.

Moreover the issues which disturb relationships in contemporary societies have been made much more complicated by modern developments in education, travel and consumer needs. They cannot be tied to the simplicities of a faith probably designed for subsistence farmers, pastoral people and early small scale forms of urban living.

Only the southern states in the United States of America with their persistent high levels of executions despite the known killings of innocent accused, seem to be within the legal framework of the Biblical injunction of 'an eye for an eye and a tooth for a tooth'. No Western system of justice bases its punishments on religious principles formulated in the middle ages or earlier.

It is only some modern states with predominantly Muslim populations that have created national codes of justice based on Islamic law and the interpretations of this by Muslim theologians. It could be said that these interpretations have been consistently retrogressive in terms of what Western thought considers to be progressive and in conformity with what the United Nations would consider to be the Rights of Man (and Woman).

The principles on which Islamic criminal law is founded seem to go against modern understandings of justice particularly in the denigration of the status of women has having the value of less than as man in giving evidence and in inferior rights to property, the custody of children and divorce. Whether this is classifiable as violence must remain liable to partisan interpretations. No modern state other than an Islamic one would allow the amputation of the hand of a thief as the sentence of a court of law, particularly when there is concern in such states over the inequality of penalties for low and high status criminals.

Iran and Saudi-Arabia have religious police enforcing prayer times and in particular the behaviour of women but the Taliban government of Afghanistan went far further in legislating against much social behaviour which was not related to modernising trends. They based these new regulations on their interpretations of Islamic law as in the Presidential Decree of November 1996 which stated 'If women are going outside with fashionable, ornamental, tight and charming clothes to show themselves, they will be cursed by the Islamic sharia and should never expect to go to heaven. The Religious Police have the responsibility and duty to struggle against these social problems and will continue their efforts until evil is finished.'

A further Presidential Decree in December1996 prohibited the playing of music in shops, hotels and vehicles, being beardless, keeping pigeons and playing with birds, kite flying, portraits of people not to be shown anywhere, women washing clothes in streams outside their homes, fashion magazines, the playing of drum music and the prohibition of music and dancing at weddings and of course not praying five times per day.

These wide-ranging prohibitions were certainly damaging to any Afghan understanding of pleasant living and even though only small numbers would have actually been prosecuted, most of the urban population felt pressured into observing these rules which went against their traditional pleasures. These interpretations were based on the assumption that if something was not specifically mentioned in the Koran, then it should be prohibited; an example of this was the statement that since zoos were not mentioned then there was no religious justification for Kabul to keep its zoo.

Iran has the Islamic Punishment (Flogging) Law, 1983 which made it an offence punishable by up to 74 lashes for women who did not cover themselves in public with a strict interpretation of the '*hejab*'; which included the showing of hair, makeup, uncovered arms or legs, clothes bearing foreign words, signs or pictures, and trousers without a covering overall. The anxieties of women used to some freedom and expecting more from the Islamic Revolution in which they had actively participated in protests against the Pahlavi regime. They were subsequently subjected to the scrutiny of the Religious Police street patrols of two men and two women who often punished women felt to be dressed improperly, and the effects cannot be overstressed (Paidar, 1995: 343).

The Bureau for Combating Corruption extended the definition of corruption to include gambling, games like chess and snooker, most types of films for entertainment, theatre, music, art and the mixing of men and women. Discotheques, clubs and bars were closed down for being dens of corruption, private parties and weddings were raided at random and the mixed occupants of cars were asked for their marriage certificates. This was accompanied by random punishments, fining, flogging and in some cases the stoning to death of adulterers and homosexuals and the execution of prostitutes. It was only in 1984 that some centralised restraint was put on the activities of the local revolutionary committees, combined with the national government making the Muslim sharia, religious law, dominant over the Penal Code (Paidar, 1995: 347).

The Iran Bill of Retribution passed by a legislature dominated by the clergy lists in Article 100 the types of adultery which would lead to execution and Article114 details how men and women convicted of adultery should be buried in pits up to their chests in order to be stoned to death (Tohidi, 1983).

The two issues here that combine to cause both personal and collective anxieties are whether these restrictions are indeed part of an authentic and necessary religious message or just modern theocratic interpretations of rules which were instituted to cope with the events of a bygone age. More importantly the anxieties which come from being liable to punishment for indulging in the commonplace pleasures known to exist in the wider world which since they are electronically based, cannot be stopped, and the arbitrary intrusions in the name of religion on personal and private behaviour.

Caste Inequalities in Hinduism and Related Violence

However, the Islamic situation of ongoing theocratic interpretations of ancient socio-religious ideas and practices being imposed on believers, is shared by Hinduism. This religion has carried through into modern life its historical social and religious structure of caste and impurity which has imposed serious difficulties on Indian political and social development.

The strict division of Hindu social life along caste lines may have had some balancing social virtues in integrated and isolated communities, but this may well have been an ideal situation for which there is little historical evidence. The positioning of people within caste boundaries may have become firmer as a feature of contemporary life because of the categorizing which always accompanies bureaucracy, requiring people to detail their own social characteristics.

Whether caste became much more fixed as a result of the earliest British censuses in India recording the caste of everyone, is probably irrelevant since any government census or form will detail occupations which often disclose caste. This also occurred in Northern Ireland where the applications for jobs required the listing of educational qualifications and where they were obtained. Since most schools there are sectarian this disclosed the religious denomination of an applicant for a job and thus is a stage in discrimination. The reality must always have been that the higher the caste, the better able its members would have been to benefit from these religious restrictions on what they could do and with whom they could associate.

The Untouchables at the bottom of the caste hierarchy who did all the dirty jobs in society whom Mahatma Gandhi called '*harijans*', the beloved of God, became a matter of serious political concern in independent India not only on moral grounds over which a secular government has little or no control since caste status is ascribed through birth, but more importantly these people were now voters of political significance because of universal adult franchise.

So the new government was faced with providing equal opportunities for millions of people whose status had been defined by birth in the Hindu religious system as 'outcastes' and 'untouchables'. The planning elite may have considered this to be a modern anachronism and in terms of Westernised and secular understandings a fading situation because of global social changes.

There was also the fact that caste based classifications suffered from want of exact data since caste data had been omitted from census recordings since 1931. What individuals may have considered their caste to be and what others accepted must always have varied particularly in urban settings and could often be safely ignored in immigrant communities of Hindus overseas.

The Rane Commission in 1983 based its recommendations on class rather than caste maintaining that the provision of special benefits by caste would do no more than perpetuate the hereditary evils of the caste system. Further to define certain groups as backward and thus entitled to certain positive advantages as a whole gave such people a vested interest in being defined as backward and of course it excluded from possible benefits deprived Indians who were not Hindus.

The Constitution of India abolished Untouchability as a classification by which such people could be deprived of social, political and economic rights but at the same time politicians were bound by the franchise and the reactions of voters. So the government did not follow these recommendations which had gone outside a specifically Hindu frame of reference and instituted the reservation of a certain proportion of places in government service and higher education for the so-called Scheduled Castes and Tribes.

It was then proposed by the Government that there should be an 18 per cent increase in the higher education reservations for the backward categories which led to widespread violence in Gujarat which the Provincial Government institutionally tolerated. This was in spite of the fact that it was accepted that this increase would make very little actual difference in the categories affected, as they would not have the necessary qualifications. In 1984, 208 out of 675 places in medical colleges were thus reserved but only 3.4 per cent were taken up. It was estimated that if the permitted 49 per cent reservations were in force the actual utilisation would be less than 15 per cent.

The result in Gujarat was organised violence involving the burning of buses and government vehicles, offices, banks and post offices about which the police did little. It was a calculated attempt by caste Hindus to prevent the extension of certain material rights to those whom they considered to be their social, political and religious inferiors. It was estimated that 68 per cent of Untouchables were still being denied access to potable water from wells which caste Hindus had defined as reserved for their use. 'No ethic of responsibility (was shown) in the public utterances of those holding high public office' (Baxi, 1990) which should have ensured public order.

The overall result of these Constitutional changes and their backing up by reserving jobs for people according to their caste affiliations produced a new dimension of anxiety not only in those who were supposed to benefit but spread these anxieties to those who were not in this way legislated for and who felt that their advantages in employment and education were being diminished since the cake of privileged and employment was not being enlarged to provide more slices. However, their anxieties as Hindus was based on a wider range of anxieties over religious pollution.

Anxieties Over Religious Pollution

In proportion to religious belief, there must be equivalent psychological pay-offs; the conviction of being in the right and getting benefits from that and proportionate fears from the consequences of going beyond mere non-conformity which must be the periodic pattern of any form of religious commitment.

When religious requirements invade social life, the degree of conformity must be correlated to the social and psychological advantages of conformity and the corresponding difficulties from non-conformity. Some religious requirements are quite specific for which there is social backup fitting in with morality since everyone believes that killing people and stealing is wrong. Most religious establishments do not have the means or the wish in many cases to act as some sort of police force. Adultery and theft are usually prohibited by religion and although common enough, most believers manage to avoid these sins for most of the time. Thou shall not steal is more or less a universal religious requirement but it is universally seen as requiring social more than religious supervision and enforcement.

Pollution is often a feature of religious beliefs and practices and when it relates to bodily functions it can usually be worked round so that its avoidance has positive rather than negative values. Hinduism copes with this by having Untouchables carrying out polluting activities so that the producers of pollution are not contaminated.

There are initiation rituals for specialised socio-religious groupings which use these extreme pollutions as a means by which human beings are released from the restrictions into which their socialisations have tied them. Tantric behaviour in Hinduism and the Mau Mau initiations in the Kikuyu revolt in Kenya (La Fontaine, 1985: 73-77) are examples.

Both Christianity and Islam with their concepts of institutionalised charity are not worried over pollution and the former has always seen the tending of the contaminating sick and overt humility as the cleaning of latrines to be signs of virtue. The avoidance of something defined as religiously polluting is not an issue except in the cases of excluding women from some monasteries as occurs in the Coptic and Greek Orthodox Churches and the exclusion of menstruating women from even church compounds in Ethiopia.

In the past there may have been anxieties in Christianity stemming from Judaic ideas, but for most of its history their worries were over the reality of hell as their after-death destiny should they break the laws of their faith is not common today; only some fundamentalist sects now rely in part on a hell and damnation theme. The theme of sin is a thin one in which acts are not related to any overall and exact scheme of social behaviour, and there has been no institutionalisation of pollution relating to religious and social classifications. Islam has always relied more on the sybaritic realities of Paradise as recorded in the Koran than on the possibilities of hell for any failure to follow the requirements of the Five Pillars of the Faith. Instructions for preparing for prayer often contain instructions about lavatory procedures.

Buddhism and Taoism are not over concerned about pollution and are more concerned with a balance of virtue at any one time should they die unexpectedly and their manipulative systems by which individuals can improve their chances of bettering their positions on the next rebirth. It may be that the Buddhist hells and the Taoist Gods of hell are circumvented at least in part by making possible a better status in the next rebirth.

Hinduism is alone in providing an all-embracing socio-religious system of ascribed status, a by birth religion in which all relationships are defined hierarchically and in terms of pollution endangering post mortem status. The Hindu conception of religious pollution, not only includes the obvious physical pollutions of death, disease and human effluent but goes much further by extending the possibilities of pollution to the inter-relationships of the castes in which touching others or being within their shadow is fraught with pollution anxieties, and restricts from whom an individual may accept food and water. It is quite possible to be contaminated by a lower-caste person without ever knowing that it has happened; a serious difficulty in any modern urban industrial situation with public transport, restaurants and currency and no doubt leading to religious anxieties among the ultra-orthodox.

Of course, in the immediate past the caste structure may have been less rigid than it is perhaps today but this rigidity may have been an indirect consequence of British colonial bureaucracy. Asking people to state to which caste they belonged made the system rigid as it was often recorded on paper and tended to come up as the individual's identity in all public dealings. It may have become more difficult to manipulate sub-caste membership by such processes as marrying daughters with substantial dowries to husbands of a slightly higher sub-caste. There is also the socio-religious agreement of sub-castes to change their practices to fit in with the public rituals of higher sub-castes than themselves; the so-called process of 'sanskritisation' by which sub-castes take on the rituals of sub-castes superior to themselves.

The contemporary position is that individuals are probably paying more horizontal attention to their caste positions than the vertical ones which could no longer be followed because of unknown and thus unavoidable pollution from contacts in public transport, the handling of money, the eating in restaurants and industrial employment.

The membership of a sub-caste became more useful as providing wide-ranging social support and a supportive religious and political environment within and independent of the social, political and economic changes which continue to disturb their lives. In visits to the towns and employment their fears over pollution can be reduced if need be, by visits to temples which cannot know the caste status of suppliants and which themselves get benefits from '*darshan*', in which visitors are seen by the Gods or their representatives in a detached but very personal way. The bilateral anxieties over pollution and other dangers are balanced out by the simple performance of rituals.

Hindu Reciprocities and Anxieties Over Pollution

In the villages the fear of pollution is bilateral and mingled with the attempts particularly by Untouchables to change their social entitlements in conformity with national laws and the Indian Constitution and the resentments of those who experience the erosion of their quasi-traditional entitlements. These personal contacts with Untouchable fellow villagers which were both polluting and inevitable were traditionally coped with by the exchange of gifts in return for the services rendered. We need you but avoid you, but we arrange that you get a reasonable return for your excluding intrusions. In many cases this system of balanced village social and religious system has been upset by new forms of elected local councils and the payment for such services as street cleaning where before the work was done in return for donations by the better off villagers.

The giving and receiving of gifts as payments for services rendered also causes anxieties over pollution. Ghosts can be passed with alms given at the time of funerals to those performing polluting actions or who are themselves polluting (Parry, 1994: 643). Bhats, a lower caste of praise singers believe that the genealogical recitations at funerals can sometimes pass on damaging spirit possession (Snodgrass, 2001). Gazah landlords distribute alms to peripheral and dependent service-cum-polluting sub-castes and by this means dispose of dangerous and inauspicious substances which they avoid by not receiving gifts themselves (Raheja, 1990).

Indeed Dumont contends that the Hindu hierarchical opposition between the pure and the impure is the sole ideology informing relationships between the castes, which explains 'the poison in the gift' (Dumont, 1970: 800). The anxieties here are not just the receiving and giving of 'gifts' which could be refused but which cannot be in the social system of necessary reciprocities as they are the means by which inter-caste relationships are kept balanced for the social good of the community. Without these danger bearing payments, the gift receivers would be impoverished and the gift givers deprived of essential services which would be ritually polluting if they had to perform them themselves.

The fear of pollution must remain as a background to many social practices but it is no longer quite so clearly contained by continuing and accepted reciprocities which have been replaced in some places by the concept of direct payments for services rendered and in its absence the failure of these services to be performed for the overall public good. The uncontrollable but ritually controllable fear of lurking pollution remains and as we have seen it continues to be a contributory factor in inter-caste tensions and violence. Another cause of anxiety is the directing of evil onto other people; the fear of witchcraft.

Anxieties Over the Existence of Witchcraft

It is worth repeating the statement that if people believe something to be true, then it is real in its consequences (Thomas and Thomas, 1928) and this applies as much to the widespread belief in witchcraft as it does to the belief in spirits and the active existence of God. Witchcraft by which humans are able by using personal and unverifiable powers to cause misfortune to others is a common enough form of aggression leading to killings in both Africa (Tanner, 1970) and Asia (Carstairs, 1983) and has led to widespread aggression against those considered to be witches and wizards (Willis, 1968; Richards, 1935). It can be assumed that this type of aggression depends on non-pragmatic powers that come within our definition of religion and magic being indistinguishable.

It is a mistake to see belief in witchcraft as a failing of reason because that would mean that many more human social activities become subject to the same premise and denigration. The whole concept that certain individuals are charismatic rests on the premise that they have not just unusual but exceptional personal power. While it is often seen to exist in its benign form, there are just as many examples of people who are charismatically evil.

The social form that charisma takes means that individuals can influence others without using the more commonplace channels of force or economics. While some may be able to exercise this power on a personal one to one basis, others in contemporary societies are thought to be able to influence what happens to others by practices when there is no personal contact at all.

After all many people pray for others to have better health and happiness and appear sufficiently well satisfied with the results or the reputation of reported results, to make this a commonplace practice in all religions. We cannot presuppose that there are not negative praying procedures so that other people would have poorer health and unhappiness and indeed that this is likely to be both common and unadvertised. Individuals have reputations for evil as others have for goodness.

So a belief in witchcraft is not just the illogical thinking of pre-industrial peoples but an acceptance of charismatic powers and one that is so widespread in both Africa and Asia as to be classifiable as a normal part of their social and personal thinking. It would be a mistake to seek a single reason or indeed reasons for specific cases of people being accused of witchcraft; since it cannot be analytically isolated. Witchcraft cannot be defined so it can be used for virtually anything which does not have socially acceptable benign explanations. Amulets and specific behaviour to ward off witchcraft are a commonplace methods to reduce these anxieties (Tanner. 1969a).

There are of course primary explanations for almost everything; people lose their jobs because of economic recessions and have accidents by carelessly crossing the road but any such explanation does not answer the question as to why specific individual's lose their jobs or get hit by a lorry. Cases of witchcraft accusations in the 1950s among the Sukuma of Tanzania (Tanner, 1955) related to a person with a generally accepted unpleasant character, an independence of spirit and a success in trading which made him independent of any necessity for local interrelationships.

When there are multiple anxieties in a tribal community as occurred recently among the Sukuma and elsewhere, then the assumption of causes which can be identify locally and thus to a certain extent manageable becomes irresistible. However for particular people to be attacked and killed, we have to start to start with some basic factors. We have shown earlier that in Tanzania between 1970 and 1984, 3693 killings of suspected witches occurred which were known to the government, of whom 62 per cent were women over 41 years of age (Mesaki, 1992: 281-87).

These are horrendous figures indeed and we see the same pattern in India (Carstairs, 1983) in which a woman was killed as a witch after a long build up of inter-personal tensions in a village community which did not appear to have much to do with the difficulties related to rapid social change. Middle aged and old women predominate as victims and we can presume that they were divorced or widowed and probably without male relatives who could have protected them or whose existence would have stopped such rumours developing in the first place.

Beyond this to make general statements or suppositions that these widespread killings in almost epidemic proportions, were reactions to rapid political and social change and a decline in living standards, begs the whole question. Far fewer killings occurred in the coastal areas near to the capital Dares Salaam where the experience of change must have been more radical.

There could be a national correlation between personally experienced dissonance and such matters as the national compulsory villagisation campaign, unfulfilled political promises, the failure to provide jobs for the educated, over centralisation, and inefficient administration combined with inflation and rapid population growth. This state of affairs is common to many new states, but the religious paradigm in north-east Tanzania was to attribute their immediate difficulties to witches and to a lesser extent to wizards.

For the Sukuma living on the cultivation steppe there came environmental deterioration and droughts, the decline of subsistence agriculture and the growth of cotton cultivation for cash. The specific change which may correlate to these witch killings was the decline in the stability of marriage, the increase in internal migration leading to the inability to attribute misfortune to malevolent ancestors and the unwillingness of women to cultivate cotton for the profit of their husbands; a structural lack of balance between men and women. The women themselves saw traditional male repression and aggressiveness as clashing with what they had been lead to expect from the idealised modernisation goals of the state.

So we can conclude that the increase in witchcraft in Tanzania and in other African states is the use of a traditional religious paradigm that people can transmit malevolence for any number of possible reasons. This fits in well enough as explanations for anything that causes personal and communal difficulties from the loss of jobs and the failure of adequate rain to fall on certain fields. It provides an explanation, releases tension and contributes to new forms of social control (Macfarlane, 1970: 241-50). Whereas it is possible for adults to off-set their anxieties about dangers based on religion, the effect on children may be much more erosive and long-lasting.

Religious Violence and the Anxieties of Children

Children must always take into their minds the realities of the neighbourhoods in which they live and for most there will be anxieties from the possible hostility of all the strangers outside their doors particularly in towns where almost everyone there is unknown socially. These fears are partially down graded as the child becomes adult but never entirely, and outsiders are always treated with some justifiable mistrust whatever their actual social roles may be. And it goes much further than this in situations in which religious hostility is part of the social lives of children.

Recently in Belfast the capital of Northern Ireland, Roman Catholic primary school children had to pass through a predominantly Protestant area as the quickest way to school from their own religiously segregated housing estate which they had done for some years without incident. Then because of a change in the political climate little children were forced to walk to the Holy Cross school through a screen of policemen in riot gear from behind whom Protestant adults were spitting at them, throwing bottles and screaming abuse—whores, sluts, Fenian bastards, animals and a chant rising in pitch and menace—'scum, scum, scum'. Even though each child was accompanied by a parent, the effect on them of such daily experiences must have been traumatic and damaging (O'Toole, 2002: 30-2) and long-lasting.

Such incidents tend to be highlighted by the media and not all children in Northern Ireland are equally affected, but the twin Christian but opposed cultures have socialised children into a position in which those who frustrate their socials needs are members of the opposite and opposing Christian denomination. Roman Catholic children in the 1950s were brought up to think that to go inside a Protestant church was to commit mortal sin. 'You could touch the grass in the churchyard provided that you did not touch the ground. They hadn't the true faith like us Catholics. God alone knew the horrible things they got up to inside the church and when they died they would all go to hell, (Hoban, 1994).

The opposite viewpoint was equally strident and clear. 'By every means in her power with all the resources at her disposal, slowly and insidiously the Church of Rome is working day and night knowing that every farm or residence that passes from the possession of a Protestant to a Roman Catholic is helping to bring about the day when our present majority shall be wiped out, placing our Protestant rights and liberties at the mercy of a power that is determined to destroy them' (Christian Irishmen, June 1945).

The practical end result of having denominational schools was that sectarian abuse became socially sanctioned and indeed rioting became the only joint activity possible between the two sectarian communities and that prejudice was beyond the reach of law and order. The children at risk were more likely to be from economically deprived large families in which the Roman Catholics had much higher unemployment rates, lived in a 'riot' area and had adults more involved in political activism; an overall environment loaded with anxieties (Fraser, 1973). Even if such children were removed from such split hostile environments, it seems that it would take years for an alternative framework of thinking and of behaviour to take over (Kav-Venaki *et al.*, 1976).

We will discuss latter in this chapter the anxieties which may be caused to children by initiation ceremonies generally, but there are other ceremonies which may be traumatic for children. The Kuzhi Thiruvizha festival occurring once in every seven years in Tamil Nadu, India has children drugged and briefly buried as a sign of devotion to local goddesses which must have had some traumatic effects for those involved. The difficulties in instituting or failing to institute change which social rather than religious ideologies consider necessary was shown in this case as the police refused to act as no one had been injured and no one complained apart from the fact that a State minister and local members of the State legislature were present (Kapoor, 2002).

Violence within a Single Religion

In thinking about any religious faith with its divine foundations, it is reasonable to hope that such accepted beliefs would lead to substantial theoretical if not practical unity. Assuming that man has developed a need for rationality over the centuries so that this would lead to some degree of ethical unity so that violence would have been avoided but this has not happened.

Historically there have been religious wars within faiths in which Christianity has predominated of which the Thirty Years War in Europe between Roman Catholics and Protestants may be the best example. It was the end of Christian violence for some centuries between the conflicting tensions of political and confessional allegiances (Parker. 1997: 196) which resulted in horrifying destruction of people and property. At this level intra-Christian fighting has all but disappeared but at a lower one, there is little unity and the potential for disputes is always there. For Christianity their holiest shrines are in Jerusalem where there have been persistent inter-denominational quarrels about their custody, so much so indeed that the Ottomans left the overall custody of access to the Church of the Holy Sepulchre in the hands of a Muslim because they were unable to get any agreement from the Christians. In July 2002 the monks of the Ethiopian Orthodox Church and the Coptic Church of Egypt came to blows over their respective rights to custody of the roof and the Israeli police had to be called in to restore order.

All the great religions have examples in the past of believers who have physically tortured or altered their bodies for religious reasons or have either killed themselves deliberately or put themselves into a position where they are killed by others because of their faith. Religious history has popularised the lives of many of these individuals so that there are statues of Jain saints who have starved themselves to death and pictures of anorexic Christian saints. Such individuals may have been remembered in sectarian histories as the overly devout while contemporary psychologists would tend to diagnose them as abnormal.

Violence between Shia and Sunni Moslems

It is not difficult to see the potential for violence between these two branches of Islam in which the majority Sunni believe that the Prophet Mohammad was the last of these divinely inspired men and the Shia who believe that divine views are kept alive through the inspired words of their *ayatollahs* while waiting for the reappearance of the descendents of the Prophet. The war between Shia Iran and Sunni controlled Iraq which was initiated by a partially secularised Baathist regime in Iraq was seen by the Iranians as a straightforward attack on their Shia faith. The Ayatollah Khomeini told the Iranians that they were fighting 'to protect Islam… There is absolutely no question of peace because the Iraqis are corrupt and the perpetrators of corruption. Those who criticise us say 'Why do you not compromise with these corrupt powers? It is because they see things through human eyes and analyse these things with a natural viewpoint. They do not know the views of God and how the prophets dealt with oppressors or else they know but pretend to be blind and deaf...That is contrary to the views of all the prophets' (Chubin and Tripp, 1988: 38).

Communal riots in Lucknow in the colonial period were between Shia and Sunni as much as between Hindus and Muslims and there has been contemporary Sunni violence against Shias in Pakistan. Also recently in Iraq Sunni predominance was assured by the execution of some Shia leaders and the persecution of Muslim Kurds from the 1970s when they were forcibly removed from frontier areas and there has been substantial violence against them, including the use of chemical weapons on racial rather than religious grounds (Sluglett & Farouk-Sluglett, 1992).

The Shia system allows for change since within it is the possibility of charismatic figures appearing who are institutionally capable of furthering divinely inspired re-interpretations of Muslim ideas. This is a system which in some ways parallels the potential ability of the Roman Catholic Church to update its doctrines through the official theological statements of the Pope. In the Shia system there is the potentiality for conflict within itself and between it and the Sunni who have no similar means of updating ideas and practices which were formulated in the seventh century.

In any religious system and indeed outside them, there is always the possibility of charismatic figures appearing who have divinely inspired messages and whose views catch on in particular situations and which erupt into violence. In northern Nigeria rapid urbanisation and the moving out of the Westernised elite into high quality suburban housing resulting from the oil boom of the 1970s, combined with the military coup of 1966 and with it the flight of southerners, made many Muslims realise their dependence on Christians and the need for reform. This rapid change and reckless spending promoted an unprecedented rural to town migration leading to many unemployed and the pushing to one side of those who had only qualifications from Koranic schools, combined with appalling living conditions and an enormous increase in crime against which the police proved impotent. Onto this scene came the charismatic Prophet Maitatsine calling for a religious war '*jihad*' against all European things and the local rich which unleashed a reign of widespread violence and possibly a thousand dead which the army had to put down (Barkindo, 1993).

Even Saudi-Arabia founded under the influence of Wahabi fundamentalists, has had violent events. In November 1979 some 400 armed militants calling themselves the Ikhwan, occupied the Great Mosque in Mecca, the centre of Islam. This resulted in many deaths and despite some horror at such sacrilege, there was widespread sympathy for their aims of making the Saudi family rulers accountable for the overindulgence of their lifestyle. A graffiti in Riyadh University referred to their leader as 'our martyr. Why did you not storm the palaces. The struggle is only beginning' (Hiro, 1989: 133). Moved by this the Saudi Arabian Shia broke the ban on publically celebrating Ashura, the festival of mourning for Ali, resulting in a riot in which some police and Shias were killed.

Hindu Violence against Untouchables

The Constitution of India which prohibits any Hindus from being deprived of their rights as citizens because of their caste status as Untouchables, was a necessary step towards social justice for the millions at the bottom of the nation's economic and social life as a result of their hereditary religious position. A constitution does not implement itself and thus requires the support of public opinion and official organisations.

These constitutional provisions in terms of Hindu social organisation have to be regarded as revolutionary in two ways. Firstly, the Untouchables themselves became aware that they had these new rights and thus even if they did not get the support of public organisations for getting these rights implemented, their attitudes to caste Hindu trying to maintain their superiority became less subservient if not publicly resentful. Secondly, caste Hindus started to object to this overt and covert assertiveness in rural communities where it was disturbing long-term social and economic interrelationships and balances.

Newspapers record in repetitive detail long lists of occasions in which Untouchables have been penalised (Kambie. 1981). Statues of Dr. Ambedkar, the long-term leader of the Untouchable political movement for improvements in their status, have been destroyed or damaged, cattle owners have not been allowed to become members of a milk co-operative, priests have refused access to temples, their marriage procession attacked by caste Hindus, village heads taking oaths to prevent them working their fields, assaults for walking on public roads, being killed over using caste wells during water shortages, over a hundred houses burnt and communities forced to leave, their women stripped and branded, their children made to sit separately in schools, and a school teacher beaten for sitting in a chair. The list is virtually endless and nation-wide.

More specifically in the year ending 1981 there were 14,306 known atrocities against Untouchables involving 493 murders and 1245 cases of arson. Many occasions for violence were caused by dressing or behaving in a way suggesting a dignity above what caste Hindus were prepared to concede to them. In one wedding procession incident fourteen Untouchables were killed including six burnt alive. On other occasions violence was started because Untouchables were wearing sandals, riding horses and having a marriage procession through certain caste Hindu localities (Commission for Scheduled Castes and Tribes, 1981: 76, 151).

Persisting Intra-religious Hostility in Northern Ireland

After the Good Friday agreement which led to some relaxation of Republican violence and to some progress in the disarming of the Irish Republican Army's stockpile of weapons, it was hoped that peace at the communal level might move forward (Tanner, M, 2001). This does not seem to have been the case with the expansion of Roman Catholic political power by democratic means leading to the loss of Protestant control of Belfast City Council and the election of a Roman Catholic mayor. There has been the corresponding decline in Protestant power which has led to further violence with the burning of Roman Catholic churches and schools.

The situation of tension has not been reduced by the Republican practice of flying Palestinian Liberation Organisation's flags and the Protestants flying those of Israel. In one case masked Protestant men asked college students to recite the alphabet because Roman Catholics with their Irish language background pronounce 'h' differently to Protestants. There is also the Protestant fear of Roman Catholics buying up houses in areas now divided by corrugated iron fences designed to keep the communities apart, once these had been removed (Economist, 15 June 2001).

Martyrdom

There are two types of martyrs which are divided historically. Firstly, those who are killed by their oppressors because they belong to another faith and would not recant their beliefs when given the opportunity to do so. This occurred in the Roman persecution of Christians who would not worship the Gods of the Roman State in the person of the Emperor and the permanently settled Muslims in mediaeval Spain who were faced with conversion to Christianity or expulsion to north Africa.

In both these cases individuals could change their faith and save their lives and livelihoods which was quite common but even then they were not trusted. For the former the number killed was not high and there was considerable sympathy for those who changed or at least pretended to do so.

The second type involves men and in some cases women as well who choose quite deliberately to go to their deaths for a religious reason or at least a reason which combines communal political as well as individual religious aims. Towards the end of second World War when the Japanese were clearly losing, some thousands of pilots out of loyalty to the Emperor as God and in the hope of being remembered as important spirits at the Yasukuni Shrine for the war dead of Japan in Tokyo, piloted bomb laden aircraft in one way flights intending to sink American and British naval shipping (Okumiya, 1980. Inoguchi & Nakajima, 1960).

There are Hindu suicide bombers involved in supporting the Tamil demands for a Hindu state in northern Sri Lanka of whom a woman killed the Indian Prime Minister Rajiv Gandhi. Then there are the Palestinian ones who kill themselves and as many Israelis as possible as part of a political resentment against the Israeli occupation of their land and in hope of entering Paradise. Suicide bombing is also a feature of current Iraqi life. Finally, the aircraft which in September 2001 were flown by Muslims into the World Trade Centre in New York killing themselves and their civilian passengers as well as some three thousand office workers, all of whom had no connection with what these suicidal men considered to be American hostility to Islam.

The religious background to these Muslims killing themselves for an Islamic reason is quite clear. It is always necessary to remember that the Koran is the literal Word of God transmitted to the Prophet

Mohammad and in this it bears little resemblance to the Holy Bible in its disputed history and many translations in which Christians may or may not believe as it does not have the basic veracity of the Koran.

Firstly, the Koran states that the dead are alive if killed fighting in the way of God (Koran 2.154, 49. 3.169, 38). The point to remember here is that death in battle for the Faith is something which might or might not happen, it has no inevitability about it whereas going to their deaths carrying a bomb, then entering Paradise is both assured and instantaneous. 'It's as if a very high impenetrable wall separated you from Paradise or Hell. Allah has promised one or the other to his creatures. So by pressing the detonator, you can immediately open the door to Paradise – it is the shortest path to Heaven' (Hassan, 2001).

Then the Koran is quite specific as to the circumstances which would greet the virtuous believer in Paradise. The abode of the just, the garden through which rivers flow, reclining on couches, eating fruit and served by ever-youthful boys (Koran, 18.32, 12-44: 2.68, 17-33). More specifically there are numerous references to wide-eyed houris with swelling breasts untouched by men or djinn, spotless virgins, amorous like of age enclosed in pavilions (Koran 37, 48, 7: 38.52: 78, 33 etc).

It is important to recognise that the social and religious processes by which these contemporary Muslims choose to go to their deaths parallel in many respects those of the early Christian martyrs (Riddle, 1931). The rewards were assured with exact specifications, salvation was immediate and personal, a guarantee of personal communication with God, foreknowledge of the support which would be given to their families and the knowledge that they would by becoming martyrs move from being nonentities to being important.

The procedure for becoming a Muslim suicide bomber is a combination of one's conviction and group support up to and alongside the point of decision. A ritualistic dialogue of question and answer about the glory of martyrdom so that 'we were in a constant state of worship' which was detailed in an Arabic document found in association with the World Trade Centre attack.

In both these ancient Christian cases and the modern Islamic ones there is no evidence that those who become martyrs had suicidal behavioural characteristics; they seem to have been normal people with normal secular behaviour so that they could not be spotted in advance as potential suicide bombers. We can be certain that Muslim suicide bombing will continue to be a repetitive feature in situations in which Muslims consider themselves unjustly treated in their political and religious aspirations which in their faith are indivisible.

The Suicide of Hindu Widows–Suttee

Traditional Hinduism has religiously sanctioned and supported the belief that the true widow burns herself to death on the funeral pier of her husband as a sign that she has no life worthy of maintaining once he has died. This certainly outraged the British who could never believe that any rational woman could voluntarily burn herself to death in this way and legally forbid the arranging of such suicides in 1829.

Since 1947 there are known to have been 28 instances in Rajasthan which was never directly ruled by the British and a number of additional cases elsewhere including that of the wife of a senior army officer. These did not cause much popular interest until that of the young Roop Kanwar in 1987 and the site of her death became almost at once a popular shrine visited by thousands.

It is believed that such self-abnegation generates a power that passes to her family and that this female power must be channelled if it is to be devoted to the betterment of men and through men to society. Fundamentalist Hindus believe that the modern world in forbidding suttee, would prevent this power from its traditional channels benefiting religion, virtue and social cohesion. This attitude of mind led to male agitation and demonstrations in its support (Hawley, 1994). There is an economic aspect to this as Roop Kanwar's village and the whole neighbourhood benefited from becoming a pilgrimage centre.

Infanticide

We will see latter that the killing of girl babies in India is not so much religious as a reaction to the cost of marrying off daughters and the fact that they go and live elsewhere which means that the cost of their upbringing gives their families no return on this investment. However, in other cultures babies are killed for religious reasons.

The most extreme case of religiously motivated infanticide must have been the Carthaginian sacrificing of their first-born children and this is likely to have affected the ability of that society to survive as first-born children tend to be the more successful. Some 20 per cent of the children of the well-to-do were killed in this way (Weyl, 1968). The Nayar sub-caste of southern India were reported at one time as sacrificing the first-born sons to the goddess of smallpox (Sherring, 1872: 81).

In a number of societies children that are born in an abnormal way or appear to be abnormal such as twins when children are normally born singly, are often killed since at least in some Bantu societies this is taken to be a sign that ancestors are displeased. Children born by breech presentation, twins, with extensively marked bodies, males without testicles and those who cut their upper teeth first are widely reported to have been killed (Krzywicki, 1934).

Religion and Body Mutilations

Pain as part of religious practices is commonplace whether self-inflicted or inflicted on individuals as part of their commitment or as a condition or illustration of religious membership. It is difficult to define as even in a religious context it can be subdivided between physical sensation, emotional responses and evaluative ideas which can be both institutional and personal (Melzack, 1975).

Rituals of self-hurting and the theological glorification of suffering occur in every society and physical pain appears as a necessary or acceptable part of pilgrimages, funerals, initiations, mystical discipline along with authoritative pronouncements from religious leaders (Glucklich, 2001). There are numerous examples from the biographies of mediaeval Christian saints which mirror the current austerities of Hindu *saddhus* (Vauchez, 1977).

Body mutilation is a common occurrence in conjunction with religion whether it is individually self-inflicted as in the extreme asceticism of some early Christians, and the anorexia of some Buddhist devotees and the self-scourging which some carry out to reduce their physical desires. The most extreme contemporary examples are Hindu and Muslim ascetics being loaded with heavy chains, being suspended upside down, piercing their tongues, cheeks, abdominal wall, neck, hammering nails into the skull and pulling out their eyeballs (Hunt, 1934).

Self-mutilation as part of mourning and grief follows a set procedure in many societies (Rosenblatt *et al.*, 1976: 234) and it was described in an Aborigine ritual in which many gashed themselves even before the man was actually dead (Durkheim, 1968: 436).

Self-mutilation is also part of some communal rituals such as the carrying of bundles of cacti on the bare backs of Mexican men during Good Friday processions and the regular beatings and piercing of their bodies by Shia Moslems in commemoration of the martyrdom of Ali. Members of the Skopsi Christian sect in 19th century Russia castrated themselves to avoid sexual sins. In this category fasting is so common among Ethiopian Copts as is their overindulgence afterwards that it has led its recognition as a special form of gastritis (Knutsson and Selinus, 1970).

The religious justifications for such self-mutilations have a cross religious similarity. A Hindu text states 'Whatever is hard to be traversed, whatever is hard to be attained, whatever is hard to be reached, whatever is hard to be performed, all may be accomplished by austerities; for austerity possesses a power which is difficult to surpass... Whatever sin men commit by thoughts, word, or deed, they speedily burn away through penance if they keep penance as their only riches' (Laws of Manu, 11: 239); such an approach might well have been written by a Christian theologian.

It forms part of pilgrimage procedures. The Roman Catholic Irish climb their sacred mountain, Croagh Patrick, often with bare feet, in order to go attend Mass at the top. A Tamil Hindu pilgrimage included walking bare foot for the forty mile route aimed at a transformation of devotional love (Daniel, E.V., 1987: 255-68).

Male Circumcision

Some mutilations such as male circumcision are necessary for a man to be considered a Muslim or a Jew but many forms are either entirely personal as the individual seeks to become closer to God or partially voluntary in group participation from which social as much as religious status is gained. Those who are mutilated are often infants whose parents go through these circumcision rituals of social and religious inclusion on their behalf, or as a necessary part of adolescent initiation rites or done by adults as part of their own religious yearnings.

Male circumcision is not mentioned in the Koran and may have been adopted from an earlier Arab custom and there are several traditions that it was favoured by the Prophet Muhammad. A group ceremony carried out in Pangani, Tanzania in the 1950s involved the overnight reading of the whole Koran over the children about to be circumcised. It may often not be performed under hygienic conditions and result in deaths from tetanus and penile mutilations (Gosden, 1935; Shulman, 1964). It can be carried out at any age from seventh days after birth in Dahomey to save expense and as late as the thirteenth year in Bosnia.

Judaism on the other hand with its concern for ritual cleanliness and for health forbids the circumcision of a child soon after birth, when ill or not fully recovered or in conditions which appear to be linked with haemophilia (Jakobovits, 1961). Also because of penile mutilations from inept circumcisers, there is the increasing use of sterile even hospital environments for the operation in which the observers can see and hear the appropriate prayers but not get near the surgery (Weiss, C, 1962).

Christianity has no direct interest in circumcision but has had to become involved in some African situations in which there is a connection of the operation with the assumption of adulthood. Most denominations ignore the issue but the Universities Mission to Central Africa in southern Tanzania tried with little success to Christianise the ritual and to introduce more hygienic procedures.

Perhaps in contemporary justification attention is given to the possibility that it protects from penile carcinoma which is a rare condition. There is a low incidence among Muslims in comparison to Hindus (Bleich, 1950) and a higher rate among uncircumcised Ugandans than among circumcised Kenyans (Dodge *et al.*, 1963).

It is also suggested that circumcision reduces the rate of cancer of the cervix and uterus but a study of European and Abyssinian women found the rates to be almost the same (Huber. 1960). There are too many other factors involved for any conclusions to be drawn except its relationship to hygiene and religious cleanliness. A Maliki text Mukhtas-aru and Al-Ghazali's The Beginning of Obedience (Watt, 1970) contain detailed instructions for personal cleanliness in relation to urine, semen and faeces, particularly in relation to the performance of the obligatory five daily prayers. Furthermore early intercourse with numerous partners has been found to be correlated to cervical cancer and so is more likely to occur in the less religious (Hulka, 1982).

Female Circumcision

This has attracted considerable attention as the inhuman mutilation of young women. It has been performed at various times and places throughout the world particularly in areas under Muslim influence in Africa and in many African traditional societies. There is no evidence that it occurred in early Egypt but it is mentioned in Strabo (1950:14, 4, 9) and Herodotus (1952: 2, 104) as occurring there in later times.

Female circumcision takes three forms. Literal circumcision in which the clitoral prepuce is removed by razor, knife or smouldering stone, the so-called 'sunna' operation. Secondly, the intermediate circumcision in which the clitoris is removed as well as the anterior or all of the labia minora and slices of the labia majora. Finally, pharaonic circumcision or infibulation involving the complete removal of the clitoris, labia minora and majora with the two sides of the wound stitched together leaving a small opening for the passage of urine and menstrual blood (Gordon, 1991).

This operation has been wrongly attributed to Islam for it antedates the origin of Islam and does not occur in Saudi Arabia, nor in Iran, Iraq or Turkey. It is not mentioned in the Koran but there are traditions based on the alleged remarks of the Prophet Mohammad that it was an embellishment for a woman but an obligation for a man.

Although it is clear that cliterodectomy has no religious justification, it is regarded by most Sudanese Muslims as part of the discipline of their faith (Cloudsley, 1983). However, infibulation seems to occur overwhelmingly among non-literates and cliterodectomy among the educated and in Egypt (El Dareer, 1982).

The Muslim theological view is that it should consist of no more than cutting off of a part of the clitoris and that any further mutilation is forbidden (Trimingham, 1949: 182). It has also been forbidden by Egyptian law since 1959. Islam has no centralised organisation which could further this view and support the secular and humane opinion that the mutilation of women by any of these methods is a dangerous and inhuman practice.

The justification for female circumcision is that it reduces sexual desire in girls and protects their morals by removing potentially erogenous parts. It can also lead to the constriction of the vaginal opening which is considered more pleasurable for the husband so that we find women being reinfibulated after childbirth or after being widowed or divorced. An alternative Somali view that women have to be protected when working in the fields or shepherding (Kwaak, 1992). All these are male views which have little consideration for the women's needs. University students in Khartoum (Nordenstam, 1968: 95-6, 205-6) regarded the practice of infibulation as unjustified but they continued to be in favour of cliterodectomy as it protected women from untimely pregnancies. Even progressive fathers opposed to circumcision would still have their own daughters circumcised.

Once this mutilating rite has been performed there may be complications beyond those connected with the operation itself (Mustafa, 1966; Worsley, A., 1938). The list of medical complications arising from infibulation are horrendous (Gordon, 1991). A Sudanese doctor (Hathout, H.M. 1963) refers to the frantic struggling of girls who are forcibly held in the lithotomy position leading to mistakes. The binding together of their legs for up to forty days afterwards adds to the potential complications.

The operation can lead to marital difficulties latter if the vaginal opening is too small or if the bride is secretly reinfibulated prior to the marriage. As a result coital injuries do occur as well as rectal intercourse, prohibited by Islamic law, occurring by default as the vaginal opening is too small. A high proportion of Sudanese women express no interest in the possibility of sexual pleasure. Later there are obstetric complications when the circumcision scar has to be cut to allow the child to be delivered (El Dareer, 1982).

From the biological point of view the whole process of male and female circumcision is perplexing. The prevention of disease is debatable and can only affect very small numbers in any population. This cutting away of skin around sensitive erogenous zones intimately connected with reproduction makes no sense at all biologically. Its dangers and its effects in reducing sexual pleasure makes the whole process of reproduction much less cost-efficient. However, peasant women in Malaysia claimed that the removal of the clitoral hood increased the woman's pleasure in sexual intercourse (Ong. 1989: 73). There are, however, the effects on the women involved of violence and the possibility of its occurrence in the creation and maintenance of pervasive and significant fear in those exposed to it within the environments in which they live.

Why then circumcision which some religions do without. The foreskin of the male cannot be biologically disadvantageous or it would have been lost in the course of human evolution. The clitoris arguably makes reproduction more efficient by making sex more enjoyable for women. Why cut off or damage either organ?

It must be seen in its social and religious context. For men it denotes membership of the Islamic faith and for women as a rite of passage into adulthood and marriage in which tightness of the vagina is valued and its decline in Egypt is related to a change from extended to nuclear families. Circumcision is widely seen as an aspect of male control over women, a reflection of the divinely ordained dominant status of men in Muslim societies but international concern to eradicate this has had limited success (Dirie, 1985).

Cannibalism and Religion: The Extremes of Cultural Dissonance

The association of religions with violence is both clear and common enough since those involved talk and write about their motivations and the destruction which occurs is noted and the names of the dead listed and mourned. The eating of human flesh would be seen generally to be immoral and its association with any religion to be very questionable.

However, cannibalism is closely related to religious practices in some communities but it seems unlikely that it has ever become socially accepted and instituted in order to supply food or more specifically to be due to a shortage of animal protein (Evans-Pritchard, 1965), although it is common enough in situations of extreme deprivation for which there is no alternative to dying but to eat the dead.

Christianity sees no sin in eating the dead in such circumstances that as the Roman Catholic Argentinian rugby football players who crashed in the Andes and ate the dead in order to survive. On going to confession for what they felt was a terrible sin, they were told that there was nothing to confess (Read, 1993).

The monotheistic faiths and their followers view cannibalism with revulsion as blurring the distinctions between humans and animals in treating human bodies like animal meat. These believers and indeed secular governments are not prepared to even consider that cannibals, the word itself is pejorative, have valid social and religious reasons for eating the flesh of dead people whether relatives or outsiders.

In Brazil both missionaries and government officials threatened to hold back food and medical help to those who continued with cannibalism. 'Eating people is wrong and that is the beginning and end of any discussion of the subject and in their failure to be able to argue against the eschatological beliefs of the people, they fall back on the logic of disease. Very true in the case of 'kuru' among the Fore of New Guinea whose women ate parts of their dead kinsmen and who suffered from a fatal degenerative disease of the central nervous system (Gajdusek, 1973).

There have been many kinds of cannibalism functionally part of specific societies which outrage the religious and secular understandings of the larger societies surrounding them. Commemorative cannibalism among the Trobriand Islanders who exhumed and dismembered the bodies of related men and were expected to display their filial piety by sucking the flesh off the bones (Malinowski, 1929, 13). Compassionate cannibalism by the New Guinea Gimi women who were expected to eat parts of the dead bodies of their male relatives in order to release their individual spirits (Strathern, 1982).

Perhaps the most important were beliefs related to fertility among the New Guinea Bimin-Kuskumin amongst whom male agnates honoured the dead by eating their bone marrow to ensure the passage of the dead men's spirits to the ancestral world, thus recycling their procreative and ritual strength within their patrilineage (Lewis, I.M. 1986: 73-4).

Finally, among the Wari of Brazil a complex amalgam of myth, eschatological ideas about the human body and social psychological and ecological concerns for whom the magic of existence lay in the commonality of human and animal identities which through cannibalism allowed human participation in the dynamics of both eating and being eaten (Conklin. 1995).

In these forms of ritual cannibalism we have the culturally acceptable behaviour in a number of small scale societies, clashing with the secular and religious values of larger societies which are prepared to exercise a variety of sanctions which could be interpreted as violence against the living for their violence against their own dead. This would seem to be extinguishing a social and religious practice which did no harm to those involved except for the Fore of New Guinea and even that could have been avoided by the injunction that the flesh should have been cooked well before eating. Let us now pass on to discuss violence between religions.

6

Violence and Fear between Religions

The Fact of Inter-religious Violence

Many outsiders to the intricacies of religious behaviour and the violence and fear connected with these practices are surprised that those within a faith do not in their own interests get together with the people of their own faith in order to prevent these eruptions. We have seen that this has not occurred in history or in contemporary life.

If that is as difficult to arrange as it been between Christians in Northern Ireland and between Shia, Sunni and the Ahmaddiya Muslims in the Middle East, then how much more difficult it is to get people who believe in different Gods or quantities of Gods and spirits and who practice their faiths in dramatically different ways, to sit down and discuss their differences. Who has theological and popular power to represent who and what are they talking about and how much of these differences are religious rather than political, social and economic ones. Perhaps we might almost suggest that considering the complications surrounding these differences, it is surprising that there is not more violence in which religions are implicated.

There has scarcely been any period since the end of Second World War in which political conflicts have not shown some elements of religious disagreement (Casanova, 1994). In the Middle East, Africa and Asia all the religions and their fundamentalisms, Jewish, Christian and Muslim fed by their old power struggles augmented by oil money and the purchase of arms, have been meeting each other in various forms of armed struggle in Palestine, the Sudan, Indonesia, the Philippines, India, and the Indo-Pakistan border.

But there is another aspect to religious involvement in violence which is that the major religions particularly Christianity and to a growing extent Islam both as institutions and through their activists, have become deeply involved in the struggles for religious liberation, political justice and various interpretations of democracy (Casanova, 1994), of which the Christian open missionary activities with its specialised personnel and training schools are an obvious example. Missionaries have been killed in several countries because of their teachings and El Salvador had the assassination of Archbishop Romero in the middle of a service in which he was the main celebrant. There was also the killings of several Jesuits and in Rhodesia presumably by those who felt threatened by their public message.

Thus religious violence has several themes. Firstly, quarrels over definitions along which lines people have become socially and politically divided historically. What is believed to be the Word of God is a difficult position from which to start negotiating changes within a faith and nearly impossible over the boundaries between faiths without initiating substantial cognitive dissonance. The Japanese reply to a question as to whether he believed in God was to enquire what God had the questioner in mind is symptomatic of such difficulties.

Secondly, where there are no definitions but a range of socio-religious differences which are so amorphous and so institutionally formless that there is no one with whom discussions can be usefully initiated such as the nature of ancestor influence and witchcraft. It is because of this that the religious thinking of non-literates has never received the intellectual equality and understanding that their pervasiveness suggests are necessary; there has always been the assumption of inferiority. In the context of violence it is salutary to remember that the Great and the Good are possibly less influential than the locally Evil and Bad whose actual and potential positions are built on the popularity of existing differences and the satisfactions which are fulfilled by these practices. In all these differences religious violence circulates between the two extremes of abstract idealism and communal tensions.

The Understandable Logic of Religious Violence

There is some truth in the theory that if power seeking individuals are unable to gain their goals through the usual political and social channels, it helps them to link their temporal struggles with religious ideas which contrast their ideological orderliness with the current social chaos. 'Those who want their use of violence to be morally sanctioned but do not have the approval of an officially recognised government, find it helpful to have access to a higher source; the meta-morality that religion provides (Juergensmeyer, 1988). Although this refers to violence in the Punjab, India, it provides useful parallels to the religious backings for violence elsewhere.

However cynical it may seem it appears again and again in societies divided by religions in which the political system has been unable to cope successfully with these divisions nor to develop satisfactory alternatives. Religion provides the possible basis for a new national consensus which is not possible while there are substantial minorities belonging to other religions who cannot be driven out or converted.

So religious leaders who combine their beliefs with the conviction that their religion must have its full development expressed in political and social control of society, develop the message to convince the devout that the religious ideal is realizable in human terms in the here and now in a geographical location and that there are actual opponents blocking this possibility. This hope is common enough in small communities such as the Amish and Hutterites and the aspirations of some African Independent Churches, but they do not involve violence. Where these hopes are national, if not global, violence is perhaps inevitable.

The violence in these situations is occasioned by the fact that this religious idealism is promoted in terms of what their founders and other historical leaders found to be appropriate in the past. A looking backward to entirely hypothetical idealised situations which are neither likely to have actually occurred then nor are capable of being reproduced in modern societies. Every feature of life has been changed by global developments which control individuals without any society and its members being able to do much about these overarching factors. Electricity and oil have revolutionised not only what religions can do but make it much more difficult if not impossible to contain ideas which implicitly and directly challenge these historical principles on which some religions were based in a bygone age.

Leaving aside the retrogressive thinking of Muslim idealists, the Sikhs provide an example of this idealism being connected to violence against those of other faiths, the surrounding Hindu majority. As in Islam there are religious texts to support violence, and Gobind the Tenth and last guru of the Sikh religion who died in 1708 stated 'God subdues enemies, so does the sword; therefore, the sword is God and the God is sword (Gobind Guru, 1909: v. 83). He even ordered that the carrying of a small dagger should be part of the everyday costume of a Sikh along with a steel bracelet, knee length under-pants and uncut hair and beard.

The Sikh religion centres on the Golden Temple and its compound in Amritsar and up to 1947 their politics was polarised between the Akali Dal who controlled the temple and the secular-cum-Hindu Congress Party and the Communists. National political developments made their main concern to distinguish Sikhs from the surrounding Hindu majority leading to campaigns for political separatism. 'Religion was reduced from being the essence and guide of life in all spheres to a sign of distinction between politically organised communities (Dumont, 1970: 91).

By 1984 residents in the temple compound included Bhindranwale a charismatic figure who introduced the idea of the righteous war in defence of the Sikh social-cum-religious identity. This was initially a popular reaction against non-uniformity, secularists, Hindus, heresy, modernisation, cultural disintegration and unacceptable political domination. He fortified the second temple in the compound from where he became the main organiser of a terrorist campaign resulting in the deaths of several hundred Hindus, while making himself the target for Central Government retribution (Leaf, 1985: 494). This resulted in Operation Blue Star in June 1984 which cleared the compound of those who had been defined as terrorists in which hundreds were killed leading to widespread further violence against Hindus as well as their opponents within the Sikh community (Madan, 1991). This attack on the temple led to the assassination of Prime Minister Gandhi by her Sikh bodyguard and nationwide attacks on Sikhs. In this series of events we can see the popular appeal of a specific religious identity being used in support of a political campaign which used violence and which in its turn provoked violence against them.

While this violence in the Punjab involved hundreds of deaths on religious grounds, it did not involve the more reputable parts of Sikh society and the Central Government's reactions were expressed in secular terms against terrorism rather than as a Hindu reaction to the killing of their co-religionists. The religious violence in the Balkans went far further than this as genocide on religious grounds.

Whether the violence in the Balkans can be described as religious or ethnic or a persistent intermingling of these two categories can be a matter of interpretation but nevertheless the Muslims who were killed in their thousands, were chosen on the basis of their religious identity. The Christian Serb politicians and the army if they did not organise the killings, certainly carried them out with the support of Christian church leaders. It was grounded in a religious mythology that characterised the targeted people as both ethnic and religious traitors and thus their extermination was a sacred act. Further the perpetrators of the violence may have been at least partially protected by the policy makers of the Western world being culturally dominated by Christianity (Sells, 1996: 144). Here again violence was carried out in an atmosphere in which religion was brought in as a support. Let us now move on to more narrowly defined religious involvements in violence, the Islamic case.

Violence Furthered by Islamic Idealism

There are many instances in the past in which religions have gone to war in the names of their faiths, but these bilateral dogmatic confrontations as in the Crusades and the expulsion of Muslim rule from Spain seem to have ended with the Thirty Years War between Christians. But this would have been a benign view of more recent history with the Ottoman Muslim genocide of the Armenians and following the Greek attack on Turkish Asia Minor, the mutual expulsion of Christian Greeks from Turkey and of Muslim Greeks from the Greek mainland and Crete. Even more recently the same thing has happened in Cyprus divided into a Muslim north and a Christian south. It is salutary to remember these events when assessing the justification and extent of more immediately contemporary Islamic support for violence, apart from the model of the Prophet Mohammad's life and the support of some sections for divinely justified violence using the word '*jihad*'.

Although the original meaning of this word was effort for the realisation of personal faith, it has now been taken to refer to the armed struggle against unbelievers and the protection of the Islamic community against unbelievers (Gieling, 1999). It has also been understood as military action with the object of expanding the Islamic world (Tyan, 1965: 11.538-40). Both stem from the fundamental principle of the universality of Islam by which this religion along with the temporal power which it implies, ought to embrace the whole universe if necessary by force.

This framework of peace with non-Muslims as opposed to Jews and Christians who would be tolerated as 'people of the book' once they have submitted to the Sunni conceived suzerainty of Islam, is a provisional state of affairs. The Shia go further than this seeing the non-acceptance of their teachings as equivalent to unbelief and '*jihad*' as a duty to rid the world of a greater evil. A substantial part of Muslim doctrine sees '*jihad*' as important as the Five Pillars of the Faith and to which each Muslim should be individually dedicated. The 'hadith' sayings of the Prophet suggest three interpretations; as a form of monastic dedication, acts of pure devotion and as one of the Gates to Paradise.

The word '*jihad*' comes up frequently today in the injunctions for Muslims to oppose America influences and the United States which the Iranian Shia have defined as the 'Great Satan'. It was used to invite support for the Turks against the Allies in first World War, and in rebellions against British authority on the North West frontier of India and in Somaliland, and indeed it is currently a common word.

However, it now seems to be the case that only Islam is collectively capable of raising support for political violence in the name of defending Islam against the indirect cultural intrusions of the West. It has less frequently used military methods to defend what it sees as the West's deliberate policy to subordinate the Muslim world to its secular dominance which to the Western way of thinking has nothing at all to do with Christianity. The West sees its leaders to be nominal Christians whose political policies have no ostensible public or private connection with religion.

The Jews and Muslims have been intermittently fighting each other since the beginning of the last century in both Israel and Palestine. Although the religious differences are clear, both have officially stayed clear as far as possible from giving their violence a specifically religious backing; mosques and synagogues have not so far been the objectives of specific violence. The exception to this is the Mosque of the Dome or Temple Mount in Jerusalem which has been periodically invaded by Israeli Jews wanting to make political or religious points of its connection with the original temple, while it remains one of the holiest sites in Islam after Mecca and Medina. Even in the Sudan the long standing civil war between the Christian-cum-traditional south against the dominance of the Muslim north has not so far been couched in overt terms of religious oppositions.

It is only with Islam that there is a model of violence in the life of the Prophet Mohammad and this has to be stressed that Muslims have him as a model of and for violence in a religious cause. No other religion has this clear religious justification for violence against non-believers In India there is the growth of Hindu nationalism as a reaction to the existence of Islamic states to both east and west and the militancy of Pakistan. There is also the one hundred million Muslim minority which the Hindu majority see as potential if not as active traitors to the Indian nation. In Sri Lanka there has been a somewhat similar growth of Buddhist nationalism in response to the demands of the Tamil Hindus for independence.

Violence Furthered by Buddhist Nationalism

Buddhist fundamentalism mirrors in some ways its Islamic counterparts with its reinterpretations of the Theravada world view as a reaction to what the Sri Lankans see as the disruptive effects of Westernisation and modernisation generally; as a model affecting their identity as Buddhists and not just as a reaction of social discontent over their lack of economic progress (Swearer, 1991). The shared ideal of a simple, homogeneous, egalitarian pre-colonial Buddhist peasant society and the hope of reintroducing a mythical past, is the aim of contemporary radical monks who think that the religion of the Buddha cannot flourish without its own sovereign territory (Tambiah, 1992: 82-99).

The Sri Lankan two party system tended to sustain Buddhist extremists since control of Parliament would inevitably go to the party which captured the most Sinhalese Buddhist votes over Tamil Hindu minority ones so that the latter were condemned to being a permanent and impotent minority. In the short-term it paid politicians under a Buddhist umbrella to attack the Tamils in terms of past Buddhist glories and to voice the goal of a religious reclamation of the island. There was also increased popularism and chauvinism among towns people who became attracted to the ideology of a politicised Buddhism and its simplified racism in an increasingly divided island.

This Buddhist-Hindu polarisation eventually developed a momentum of its own with intermittent murderous rioting against the Tamil Hindus from 1956 to 1983 in which some of the violence was partly directed by agents of the state. The language riots of 1951 over the making of Sinhalese the national language as well as other disturbances which turned into a persisting civil war led by the Tamil Tigers. Senior Sri Lankan army officers worship at the temple of the Tooth in Kandy and receive the blessings of senior monks, so that the fighting is dichotomised along both religious and ethnic divisions.

Buddhist monks are not so much religious leaders as objects of worship which makes it difficult for believers to dissent from what monks are preaching when they mix in their sermons the Enlightenment of the Buddha and the need to fight Tamil terrorism. As individual monks they have considerable autonomy to engage in whatever religious or political activities they choose in the absence of institutional control outside the particular monastery to which they are affiliated. Their activities can be sectarian and territorial at various levels from that of the neighbourhood to the nation as well as furthering their own special interests (Manor, 1994).

The political and violent involvement of monks is clear since they were believed to have been involved in the assassination of the first Prime Minister and have participated in large numbers in political demonstrations. Monks recite prayers at public ceremonies and political rallies, and they are sought to provide blessings to ensure the safety of military personnel as well as in aiding the building of pagodas in army cantonments.

Extra-territorial Support for Religious Violence

Many long-term periods of violence between people of different religions have the support of similar people and their communities who have emigrated because they are of the same religion. Others who have emigrated still feel some obligation to support those left behind in their ongoing difficulties. This hostility to those of the other religion may have been related to current difficulties or be based on folk memories which have been passed onto them by relatives and community members whose ancestors have left that area generations ago. These supportive outsiders may have no personal experience of this inter-religious violence or its antecedents.

In Northern Ireland as a predominantly Protestant area, was separated from the predominantly Roman Catholic south in 1921 and there have been much periodic violence both before and after this separation culminating in the current troubles which started in 1969. Roman Catholic Americans of Irish descent are reputed to have consistently funded the violent Irish Republican Army rather than the political parties attempting to achieve some practical political accommodation between the two warring religious factions. It is also reported that the Libyan leader Colonel Gaddafi has supplied them with large quantities of arms.

In Israel the Jews have received constant and massive support officially from the United States as well as from Jewish organisations just as the Palestinian Muslims have received similar support from all the surrounding and more distant Arab states. It may be that this American support has increased the Israeli reluctance to be less aggressive towards the Palestinians whom they evicted from their centuries old land-holdings and houses.

The continuing trouble in Kashmir between Hindus and Muslims over the cease-fire line has certainly been consistently supported by Pakistan. Just as the southern Sudanese are getting outside help in their resistance to the military power of the Muslim north and no doubt the same is occurring in Chechnya, Kurdistan and the Christian Karen opposition to the Myanmar military government. All these violent religious confrontations illustrate that it is impossible to contain such conflicts.

Thus in all these on-going inter-religious confrontations those involved have received the continuing support of outsiders who are not directly involved through the passage of money through banking links as well as the smuggling of arms through sympathetic channels. There will always be people on the ground who wish to keep such conflicts going in the hope that they will eventually receive some lasting political advantages.

Much of this outside support comes from a form of detached romanticism about the past and is even less likely to be a possibility in the future. 'There are Sikhs in Toronto, Muslims in Britain and France, Jews in Brooklyn and many others.... who seek to sooth ancestral voices by encouraging barbarism far from home. Some are prepared to die for their causes. Most are content to let others do the dying while they work on their identities at home' (Buruma, 2002). There is often a litigious aspect to this violence in that participants often want religious leaders to rule on the righteousness of their cause.

Religious Rulings Supporting Inter-religious Violence

With Judaism religious rulings about the justification for violence in Israel were brought into prominence by Goldstein's killing of twenty-nine unarmed Moslems while they were praying in the mosque on Temple Mount in Jerusalem. In a memorial book of religious rulings which referred to Goldstein as a saint, a rabbinical proposal was that 'The prohibition of 'thou shall not kill' and 'he who sheds human blood' do not apply to a Jew who kills a Gentile and no authoritative prohibition is involved at all. An offensive war, launched in order to kill Gentiles for fear that they may attack Jews is a legitimate option' (Elba, 1995: 127).

Another rabbinical proposal in support of Goldstein's murders listed 'five virtuous aspects of these murders; sanctification of the name of God, saving the life of Jews, revenge against Hebron's Palestinians, cleansing evil and the struggle for the Kingdom of Israel' (Elba, 1995: 20).

These rulings can be assessed from the statements of Yigal Amir, who murdered the Israeli Prime Minister Rabin, said 'Once it is a ruling, there is no longer a problem of morality. If I were involved now in the biblical conquest of the land and as said in Joshua, I would have had to kill babies and children, I would have done so regardless of the problem of morality. Once it is a ruling I do not have a problem with it' (Gvitz., 1996). This way of thinking parallels the Muslim '*fatwa*' ruling by the Ayatollah Khomeini that the killing of the novelist Salman Rushdie for apostasy was a religious obligation on all Muslims. Muslims do not have to ask their theologians for tortuous elaborations of religious thinking on the issues involved in inter-religious violence since the verses of the Koran, the literal Word of God, are clear enough for all to read.

Violence and the Need to belong Somewhere

Violence by the members of one religion against those of another faith is only made clear by taking it as a single element in the social lives of those involved. Everyone is made up of multiple loyalties and identifications which are never simple and are always changing. In certain circumstances religious hostility is made salient so that those involved feel threatened at the same time there is always the need to belong. In the Western world individuals have few problems with multiple identities which usually keep roles in business, politics and religion separate and this has been the result of a long process of social differentiation in developed and quite well off societies.

In Western societies Christians no longer expect to have civil and criminal law based on religious principles, but Islamic societies attempt to apply Islamic law as interpreted by their theologically trained leaders to every aspect of their lives from the prohibition of interest in banking to forms of inheritance linked to blood and marriage relationships and limiting the independent allocation of property.

Perhaps most individuals have always felt that they belonged somewhere traditionally and that they were members of communities which had some stability providing them with identities as tribesmen, believers or whatever. Even if this state was always changing because of factors outside their control, it was felt to be stable because the changes from natural disasters and political upheavals did not effect this sense of identity.

For non-westerners much that has happened in their lifetimes has been indirectly threatened by the superiority of the West, scientific discoveries, political freedoms, economic enterprises and what they see as cultural if not physical aggression. 'In a world which belongs to others and obeys rules made by others. A world in which they are orphans, strangers, intruders or pariahs… What can be done to prevent some of these feelings; they have been bereft of everything and have nothing more to loose, so that they come like Samson, to pray to God for the temple to collapse on top of them and their enemies alike' (Maaluf, 2002). It is Muslims in particular who have felt these intrusions on their identity because a specifically Islamic state was created by the Prophet Mohammad and provided for in the Koran as the Word of God.

This is even more so for the contemporary Palestinians of whom most are caught between being migrants and exiles. In their experience they have become exiles even when remaining on their own soil. There is no concept to describe the phenomenon of 'exile without moving', a wrenching discontinuity in which these individuals have become strangers in their own country.

Only a small proportion alive today actually experienced the trauma in either 1948 of becoming unwanted residual residents in Israel or in 1967 becoming exiles. So most now born in exile have an inherited lack of status as they have never known their 'native place' and more importantly have never experienced a physical and/or social environment to which they naturally belong.

At least 5.2 million Muslims now claim descent from the 1.4 million who were living in Palestine in 1948. Those remaining in Israel are not accepted as full members of the Israeli social and political community and who suffer discrimination in education, employment and having no rights to buy land. Those in exile have neither citizenship nor the protection of any state (Abu-Lughod, J.L., 1996: 6-69). This is combined with a sense of despair from the ninety thousand Russian Jews settled in some 150 new settlements on the West bank combined with a further hundred thousand settled in East Jerusalem, augmenting their universal experience of Israeli brutality.

It is not surprising therefore to find that Islamization from both above and below has occurred almost as if there were no other alternatives available for the Palestinians as a whole. The 'intifada' protest uprisings merging into an Islamic '*jihad*' in which Palestinians of all ages participated both actively and passively seeking to throw off Israeli occupation and a less important fundamentalist movement to initiate Islamization from below with attacks on unveiled women and places of public entertainment defined as 'places of perdition' (Legrain., 1994).

In such social environments violence against another religion provides both a sense of identity and for the expression of genuine feelings that they are being menaced by the members of the other religion. In situations such as Kossovo those who kill others are morally convinced they are in the long-term saving the lives of their own nearest and dearest. At the same time participatory violence gives them an entry into groups which provide them with both identity and commitment. It is deliberate missionary activities, independent of disinterested charitable work which can provide its recipients with a sense of violation and in some earlier cases actual violence to their traditional religions.

Obvious Differences Leading to Inter-religious Violence

Where the practitioners of a particular faith have a distinctive physical appearance this is likely to attract violence whether it is the hair arrangements and clothing of Orthodox Jews and the Amish or any marked differences which become associated in people's minds with those who have become socially and religiously defined as a hostile 'other'. The Copts in Egypt and Christians in Pakistan avoid looking different and thus attract Muslim violence only when they go to worship. Sikh men cannot avoid looking different and are thus likely to be socially and religiously segregated because of their beards and turbans.

In India where there is persisting tension between Hindus and Muslims, the costumes and appearance of professional men rather than women may be indistinguishable but in general both men and women are religiously distinguishable by the way they dress; whether this makes them aggressors or victims will depend on time and place but their religious commitment will always be obvious.

For fear to exist there may not be more than an undercurrent of anxiety. Jews are well aware of the amount of direct and indirect anti-Semitism to which they are exposed or indeed might be at any time. Crypto-Jews in New Mexico in the United States have secretly maintained their beliefs and customs in fear of social sanctions from the surrounding society (Teltsch, 1990).

Distinctive religious buildings have always invited violence and sometimes as in southern Egypt the lurking violence of Muslims against the Coptic minority is somewhat reduced by the unpretentiousness of their churches so that even their cathedral in Assuan does not obviously seem to be a church. The minaret of the mosque and the spire of the church are visually reminders of particular faiths and are thus often the objects of violence in Indonesia. Thus we can see that religious violence focuses on symbols which are either conveniently static and thus can be attacked and destroyed or on visibly committed people and animals against which violence can be more easily mobilised.

Cow Protection and Inter-religious Hostility

Using or avoiding animals in social and religious practices is often a cause of tension and violence since they can be seen, smelt, touched and eaten. While families, lineages and clans may have particular animals or species dedicated to their ancestors, and spirits, but these are not often the cause of religious violence because they are varied and well distributed in any social environment. Some people may have taboos concerning certain animals which they are no longer ever likely to meet. Only Christianity does not have religion-wide restrictions on what can be eaten and under what conditions of preparation. Islam and Judaism forbid the eating of pork but it is Hinduism which goes furthest in this respect in its veneration of the cow as a symbol of the Divine, which makes its religious significance of particular importance as an occasional but regular focus of violence.

Many Hindus would describe the sacredness of the cow as the most important element in their faith although the theological discussion of this protection is related to the protection of all living things '*ahimsa*'. It seems more likely that this ascribed sacredness developed from its widespread uses and usefulness. There can be no doubt that both historically and today the cow is central to any understanding of Hinduism. Any observer can see the cow depicted in colourful popular religious art and in temple statuary and even more obviously wandering the streets of many towns.

Cow killing or public affronts related to the cow have been at the root of many Hindu-Muslim riots and since this veneration is widely known, the conclusion must be that it is done deliberately by Muslims just as the Hindu use of pork is done to deliberately provoke Muslims. It would seem almost childish to react violently to such provocations were it not for the deeply rooted religious commitment to avoid or protect these two domesticated animals.

The cow is such an essential element in the Indian economy where its dried dung as a fuel is the equivalent of many million tons of firewood and coal and the relationship to this of the half a million or so cows which are kept alive in religious institutions in which the sale of their products may only pay a fifth of the cost of their maintenance (Lodrick, 1981: 199).

The fact remains that Muslims slaughter cows and eat beef and since every town contains a mixed population of Hindus and Muslims which in effect means a universal visual awareness of cow related problems and the constant possibility of Hindu outrage. Thus it would seem that the public views that Hindus preserve cows if they possibly can and Muslims kill and eat them is a paradigmatic basis for inter-religious hostility. This is despite the fact that Hindus will sell their cows for slaughter when famine or drought make it impossible to keep them alive and that Muslims rarely eat beef because of the expense. Let us now consider the fears that people may have of those who practice different faiths.

Fear of Those Practising a Different Faith

In any society where there is a dominant religion, it will inevitably spill over into political, social and economic life. Those belonging to minority faiths are going to be indirectly penalised regardless of their legal and perhaps common sense rights to have their personal talents utilised. Copts in Egypt keep their religious affiliation as quiet as possible when seeking employment in the public sector and outside the areas in which their fellow believers are sufficiently numerous to provide at least some measure of protection. A Muslim soldier in

India might well find it difficult to reach the higher levels of authority in the defence services after several high level defections to Pakistan and in that country Christians are reluctant to go to church services for fear of being attacked. This is apart from periodic violence which the Sunni majority perpetrate on Shias and Ahmaddiyas when they worship communally.

Wherever there is a dominant way of behaviour particularly when it relates to the public expression of religion, those who do not conform are under some degree of anxiety as to the consequences. This lurks in the backs of their minds as an explanation of events which affect their livelihoods and pleasures which may have nothing to do with their religion or that of the dominant culture. In the situation in which the society is in practical terms divided along religious lines, it becomes the understanding and explanation of all that goes on particularly when such societies are not divided on observably different ethnic lines or when public opinion concludes that the important divisions in a society are based on economic or class divisions.

Hindu Hostility to Muslims

In India Hindus and Muslims look different, often living in different areas and having different occupations although they may share the same language and have lived in this way for longer than anyone can remember, nevertheless hostility and violence are never far away. Violent riots between Hindus and Muslims have been a feature of India's religious environment since the Muslim Moghul conquest of the northern part of the subcontinent, but neither religion can be treated as a single unit either socially or religiously.

It would seem however that for most of the time there is an inter-religious truce as both religious communities are useful to each other economically if not socially. Periodically there are eruptions of hostility occasioned by local commonplace tensions and national issues such as partisan sympathy for the separate communities involved in Kashmir, reactions to the destruction of the Ayodha mosque and the Sikh assassination of Indira Gandhi. It is also possible that Hindus need Muslims to provide them with the social, political and religious cohesion which does not come automatically from Hinduism as a religion.

In this situation of almost paradigmatic hostility between these dichotomised communities that Hindu women possessed by disabling spirits are found by diviners to have a high proportion of Muslim ones responsible for their illnesses (Freed and Freed, 1964). Long standing hostilities can thus emerge out of the subconscious.

The Shia Bohras are a mercantile community with a strong work ethic and a marked avoidance of spendthrift ostentation; they keep themselves to themselves. In the 1993 Bombay riots after the destruction of the Ayodha mosque by Hindu zealots, they were often targeted because of their distinctive 'Muslim' appearance and indeed to the average Hindu they looked more Muslim than the Sunni Muslims who were protesting against what they saw as Hindu sacrilege. This resulted for the Bohras in the strengthening of their Islamic identity and their communalism was invigorated by the heightened tension in the surrounding Indian society (Blank, 2001: 259-68). By reason of their appearance and mercantile professionalism rather than their beliefs these Bohras bore a disproportionate share of the anti-Muslim riots in India. In Pakistan they have been caught in Sindhi-Muhajir (ex-India immigrants) tensions (Shaheed, 1990) as well as Sunni-Shia quarrelling so that the feeling of victimisation has become a fact of their communal lives.

Missionary Imposed Ideological Changes

Most people only see or consider religious violence to occur when it is obviously extreme, the destruction of people, their communities and their buildings in religious wars. If religious violence is taken to be the imposition of the ideas and practices of one religion onto individuals of another faith who may not have their beliefs sufficiently well articulated or indeed understood to oppose an ideological and material attack from outside, then the examples of religious violence multiply.

Only Christianity over the centuries has made an institutionalised effort to convert others away from their existing faiths and practices. Islam spread along the lines of trade and is done by a simple public affirmation of belief in the Prophet Mohammad and Allah. Buddhism did so through the personal example of individual monks but it has no ceremony of conversion because that would be yet another sign of attachment from which individuals aim to free themselves by meditation. Hinduism as an ascribed religion can have no process of conversion.

We have already noted that forced conversions have occurred sporadically in the past such as that of the Spanish Muslims who were faced with the alternative of conversion to Christianity or expulsion to Morocco and earlier in Central Asia where it was conversion to Islam or death. In general conversion from one faith to another is a long process of seeing religious reality in a new way and/or some feeling that it is to their social, economic or political advantage.

It is a mute question as to the degree to which conversion to Christianity with its past association with dominant political and economic forces and its general air of being an example of and in association with modernity, can be described as choice or rather in certain circumstances as a form of psychological or physical violence. The notion of 'rice Christians' in the past socio-religious environment suggests that those without sufficient social support to cope with famine may have become Christians. Since for most Chinese their religion was a matter of maintaining relationships with their ancestors and thus it may have been easy for them to practice the two systems at the same time. In the absence of sustaining and supporting families, some would have seen the missionaries as surrogate families with the Roman Catholic nomenclature of 'fathers', 'sisters' and 'brothers' aiding this supposition and conversion as a rational alternative to starvation.

The possibility of violence based on ideology is easy enough to see when the opposing religions in their Great Traditions have written theologies and identifiable institutions but then both sides can indeed defend themselves from an imposed erosion of their religion should they so wish to do so.

The missionary situation in which outsiders provide a new faith for a traditional non-literate people which substantially modifies their way of life under the guise of providing the Truth, then we have ideological violence in which their respective powers are unequal. Missions and their initiation of schools in the context of Western colonial power seems to show clearly the use of alien ideologies to achieve effective control over formerly independent ways of thinking and behaving (Berndt, 1962: 423).

Only rarely is the missionary effort not combined with political, economic and social factors which make the choice and the pressures to change not quite so ideological as it might seem. Christian missionary efforts however well intentioned made substantial and violently disruptive changes in the lives of converts. On the other hand Islam has conversion by a simple affirmation without the supervisory structure to allow for the imposition of its religious legal system so it would seem that only Christianity has the clearest potential to disrupt with its supervisory staff and ancillary secular supports.

On the fringes of the major faiths particularly Christianity with its record of missionary efforts to pull in converts, there are confrontations with identifiable traditional faiths which have no equivalent public face. Short of rebellion there are no means of resisting these ideological invasions except by going underground on the basis of individual needs. Latin-American Indians were converted wholesale into Catholic Christianity but they merged their traditional ideas into Christian practices so it became a private and a public syncretic faith. These traditional religions were not given any ideological status worthy of some intellectual acceptance and they were usually seen as the work of the devil making itself manifest in inferior and misguided magical and social rather than religious practices.

The missionaries were backed not only by the colonial power but by a material culture of great attraction to materially deprived people. Their own standards of living however low it may have been in terms of their home cultures, was certainly much higher than that of the persons with whom they were working. They were thus in a position to be quite violent both physically and personally on religious grounds.

It was often a condition of acceptance into Christianity that objects associated with traditional beliefs should be destroyed or handed over to the missionaries. But the existence of violence as part of the process of conversion may often have gone further than this burning of symbols. The requirement of monogamy meant the expulsion of extra wives from their existing social support as did the prohibition of already married men inheriting the widows of their dead brothers. In Alaska the Presbyterian authorities forced Tlingit parents to sign five year indenture contracts if they wanted the children admitted to their schools which was contrary to their customs as they were matrilineal and a male parent had no such powers (Kan, 1999: 243).

Overall the traditional religions were so socially invisible that they were not able to require Christian institutions to adapt to their deeply implanted practices which Christianity had to do in India as a prerequisite for making any progress at all where it accepted the parochial realities of caste up to quite recently.

An individual accepting Christianity is debarred from entering or continuing polygynous or polyandrous marriages so that conversion leads to the abandonment of extra wives or husbands and despite its occurrence in the Old Testament, the prohibition of widow inheritance by men who are already married which makes for the destitution of older widows who cannot otherwise find support.

The indívidualism of Christian obligations makes it difficult for them to participate in non-Christian ceremonies for the cohesion of the community, extended family, lineage or clan. This means some degree of isolation and the requirement for Christians to bunch together for their own forms of social life; the more particularised the requirements of the denominational faith, the greater the degree of necessary isolation.

Both Christianity and Islam are matrilineal faiths so matrilineal cultures which might be attracted by a prayer which could have started with 'our mother's brother which art in heaven' can no longer have any moral support for a mother expecting her mother's brother to be responsible for her children rather than her husband who in turn is responsible for his sister's children; Christianity would see such practices as both immoral and illogical.

The abandonment of ritual concern for family ancestors and the denial that they have any influence on the material welfare of their descendents, is a violent disruption of lineal unity, making the convert adrift in a religion of detached concern by a very distant deity. The remembrance of ancestors has only recently been allowed in the Roman Catholic Church as in side altars in some American churches with Chinese members by theologically ceasing to regard it as worship but as remembrance.

This is not to suggest that many such changes in social practices may not have been inevitable or in the process of disappearing because of economic changes anyway, but conversion or membership of a Church makes these changes attributable to Christian influence and not to social change in general.

Certainly in colonial situations there was often a tendency if not the inevitability of Christian practices being incorporated into statute law and thus getting secular endorsement. So the person who wants to continue with a traditional practice endorsed by its religion may be forced into violating secular law. Widow inheritance was forbidden by law in Musoma, Tanzania in 1929 but was still widely practised as an accepted social necessity in the 1960s.

Monogamy as a Christian requirement is reasonable when there is some numerical equality between the sexes but where many men leave subsistence farming for work elsewhere, the surplus of women who can never get married monogamously are forced into concubinage or remain socially isolated. The adult sex ratio in Musoma in the 1960s was 100 women to 70 men. In any religious conversion process, whatever the ascertainable degree of personal choice there are violent disruptions to social life which have been imposed on rather than created by those involved. Unless converts became part of a socially self-sustaining community as did Seventh Day Adventists in Sukumaland, Tanzania, it must always have been the occasion of anxiety and fear because of its disruption of traditional ways of coping with their difficulties within a new religious framework of thinking.

Traumatic Conversion and the Breaking of Social Conventions

Conversion is often seen as a steady rather than traumatic change from one system of belief to another but except in the intellectual sense not one which could be classified as violent. On the other hand conversion to millenarian beliefs often involves a period of excesses when all social boundaries are transgressed often materially as well as symbolically, in order to start again (Burridge, 1969: 296). This occurs within Hinduism where there are sub-caste sects in which potential members commit incest, in order to be free of bodily constraints.

In the Mau Mau civil war and rebellion against the British colonial power in Kenya, oath taking was a necessity for Kikuyu wanting to gain full membership of rebel groups. These ceremonies involved the drinking of blood, the eating of excrement and having intercourse with animals with the effects in the words of one leader. 'I had been born again in a new society and a new faith' (Buijtenhuijs, 1971: 98).

State Religions and Psychological Pressures

A state religion may have nominal and peripheral relationships to a particular religion as with the Queen of England as head of the Church of England and the coins all have her denoted as FD–Defender of the Faith. This religion has an intermittent and seemingly unimportant influence on national social and political movements. There is national legislation prohibiting bias for or against any type of religious commitment. This nominal affiliation to a national faith is duplicated by the role of the King of Siam as a publicly practising Buddhist in a state in which that faith predominates.

Much the same would apply to religious affiliation in the United States in which the Constitution prohibits any specific connection between religions and the state; hence the legal challenge brought by a small number of litigious parents over prayers in state schools as unconstitutional. This is not a nominal commitment to religiouslessness but a constitutional provision for a religious free-for-all aimed at preventing the religious problems which they had seen in 17th century Europe.

There are obvious differences in non-Western states. Saudi Arabia which contains the basic shrines of Islam offers no public places anywhere for any non-Islamic worship and prohibits non-Muslims from entering the environment of Mecca. With their employment of many Roman Catholic Philippine citizens it can only be presupposed that they keep their beliefs well hidden. The Gulf War and the presence of many thousands of American men and women soldiers and their chaplains must have been as severe blow to Saudi political and religious prestige. It could be said that Saudi Arabia does not have an inter-religious problem because it has never provided a religious opening for it to occur, nevertheless there has been violence there between Sunni fundamentalists and Shia citizens and Hajj pilgrims. In Iran, however, after the Revolution non-Islamic believers were persecuted and under considerable pressure to hide their affiliations.

In any state in which there is an official state religion which is prominently part of its political system whether it is theoretically ruled or not, is going to benefit those who are known believers. Sri Lankan politicians on appointment make a special pilgrimage to offer thanks at the shrine of the Buddha's Tooth in Kandy. The extent to which less active practitioners are penalised will depend on internal pressures to change to a more exacting religious dependency and their need to pay some attention to international public opinion.

The Factor of Persistent Fear from Those of Another Religion

There are two forms of psychological violence at the level of either persistent fear because of some historical events which were not experienced by anyone currently alive and the fear of contemporary people which is part of the current lives.

The Balkans have been the scene of intermittent and indeed persistent violence for more than a century from internal revolutions, Ottoman violence in support of its suzerainty, foreign invasions from both Germany and Italy, two periods of civil war separated by the Tito era of internal stability, culminating in the NATO attack to prevent further ethnic-cum-religious violence. However, ethnically divided these people may be, they are not biologically distinguishable, so they see themselves as divided by religion.

In various periods and places, the state of mind of the people has been described as fearful to the extent that some people may have been physically ill because of fear. 'It becomes the key to half the circumstances of existence. Fear is the dominant, the ever-present motive. It builds villages. It dictates migration. It explains deceits. It has created the morals of a country' (Brailsford. 1906: 367).

In attributing to people in the Balkans that they are Muslims or Christians often places excessive emphasis on the formal requirements of those faiths particularly as the then Yugoslav state took the official view that both ethnicity and religion were no longer of any contemporary significance. This classification had remained dormant for nearly half a century until the break-up of the country until it became of prime importance again; it was as if the Communist era of unification had never existed.

In most areas the violence which developed into a civil war for the subdivision of the state on religious-cum-ethnic lines, seemed to have been started by those from outside each community and it developed into one in which neighbours were pitted against neighbours often the familiar persons next door who were made into depersonalised aliens, members of the enemy ranks. Names disclosing religious affiliation became important on a generational basis for those from before second World War and for those who came of age in the 1980s but it was not an issue for those born in between (Bringa, 1995: 1-7).

In many cases Muslim religious identity was determined strictly by external criteria so that a Bosnian Muslim in a Serb or Croat concentration camp was not there because of any particular act, expression or thought. Some were not practising, others were atheists and many observed some Islamic rituals on cultural grounds and considered themselves sceptics. Many were there because they were Bosnians and had recorded themselves as Muslims in the 1971 Census in order to avoid being classified as Serbs or Croats which could have had religious implications (Sells, 1996: 14). So there was no basis for distinguishing 'Muslim' other than religious self-selection (Irwin, 1984: 438).

The Religious Divide in Israel between Jews and Muslims

While there may be persons on both sides of this religious divide who attempt individually to bridge the gap in understandings between the peoples of these two faiths, it has gone on too long and too far for it to be anything else than a persistent background fact for both behaviour and thought. It shapes the thinking of all adults and children as in Palestinian Gaza where children as young as three years play games as martyrs attacking Israeli police posts.

Palestinian violence against Israeli targets is an intermittent but persistent part of their lives against which they are legally armed and protected as far as possible by the Israeli state. Palestinians are forced to stomach Israeli physical dominance of their lives and their existence as second class citizens is permanent. It must form part of their conscious as well as unconscious thinking.

In Palestinian areas calendars are printed with martyr of the month motifs and children who cannot read chant the names of martyrs who have died in suicide bomb attacks, and whatever their personal feelings the families of suicide bombers are rewarded in cash and celebrate the death with public festivities. Public Opinion Surveys in 2001 showed that of the Palestinians responding, 76 per cent approved of the suicide bombings of Israeli targets.

We have to conclude that violence between believers in different Great Traditions either as a primary factor in violence or as one which is a convenient summary for differences stretching across a broad spectrum of social, economic and political differences; a religious label attached to a person is a more exact distinction than ones in other fields of social life. Moreover the Great Traditions since they have institutional and literate foundations have much to defend which is seemingly obvious, while the Little Traditions despite their popularity and more local distinctiveness carry on in the shadows of social life and are less the occasion of violence, except in their defencelessness against the intellectual and physical superiority of the over-arching Great Traditions.

7

Secular Violence and Fear Against Religions

The distinction between secular and religious systems of government is not clear cut. On the one hand there are Islamic republics and kingdoms either stated to be so in their titles as Iran or so dominated by Islam as to be seen as a religious political system.

On the secular side there are governments such as that of the United States in which God is mentioned in their constitutional documents but is not allied to any particular religion and that of the United Kingdom in which the Queen is the 'secular' head of the Church of England and her appointment as Queen is validated by a Protestant rite of passage and much the same would apply to the King of Siam in his connection with Buddhism. So most governments are not so much secular as secular with religious overtones which exercise considerable care to keep clear of religious issues and complications as far as they can. They avoid any attacks on religion unless it is within the narrower definitions of terrorism, health and safety regulations, care of animals and human rights in which the laws involved are not specifically directed at a religion but apply to the population in general.

This leaves Communist states as the only systems of government which not only steer clear of any official connections with religion but go to considerable lengths to penalise and restrict as far as they possibly can any public expressions of religious commitment. By definition they see all expressions of religion as a combination of superstition, mental backwardness, confidence tricks, feudal leftovers, counter-revolutionary tendencies and a misuse of time and resources which should be put towards national economic and political development.

Secular Violence against Religious Institutions and People

This has to be divided between secular mobs acting against religious communities of which they disapprove and the actions of secular states, communist regimes of China and Russia and the extreme example of Nazi actions against the Jews between 1935 and 1944..

Mob action against members of religious communities have been common enough in history and we can presuppose that most of these events occurred with the tacit approval of the authorities who saw no reason to intervene even if the mobs were acting against the long-term interests of the community and the elite. A case in point would be the killing of the Jewish community in mediaeval York, England which is thought to have been a way of destroying the records of the indebtedness to them of small traders, while the elite would have seen no advantage in getting rid of convenient financiers.

When states are involved in persecution there is a bureaucratic apparatus as well as political will involved within an ideology which sees advantages in the persecution of their fellow citizens who practice religion. Only the Nazi regime attempted the systematic extermination of an entire Jewish community group under the heading of the 'final solution'.

The Persecution and Killing of Jews

Anti-semitism has been a commonplace in the Western world but not in the Islamic states (Lewis, B., 1982). In Tsarist Russia it had the tacit approval of officialdom but took the form of popular communal outbursts; 300 Jews were killed in Odessa in 1905 and 80 in Bialystoil in 1906. During the period 1917-21, mainly by the White Ukrainian Army possibly as many as 60,000 Jews were killed in 887 major and 349 minor programmes (Encyc Judaica, 1974.13: 694-701).

It is only with the Jewish Holocaust during the Second World War that we have more detailed figures when the Nazis applied factory conveyor belt methods to the killing of something like six million Jews (Encyc Judaica, 1974.8: 889). The virtual obliteration of Jewish urban communities; the city of Krakow had a large Jewish population in 1939 but 55,000 were killed and only a few hundred live in that city today.

In 1900 Warsaw had the highest concentration of Jews in the world totalling about half of the population who were forced into a walled ghetto by the German occupiers of Poland during Second

World War leading to deaths from overcrowding while 312,000 were gassed in 1942 and a further 80,000 lost their lives in the ghetto uprising of April 1943.

It is not so much the sheer totals of the dead which is appalling as its deliberateness in a society which prided itself in its numerous contributions to civilisation because more died of the devastation caused by the Taiping Rebellion. Perhaps only Tamurlane may have killed as many for religious reasons. But it was not only Germany which was involved and the governments of several states occupied by the Germans actively contributed to the decimation of their own Jewish communities. This extraordinary episode in which the Nazis virtually eliminated an entire religious community must remain inexplicable.

The Russian Communist Violence against Religion

It is easy to see the Communist attacks on religion as one belief system clearing away another one with which there would always be ideological differences, but it was not like this and it cannot be classified as competing religions in which the stronger attempted to get rid of the weaker.

The Communists in Russia followed the reasoning of Marx that 'religion was the opium of the people' and that it was no more than an historical stage which would be superseded by economic reasoning. As much as anything the Communists believed that their people must be protected from the agents of superstition holding them back from the inevitable processes of material progress which the Communist governments would deliver.

Whilst it is generally accepted that the early Stalinist regime went to considerable lengths to persecute religious people and the religious activists who provided them with religious services, it was not a process of deliberate extermination. During the Second World War there was a partial rapprochement in order to get additional religious support for opposing the German invasion.

A fresh anti-religious campaign was initiated by Khruschev in which considerable violence occurred. In January 1958, there were 18,521 registered places of worship which by January 1964 had been reduced by 37 per cent to 11,687. The Orthodox Church (Ellis, 1986) bore the brunt of this reduction losing 40 per cent of its churches but many were churches which had been reopened during the German occupation of the Ukraine. These closures were generally imposed upon unwilling congregations through different legal devices; the priest as the 'local cult servant' would be charged with an offence and removed from his parish, then some of the minimum twenty believers required for registration would be pressured to resign and the church then closed as not having the requisite minimum supporters. Some sects were denied registration altogether such as the Pentecostals, the Jehovah's Witnesses and the Seventh Day Adventists.

Five out of the ten surviving Orthodox seminaries were closed down as were three-quarters of the 69 monasteries and convents which in some cases were accompanied by considerable brutality with the monks being forcibly evicted, arraigned in court and sent to labour camps (Bourdeaux, 1970: 96-115).

There were similar attacks on the Muslim religion with only 312 registered mosques and 1310 unregistered ones for a believing population of several millions. The Communist authorities seem to have particularly targeted Muslim places of pilgrimage which were reduced between 1958 and 1964 from 275 to 178.

The archival material available after the end of Communist domination showed that during the Khruschev era, the Communist Party approved all possible methods in their struggle against religion; raids on churches, seizure of icons, the public ridiculing of believers by Komsomol groups, illegal searches, the seizure of literature and the constitutional rights of believers violated by the refusal of the authorities to register actual functioning religious communities (Anderson, 1994: 38-67).

Even without the opening up of official records, the newspapers provide evidence of this prolonged and recent repressive campaign. *The Moscow News* reported that between 1962-70 the Baptists alone had been fined by the state 94,300 roubles for holding illegal prayer meetings and that such meetings were broken up by the police on 986 occasions.

Under article 227 of the Penal Code 'infringement of the rights of citizens under the guise of performing religious rituals', 350 Baptists, 260 Pentecostals, 215 Jehovah's Witnesses and so on were sentenced to imprisonment (Moscow News, 1990: 18, 16). In addition thousands were sentenced to administrative punishments, short sentences of imprisonment and fines. There were also Muslims sentenced for participation in Islamic related customs, the paying of bride-wealth and polygyny for which there were 709 convictions in Turkmenistan alone in 1962-64.

Much of this repressive brutality has to be evaluated in the context of a long official inheritance of arbitrary bureaucratic action against non-conformists of which religious activists by their public behaviour would have drawn attention to themselves, and at the highest level there was an ideological refusal to accept the individuality which had at least become a commonplace global understanding as part of the Rights of Man.

Chinese Communist Persecution of Religion

As a Communist government based on Marxism it was inevitable that they would take hostile action against all religions particularly the specifically Chinese ones with their landholdings. Whereas in Russia the Orthodox Church with its past connections with Tsarism was seen as a focus for counter-revolutionary activities and at the least thinking in opposition to communism, the Chinese actions were based on different thinking.

The Chinese government's attitude to religions after they had gained suzerainty over the country, was based on their own historical experiences. Their national ideology as much as that of the previous republican and imperial regimes saw the state as a sacred or at least an inviolable whole. Set against this was their recent history which saw religions as at the least disruptive and often providing the motivation for rebellion which must have remained part of their thinking (De Groot, 1903-4: 559).

There was also the fact that their thinking although political was nevertheless based on rational economic planning. A Communist official in explaining their government's opposition to what they saw as feudal superstitions, commented that in every community 100-138 days per year were wasted on religious festivals (MacInnis, 1972: 183-86). The Taiwanese government which was certainly not Communist, took much the same view and tried to organise a single limited series of religious festivals for the whole island.

The enormous costs in terms of lives and materials of the Taiping Rebellion, the Yellow Turban revolt, the Panthay Muslim Rebellion 1855-73 and the Boxers and more importantly in the damage that they did to Chinese national dignity, must have made the Communist State all the more sensitive to and reactive to the possibilities of further religion based rebellions particularly when a religion was linked to ethnicity as with Islam and the northern peoples.

In this their reactions to Christianity and Islam were different in which the latter was seen as Chinese without any organisational links to outside bodies or to nations which were thought of as ideologically hostile to China and its aspirations. It had existed for many centuries without foreign support or missionary organisations and in all its forms it was run by Chinese personnel (Israeli, 1979).

Although there may have been small and ancient Christian communities in China dating back many centuries, it was in their modern eyes an imported religion and imported moreover by Westerners who could not even agree amongst themselves as to what they were teaching. Christian missionaries were always unpopular despite their important social work, because they were connected to the extra-territorial rights of European powers, their habit of going to court on behalf of their converts which was a non-Chinese pattern of behaviour and finally, their cultural crudity (Fried, 1987). The rivalry of the missionaries mirrored that between their countries of origin and there were clashes between Protestants and Roman Catholics as in the 1901 riots in Nanchang in which the Methodists looted the Catholic shops and the Catholics counter-attacked the next day resulting in numerous deaths (Young, 1996: 100-105).

So the Communist authorities saw the Christians as basically disruptive and went as far as they could to make every denomination including the Roman Catholic Church into purely Chinese Churches which they could not do with the Muslims who had a focus for their faith in Mecca which was quite independent of any Western influences centred as it was in an independent Arabian state.

The Cultural Revolution's 'Smash the Four Olds' attack on 'feudalist' practices included religion and the Muslim communities were an obvious target, more so than Christians who had no specific Christian communities. The Shadian incident in a Muslim village in Yunnan on the Vietnamese border was perhaps exceptional and subsequently regretted but nevertheless symptomatic of hostility to any communally concentrated religion (Dillon, 1999).

There was a split in this community between the traditional Islamic majority and the actively Communist minority in 1968 so that the village leaders called in a propaganda team from the Peoples Liberation Army who went about their work in the full spirit of the Cultural Revolution. Under the slogan 'purify class ranks', those criticised were required not only to denounce themselves but also to eat pork and pork bones were thrown into the mosque well from which most of the community drew its water and which they closed for worship.

In 1973 when the elders thought that the political climate had eased, they applied for the mosque to be reopened but this was refused as Islam was equated with local nationalism which led to several clashes with local militias. These escalated involving both the provincial and central governments which led in July 1975 to the Peoples Liberation Army invading the village in force destroying the whole village and killing over a thousand people.

Although in early 1979 the Government apologised for the destruction, rebuilding the village with new mosques and compensating survivors (Gladney, 1996: 137-140) these Muslims were reportedly sceptical that there has been any permanent change for the better as the same provincial officials were still in office.

In the north where Muslims were numbered in millions the Red Guards during the Cultural Revolution desecrated many tombs and graveyards and closed all mosques which led to numerous confrontations which started in the Religious Systems Reform Campaign of 1958-66. All of these hostile activities took place in the political environment of the Communists considering not only that religion was outdated but that at least in the north was dangerously linked to ethnic expressions of identity implicitly opposing the dominance of the Han majority ruling from Beijing.

Symbolic Violence in the Spanish Civil War and Some Parallels

Break-outs of violence against the dominant Roman Catholic Church in Spain have often occurred in Spanish history. Mobs burnt churches and convents in both the First Carlist (1833-35) and Second Carlist (1868) wars, in Catalonia in 1909 and in the first months of the Civil War in 1931. The 1931 Constitution of the revolutionary government abolished Church schools, forbade the Church from acquiring property, dissolved the Jesuit Order so that of necessity the Church shifted to becoming the religion of the counter-revolution.

The militants from the main labour federations then turned on the Church as the chief remaining representative of the Right as the dominant class had materially supported the Church which had then furthered their interests. But this violence went far further than the direct violence of previous outbreaks (Thomas, 1961: 171-180).

These revolutionaries wanted to show that they were outside the social rules which had previously dominated society. There were exhumations of the bodies of priests and nuns and their exposure in the violated churches of many towns and cities as well as posing themselves in vestments for publicity photographs. These were spontaneous acts against the social order represented by the Church and were neither officially organised or motivated.

'It is in millenarian movements that the deliberate flouting of such fundamental taboos as incest, cannibalism and abuse of the dead has been best attested. (In Spain) a militant, almost ecstatic egalitarianism was evident in which all signs of social hierarchy or dress and demeanour were abolished. The state for all intents and purposes ceased to exist. But between new rules and old, there was a violent and disquieting phase of no rules in summer 1936. A spontaneous dramatisation of absolute liberation from all the constraints of the past including those of 'common decency' (Lincoln, 1985).

Fear Induced by the Secular Authorities against Religious Practitioners

In Spain the republican attacks were accompanied by a widespread and uncontrollable onslaught on the lives of members of the Church. Whatever may have been the overall total of executions carried in Republican Spain in the late summer of 1936, 7937 were religious personnel including 12 bishops, 283 nuns, 5255 priests, 2492 monks and 249 novices (Thomas, 1961). This extraordinary and passionate hatred of Roman Catholicism by the Spanish working class can only be partially explained by the Church involvement with the middle and upper classes on whom they relied for financial support and who were given preferential treatment in return. It would seem that nothing like this has occurred elsewhere and that in the Holocaust rabbis would have been killed as part of the Jewish communities in which they served and not killed separately.

A Communist government with its formal structure has always been hostile to any form of religious practice and particularly so to those faiths which have institutional structures potentially if not inevitably thought to be allied to or to become the means for widespread counter-revolutionary activity. This may well have been true at an ideological level but there is little or no evidence that the Vatican or any other institutionally centralised faith acted in any such direct way. After the initial anti-religious violence, these governments could relax such direct actions and rely on fear to further their aims to extinguish the practices of any faith.

The procedure by which an authoritarian regime can subvert a religious organisation and its members is shown in a Russian Cheka internal document dated to the early 1920s on how they should get agents and information from among the clergy. 'Use the clergy in key positions by making them fearful of a strict interpretation of their responsibilities under the law and that this applies as much to their subordinates. Then find out the characters of individual clergy in order to play on their ambitions. Finally, recruit informers among the clergy gaining materials in various ways through the removal of correspondence during searches. Any authoritarian regime in this way will create a network of informers throughout society so that an atmosphere of unease if not fear, will permeate each and every group so that there is an atmosphere of paranoia leading to distrust.'

During the Khruschev era the hostility of most local authorities would have made it likely that only a few priests and pastors would have carried on when bishops were retired and two Archbishops of the Orthodox Church were imprisoned. The opening up of records has disclosed that large numbers of religious personnel were informers for the secret police with their own code names, but this may only have been a qualified response to state pressure. Nevertheless priests would have been very cautious over what they did so as not to risk their registered status, their livelihoods and indeed their religious vocations.

Dangerous as the Russian persecution may have been, it was not as dangerous as the revolutionaries in the initial stages of the Spanish Civil War with their killing of priests and nuns. There was also the Mexican government in the early 1920s which was strongly anti-clerical and drove Roman Catholics underground so well described in Graham Green's novel '*The power and the glory*' or into open rebellion as in the Cristero movement (Wilkie, 1966). The Muslims being less institutionalised certainly continued their prayers in private despite being denied the opportunities for collective worship and Christian baptism continued.

For a minority these state actions went far beyond what they could accept as a necessary part of citizenship and despite the fear raised by the very real possibility of direct persecution, both Christians and Muslims continued to practice in private and in small groups with smuggled copies of the Bible and the Koran.

We see that Communism as a Great Tradition which despite its ideological pragmatism, ends up in what are in effect eschatological hopes, has everywhere seen organised religions as both an ideological and factual enemy of their plans and Communist governments have persistently persecuted any public forms of religious practice. The effect of these persecutions was generally to increase religious practices which could not be so easily noticed and thus pushing people into more individual and less noticeable forms of worship which anyway had been a tendency in Western societies since the Reformation.

8

Religious Violence and its Destructiveness

A detached view of religious violence which neither opposes or promotes religious interests or viewpoints, has already shown that violence has occurred and is occurring in which religion has played a substantial part. What have been the consequences of this violence to humans, materials and animals.

Any argument that involves religious views and rulings on the morality of this violence detaches itself from the realities of what has occurred; justifications and meanings are variable and environmental in the intellectual sense as we have shown in chapter 2. It is necessary to evaluate what human beings have been killed or mutilated because of religious involvements, how much property has been destroyed and how many animals killed for religious reasons rather than for human consumption.

We have taken violence to mean religious activities that have abruptly changed the slow processes by which societies alter themselves or are altered, which would not have occurred but for this religiously motivated intervention. What people have died or been crippled before their expected time of death because of religious violence, what religious buildings, not just places of worship but the buildings used in welfare and educational programmes for which religions have made themselves responsible, been destroyed rather than just decaying with age or lack of use What animals sacrificed for religious purposes rather than being use for food and finally, overall have religions by violent means altered human environments.

In this assessment there are two dimensions. Religious activity of any sort alters the environment in which it takes place. Even the most ordinary of religious processes has some effect so that the first dimension is for how long has this religious practice been carried out. The pilgrimage process has actively altered every environment through which pilgrims have passed carrying disease and they have used up resources. The rare sacrificing of an animal in a London suburb for a traditional African ritual has no significance but the sacrificing of goats to the Goddess Kali in Calcutta is a long standing ritual involving many people and animals.

The second dimension is for how many people and for what area does this religious violence or abridgement of rights affect. The refusal of the Jehovah's Witnesses to allow blood transfusions for their sick or injured children and for some Christian fundamentalists in the United States to refuse to accept disease immunisation for their children on religious grounds, only affects a few people and involves very few deaths as does the poisonous snake handling Christian cults who believe that freedom from sin protects them (Alther, 1975). These activities are culturally bizarre but numerically insignificant. In both these categories it is the magnitude of these changes brought about by religions, not their apparent religious dangerousness or eccentricity which is important.

Religious Violence Affecting Human Beings

The Spanish Civil War 1935-39 between the anti-Roman Catholic Republicans and the Roman Catholic Nationalists involved substantial killings for ideological reasons. A nationalist leader remarked to Dr. Junod the Swiss Red Cross representative, on passing what he called a Red village 'I am afraid that we had to put everyone in prison and execute very many people' (Junod, 1951: 89). Their families had their heads shaved, had slogans daubed in their foreheads and the women were sometimes raped. A priest commented that 'happy is the condemned man for he is the only one who knows when he must die. He has the best chance of putting his soul in order before he dies' (Alba, 1948: 371). After the war it was estimated that the Nationalists executed or murdered at least 40,000 and the Republicans some 85,000 (General Cause., 1953: 402).

In the 1965-66 Indonesian massacres of atheist Communists even larger numbers were killed. In Java this approached an Islamic '*jihad*' against unbelievers in which perhaps a quarter of a million were killed (Cribb, 1991: 8) and in Hindu Bali 20-60,000 Communists were killed (Cribb *et al.*, 1991: 246).

The first aspect to appreciate in such massive and widespread killings even when they occur over a relatively short period of time, is that there is no means of knowing how many died. After one inter-religious riot in Calcutta during the period surrounding the Partition of India in 1948 the police stated that 3000 bodies had been collected off the streets. So in all these large scale instances of religious violence, the accurate scale of human loss is unknown and there are no details of the age and sex of those killed. A single murder victim would have a single file but mass killings are bunched together without providing such individual details. But in demographic terms there have been massive unexpected distortions of these populations.

So from the crudity of these figures we can accept that many more will have been injured even crippled, others orphaned and widowed, the so-called survivors who will have had their livelihoods destroyed. Even larger scale events such as the Holocaust killing of the Jews, there were so few survivors as to minimize this aspect. Only the dead have to be considered.

The Pol Pot Communist regime in Cambodia 1975-79 had a policy of abolishing religion, removing all Buddhist monks from their monasteries and forbidding religious festivals apart from evacuating all towns and abolishing all markets. They instituted communal feeding in all communities which included the cooking of pork and Muslims refusing to eat this food were called 'class enemies resisting the revolution'. This killed enormous numbers approaching holocaust proportions for which details are only known for the Cham Muslims (Kiernan. 1996: 271) of whom only 36 per cent of the 250,000 community survived. More specifically the Muslim elite were killed off as only 30 survived of the 1000 who had gone on the Hajj to Mecca, 38 out of some 300 teachers in Koranic schools. Overall it has been estimated that only 21 per cent of the Cambodian population survived execution, starvation and death from overwork (Becker, 1993; Chandler, 1991; Jackson, 1989; Moyer, N., 1991; Thion, 1993).

Then there are the refugees from religious violence such as Muslims in camps in Rajasthan because of fears of Hindu violence, both Christian and Muslim refugees in ex-Yugo-Slavia, Christian and traditionalist refugees in the Sudan and Uganda so that the refugee totals involved are in millions. In these uprooted populations the young and the old will have died in disproportionate numbers and women will not become fecund because of the disruption of their menstrual cycles from malnutrition. There are high morbidity and mortality rates from these massive socio-religious disruptions.

Violence to Property by a Religion

It is often assumed that the use of property is governed principally by economic considerations of some immediacy. The time span of subsistence farmers foresight is usually no more than a year and it is those with higher status and wider ranging commitments who can take a longer view of the use of their property and who invest in religious constructions.

Thus there is a distinction between buildings and monuments which are constructed by and for the use of specific believers and while they may be changed from time to time, they are rarely destroyed. If religious buildings are destroyed it is done either by secular powers for secular needs such as road widening in Gujarat which was regularly obstructed by the tombs of Muslim saints along the projected routes. Some can be destroyed by the members of other faiths such as the dynamiting of the gigantic statue of the Buddha at Bamian by the Afghan Taliban who considered it to be an idolatrous survival which true Muslims could not tolerate in perpetuity as 'insults to Allah, regardless of its great age and that it was no longer the object of any religious veneration. Then there is revenge destruction of religious buildings as in the burning of a mosque in Kathmandu in retaliation for the killing of Nepalese workers in Iraq.'

Religious constructions are thought to be always in the form of special buildings and shrines which are distinctive for each faith but the South Pacific provided a new dimension. The people had experienced a series of radical changes from successive colonial governments and world economics in which many men had the unsettling experience of being employed by outsiders and away from home as well as Second World War in which everything that they saw and used came from the sea in ships and then in aircraft. It was particularly the war which affected them deeply when most of the American servicemen in base camps were black and the goods they handled appeared unlimited and quite freely given away. From this developed the so-called 'Cargo Cults' (Worsley, P., 1968: 38). Under charismatic leaders religious cults developed which involved a return to ancestor worship, elaborate religious practices and material preparation for the arrival of 'cargo' such as the building of docks, roads and latter airfields with bamboo control towers and wireless masts as in the 1945 revived Malekula Cargo Cooperative. A material disruption of those societies.

Then there is the destruction of property by individuals as part of their religious rituals or assign of their commitment to an existing or new religious ideology. In Papua New Guinea there have been a number of quite recent religious movements in which there has been the competitive destruction of property in anticipation of an increased return through religious power such as the Milne Bay Prophet Movement, the Assissi Cult, Buha Movement, the Naked Cult and the Tanna Movement.

In the Spanish Civil War several thousand churches were destroyed or severally damaged and the contents looted, but not cathedrals so that there was no focus on all centres of religious devotion. The destruction of the mosque at Ayodha in India was a special and inflammatory event. For several centuries a mosque has stood at Ayodha on the site of the alleged birthplace of the Hindu God Rama. This had caused no particular difficulties or tensions until the Hindu nationalist party sought in Hinduism a specific socio-religious political identity for India despite its secular constitution by appealing to voters as Hindus rather than as supporters for less ideological and more practical politics.

As a result of this heightened tension a Hindu mob demolished the mosque in anticipation of its replacement by a Hindu temple and this inevitably led to widespread Hindu-Muslim rioting. Public religious opinion egged on by politicians interested in this destruction which the Government of India had ineffectually protected.

Some may use their property to enhance their status in religious organisation such as the annual parades of venerated statues in Hinduism, Islam and Roman Catholicism. These activities would take property and those involved out of economic circulation for the days of religious obligation. This can be dangerous indeed for survival as when whales are only available for inshore hunting by the Tlingit Alaskans for a few weeks every year and Protestant converts were forbidden to work on Sundays thus penalising their ability to accumulate food for the coming winter (Kan, 1999).

A considerable amount of property is destroyed in offerings at shrines as part of petitioning saints, spirits or ancestors hoping for their intervention. A popular Roman Catholic shrine near Nijmegan in the Netherlands may have at any time some hundred or more candles burning with substantial loss of materials and their heat and light bringing potential. It was reported on China central television that the money spent by pilgrims on incense during visits to Mount Hengshan, one of China's four sacred mountains amounted to 100 million yuan equal to the annual budget of China's Natural Science Foundation (Shi Meifen, 1989). In general places of worship are marked by the constant burning of devotional objects.

Then there is the care and disposal of the dead. In many cases this uses up substantial areas of urban land and in overpopulated countries such as China with a shortage of arable land, graves take up areas of fields round which peasants have to plough. In Shantung province it was estimated that 3 per cent of arable land was occupied by graves and tombs, the lumber used for coffins would build 200,000 homes and that burial clothing used up 24 million feet of cotton cloth per year (Chao Chien-Min, 1958). The burning of the dead in funeral pyres at Banaras is inefficiently done with scarce wood rather than in subsidised technically efficient crematoria. Apart from this there is the incense and paper burnt at funerals which involves the destruction of wood pulp. In Bali, Myanmar and Thailand the well-to-do dead are cremated in enormous paper and wood constructions requiring effort, expertise and expense.

On a global scale the care of the dead rather than their more economic disposal involves the destruction of enormous quantities of materials which could have been used for some communal betterment. In Western societies this amount must far exceed the totals involved in the construction of tombs for rulers such as the Pyramids of Egypt, Moghul monuments of India and those of Chinese emperors since money spent on funerals there extends right down the social scale and certainly involves substantial indebtedness.

There are also places of worship which take up land of economic value near to population centres which in Egypt is along the Nile fringe of usable land and in their towns there are over thirty thousand mosques. Taking comparable rural areas in England and Myanmar, the density of churches and monasteries is about the same and their current environmental value in protecting land and species can only be seen as a small return on the amount of materials used on their construction and the reservation of such areas for religious usages.

The construction of religious buildings is an ongoing use of materials and labour for churches, mosques, temples and synagogues which are rarely if ever used to anything like their full operational capacity either in time or numbers. With the relaxation of Communist hostility to religion in China, a report noted that in one county alone there were 837 newly built temples and 498 newly built lineage ones (Fu Tie-Zhu. 1989).

Finally, there is the use of materials involved in supporting worship such as the beaten gold on statues of the Lord Buddha, the gilding of altars and the use of jewels on ritual utensils. There is also an enormous output of religious reading material and pictures using up significant quantities of wood pulp.

Inter-religious Violence to Property

In situations of religious tension there is no better way of expressing hostility than the destruction of places where another religion practices its devotions. In Northern Ireland there has been a continuous process of burning or blowing up churches, just as in India there has always been the mutual attempts to destroy and damage mosques and temples and in Pakistan and Indonesia Muslims have destroyed churches.

Missionaries have to be seen as representatives of an outside and uninvolved but influential culture which often combines religious dogmatism with ignorance of the people with whom they are working. This ignorance is a combination of the perennial difficulty of knowing about and understanding another culture in another language and if they do know objecting to such behaviour on moral grounds and thus feeling that they are obliged to seek its physical destruction. In the past celibate Roman Catholic missionaries may have had only one leave during their whole working lives which they spent in one area but now all missionaries have regular leaves and their commitment to a particular cultural area is much shorter so that they are less linguistically competent and less understanding of the cultures in which they work.

In Alaska Christianity runs parallel with an intrusive 'progressive' ideology so that in 1912 there was both missionary and local Protestant pressure for the Tlingit to cut down and burn their mortuary and memorial poles and this remains a contemporary controversial issue (Kan, 1999: 461). In Tanzania baptism to Christianity was often conditional on burning objects associated with 'paganism' which was at least among the Sukuma associated as much with family welfare and their ancestors as with worship in any theological sense. Early missionaries in Uganda on occasions destroyed the ancestor shrines in compounds which they passed.

Secular Violence to Religious Property: Government Seizure of Religious Property

While it is understood that much religious activism is correlated to economic, social and political events, it is often thought that violent actions against religious institutions and activities are the result of some coherent atheistic policy of an authoritarian government as was clearly the case of Soviet Russia under both Stalin and Khruschev, but this has not always been the case. While the Pol Pot attack on religion was both crude and wholesale, the Russian opposition to religion was both more systematic, long term and institutionalised. The Academy of Sciences adopting a resolution in '1959 for the intensification of the scientific work on atheism and the All Union Atheistic Conference of that year recommending that this work must be linked to the tasks of Communist reconstruction.

Soon after the Revolution it was decided to confiscate all church bells as it was announced that their metal was needed for economic progress with the underlying reason that their sound announced the persistence of Christian practices, just as later in the 1960s the Muslim call to prayer was prohibited in the North Caucasus for the same reason (Anderson, 1994). Few churches were physically destroyed unless they could not be used for social purposes, but thousands were closed and turned into stores, schools and secular meeting halls. By 1936 some 41,868 religious buildings which existed before the 1917 Revolution had been legally closed out of 73,963. In China during the Cultural Revolution the Red Guards destroyed a considerable number of temples as well as mosques as they represented ideas which were obstacles to revolutionary change.

Religious Violence to Animals in Sacrifices

As far back as archaeology can discover or writen record provide details animals have been killed for religious reasons, but this cannot be seen in religious terms alone. Objects are certainly destroyed regularly for religious reasons and the consequences can affect mental processes and the subsequent economic, political and economic lives of those involved.

Animal sacrifices are different. The animal is killed but the meat us usually eaten. The sacrifices provide an immediate intake of animal protein and in this they may irregularly contribute to human biological well-being. Thus there is a certain underlying rationality in both the preservation of and the killing of animals for religious reasons.

The main use of animals has always been for food, agriculture and draft but they are now as always used for sacrifice and the significance of these violent acts lies in the quantity of animals involved and the periodicity of the sacrifices related to rites of passage and the crises of individuals and groups. We can see contemporary examples of sacrifices in the temples to the Goddess Kali in Calcutta and in the tribal societies of Africa in their propitiation of their ancestors and unrelated spirits combined with the mass killing of animals of the Muslim Hajj pilgrimage to Mecca.

The use of animals in religious sacrifices is a calculated act of some precision which involves the value of the animal against the difficulties which its sacrifice might allay. One suspects that exactly the same calculations go into Christian and Buddhist donations to charity. Thus in eastern Africa and the southern Sudan the need to conserve stock, the uncertainties in their environment and the need to accumulate as many head of cattle as possible for prestige and their use in negotiations for more women, are balanced against anticipated or experienced misfortune which might be alleviated by animal sacrifices.

The Nuer for instance are quite capable of substituting a wild cucumber for a cow as a sacrifice on the grounds that their 'kwoth' the sky spirit had not paid sufficient attention to their previous requests which had been accompanied by the sacrifice of a cow. Cattle are too economically valuable and prestigious to be used in regular religious ceremonies. They tend to be used for serious situations although of course they will eat the carcasses of animals whose deaths were unforeseen (Evans-Pritchard, 1940).

Some New Guinea communities accumulate pigs until they start to become a liability breaking into cultivation and proving too much for the women to control and they then hold ceremonial feasts in which there is the mass eating of pork. They maintain a balance between pigs numbers beginning to overrun each community's habitat and the capacity of the social and natural environment to sustain them (Rappaport, 1967: 17-30). Similarly the Chukchee tribe of north-eastern Siberia used sacrifices to reduce their caribou herds and providing themselves with protein. They killed male fawns and big bucks pairing each with a female fawn, thus holding down herd accumulation which at the same time prevented sharp status differences developing in the community had a large number of breeding females being retained (Bogoras, 1904: 9).

Haruspiciation is a method of predicting the future or finding out the answers relating to particular problems by examining the entrails of specially killed animals or fowls which have been ritually connected with those in trouble before being killed. It is quite common as a way of finding out what to do next (Murra, 1965: 186), but the Sukuma of Tanzania use chickens to cut down on the costs of such sacrifices.

The Mass Sacrifices on the *Muslim Pilgrimage to Mecca*

The obligatory killing of an animal for each Muslim pilgrim on the Hajj to Mecca is the most important and conspicuous contemporary mass killing of animals for a purely religious purpose and one moreover which is an annual event. Every pilgrim is obliged to kill an animal as part of their religious obligation in fulfilment of the once in a lifetime pilgrimage which is one of the required Five Pillars of Islam. Since the Hajj now involves about two million people at Mecca the problems of killing an enormous number of animals in a small area over a short period of time are obvious.

Even in the late nineteenth century the sacrifices of some 30,000 pilgrims had made the number of carcasses a health hazard. The earlier religious requirement that pilgrims give to the poor what they could not eat themselves became unworkable and the authorities in Mecca had to organise burial pits and the lavish use of lime. The small resident Meccan population of a few thousand harvesting the annual influx of pilgrims could not possibly cope with this level of sacrifices. There are now centralized efforts to cold-store the meat from perhaps half a million animals and to move it in bulk to countries in which there is a shortage of animal protein.

Apart from the conditions under which these animals are killed *en masse*, considerable damage is done to the environment to get them to Mecca which is a volcanic environment with little water and no vegetation. Enormous quantities of imported fodder are used up by these animals prior to their sacrifice and the areas from which they come get little benefit from this religious trade. This typifies a violent religious activity with no immediate secular correlations which is carried on in a religiously defined and exclusive area.

Millennarian Holocausts of Animals

There are certain situations in which tensions are so widespread that the hope of an immediate improvement is bound to attract. A millennium understanding takes over a whole society which would lead to the instantaneous improvement in the lives of all involved. This has happened with the Ghost Dance movement among the American Indians and repeatedly in the many Cargo movements of the South Pacific but only in one has there been a mass killing of animals for such a religious reason.

In 1853 a South African Xhosa Christian convert returned to his home area and began preaching a religious message that involved killing all their cattle in return for immediate earthly benefits. His niece Nongqawuse of whom he was guardian, developed this theme stating that her prophecies came from her conversations with the spirits. She said that these spirits had told her that the Xhosa dead were preparing to rise again bringing with them wonderful new cattle, but the living members of the tribe must prepare for this by slaughtering their own cattle and destroy their food stocks as these were all contaminated and impure.

Furthermore they should not cultivate in the coming season but instead build new cattle enclosures and grain storage pits for the cattle and corn which would appear miraculously. Also they should build new houses and wear new ornaments. On top of this the blind would see again, the deaf hear, cripples walk and the old would be young again.

In support of her message was the fact that the 1855 lung disease epidemic which had killed about half of their cattle, was taken as a sign that their ancestors were both troubled and wished to communicate with them. With such generalised beliefs it was not difficult for this charismatic prophetess to develop her message stating that if all impure and evil things disappeared, the Xhosa world would become a better place.

Other factors added impetus to their general feelings of disquiet. The Xhosa has been in violent conflict with not only the colonial government but also with the local European settlers on and off for the preceding half century. They were being progressively squeezed off their ancestral lands into the territories of other tribal groups to the north. While the Xhosa men would have responded to this aspect of the prophetess' message, it was particularly attractive to the women to whom it promised a different liberation. They bore the main burden of cultivation and they rejoiced that they would get crops without having to work the fields at all (Soga. 1857) and they became the most enthusiastic of her followers.

The consequences of this mass slaughter of cattle were catastrophic. By January 1857 the Xhosa were estimated to have slaughtered 400,000 head and many did not cultivate at all. The population dropped from 105,000 to 25,000 in a year. As a result they no longer had enough people to occupy their traditional lands and could no longer expect the support of the colonial government for their claims to ownership. The resulting environmental vacuum allowed the expansion of white settlement and the retraction of the area of land which they had previously cultivated quite adequately by traditional methods. 'Their national, cultural and economic integrity, long penetrated and undermined by colonial pressure finally collapsed. Nongqawuse and Sir George Grey (the Governor) had irrevocably transformed the Xhosa nation into South Africans' (Peires, 1989: 310-13, 321).

These ideas were a development of existing Xhosa religious beliefs and indeed are the contemporary framework of much Bantu religious belief. They believed that the dead did not really die in the biological sense but were a continuum with their living descendants and that if they were dissatisfied, they could impose misfortunes on the living. This disaster therefore replaced one religious and cultural utilization for the environment with another which was more productive than the former but largely for the benefit of other groups. Some aspects of this correlate with contemporary Islamic fundamentalist thinking that by destruction of Western property their return to a purer earlier age can be assured. Let us now look at the extent which religious violence has affected the environment.

9

Religious Violence and the Environment

The implications of current approaches to changes in the environment are that reason and voluntary actions are the only acceptable ways of offsetting destructive environmental actions. Thus any form of biological regulation is to be deplored and prevented, and further that any Malthusian checks on environmental deterioration by means of war, famine and disease cannot be considered as viable, valuable and promotional options. Nevertheless it has been the case that the followers of a religion have deliberately laid waste to an area such as the demolition of the World Trade Centre, New York in September 2001 and in other cases religious practices have inadvertently decreased populations to the relief of the environment. Morally questionable religious activities which their theologians might well deplore, have benign and malign consequences.

There is also the possibly in much thinking of the remnants of nineteenth century 'ascent of man' optimism that the decisions of man, collectively and individually, are based on the calm considerations of logic and compromise. It is necessary to consider these views in the light of current affairs in which religion is the principal component and this has actively affected the environment.

We have taken religion in this work to be any action which is based on some supernatural idea or proposition which is not susceptible to proof. This definition would thus cover the activities of those acting according to the beliefs of the major religions, smaller denominations as well as small sects, and those acting in response to what outsiders would consider to be magical assumptions; thus recently in Uganda the leaders of the Holy Spirit rebellion have been providing their soldiers with amulets against being hit by bullets as was the case in the 1905 Maji Maji rebellion in Tanzania against the Germans. Whether these religious actions are to be considered moral or immoral is not relevant in respect of their effects on the environment.

Environmental Factors in Religious Violence

It is generally assumed in developed societies that religion as a motivating force is of diminishing importance. This comfortable theory based on rational man ignores the destructive power of religion in contemporary wars and civil wars and its consumption of materials. Thus it is a fact in the contemporary world that religious motivations can have an active effect on the environment. Furthermore this effect is in the main destructive, while the benign are more incidental and less obvious and do not reach the head-lines.

Violence in the context of the environment is taken to be the killing or destruction of any animate or inanimate object for which the primary reason is religious and which goes beyond the religious eccentricities of individuals, families and small exclusive groups. This would include crusades, pilgrimages, martyrdoms, terrorism, sacrifices, wars, civil wars and genocide.

The Problem of Defining Environmental Influences

This assessment of the environmental impact of religious violence is based on the assumption that its effects are not directly or indirectly related to the survival of humans alone. There are difficult questions as to what constitutes an environment over which we have collective anxieties other than some generality in which we as individuals and groups are involved.

Some questions that need to be addressed are:

(a) When does a small almost individual environment become a major one in which we should have legitimate concern? The kissing of an ikon by a series of people in a Greek Orthodox church prior to warfare against Muslims at least prepares them for violence and environmental damage. This should be assessed as preparation for destructive violence apart from the spreading of disease from the transfer of moisture from one believer to another.

(b) There is the question of how far a destructive influence operates from its initial point. The range of influence be it in terms of square kilometres, the number of species or the number of humans affected; land mines in the civil wars in Bosnia, Croatia and Afghanistan which have not been removed, have created nature reserves avoided by humans and killing off the larger animals that stray into those areas. Refugees from religiously based warfare spread diseases and destroy environments from their concentrations and the sheer number of their contacts. Ngara district of Tanzania with a peace-time population of a hundred thousand, received four hundred thousand refugees from Ruanda in 1994-96 (Waters, 1999)

(c) In addition these same influences have to be assessed in terms of how long they will last. The killing of large numbers of young men in religious conflicts has an effect which lasts for at least a generation for they cannot breed. Unexploded munitions remain dangerous indefinitely as we have seen in Afghanistan and Croatia.

(d) Finally, an effect on the environment for religious reasons can fluctuate between benign and malign depending on the range of its effects and the time span of these effects. There is no doubt that the indiscriminate sowing of landmines in Afghanistan is good for the environment on both counts as it allows the natural regeneration of impoverished soils and vegetation and restricts population growth, but bad in the short-term for humans and livestock.

Religions and the Environment: An Overview

There appear to be three types of religions which can have effects on the environment. Firstly, the 'religions of the book', Christianity, Islam and Judaism. These religions based on sacred writings are used during a single life from which there are eschatological benefits. Their tenets are individualistic and relate to a single life-time. Any behaviour which is going to have an effect on the environment is likely to be based on small theocratic Christian communities such as the Amish (Hostetler, 1993), the Hutterites (Hostetler and Huntington, 1974) and the Mormons (Francaviglia, 1978). With Jews there are the imposed urban ghettoes and in Israel some collective farms based on religious principles. Islam other than some concern over the use of water supplies, does not have such communities farming on religious principles. It is not the aim of these faiths to have an environmental effect as they are one-human-life centred. Direct influence with long-term indifference since concepts of heaven are not this worldly related.

The second type of religions which have some direct environmental influence are the Eastern religions, Buddhism and Hinduism in which the individuals through some form of after-death transmigration have an infinite number of some sort of future lives. Individuals by their behaviour can improve their position in their futures lives. This leads to religious centres becoming nature reserves, vegetarianism, the avoidance of killing even insects by accident as with the Jains (Dundas, 1992), and in the return to their habitats of captured birds and other animals. Seeing cows on the streets of Indian cities immediately raises environmental issues, whereas the consequences of Jain behaviour is socially and biologically invisible. Similarly, some widespread direct influence within long-term indifference. The problem for environmental concern is the enormous number of future lives which the individual will have to go through and efforts for immediate benefit are for the individual, not for the environment in which they live; the fact that a few fish, birds survive for longer than naturally may have little effect on the environment.

A possible third type are the pre-literate religions of tribal peoples in which the living, the dead and the unborn form a familial continuum. Environmental success for such groups is at the expense of other groups. There are no overall beliefs or practices which could have widespread effects, but for the small group there is an environmental balance supported by their religions correlating to survival. The tribal community operating within a circle of their own social horizon, may seem to have evolved a socio-religious system balancing their subsistence needs with their environment, except when it is invaded by external disease and inter-tribal warfare. The theoretically isolated and environmentally self-sufficient traditional community is probably an illusion.

Religious Violence and the Environment in History

Historically religions have been extremely destructive of human populations and their environment apart from their responsibility for the spread of disease (Reynolds and Tanner, 1983; 1995: Chapter 13). In 1893, 33 thousand pilgrims died from cholera in and around Mecca and the dead remained unburied (Izzedine, no date).

It is not so much the numbers who have been killed for religious reasons but their proportion to whole populations. The Taiping Rebellion in China, 1851-64 under a leader claiming to be the brother of Jesus Christ (Boardman, 1952) may have killed or been indirectly responsible for the deaths of up to 20 million people so that in some cities only dogs survived (Spence, 1996; Yu-Wen, 1973; Michall, 1966; Wakeman, 1966). Tamurlane killed from piety (Groussert. 1970) about 80 per cent of the population along the belt of Arab-Iranian civilisations (Lamb, 1932); his men are said to have piled 70 thousand heads outside the walls of Isfahan. This war destroyed the finely balanced environments of these societies in quasi-desert oases from which they have never recovered (Hookham, 1969). At the Christian siege of Damietta in 1219 only 3000 Muslims out of a population of 80 thousand survived suffering starvation and disease (Oliver, 1894). These are very high proportions of these populations significantly reducing their pressure on their environment from one point of view but from another left these societies without sufficient manpower to maintain their existing environmental balances by irrigation.

More recently the Turkish killing of some 35 per cent of Armenians in 1915-17 (Boyajian, 1972) does not quite reach up to the same levels of environmental relief although the figures will be higher if emigration is included. The killing of over ten thousand Mahdists in the Sudan at the battle of Omdurman in 1893 (Levy, 1974) would probably be about the same level of population reduction.

Some better known historical massacres would have had little environmental effect. The St. Bartholemew's massacre of Protestants by Roman Catholics in France in 1572 only killed 1 per cent of that population (Benedict, 1991; Erlanger, 1962). Much the same applies to Jewish pogroms in Russia and Poland over the end of the last century (Enyclopaedia Judaica, 1971,13: 694-701). Finally, the Holocaust killed off whole Jewish communities in a return to the population obliterations of Tamurlane, with an estimated 6-1/2 million Jews killed between 1933 and 1945.

In cities in which there were Jewish ghettoes this will have cleared substantial urban areas for post-war renewal. The Iran-Iraq war perhaps killed a quarter of a million men, but as it occurred in a desert, there were few environmental consequences. On balance it would seem that religious wars except for Tamurlane's exterminations and the Jewish Holocaust, have provided no more than a single generation's relief from population expansion since it is usually young men rather than young women who are killed.

Religious Violence: The Continuation in History

A study of 106 wars between 1820 and 1952 (Wilkinson, 1980, Richardson, 1960) showed that differences of religion were frequently cited in the sources as a cause of fighting. Three quarters of all inter-religious pairs had a Christian member and 90 per cent of all fighting between co-religionists were Christian. Only 10 per cent of wars had neither a Christian nor Muslim component. This has led some commentators to conclude (Wilkinson, 1980; Wright, 1964) that Christianity and Islam strongly incited their members to fight those of other religions or incited those other religions to fight them or that these two faiths especially incited their members to fight one another.

Are current religions associated with warfare to any lesser or greater degree? Lebanon (Christian *versus* Muslim), Israel (Judaism *versus* Islam), Sudan (Islam *versus* Christianity and African traditional religions), Sri Lanka (Buddhism *versus* Hinduism), Iran/Iraq (Shia Islam *versus* Sunni Islam), Afghanistan (Islamic civil war), Yugoslavia (Christian *versus* Islam), Cyprus (Christian *versus* Muslim), Northern Ireland (Roman Catholic *versus* Protestant Christians) and south-eastern Russia (Christian *versus* Islam). This list could be extended further by including conflicts in which Christianity fights Communism as well as in Kashmir and India/Pakistan (secular Hinduism *versus* Islam) where there have been three wars and continuing tensions.

The attack on the World Trade Centre in New York in September 2001 killing some three thousand people was religiously motivated as was an early gas attack in a Tokyo subway. Thus it would seem that there has been no let-up in what might be categorized as wars in which differences of religious beliefs are at least one of the principal motivating forces. There are newspaper photographs of weapon training in Iranian mosques and mullahs with their kalashnikovs just as there are pictures of Christian priests in the Lebanese civil war with pictures of the Virgin Mary on their rifles.

Some of these current religious wars are no more than continuations of older quarrels dating back centuries as in the ex-Yugoslavia where Christians and Muslims are still reacting to each other in terms of past Turkish dominance. Others in the Lebanon are continuations of circulating tensions between Christian, Druzes, Jew and Muslims in which each religious community has been the object of periodic massacres. In that country communal population levels from increases and decreases in the birth rates provoke tensions which have been avoided to some extent by not holding regular population censuses. The present latent, continual and widespread tension between Greece and Turkey in the Aegean and Cyprus dates from the Middle Ages. This hatred was revitalised by the Greek invasion of Asia Minor in 1920 and recently by the Turkish army invading Cyprus to assist in the division of the island on religious and ethnic grounds.

Have there been any changes since 1945? In the past Christians have been way ahead in belligerence with Islam some way behind. This balance appears to be changing so that Islam may be becoming the most violent religion, whether or not terrorism is included in Israel, Egypt, Algeria and Northern Ireland in which religion is the main category distinguishing protagonists.

In sociological terms Islam with its small range of religious requirements fulfilled by action rather than attitude, appeals far more to those who have not benefited from economic and social development. Islam is likely to appeal much more in the future and to cause more ideological trouble with environmental effects than the ex-Christian societies of the West. These do not appear collectively to believe in anything sufficiently strongly to fight for it on religious grounds except for a few small fundamentalist groups. Islamic Iraq invaded Islamic Kuwait and on retreating did not hesitate to set fire to oil wells which caused immense environmental damage to the Persian Gulf.

Nevertheless in Christianity there is the incitement to violence which has an important current part in its religious rhetoric (Juergensmeyer, 1993). 'Onward Christian soldiers' and 'Fight the good fight' are still popular Protestant hymns in English. Overall there are no grounds for thinking or planning on the assumption that such quarrels based on religious differences are becoming less vicious and destructive.

Only in one respect are religions less environmentally destructive than they used to be and that is in the spread of known epidemic diseases. Refugee routes may be no longer the channels along which diseases flow and refugee centres are no longer the focus for the outbreaks of so many mass diseases. This control of epidemic diseases has been through secular agencies; no religious authorities have acted to control the taking of water from holy but polluted sources.

Contemporary Warfare and the Environment

The environmental effects of such extensive wars are often visually obvious as with the devastation of Gaza, Beirut and Sarajevo (Vukovic, 1993) after years of civil war with sophisticated weapons. Firstly, it takes certain areas out of human use for variable periods. In terms of biology the destructive effects of warfare are surprisingly short-term; nature recovers remarkably quickly. In the tropics a battlefield is nearly unrecognisable after two years; the effects have to be looked for. In deserts warfare does not matter and indeed it is probably the best place for fighting as groups of breeding males only destroy themselves in waterless wastelands. In terms of species survival, warfare is no more than a hiccup in time, infinitely less destructive of environments than the omnivorous goat.

Secondly, it reduces population pressure by destroying surplus numbers of young men who are unable to reproduce. The killing of an estimated hundred thousand men in the Iraq-Iran war could be seen as an environmental success allowing those countries a breathing space to develop more for the maintenance of their too rapidly expanding populations. However, as in the continuing Afghan unrest dead fighters would have their widows absorbed into polygynous marriages ever since the battle of Badr in which the Prophet Mohammad encouraged the surviving men to marry the widows of those killed for their new faith.

Since the rapidly expanding population of Sri Lanka caused by the 1947 DDT campaign against the malarial mosquito which doubled the island's people in 17 years, the civil war between Buddhists and Hindus could also be seen as environmentally advantageous except in the sense that the killing has not yet reached high enough levels to relieve overcrowding.

Warfare in populated areas also reduces livestock pressure on land. Armies are often either poorly fed or want variety so that any edible animal in the fighting area tends to be killed off if not hidden; chickens, pigs, sheep, goats and cattle are eliminated. Many third world areas are grossly overstocked and in this respect civil wars are better as they tend to last longer than wars and their effects are more widespread. The recent civil war in Ruanda between Christianised tribal categories has killed off both livestock and large numbers of people in a country with very high population densities. In the sense that Christian values had no effect on this mass killing, its lack of influence was environmentally benign.

Finally, warfare moves populations away from the areas of fighting into refugee camps in which they would die in larger numbers than they do but for aid motivated at least in part and in origin by Christian obligations to help those to whom they are not related; in this sense Christian aid prolongs the population in marginal areas incapable of sustaining high population densities as in Somalia.

The significance of contemporary religious warfare on population levels has perhaps not been fully recognised because the totals are not high enough to merit mass media attention. If the Northern Ireland Protestant *versus* Roman Catholic figures for 1969-81 were applied proportionately to the United States, they would have had 282 thousand killed, two million injured and if applied to mainland Britain 75 thousand killed and three-quarters of a million injured (Hickey, 1984).

If economic waste is related to what might have been done to the environment in Northern Ireland the totals are horrendous. Over a hundred churches damaged or destroyed 1971-82, 28,500 shooting incidents, 7200 bomb explosions plus 3200 bombs defused, 2300 deaths (O'Malley, 1983). This is a civil war between two Christian groups of more or less fundamentalist Christians led by their clergy who talk in terms of 'no surrender' and Roman Catholics who take little notice of their own clergy's admonitions to stop violence. In environmental terms this prolonged low-key civil war may well have had few effects since the economy is maintained by outside help and those most affected by the tensions can emigrate or move to less intense areas of direct confrontation.

Religious terrorism in which the initiators give their lives in a struggle on God's behalf (Rapoport, 1982) thus gaining immortality as with the Hamas bombings in Israel have had little direct effect on the environment as the two religious communities involved are already segregated. Since the United States, State Department estimated that only 8700 had been killed by terrorism in 1968-95, the numbers killed are too small to have any direct environmental effect and the devastation is local and temporary. The crashing of aircraft into the World Trade Centre and the Pentagon killed off only fecund men and women but the placement of millions of tons of the rubble from the former buildings has had a major environmental effect near to New York wherever it has been dumped.

Religious violence if it does not kill, separates populations. Like moves towards like and in anticipation of the 'other' taking over their property and land, as much as possible is destroyed; in Israel Jews have destroyed property in areas to be taken over by the Palestinians, and evacuating Christians in ex-Yugoslavia have burnt their houses rather than let them be taken over by the incoming Muslims. Such areas are environmentally neutralised for a time from human occupation and their populations have to be supported by others.

The effect of the Greek Christian attempt to dominate Cyprus and the mainland Turkish counter-invasion, effectively divided the island with very few Christians in the north and even fewer Muslims in the south, much the same as in Asia Minor where Greek Christian villages are still empty after the flight of their inhabitants in the early 20s. The result of these population movements of 20 years ago in Cyprus is still visible in the north with empty farms, closed shops, idle factories, and desecrated Christian cemeteries, whereas the forced evacuation of Cretan Moslems in the mid 20s is not so visible except architecturally. In both these cases the totals of killings were not enormous but the amount of land taken out of agriculture must have been high in terms of harvest yields. Farming in the open exposes workers to danger and little agriculture is carried out in war zones so that the affected populations depend for survival on hidden stocks, other people and international aid. Thus such exchanges of populations on religious grounds may have been in the short run environmentally beneficial, while causing productive strain on other areas.

There is possibly another factor in religious segregation as in Belfast where 70 per cent of the population lives in religious ghettoes of their own choosing after decades of harassment. Any religiously segregated community like the Amish has increased inbreeding and the gene pool becomes restricted. This may well have environmental effects in reducing their reproductive rate if it is prolonged.

Invasions of one religion into the territory of another may result in the unequal use of environmental resources. The Israeli occupation of Arab land has resulted in the unequal development in which the two communities in close proximity do not have equal access to resources. Newly created Israeli settlements will have clean piped water supplies and indeed swimming pools while the nearby Arab villages will have the women drawing impure water from wells with buckets and rope. This division is carried out by the power of the religiously motivated gun and remains a visual incitement to continuing violence.

Religious violence takes two forms. One, in which humans destroy humans and second, in which humans destroy inanimate and animate materials and living matter. In both cases there are immediately visible as well as long-lasting environmental effects.

It would seem that religious violence, human to human, affecting the environment is now on the increase after a lull in the second half of the 20th century. This increase may be due to the failure of secular economic and political systems to deliver their somewhat optimistic forecasts; the ideology of inevitable development as an individual right.

This religious fighting is probably environmentally benign in both the short and long term as it reduces human and animal populations as well as periodically taking large areas out of human use.

Humans destroying non-human materials and animals for religious reasons has been and continues to be important. It may in fact be on the increase as the developed societies use up more materials for religious purposes without replacing these environmentally. This indirect religious violence must be considered environmentally malign in both the short and long term.

In practice rather than in theory religions tend to be environmentally destructive in the short-term but benign in the long-term. Where religious are involved in mass activities, they destroy rather than preserve. The more passive influences of religious practices on individuals and groups (Reynolds and Tanner. 1983) tends to preserve them and thus possibly threaten the environment in the long-term. Where they do preserve the environment it tends to be in the form of religiously motivated 'zoos', small enclaves of accidental preservation.

PART C

The Prevention or Mitigation of Violence— The Reverse of Religious Violence

We have seen the extent of religiously motivated violence and perhaps realise that it is far more frequent and in many more forms than the occasions in which it is reported in the mass media. When religious violence appears on television or in pictures in the press it may be due to its political usefulness and personal ambitions of contesting elites who may have little personal commitment to any religious agenda.

But although religions may be involved in sporadic and in some cases institutionalised violence, they are also involved directly or indirectly in the prevention of violence and also with repairing the damage done in the name of religion. While much required religious behaviour could be described as both theoretical and impractical, Christianity more than other religions in terms of committed personnel and resources, has always concerned itself directly with mitigating the effects of violence with special institutions for the relief of suffering brought about by violence or neglect. Any study of religious behaviour and its influence would be seriously biased if it failed to balance accounts of violence with details of its direct or indirect influences to reduce violence or mitigating its effects.

The major religions all have their messages within their Great Traditions which require activity or inactivity by individuals and institutions in order to fulfil their religious obligations. They are required to initiate and maintain personal behaviour patterns in accordance with these doctrines, but this is always a question of degree for individuals and the extent to which the control of this religiously required behaviour has become institutionalised.

But there is an another aspect ; what do individuals or the religious institutions of their faiths do to prevent others misbehaving according to the tenets of their own faiths or the faiths of outsiders. Clearly Buddhism despite its dominant characteristic of passivity, has an obligation to prevent violence, particularly the killing of any living thing. But this aim of passivity has no objectives involving Buddhists in the practicalities of human affairs; doing nothing can of course prevent violence, but this for the Buddhist must be an accident not the following out of a deliberate policy since this would not aid the elimination of all wishes. Of course, there is a subtle dividing line between actively pursuing your faith in ways that may be directly or indirectly violent and acting in accordance with your beliefs without seeing it as a means to directly gaining adherents.

It would often appear to be the case that people in religions with doctrines of peacefulness however devoted they may be to the beliefs and practices of their faith, are usually too tied into the immediacies of their social, economic and political environments to be able to take a religious line as individuals opposing the development or mitigation of violence. For religious behaviour as such to be widely influential if it did not coincide with what any community and its people want, would require their subsistence to be guaranteed and for such a society to have the time, the resources and the personnel to take up religious occupations independent of any immediate need to survive. It may be that few in any religion are prepared to go outside their usual social patterns of behaviour in order to support something which has little or no local support. This would usually require living in specially dedicated communities.

However, organisations associated with particular faiths or denominations which are run by professionals and committed volunteers are sometimes able to step in after secular and religious violence has occurred to ameliorate some of the damage to lives and the property needed for their survival. An after the event showing of commitment to the brotherhood of man despite an inability to prevent the events themselves.

We need therefore to examine the roles of religious people in the direct or indirect prevention of violence to other living beings and property regardless of their religious or secular affiliations and more specifically their failure to do so.

10

The Preservation of Human Lives

In any society there are individuals however defined who are in danger of being killed or who would die because of deliberate neglect and most religions are concerned with this. Depending on definitions of what constitutes human life, the major religions have been actively against abortion as a form of murder for Christians and for Buddhists the prevention of a person continuing with the interminable cycle of rebirths.

Religious concerns are filtered through social practices which favour men over women and which often lead to cruelty and neglect. In many cultures boys are fed before girls and they are taken for medical treatment at a latter stages of their illnesses than boys (Dubois, 1972: 606). Infanticide is an ever present danger for unwanted children, usually girls for whom families may not see that any investment in them brings no return on this expenditure. They eat and have to be clothed but marry into other families and for them to be married at all means the cost and indebtedness of providing adequate dowries. When the husband's family thinks that the dowry is inadequate, then the wife is in danger of being harassed into suicide or being murdered so that the widower can remarry for the greater financial advantage of his family. In addition unwanted children are always at risk and religions may be important in preserving their lives.

The Prevention of Infanticide

The Islamic view of female infanticide is quite clear; the practice is forbidden. The Prophet Mohammad made several straightforward statements that the care of daughters is a cause for glorifying Allah and referred to them in the Koran as 'Allah's daughters'. He accompanied this by stating in the Koran that 'the female child buried alive shall be asked for what sin she was put to death'(Sura, 6: 141 and 152).

This change in attitude towards female infanticide which Mohammad instituted cannot be obviously explained in terms of any prospective advantages to the new Muslims from an expansion in the female population. The earlier casualties had left this small new religiously motivated community with a surplus of widows. It was initiated by the Prophet for other than economic or social reasons and later this became part of the dogma of Islam.

There is a constant tendency for Muslim leaders to go back to 'the word of Allah' as recorded in the Koran and this has perhaps modified rather than controlled contemporary Muslim behaviour. Today there is no public comment on the neglect of girl babies but it probably occurs to some extent as in some failure to register the births of females in Algeria (Breil, 1959: 74ff) and in Egypt (Mboria, 1938).

The British administration in India waged a long campaign against infanticide based on the Christian premise that it was murder without really understanding the Hindu preference for sons. The 1852 census of Mysore showed that in the Thakoor sub-caste there were 10,695 male and 5,865 female children. It took many years for such practices to be reduced so that they were at least no longer so obvious. A police post in one village in which there was a massive imbalance between girls and boys was apparently responsible for the survival of ten out of thirteen girls born in the next year (Chevers, 1870: 752, 759). The Government of India Census Report 1901 showed that the deliberate killing of female babies had been largely stopped although it is still practised in rural communities where it is largely condoned (Pakrasi, 1970; Chandrasekhar, 1959).

If there is a narrow dividing line between survival and death in small communities the religious system may allow for the killing or abandonment of not only children not required for survival possibilities since boys grow up into hunters and girls have no direct roles essential for survival, but for the elderly as well.

Hunters and gatherers with their narrow margins between survival and starvation and religions related to this, have usually taken a harsh line with the long-term liabilities from having more women than men and indeed babies who are not needed for survival. In the 1920s of 108 babies born to Netsilik Eskimo women, 40 were killed of which 38 were girls (Rasmussen, 1931). The Yanomamo Indians of the Amazon (Chagnon, 1977: 75-76) often killed girl babies since they would not develop into warriors needed for both offence and defence. In both these societies the spirits would seem to have preferred the survival of the group to that of individuals.

The Treatment of Orphans

Unless arrangements are made through family connections or special institutions the chances of orphans surviving has always been limited. However, Islam has always shown special concern for orphans because the Prophet Mohammad himself was an orphan having lost his father before his birth. The uncertainty of his own birth and that he might not have been born at all certainly influenced him as he repeatedly refers to the wonder of procreation as one of the awesome signs of God 'Blessed be Allah, the best of creators' (Koran, 23: 12-24), so it is not surprising that he instituted not only the prohibition of female infanticide but also the care of orphans. The Koran which is a relatively short book mentions them 23 times as in the list of those who should benefit from property seized in war (Koran, 8: 41). The very much larger Old Testament has 30 mentions of orphans and the New Testament no mentions at all.

While Islamic law does not seem to give full property rights to adopted children as adoption gives no right of inheritance, but considerable attention is paid to protecting of such property as they have; 'To orphans restore their property when they reach their age nor substitute your worthless things for their good ones and devour not their substance by mixing it up with your own' (Koran 4: 2). Muslim lawyers have given considerable attention to the care of orphans when widows have been left without sufficient means to keep themselves and their children. The Koran gives general injunctions for their care (Koran, 2: 218. 93: 6 and 9).

Christianity from early times had institutions for the care of orphans who were abandoned without any family connections which were run by religious orders but in the absence of wet nurses they had very high death rates. There are no Christian objection to adoption with such children having full familial rights. Hindu religious law makes it imperative for a childless man to adopt a son 'because a son delivers his father from the hell called *Put*' (Laws of Manu, 1969). There appears to be no Hindu provision for the adoption of foundlings in a more general sense and thus fails to care for orphans.

Only Judaism has canonical difficulty over the adoption of orphans as there is no provision in Judaic law for artificially creating a kin relationship by a legal act or fiction but does allow for guardianship as something approaching adoption but without any inheritance rights. The Lubavitch as an extreme orthodox sect, is opposed to even this as physical expressions of affection with adopted children would automatically involve a couple in forbidden contacts with members of the opposite sex to whom they are not blood relatives (Enc Jud, 1974, 302).

The Survival of Retarded Children

In subsistence societies such children have very little chance of survival because keeping them alive has no long term return for those who feed them by the work that they might be able to do latter in life. Various grades of handicapped children may still survive because they have some social value; a blind girl may still get married to a man who would not otherwise get a wife as she is still capable of bearing children.

Most children who are obviously handicapped would be killed at birth and none of the Great Traditions have developed institutions for their care until quite late in their development. As societies become wealthier their religious organisations are better able to preserve such people who would not have otherwise survived.

Even though care of the retarded becomes more institutionally recognised with affluence there are grades with which such care is put into action. It is among the religiously motivated that such an abnormal child is more easily accepted. An American study found Roman Catholic mothers more easily accepting their retarded children than those from other denominations. It was concluded that their beliefs gave explicit absolution from any feelings of personal guilt and that it could be seen as a unique test of religious faith (Zuk *et al.*, 1961).

The Prevention of Abortion

Leaving aside discussions as to whether the unborn child is considered to be a living being or not, there is general religious agreement as to the unacceptability of abortion. Both Buddhism and Hinduism with their beliefs in an almost endless succession of rebirths, have every reason to oppose the idea of aborting a potential human already started on another turn of the Wheel of Existence. The teachings of the

Gautama Buddha state that 'rebirth takes place when a father and a mother come together and the one to be born is present' (Suriyabongse, 1954). Modern views in Thailand (Hanks, 1968) and Sri Lanka (Ryan, 1953) conform to the views that an abortion is not only impeding rebirth but involves the prohibited taking of life.

However in Japan with its syncretic religious beliefs mixing Buddhism with other faiths, have births influenced by astrology overriding ethical objections to abortion. It is widely believed that girls born in the Year of the Horse would grow up to be bad natured and difficult to marry off. In 1906 the sex ratio of officially reported births was 107.6 males to 100 females against a long constant sex ratio ranging between 104-105 to 100 females (Tak, 1974). In 1966 the overall birth rate dropped precipitously and the induced abortion rate rose from an expected 30.6 per 1000 birth as to 43.1 and the neonatal death rate for girls was 20 per cent (Kaku, 1975). The probable deaths of such babies may have been due to benign neglect rather than deliberate killing.

In Taoism and Shintoism it is held that the baby does not have a soul until it has seen the light of day. However, in both China and Japan the moral repugnance over abortion is shown in the common practice of making offerings for the souls of aborted babies who are thought to be capable of revenge on the living for what has happened to them.

In Taiwan an increasing number of abortions have come to be associated with misfortunes that have subsequently happened to the families of those involved and Taoist ceremonies have been created to placate these angry ghosts. The Dragon Lake Temple has Red Contracts 'for pacifying resentment and undoing entanglements by providing salvation for foetus ghosts' with the initial paragraph stating 'I (the person appeasing the ghost) prostrate myself so that the majesty of sagely virtues, whose divine benevolence is vast, may wash away a millennium of hatred' and ends 'may the Bodhisattva on the lotus throne, the Bodhisattva Ksitgarbha, as well as his majesty the Supreme Emperor of the eastern peak, and the Ten Luminous Kings of the Underworld inspect and receive this offering. May they show pity and mercy towards me and be lenient, accepting responsibility on my behalf. I respectfully beseech you to grant special favour to me to escape the foetus ghost's resentful hatred and to eliminate the bad *karma* that my wrongs have created so that I am freed from past resentful hatred (Moskowitz, 2001: 171-73).

From the start Christianity has considered that the destruction of the foetus to be sinful as it considered all forms of human life to be sacred and it remains punishable under religious law. In the official Roman Catholic and that of the Jehovah's Witnesses views any induced abortion is the equivalent of murder regardless of the duration of the pregnancy. This view has meant that in many cases abortion is resorted to illegally and it has been estimated that bungled abortions account for more than 40 per cent of female hospital admissions in Santiago, Chile and that one-third of all pregnancies ended in abortion (Ehrlich and Ehrlich, 1972: 291).

In most developed countries religious opposition to the legalising of abortion seems only to have been a delaying factor, but opposition continues from a vociferous and sometimes violent group of Christians and others calling themselves the 'pro-life' lobby.

Islam with its strong procreative orientation regards abortion as killing (Hathout. 1972) as does both Christianity and Judaism but there are divided opinions as to when the foetus is alive paralleling modern medical understandings and the numbers of abortions generally rise with the standard and individualism of education (Yaukey, 1961: 31).

The Indirect Failure to Preserve Human Lives

At all levels of social behaviour religious beliefs are going to have some influence on social behaviour which is particularly noticeable in small religious sects such as the Amish who combine their understandings of the Bible with an agricultural way of life. They feel a supportive obligation to all within their communities and will not move the mentally disturbed out of their communal care unless they are dangerous.

Other major religions who either control the political thinking of the states in which they operate or form the background to the moral understandings on which politicians create laws for the protection of life. Popular opinion within which people tend to think, have some potential influence on the survival of their people whether they are believers and practitioners or just indifferent to such moral issues. Any religious distinctions between sinning and moral behaviour or between concepts of pure and impure will have some effect on the survival chances of these people.

Illegitimacy

Religions which have clear cut moral requirements create distinctions between legitimate and illegitimate activities which are carried into social life. Those who are married according to the moral understandings of the communities in which they live, have advantages over those who do not have this combined religious and social status and the children born from such unrecognised unions are particularly vulnerable. This is particularly so with the Christian definition of children born from sacramental marriage resulting in much higher death rates of those classified as illegitimate and of courser the intention was to stress the importance of religious marriage. In Italy death rates for legitimate and illegitimate children only became equal in the mid 1960s after a 40 per cent difference in 1950 (Nodari and Piruvane. 1970) while in the United States there has remained a difference for both black and white babies which correlates to illegitimacy (Scurletis *et al.*, 1969).

Of course, the Christian Church has been concerned with the care of abandoned children but before the creation of vulcanised rubber allowing the feeding of babies independent of the breast, the death rates were excessively high. Of the 315 children taken in by a Montreal hospital in the years 1760-71, 290 died (Fortier, 1963).

Other religions in their Great Traditions do not make such disadvantageous distinctions. Buddhism has no marriage service since it would show greater involvement with the world and thus could not be seen as a stage in the progressive detachment which might lead to *nirvana*; marriage ceremonies are only recognised by the feeding of monks.

Hinduism has such strong concepts of legitimacy that the Laws of Manu contain no reference to illegitimacy even as a possibility to be punished by legislation. Dumont has stated that it was 'a universal principal that the illegitimate child has a status markedly inferior to that of legitimate children' (Dumont, 1970: 115) and Hinduism shows itself to be the extreme example of this situation. Enormous social difficulties ensue if there are such occurrences in the higher castes, where neither premarital sex nor adultery is tolerated ; degradation of status and excommunication from one's caste would almost certainly follow.

This is not only the case of the deserted unmarried woman and her child but also of the offspring of less than legal unions that contravene sub-caste endogamy and the ideas of ritual purity involved in this. Such unions are or were, common enough to create sub-castes which had distinct but inferior status (O'Malley, L.S.S., 1935: 94-95). For a Hindu to conceive a child by a Muslim may be seen as beyond any possibility of legitimation and such women have been disowned by their families. Many Hindu women abducted by Muslims during the 1948 Partition of India disturbances were unwilling to seek repatriation as their ritual impurity could not be removed in such away that they could ever be legitimately married within their own sub-caste.

Islam has marriage as a civil contract preferred by Allah permitting both polygyny and concubinage so that illegitimacy is rarely an issue. The Shia have a short term form of contractual 'mutaa' marriage even for a university term which from a western point of view would seem to be immoral. The recent Shia encouragement of '*mutaa*' marriages for periods of a few minutes to ninety-nine years in return for a payment to the woman and the recitation of a verse from the Koran has been described as the encouragement of prostitution (Tohidi, 1983).

It is sufficient for the father to acknowledge cohabitation with a wife or concubine to establish the legitimacy of the child (Levy, R., 1969: 136). The only distinction between children born of wives and concubines is that the latter have no property rights. Different schools of law have defined the length of pregnancy with little regard to biological facts. In the Shafi and Maliki schools of law a man can acknowledge as legitimate a child conceived before his marriage and one conceived up to four years after his marriage has been terminated.

Traditional societies have wide variations in what they consider to be socially acceptable unions which would be recognised as such by the ancestors. The Sukuma of Tanzania have more than ten types of marriages with specific titles and avoid the concept of illegitimacy by having children born from illicit unions carrying the matrilineal names of their grandfather as would be the case with Christian illegitimacies.

The rigidity of the Christian concept of sacramental marriage and thus creating the reality of illegitimacy is an example of a religion failing to preserve human lives despite its charitable efforts to care for abandoned children. In general Christian societies impose penalties on unmarried mothers and their children so that the death rates of illegitimate children has been and is higher than for legitimate children. In the 1950s in New York the death rate for illegitimate children was 24.9 per thousand deliveries and for legitimate ones 13.2 per cent (Pakter, 1961) and a parallel German study found the difference to be 37.3 per cent as against 26.8 per cent for legitimate children (Maier, 1964). We can see that the social differences founded on religious definitions have been responsible for the very high death rates of children defined as illegitimate.

The Practical Aspects of Religiously Defined Pollution

If a religion destroys some part of the environment affecting human survival without consciously being aware that this is happening, this could be described as accidental or at best inadvertent. There are limits to what is acceptable when religious thinkers argue that the lethal results of their practices are the unfortunate consequences of the pursuit of the greater 'good' being sought through these religious actions.

The River Ganges is sacred from source to sea and no other river carries this amount of sanctity in both length and quantity of water. The Nile was certainly sacred in dynastic times as the annual floods were responsible for the survival of the inhabitants of all those living in the Nile valley and its development into a complex society. This religious connection disappeared with that of the historical Egyptian civilisation with which it was interwoven and in any case it was not associated with wide-ranging ideas of religious pollution. Contemporary Egyptian Islam and Coptic Christianity pay no religious attention to the Nile.

The Ganges on the other hand is still an essential part of Hinduism with its concern over various aspects of ritual pollution and yet this river receives each day an enormous quantity of untreated sewage and at Banaras a considerable number of unburnt or partially burnt bodies. If in Hindu terms human effluent is polluting and the river water sacred, then there can only be a partial coincidence with modern understandings of hygiene.

It must be clear to Hindus that there is little contradiction between religious and modern ideas on what is sanitary since human effluent is handled by Untouchables who also dispose of human and animal dead bodies. In a city such as Banaras where perhaps three-quarters of the half million population are dependent on Hindu practices

(Saraswati, 1975: 45), the blocks on any sort of hygienic planning are created by Hindu orthodoxy. This maintains that the river is pure and that the after-death status of Hindus is affected by bathing in it and being immersed there after death. Even with subsidised cremation, there has been a steady increase of the numbers of bodies brought there by modern transport for cremation at the river's edge rising from a daily average of 32 in 1917-18 to 82 in 1989. There is also the fact that many bodies are only partially burnt and some bodies have been put directly in the river without any attempt at cremation. This has led the city authorities to put flesh eating turtles into the river as a measure to combat pollution (Parry, 1994: 56).

In this situation it is not a religion promoting water-born diseases but failing to do anything about reducing such dangers particularly as the understanding of the connection between polluted water and disease has been widely known for centuries. The Kumbh Mela in AD 2001 probably had seven millions bathing in the Ganges in a restricted area over a short period which despite the enormous investment in planning and control by the civil authorities, must have been heavily polluted. These mass bathings for a religious purpose has been described as the best possible way of distributing water-born diseases (Rogers, 1926).

Although the connection between polluted water and cholera has been known for some time, pilgrims have taken home polluted water and themselves as carriers so that despite the availability of protective inoculations in 1938 70,662 deaths were attributed to cholera at Hardwar and in 1948 52,604 deaths at Allahabad (Bannerjea, 1951). Such epidemics followed the line of the railways taking the pilgrims back to their homes. So we can conclude that the Hindu devotion to the Ganges, mother Ganga, continues to be a source of enhanced morbidity and mortality for the devout.

Religious Pilgrimages and Disease

We have seen that Hindu devotion to and use of the Ganges is a dangerous practice, violating virtually every scientific concept of hygiene and against the interest of the population in general. However, pilgrimages generally must be accepted as one of the easiest and most efficient ways of spreading diseases along the routes to the places of pilgrimage, at the pilgrimage site and on the way back home.

Between 1927 and 1961 a whole range of epidemic diseases in the Sudan, relapsing fever, smallpox, yellow fever and cerebrospinal meningitis were attributed to West African pilgrims passing through on the way to Mecca (El Tayeb, 1976). In the 1800s the average number of pilgrims may have been in the 30,000s, whereas now the annual number of Muslims from outside Saudi Arabia coming to Mecca on the Hajj will always exceed a million. The contemporary excellence of the medical arrangements now include medical teams from the pilgrims' own countries. Such concentrations of the devout will always allow for diseases to spread and deaths to occur from heat exhaustion, accidents, crowd panics and the high average age of pilgrims perhaps wanting to die at Mecca during the Hajj.

Almost every country has a number of pilgrimage sites and their territories are criss-crossed by groups of pilgrims who are perhaps checked for their sanctity rather than for their healthiness (Bhardwaj, 1973). All pilgrimage networks have to be seen as a system for the direct distribution of disease. India is reported to have some 400 religious fairs annually involving more than 5000 pilgrims. Latin America is reported to have more than 900 pilgrimage centres (Nolan, 1991) and there are a growing number of non-Roman Catholic places of pilgrimage in Europe (Nolan, and Nolan, 1989; Uden and Pieper, 1990).

We can therefore conclude that in a variety of social situations religions have directly been related to higher than expected morbidity and mortality rates because of dominating religious considerations. There are others situations in which dominant religions have shown a direct failure to preserve human lives as in the Ruanda genocide.

The Roman Catholic Church in Ruanda and Genocide

The context of religion and violence is usually thought of as a situation made worse by the appeal of irrational ideas and practices. However there are situations in which believers in a particular religion have acted as successful arbitrators between violently disposed groups such as the Franciscan friars in the Church of the Nativity in Bethlehem when they were sheltering Palestinians wanted by the invading Israeli army in AD 2002. There are also situations in which the members of a religion have conspicuously failed to reduce violence and have been conspicuously silent in their attempts to restrain erupting violence.

Ruanda is a mainly Christian country with Roman Catholicism predominating with its visible institutions in most localities with churches, schools, hospitals and convents largely run and controlled by Ruandan bishops, priests and nuns. Yet that Christian population divided politically and socially between Tutsi rulers and Hutu peasants in early 1994 erupted into widespread horrifying violence along these caste/class lines ending with an estimated 800,000 dead, killed in two months totalling about 11 per cent of the population; 60,000 bodies were collected by garbage trucks in Kigali, the capital and some 40,000 bodies which had floated down the Kagera River into Lake Victoria were buried in Uganda; a daily rate of killing higher than that of the Nazi killing of Jews in the Holocaust. Many more were displaced as refugees with their camp in Ngara, Tanzania becoming the largest refugee concentration in the world. The Roman Catholic and Protestant Churches were not actively involved in reducing or restraining violence and in some cases with their leading members being sufficiently involved to be prosecuted. How did this situation come about in a country so extensively Christianised?

Ruanda was a small overcrowded country with a population about eight times higher than it had been at the beginning of the century. Their traditional culture stressed obedience to authority and conformity to family activities, both of which ideals were reinforced by subsequent colonial administrators. The kingdom had been abolished and replaced by a corrupt military ruling through a well structured local government hierarchy of whom 'the majority carried out their murderous duties with attitudes varying from careerist eagerness to sullen obedience' (Prunier, 1995: 245).

The Roman Catholic Church predominated and somewhat naturally had initially concentrated their educational efforts on the Tutsi ruling caste and then turning to an equally biased education of the Hutu and finally, to the support of the Hutu dominated republic. Indeed the country has been described as having being co-administered by the Roman Catholic Church and a corrupt Hutu clique (Prunier, 1995: 351).

However organised it may have been initially, the main agents of the genocide were the ordinary peasants themselves under the requirements of obedience, so that they killed all the Tutsi whom they could find of any age and sex as well as supposed supporters of opposition parties and a broad class of intellectuals including doctors, teachers and clergy.

A small number of Christians did try and protect those who took refuge in churches but 'most of the Church hierarchies were at best useless and at worst accomplices.... There was not the slightest trace of collective guilt among the Christian clergy. The Church (had) placed itself in an advantageous moral position... (and) had paid heavily... in the killing of staff and the destruction and looting of its institutions. Most of the Hutu priests looked the other way because of the close association between the Hutu republic and the Catholic Church' (Prunier, 1995: 250-51).

This was not a situation in which people were taken away and killed centrally but massacres of neighbours wherever they were sheltering or could be hunted down. Very obviously practising Christians killed practising fellow believers and that the moral teachings of that faith were almost universally ignored. Further that the Christian leaders made virtually no effort to stop the slaughter because of their closeness to the political leaders. It is too easy to moralise and to suggest that the Christians should have done more when the social environment entangled them much too closely for them to take any more than nominal initiatives. However, the small Muslim community less than 2 per cent of the total population sheltered each other which was combined with their refusal to divide themselves ethnically into Hutu and Tutsi and their small numbers and minority status made this moral cohesiveness possible.

Once violence has broken out for reasons which are not directly religious, the larger the religious group the more difficult it becomes to exercise effective control over moral behaviour and it is at best left to individuals of firm beliefs in moral rectitude to put them into practise at some cost to themselves. Few have the character for unrecognised martyrdom. Let us now look at the roles of religions in the preservation of non-human life, the environment and property.

11

Religions and the Preservation of Non-human Life, Property and the Environment

We have seen that religious behaviour has significant influences on how long humans live and the diseases from which they suffer as the result of religious practices following both the Great and Little Traditions in most societies. These influences also extend to animal life which may be directly or indirectly preserved by religious practices. Religious believers have many food taboos which avoid killing at all such as the Jains or the killing of certain species, particularly the Hindu devotion to the cow. Religions which have become institutionalised have areas devoted to their religious practices which become in effect nature reserves. Of course religions in their buildings and their surroundings preserve large areas from industrial development and in many cases provide breathing spaces for urban populations while in many areas religious beliefs protect water resources and certain forests from exploitation.

The Religious Protection of Animal Life

The religious protection of animal life has a very long history. Since Hinduism and Buddhism believe in the transmigration into another living thing of something when the human dies, their followers for centuries have protected and freed animals which they believe might be the repositories of some transmigrating element in the search for detachment from worldly desires. This has preserved certain species which might otherwise have disappeared or at least diminished in numbers; large numbers of fish congregate round the steps of monasteries on the Bangkok river where fishing does not take place.

Some Buddhist monasteries near Bangkok protect large numbers of monkeys as do Hindus in Ajmer and in both cases these animals adopt quite aggressive behaviour in getting their food from visitors, market stalls and houses and the devout hold funeral services for those which have been electrocuted by overhead power lines. So do the deer in the Buddhist temples of Nara, Japan snatching foods from visitors and they are to be seen at night feeding on the central reservations of the main city roads. The meditation caves of Buddhism and Taoism in India and China are the living and nesting sites of bats and birds as are the belfries of many Christian churches.

The Chinese treated the grounds around the tombs of the sacred emperors as parks in which all living creatures had some part of the sacred character of the dead, thus serving religious and recreational purposes at the same time (Schafer, 1962: 280-1). The area in which Confucius and his descendants are buried remains today a natural area in which only the stone monuments have altered the light forest environment.

Even if there is no specific prohibition of killing animals, respect for religious areas continues to inhibit such action. Christian churches discourage pigeons and bats by fitting special doors and wire mesh rather killing them. Some mammals particularly in urban areas favour churches and churchyards as habitats. Out of 285 church porches in Northhamptonshire, Britain, 87 were occupied by bats of four different species (Greenoak, 1985).

Thus fauna will invade areas where religions either encourage or enable their presence. The holiest parts of some Hindu temples are only entered by a few priests but contain bats and birds. Some temples not only protect monkeys but other animals as well. The temple dedicated to the goddess Karni Ma in Bikaner, India is estimated to be the home of thousands of rats which has certainly gone on for several centuries (Reynolds and Tanner, 1983: 227). Here again there is no boundary between these rats and the outside world; they come and go as they please over the borders of the sacred area.

The sacred area surrounding the pilgrimage centre of Katagarama in southern Sri Lanka covers about 12 square kilometres and contains Buddhist, Hindu and Muslim shrines with moneys, birds and lizards in abundance living under protected conditions. These animals gain their livelihoods from the rubbish left behind by the thousands of pilgrims as well as from religion-inspired benevolence.

The Religious Challenge of Animals Produced for Food

People have always raised animals for food but the large scale industrialization of the processes is largely a modern product of the Christian West. It has brought serious challenges to all main religions over the treatment of animals. There is a tension between the pressures to achieve an even more efficient production of low-cost food and growing concern for animal suffering. Although some restraints do exist through secular legislation, there are often cruel distortions in the lives of animals through factory farming. Dairy farming demands methods to increase milk production and the cow is robbed of her calf at an unnaturally early stage. Pork and bacon producers produce large pigs which have proved to be chronic invalids (Midgely, 1992: 28). Chickens spend their lives in tiny enclosures in vast batteries to increase and facilitate egg production.

Such animal production has profound effects on land and water use. It takes something like ten times as much land and many times as much water to obtain the same amount of protein from animal than from plant foods. This has greatly distorted land use patterns, turning much potential arable land and forest into pasture and where irrigation is needed, diverting much water. The overproduction of cattle in arid lands leads to their concentration round artificial water-points and causing nearby erosion. The accumulation of large amounts of dung in crowded cattle feeding lots poses serious disposal problems.

It is partially due to a religious inspired conscience about this organised violence to the natural lives of animals that public opinion over these problems is now moving in a more humane and constructive direction. It is in Christian lands that the main pressure for improving the care and protection of animals has come about and not as in Eastern religions where it is a product of belief in transmigration and not as concern for the lives of animals as such.

The Effects of Religion on the Keeping of Cows

The protection of cows from the violence of meat-eaters is prominent in Hinduism. Their veneration of the cow is ancient and may have grown out of its utility for farmers as an essential draught animal which also provided meat, hides, milk, manure and fuel as well as complex religious ideas unknown and unneeded by modern Hindus. The protection of cows probably grew in importance with urbanization and the shortage of fuel so that its dried dung became valuable for cooking.

There has also been the stressing of this veneration by a succession of historic charismatic figures who related this to both moral and ritual importance. Mahatma Gandhi called the cow a companion and its veneration the distinguishing mark of the Hindu (Gandhi, 1954: 3). 'Cow protection is the dearest possession of the Hindu heart. It is the one concrete belief common to all Hindus. He who does not believe in cow protection cannot possibly be a Hindu' (Manley and Neech, 1950: 111-12). The pro-cow movement was also politically useful in the wider campaigns against beef-eating Muslims and British.

Hindu cow worship however goes further than protection; to eat its five products is the most powerful means of ritual purification. The religious importance of the cow will probably continue as it provides a popular ritual focus and must remain a centre of a network of economic usages. It is unlikely that supporters and organisers of this opposition to the killing of cows anticipated the problems that it would cause.

This contemporary religious view of the cow appears anachronistic and ignorant of effective animal husbandry. To Western even religiously sensitive eyes it presents a ridiculous picture of cows wandering the main streets of many Indian towns so that other aspects of its protection tend to be forgotten and thought irrelevant. Various Hindi phrases in current use speak of the cow as being like a mother and as a channel to heaven, giving it a uniqueness without any parallels in Western languages and their cultural appreciation of certain animals.

On the other hand this veneration is seldom accompanied by the high standards of animal husbandry required by modern farming methods. In India even the accidental killing of a cow has caused communal rioting. Devout caste Hindus perform cow worshipping ceremonies at funerals and at festivals relating to Krishna and Lakshmi.

Keeping the cow alive has important social and economic consequences. The Indian Government's Expert Committee on the

Prevention of the Slaughter of Cattle estimated that there were 20 million uneconomic cattle in the country (Nandra *et al.*, 1955), although this is thought to be an exaggeration since uselessness is a matter of degree. Even a decrepit animal will produce dung to be used as a household fuel and can be grazed on otherwise useless land such as road verges. It has been estimated that the amount of dung used as fuel annually in India is the equivalent of between 35 and 131 million tons of coal or 68 million tons of firewood (Parrack, 1969: 53).

The cow is a more costly milk producer than the water buffalo. The latter are important for ploughing as there are not enough cows to provide a pair of bullocks for as many as one-third of all small farmers (Harris, M. 1966: 53). This is partly because the demand comes at the peak season for ploughing (Shastri, 1960: 159). Despite this distinction Hindus tend to keep cows and Muslims water buffaloes, even though as milk producing animals there is a 20 per cent lower cash return (Lodrick, 1981: 241-2).

This does not mean that cows are not killed and eaten apart from food shortages. Indian Christians, Muslims, lower caste Hindus, eat beef whenever the opportunity arises. The Untouchables have beef in their diet more frequently as they dispose of the carcasses of dead animals.

Even this veneration for the cow does not mean that economic factors are ignored and Hindu farmers are careful in husbanding resources; they calculate what forage to give what animals and do not feed the whole herd equally (Srinivas, 1958: 4). In one Hindu village the only exploitation was by powerful well-to-do men with too many cows and landless people wanting to get into cattle ownership who grazed their animals on common land (Freed and Freed (1972: 399-408). Furthermore the concept of cow sanctity often induces farmers to borrow money to replace those which have died and risk the dangers of indebtedness.

The veneration of the cow has led to the survival of large numbers of partially useless animals which are allowed considerable public licence wandering the streets and eating food exposed in shops. In the crowded Ganges valley which has a chromic shortage of fodder abandoned cows are a costly nuisance in the countryside where they break into the fields of growing crops (Mayadas, 1954: 29).

Inevitably there is a scale of utility against which the preservation of the cow is measured. When possible starvation and deprivation face the owners of cows, they will sacrifice animals not essential for their survival (Dandekar, 1959: 352) and even these will go for slaughter if the pressure is extreme enough (Parrack, 1969: 36-8). The 1943 Bengal Famine coincided with an increased demands for beef from the armed forces fighting Japan and there was a rush to sell animals for slaughter. This led to the legal prohibition of killing cattle needed for ploughing, milk production and the breeding of bullocks (Knight, 1954: 141). In general Hindu cattle owners will neglect their animals to dèath rather than slaughter them and will only sell them under duress directly or indirectly to Muslim butchers (Roy, 1955: 15).

Where the cow has economic uses these are subordinated to religious considerations. Certainly cows are slaughtered but those involved in this are both socially and religiously segregated from mainstream Hindu society as Outcastes or Muslims. There are sanctions against even the reasonable need to shoo cows out of shops where they are eating grain on display for sale. Although the dung is always useful and it is collected immediately from the streets wherever it is deposited, religious and social norms prevent the full rational utilization of the cow.

Hindu Refuges for Keeping Cows Alive

Hinduism is unique in having large numbers of refuges 'gowshalas, pinjrapoles or gosadans' for neglected cows. These are complex institutions maintained by contributions from the devout, somewhat analogous to homes for dogs and horses supported by Westerners with the difference than none are ever humanly destroyed. Data from the 1980s showed that in India they accommodated 550,000 cows of whom some 174,000 were kept there until they died. They contribute nothing to their own maintenance other than the residual value of their carcasses, hides and dung (Lodrick, 1981: 201).

The importance of these refuges has long been recognised by the Indian Government and the First Five Year Plan anticipated that there would be an increased of 160 such refuges maintaining a further 320,000 cows. It is certain that there will be a further increase in the number of such refuges coinciding with the political and religious pressures from Hindu nationalists.

It is estimated that each animal eats 10 kg of forage per day amounting to an annual consumption of 1.66 millions kilograms of fodder in a country facing chronic as well as seasonal shortages of fodder. They compete directly with more useful cattle for available supplies in times of scarcity and the administrators of these refuges with their greater purchasing power can effectively outbid local farmers.

On the other hand during the 1972-74 Gujarat drought these refuges were able to keep alive some useful animals placed there by farmers who could no longer maintain them. Although many died some were returned to farming when the rains finally came. Some farmers pay rent to these institutions for keeping their cows on the understanding that if their cows begin to produce milk, they can be reclaimed (Gourou, 1963: 125). Overall we can see the prevention of commercialised violence to cows is a result of their fundamental religious importance for millions of caste Hindus and this influences the political as well as the ecology environment of India.

Cattle in Tribal Religions

Cattle as centres around which the ritual lives of tribal peoples are maintained is quite common. The Nilotic tribes of the southern Sudan, the Dinka, the Nuer and the Shilluk as well as the Maasai, the Karamajong and other tribes of eastern Africa depend for their livelihoods on cattle and they have been described as 'cattle cultures' (Herskovitz, 1926).

Cattle keeping is the connecting link between many social, political, economic and religious functions and they are too emotionally valuable to be raised just to be slaughtered for food; they are used in the ceremonies for the initiation of men and in sacrifices for displeased gods and ancestors, but even in this something less important can be sacrificed but represents a cow. The Dinka reverence their cattle and call them 'brothers' dividing up the carcass into shares reflecting the recipient's relationship to the owner as happens in most cattle owning cultures such as the Chins of Myanmar (Stevenson, 1943: 132). On reaching puberty each Dinka youth receives a bullock dedicated to his ancestors.

The economic and religious life of the non-Hindu Todas of the Nilgiri hills in southern India (Mandelbaum, 1941: 22-3) centres on their sacred buffaloes and the Chins of north-western Myanmar use their semi-domesticated mithun, the wild ox, as sacred links in sacrifices to obtain better fertility and in placating the spirits (Simoons, 1968: 260). The Sukuma of Tanzania dedicate goats and cows to their ancestors and their milk can only be drunk by patrilineal relatives.

The General Protection of Animals by Religions

Perhaps only in Hinduism is there a close and practical connection between beliefs and the protection of animals particularly the cow so that the general reluctance of both Buddhists and Hindus to kill is part of a general distaste for killing. In Hinduism the non-violent concept of '*ahimsa*' forbids the taking of the life of any living thing (Laws of Manu, 1969.6: 45-81) and is an important determinant of wider Hindu behaviour (Brandon 1970: 48).

Jainism also believes this and its more orthodox believers go to great lengths to avoid killing even insects and earth worms so they do not cultivate and even wear veils over their mouths to avoid the possibility of killing insects. These religions and Buddhism get no material rewards from their avoidance of killing but is seen as meritorious acts which in the long run contribute to the release of individuals from the cycle of constantly changing but seemingly endless Wheel of Existence.

The reluctance of Buddhists and Hindus to kill has arguably contributed to making them less environmentally aggressive than either Christians or Moslems. They protect rabid dogs and disease carrying insects and U Nu the sometime premier of Myanmar records in his autobiography is reluctance to flush his lavatory after use because of the ants in its basin. Tibetan monks may put their robes out of doors at night so that the low temperatures will kill the bugs (Ekvall, 1964: 76), but even this action would send the perpetrator to one of the eight cold Buddhist hells.

Along with the Jains many people are vegetarians, although in some societies such as the Orang Asli of Malaysia (Bolton, 1972: 789-99) the eating of animal protein is confined to men. However, many people in all religions avoid eating meat although their reasons may be philosophical as much as religious, economic and personal but the repercussions of these avoidances are widespread and important.

The Selective Protection of Wild Animals by Religions

We have seen that the Eastern religions are reluctant to kill any animals but almost all believers may eat meat on special occasions in which economics and availability are important correlates. The Hindu protection of the cow is a special case because it is so widespread and is not the taboo of a particular tribe, clan or lineage. Muslims will not eat pork which would in any case have been difficult to raise in dry environments but they eat camels. In Indonesia where conversion to one of the Great Traditions was politically required, discussion about which religion to choose often related to whether the prospective convert wanted to eat pork or not. Christians have no religious restrictions on what they can eat perhaps as a reflection of the low status of early Christian groups and such restrictions would have handicapped the possibilities of conversion.

At the lower levels of social organisation and personal relationships there are individuals with personal preferences and taboos which may be common enough if assessed for a whole society but not of much ecological significance. In many parts of the world where people see themselves as members of lineages, clans and tribes, certain animals will not be killed or eaten. But whatever the classification employed, it would be unlikely if not impossible that an area would be occupied by a single endogamous human group with similar taboo restrictions in their diets.

A sacralised animal may be protected in one area predominantly occupied by a clan with this taboo but will be killed and eaten in neighbouring areas; thus there would be an ecological levelling out. In some cases there is a coincidence of environmental benefits and totemic beliefs. The Australian Ananda tribe's major totemic sites are the most favourable ones for the Red Kangaroo which they do not eat (Newsome, 1980), so that their taboo has ensured the survival of this rarer type of animal.

The Absence of Any Traditional Concept of Environmental Conservation

The respect for nature as a theme has been capitalised by contemporary American Indians as the antithesis of modern quasi-Christian destructiveness is probably an illusion. The American Nastazi Indians' religion did not prevent their destruction of their environment and their own social extinction despite their extensive irrigation systems. The Plains Indians depended on the buffalo which was incorporated in their religious rituals, but they participated in overkills as soon as horses and guns enabled them to do so. There was no controlling ideology of restraint since they believed that the seasonal appearance of the buffalo herds was attributed to their re-emergence from below a northern lake. Their beliefs about the buffalo were unrelated to any conception that stocks of animals were limited and had to be conserved.

Thus it seems unlikely that any religious taboo against the killing and eating of a particular animal was related to the concept of conservation in general or in particular. Among the Australian Aborigines the restriction on eating one's own totem animal was out of respect for their ancestors and their future spirit children who may be currently living in them. The original pressure for the conservation of any animal must have been a combination of social and religious factors under the impetus of a long forgotten charismatic personality.

Of course, some societies may have a feeling of the need to protect an environment by not behaving badly within its boundaries as the Sherpas do as far as possible when they accompany climbers on the Himalayan mountains but this has very little or any influence on conserving that environment which is being progressively threatened by outsiders.

For religion to combine with social needs so that an environment is protected rather than progressively destroyed, there would seem to be a need for a restricted living space and a religion that allows for a combination of both inexactness and exactness. Bali is a special case in which the local form of Hinduism has provided a system of religious practices which fitted into the agricultural needs of a crowded island depending on irrigated rice growing.

As an island they have been able to retain their traditional interpretation of Hinduism. This faith defines time as a structure composed of many interlocking cycles based on a rhythm of growth of both the agricultural and social worlds. It rejects the concept of a linear scientific agricultural cycle and any direct relationship between this and a particular god.

It is a religion of holy water centred on a supreme water temple on the one dominating mountain which contains shrines to 147 different deities (Grader, 1969). Each farmer has his own shrine and there are further temples where water enters a group of fields. Rituals follow catchment areas not political boundaries. Regional water temple's containing many different social associations set the crop patterns and irrigation schedules (Lansing, 1991: 44-54). The replacement of this system by modern secular agricultural methods led to a progressive deterioration in crop yields and field and water channel maintenance.

Religious Prevention of Violence to the Environment

For religious actions to prevent violence to the environment the rituals have to be seen as personal and not just something in fulfilment of an abstract idea that the environment is something which should be protected for the good of all. All societies contain divisive and divided social groups who may agree about very little.

The doctrine of '*ahimsa*', the protection of life has been extended by both Buddhist and Hindus to the protection of trees. In the foot hills of the Himalayas the *Chipko* movement of women has conserved forest areas in a combination of Hindu reasoning and their own interests as women who if nearby forests are destroyed for commercial reasons, would have to walk longer distances to collect firewood and fodder (Dwivedi, 1990: 209). When a large commercial felling was planned in Bad Yargana, the local leader went on hunger strike and some thousands kept guard on every tree scheduled for felling and after three weeks the contractor capitulated. In another case women kept watch on the threatened trees for a week accompanied by readings from the *Bhagavad Gita* (Guha, 1990: 162-70).

The Lord Buddha was born, achieved Enlightenment and taught under trees so that they have a special significance for Buddhists. The idea of ordaining trees into Buddhist monasticism is alleged to have come from a monk who cut down a tree in a monastery compound and then died unexpectedly which was interpreted as the result of his sacrilege.

As this was combined with the belief that mature trees had individual spirits, this ritual of ordaining trees culminating in wrapping round them the yellow robes worn by monks has spread throughout Thailand since cutting down such trees is now the equivalent of murdering monks (Callicott, 1994: 234). At the request of the King, tree ordination was made part of the celebrations of the 50th anniversary of his coronation. Ceremonies of tree ordination now involve representatives of provincial governments, ministries and international aid agencies which combines political and ecological correctness with Buddhist and animist understandings (Tannenbaum, 2000).

In addition the idea that certain places such as burial grounds and parts of forests should be protected from the violence of destroying anything living there is widespread and they are more protected by the acceptance that some undefined religious essence is in occupation than by any legislation.

Religious cemeteries may become intentionally or unintentionally nature reserves. There are 103 cemeteries in London and that of the 33 acre one at Bow is astonishingly overgrown (Meller, 1999: 280) and Highgate even more so and now has probably reverted to the type of woodland which existed there in medieval times. Some of these cemeteries have parts managed as nature reserves.

Perhaps more important are sacred groves in both Africa and Asia in which only dead wood may be collected, surrounding springs and along watersheds. The large number of such sacred groves in India have preserved plant species which have become very rare or extinct elsewhere (Gadgil and Vartak, 1975: 314-20). In the Pare mountains of northern Tanzania there are sacred groves varying in size with the importance of the matters with which they are related and have become important as contemporary political rallying places (Kimambo and Omari, 1972: 111-21). Many large forest trees in Myanmar have spirit shrines attached to them and in Thailand there are sacred groves at prominent places in National Parks in which there are contemporary spirit shrines filled with recent offerings.

This religious revulsion for the destruction of living things is more extreme with Jainism in which believers are asked to appreciate the pain of the tree being cut into planks. Overall it seems that where religious beliefs coincide with material advantages for those involved, they are likely to be followed. The protection of a traditional sacred spring in Bukoba, Tanzania was turned into a Roman Catholic shrine to the Virgin Mary, providing clean water to the advantage of both secular and religious users and indeed this type of protection is common.

This type of environmental protection which can only cover small pockets of land but in Timor large areas of forest were traditionally regarded as sacred and protected from everyday cultivation and timber exploitation. The newly independent government is attempting to make these areas coincide with official forest reserves in order to preserve their diminishing areas of primary forest (Mc William. 2001). Overall it can be seen that religious practices have a significant and restraining influence on the violent exploitation of the environment and the use of animals.

PART D

Comparative Factors in Considering Religious Violence

Violence that correlates in some way to religious beliefs and practices is both complex in its isolatable showings and immensely varied in the forms which it takes. It would be inadequate to seek explanations working back from the extremes of contemporary horrors which the mass media have headlined and kept in the forefront of local, national and international public opinion.

Except for psychotic and chemically induced behaviour which we have not attempted to include since it is too individual, sporadic and difficult to define, violence of any sort is the result of complex intermingling of innumerable factors which come to the point of observable action, infrequently and in certain circumstances.

Among children at least four types of aggressiveness have been isolated, instrumental, hostile/teasing, defensive and games aggression and these would differ in the motivating circumstances, methods used, their association with other types of behaviour in the individual and how they fit into that individual's concepts (Feshbach, 1970). If that was complex enough that of adults is certainly more difficult.

In adults the diversity is so great that there is no general agreement as to how it should be categorized for individual aggressiveness and the problem becomes even more complex when masses of people are involved; instrumental or planned aggression, emotional aggression, felonious aggression, psychopathic violence and for our purposes the anti-social violence approved by the reference group (Tinklenberg and Ochberg, 1981).

Those in positions of authority in politics, social welfare, religious institutions and those involved in law and order will always want to know when violence of any sort is likely to occur and they seek exactness. Certainly it is possible to state that Hindu-Muslim violence is more likely to occur at the times of the major festivals with the proviso that it can occur at any time and in any locality. This is just about as accurate as saying that violence may occur at football and cricket matches.

We also need to know what makes this or that inter-or-intra religious violence noticeable when violent incidents with similar backgrounds occur in great numbers and are solved within communities without being classified as religious or indeed anything out of the normal since drunkards will always abuse others, quarrels will always erupt and children misbehave.

This leaves us with a sub-stratum of persistent violence correlated to religion in India, Israel, Croatia and Serbia, just as the physical abuse of women under a cloak of religious justifications is commonplace in nominally Christian and actively Islamic societies.

Suicide 'bombers' for religious reasons are not uncommon but their profiles are not similar to 'normal' suicides so that again a sub-stratum background provides the motivation and the necessary means but to presuppose similarity in their actions rather than in the horrific results is to go beyond the available evidence.

So we always have an enabling environment. A framework of religious thinking, a perceived target and certain people who see violence as a means to an end and if we accept as indeed we must that the people who are involved in religious violence are not out of their minds, then there has to be an assessment of the credits and debits for being involved in violence. Obviously these people are not going to be violent unless there is some conscious or unconscious assessment of the profits that are likely to be gained by such potentially dangerous actions.

Any possible typology of violence correlated to religion has to integrate the killing of some three thousand suspected witches and wizards in Usukuma, Tanzania over a ten year period with the killing of the same number in the destruction of the World Trade Centre. But these are small scale killings in comparison to the grotesque enormity of the Holocaust killings of millions of Jews and the Indonesian and Cambodian killings of the mid 1960s and late 1970s.

12

The Problem of Logic and Social Behaviour

Preconceived Conclusions and Religious Violence

There are a number of interrelated issues in reaching conclusions about religious violence which merit closer attention. If government officials and even researchers are convinced that religion is at the basis of violence, it is not surprising that this is what they find to be a fact to the exclusion of other considerations. Of course, for political and administrative reasons there is usually a rush to conclude so as to take action and to avoid further disruptions. There is often a reluctance to accept that religion may be a factor.

Sometimes the evidence is quite clear as in the attribution of Hindu-Muslim rioting in Varanasi in October 1809 which was stated in official documents to have been caused by a quarrel over the Muharram processions. In fact Muharram occurred in February 1810 (Pandey, 1990: 34-6). This is not to state that such processions are not the occasion for Hindu-Muslim hostility but that it could not have been the cause of that specific riot. The writers of this report found what they expected to find.

Much the same could be said of the killing or suicide of the Jewish community in York, England in 1190 which has been attributed to anti-Semitism but subsequent research has suggested that a more probable reason was the accumulation of small scale indebtedness which could be cleared by killing the money lenders and burning their houses with their records of indebtedness and that the well-to-do who depended on Jewish business acumen were not involved. All we get from that is the knowledge that Jews were then good at business and were probably more approachable than rich Christian business men and landlords.

For some decades after the end of the colonial era there was a general tendency to attribute communal tensions to divide and rule policies which had led to Hindu-Muslim tensions. However, it was the Muslims who had pressured the British government for separate representations to prevent being outvoted by the Hindu majority as well as the Hindu demands for their religious laws to be given formal legal recognition. This view also forgets that the horrors of the Partition of India and the contemporary increasing demands that Hindu rather than secular principles should dominate the Indian government's overall policies.

Up to quite recently the predominating influence on average Hindus was on the local status of their sub-caste and their more individualised religious practices and for ordinary Muslims to have their own communal worship. In such situations it would have been more likely that a wide range of social, political and economic factors would have contributed to violence. This would have been more easily classifiable as inter-religious on a national framework of some definitional simplicity which obviated the need for more detailed and local investigations (Pandey, 1990: 198-200).

There is also the fact that the social sciences with their European theoretical foundations rest very much on the assumption that if an individual adheres to or belongs to one classification of behaviour, he or she cannot belong to one which is by definition basically different. In Gujarat there were at one time numbers of Indians who considered themselves to be both Hindus and Muslims and that this was sufficiently obvious socially for them to see no difficulty in telling census enumerators that they belonged to two diametrically opposed religions at the same time. In the 1911 Census over 200,000 stated that they belonged to both religions.

The social sciences in their aim to be as scientific as possible have great difficulties in coping with multiple causations and the necessities of formal logic. Individuals rather more than communities will have fluctuating understandings and commitments which are constantly varying without much realisation that this has occurred.

But then of course it was not at the same time since they followed the public practices of each faith when it was convenient to do so. In general it can be said that obvious Hindus would not be allowed into mosques and obviously Muslims not into Hindu temples. But beyond that communities and communal festivals in which almost everyone would participate as much for fun as for religious reasons. Perhaps it is more likely that where there is a felt need Christians, Hindus and Muslims will be found in the sacred places of many different faiths and that the guardians of these places would not be so foolish as to bar their shrines to petitioners contributing gifts on the grounds of attributed affiliation, apart from the fact that their presence there might be sowing the seeds of conversion. It is an individual search for relief from misfortune and as such there would not be any need to parade any more overall commitment to a particular Great Tradition. Christians and Muslims came to the Kumbha Mela to bathe in the Ganges at an auspicious time, just as Buddhists, Hindus and Muslims came to the shrine of the Christian saint in a Columbo Roman Catholic church.

There is also the fact that if such activities are divided into religion and magic with the practices of the Great Traditions being aimed at the more abstract and impersonal attainments of these faiths, then almost all believers are to some extent always involved in the magical practices of the Little Traditions, part of more traditional and ancient faiths which are supposed to have been superseded by the major faiths. Thus 'luck' is constantly in the thinking and practices of Christians and Muslims and since Buddhism is in essence not a religion but a system of philosophy, its contemporary forms in Myanmar are almost entirely magical. It must be extremely difficult for the ultra-orthodox to confine themselves to religious precepts in all that they do.

When it comes to religious and indeed any sort of collective violence, there is no such thing as a uniform crowd with its members all participating in similar ways and the justifications for their presence in a violent crowd will be different. Some people derive direct satisfaction from participation in collective violence on religious theme such as adolescents and the poor who are usually available; they are the participants in widespread looting which is always selective in what is taken and from whom (Quarantelli and Dynes, 1970: 168-82) and so are the permanent minority who always ready to confront the police as the local symbols of authority (Momboise, 1969: 12-14).

Then there are those who are personally involved with some broad feeling of religious empowerment and feel that something must be done without having a picture of what should be done; those who are there out of group loyalty and may find it difficult not be out on the street, and the spectators for whom a religious riot is an exciting break in a dull life. Finally and most importantly the exploiters with a depersonalised perspective who may organise but do not participate (Turner & Killian, 1972: 28).

This perspective of dividing up the violent crowd by its personalised characteristics can only apply to 'flare-ups' and the seasonal rioting, the so-called 'marching season' which marks out inter-Christian rioting in Northern Ireland. While in the Palestinian situation there may be a distinction between those who are persistently involved in violence, the stone throwers who have probably been arrested and beaten by the Israeli police and those who wish that the whole problem would disappear even if it means the stability from permanent Israeli dominance, the substratum of support for a nearly universal Arab feeling of injustice must remain. In northern Nigeria and the southern Sudan the attempted imposition of Islamic law and political suzerainty can only have led to a similar substratum of persistent opposition.

It seems clear that modern Islam and Hinduism rather than divided and denominational Christianity has been enabled and bolstered if not created by the ease of modern communication. Electronics provide national and international news priority over localism unless it is in the national interest to bring it to the fore and that the complexity of religious violence recognised. Any understanding of the persistence of the potential of religion to be a factor in violence is not helped by intellectual secular sense of superiority which Nehru expressed so well 'Religion whether it was Hinduism or Islam or Buddhism or Christianity did not attract me. It seemed to be closely associated with superstitious practices and dogmatic beliefs, and behind it lay a method of approach to life's problems which was certainly not that of science. There was an element of magic about it, an uncritical credulousness, a reliance on the supernatural' (Nehru, 1991: 26). Whether the inhabitants of India read this or have just reacted to their government's secularist policies, it must have been a major contribution to their religious reactions. It is perhaps salutary to remind ourselves that 'the world view (of science) itself is not less abstract than the traditional and consequently understood by a few, the rest claiming it on the basis of hearsay' (Singh, 1995: 59) and that this applies globally and not just to less economically developed societies.

The Creation of Facts from Belief

It is basic to any religion that its beliefs are believed in and that these beliefs by individuals and groups form the bases on which the social consequences of religion affect its practitioners, others surrounding them and the general social and physical environments in which these people live. This much is clear and it is only in Islam with its global commitments and politico-religious aspirations with its divine injunctions enshrined in the Koran that beliefs correlate with certain inter- and intra-religious violence; the macro level of theological understandings.

In any search for accurate correlations between violence and religion there is a necessary concentration on obtaining and evaluating facts and in all situations the only facts which are often known with some certainty may be published but inaccurate casualty figures. Similarly, affirmations to a particular faith that they are Christians, Hindus or Muslims do not give any details of the degrees of commitment from a near total involvement of a hermit or *saddhu* to the nominal attendance at religious rites of passage of many who go along with these religious ceremonies because it is what their relatives wish and the community expect. Often these casualty figures and damage to property assessments have little accuracy since they are created by agencies which have a reason to escalate or diminish the damage that has been caused; there is nothing impartial in statistics that relate to religious activities particularly violent ones. Figures for road accidents come from the police, hospitals and insurance companies so that there is the possibility of some accuracy. Figures for murder and serious assault in any society, particularly when these are related to religious confrontations are probably more imaginative than accurate and at the back of such figures there are worries about public opinion.

Much religious activity is the result of stories which are passed from one individual to another without any malicious intent or the wish to make situations worse. Every society has well-worn social channels of gossip which are as likely to be about religion as any other topic. But they are nevertheless stories and a story is defined as 'a narrative, true or presumed to be true, relating to important events and celebrated persons of a more or less remote past' (Oxford English Dictionary, 1965: 1041).

Many of these stories have benign effects such as the story of successful prayers at particular shrines or provided by particular religious practitioners which give comfort to those who go there or who have gone there and used these opportunities for reducing their own difficulties. It would be incorrect to parallel these stories too closely with gossip as they are believed to be important and accepted as facts which can never have the presumed accuracy of a bank statement.

Those who record these stories which are told to them by religious believers, tend to treat them with some scepticism as at least being questionable until confirmed with other data. They are probably classifiable as a form of oral history which from all the work which has been done on the accuracy of both long and short term human memory, must not rate highly as evidence. Most recorders of such data will feel that they are free to speculate on what may have happened; that the numbers of miraculous cures at a particular shrine are based on human cupidity rather than on some sort of divine action for the benefit of particular petitioners or penitents or a form of psycho-biological coincidence which has worked in ways which are not yet understood by scientists.

Unless the teller of stories relating to religious issues is a professional story-teller, these men and women believe what they are retailing to be true. There may be an element of doubt but that is no more than part of the weakness of belief which they are taught to withstand even if they do not do so for innumerable personal and social reasons. Among the Bulo of Mindoro in the Philippines there is 'the constant participation in obligatory collective rituals in which the legitimacy of religious belief derives from personal experience of the spirit world and not from tradition as interpreted by elders and specialists, from sacred texts and from the privileged experience of a charismatic figure' (Gibson, 1986: 148). It perhaps the more commonplace understandings of religion whether traditional or multinational that these are the experiences which are confirmed to others in stories that 'it happened to me and I tell you in faith'. Large numbers of people at all levels of intellectual capacity and in all cultures have had experiences which they have defined for themselves as religious which now form part of their personal understandings of reality.

It must be kept in mind that 'if men define situations as real, they are real in the consequences' (Thomas and Thomas, 1928: 572), thus stories whatever the bases for their telling are facts; they are received in a framework of thinking and acting which does not usually include the speculative thinking of professional outsiders. It requires a certain intellectual and social detachment to classify a story as rumour and thus to degrade its social usefulness and the social status of the retailer.

So defining a story as no more than rumour provides the evaluator with status and leaves the story intact in the minds of the listeners. The collection of 'rumours' immediately after the Buganda *coup d'etat* in 1966 (Tanner, 1978) showed 'many to have had religious elements. 'Some of these were explicable in terms of the tribal past, but others were modern in tone, and may be an expression of the self-deception of those who wished to escape from the present and were unable to find solace in the past'. However these 'rumours' were retailed as facts, not just as something which it was rather amusing to retail since they clearly could not have happened. If there was any scepticism at all it correlated to social status; farmers believed farmers and the educated believed the stories of the educated.

It is not only in the Cargo Cults that improbable events are remembered as facts on which people acted. 'In the Vailala Madness, the cult activities were remembered as true happenings, not frauds. The leaders had received messages via the flagpoles...Informants 'remembered' hearing a warning hum in the (bamboo wireless) poles... The steamer of the dead, moreover, actually had appeared...noises were heard as it disappeared without ever actually having been seen. Others remembered seeing her large red funnel and three masts and many saw her lights...As time passed the era of the Madness became more wonderful in memory' (Worsley, P., 1968: 91-92).

We have seen that news of a stressful religious event often spreads quickly and becomes the ignition for inter- and intra-religious fighting. The theoretical explanations for such crowd behaviour including epidemic hysteria, circular reactions, convergence, interpretive interaction, unconscious desire for aggression, conformity and emergent norms (Allport and Postman, 1947; Shibutani, 1966; Meerloo, 1950), are all interesting but speculative ideas which those who create such theories would rarely if ever apply to themselves in their own emotional commitments.

These theoretical explanations all start with the word rumour and assumes that those reacting to what they are told are acting in some ways that are deviant from the 'truth' and neither logical nor in the best interests of those reacting in this way. They all appear to ignore that those involved are not responding to rumours but to personally accepted and acceptable facts. When people are told of a 'good' priest or diviner or indeed a 'good' doctor they are always and inevitably acting in an almost complete absence of facts. We must conclude that personal beliefs in their consequences have to be seen as facts, however, much they can be discredited by analysis. Rumours are not to be thought of as such as belief in them involves various hopes.

So on occasions of religious violence, there will be certain facts but to search for them as creating anything more than primary causations is probably a waste of time related to the hope of obtaining a clear cut picture of a riot. The search for these 'facts' and their potential usefulness is always overshadowed by the intrusion of beliefs and rumours. The fact that an outsider reaches these evaluations rather than conclusions because they are just that, created by those who usually consider themselves intellectually superior to those involved, is rarely accepted. Religious violence and its correlates can never be reduced to facts. No more than possible factors which create an atmosphere helpful to violence.

Religions Enabling or Restricting Revolutions and their Violence

Most modern societies ostensibly if not in reality base their policies on some form of assessable logic; development plans are based as far as possible on economic realities and possibilities, no doubt guided by secular hopes; debated and discussed on the basis of their careful preparation and backed with statistical appendices.

These secular hopes which dominate the thinking of all planners even in those states dominated by Islamic theological utopianism, have to deal with the realities of food prices and the costs of providing social services. They have their appeal and indeed may be successful when there is some effective connection between the policies and what happens to the people for whom these policies are expected to make a difference.

The memories of the public unless it is kept alive by more recent events, soon forgets the misfortunes of the past. The disorder and humiliations of China in the last century prior to the introduction of Communist control, probably form no part of the thinking of ordinary contemporary peasants; cost of living and the ownership of property and land will dominate their thinking as much as it is likely to dominate the concerns of most people everywhere.

Most people have some concept of the ideal conditions in which they would like to live but their everydayness makes them to be of limited attractiveness to the population as a whole since they would be different for different human categories. These heterotopias (Foucault, 1986) are places that do exist and are reflected in the lives of the visibly rich and, of course, in some Christian religious communities trying to create the kingdom of God on earth such as the Mormons, Amish and some of the earlier monastic ones. These places enable, compel, and invite people to see themselves reflected in some specific utopias.

Human thinking and emotions need something more than this secular or religious-cum-secular realisations as a stimulus to hope and effort. So the major religions perform the important role of providing the images of utopias whether millennial or in the longer but still primary foreseeable future and in this they have the potential to be revolutionary and in some ways accidentally violent.

These religious utopias take many different forms in which the Islamic one is specifically detailed in the Koran with realities which are male oriented; the sexual delights provided there for men are not likely to appeal to women. The Christian one is not detailed and has denominational differences in how it may be interpreted. Hinduism has unity with some ill-defined deistic element and Buddhism which in its ideal form could not have a utopia as it would involve desire rather than detachment, has created an ill-defined paradise '*nirvana*' in its attributable 'nothingness'; individuals would certainly have to take a very miserable view of the possibilities and hopes of their own lives to aim at their own total extinction.

Traditional religions as they appeal to and involve circumscribed social groups have heterotopias which are domestically limited and do not go beyond social and to some extent achievable horizons; the successful appeasement of and involvement with the ancestors in African and Asian religions or more specifically cults, could only benefit a few. It would be pointless to burn incense at the shrine of another family's ancestors. In such situations communal religious violence could not arise as their worries and concerns would not be the same as other families and their neighbours. Ancestors would also not approve of disturbing whole neighbourhoods from which they would not gain. If there should be violence it would be primarily correlated to supra-communal economic, political and social difficulties and rivalries.

The major religions although they provide personal returns for the devout, provide utopias of wider range as well as having the appeal of being abstract, they can be woven into many different imaginations and the Islamic one with its specificities even more so. So religious utopianism can provide the impetus for changing what people experience as static social environments.

Peoples in developing societies have been particularly prone to utopian ideas; the colonial era provided the image of the higher standard of living of their rulers and their departure led to unfulfilled hopes of immediate betterment constantly rubbed in by the images shown in the mass media, the floods of well-to-do tourists and aid workers. In this failure lay the religious and other motivated eruptions in Zaíre, Zambia and Nigeria. The appeal of the Islamic utopia lies in its exactness and the uniformity with which it has been popularised by the printing of the Koran in Arabic and then in other languages; revolutionary fundamentalism has the backing of a uniform concept of utopia which is absent as a stimulus from all other religions.

So in 19th century China reinterpretation of Christianity led to the Taiping rebellion aiming at the creation of a heavenly kingdom in the here and now and in the process wiped out an estimated twenty million people which was certainly not foreseen nor would it have made any difference to the compulsions of its leader and the appeal of his message to enormous numbers of Chinese. This was certainly exceptional but there have been other less horrendous examples of revolutionary and violent religious utopianism such as the Saya San rebellion in 1930 Burma with all its paraphernalia of hope-creating rituals.

The creation of Israel as the fulfilment of as religious hope for a Jewish homeland in 1947 which was clearly realised through the support of the Western nations who had failed to stop or mitigate the Holocaust but its existence on Arab land has led to persisting inter-religious violence which can only have secular solutions.

We can see that throughout history religious ideas of utopia have been a major element in initiating secular changes and that in the main this has been a violent process. Purely secular ideas of utopia as in Communism rooted in immediate improvement in standards of living have not been successful. The success of the Western societies in providing better living conditions for their people and the failure of their own new leaders to be similarly successful except for their own personal betterment is a constant push towards revolutionary and violent religious movements.

13

Some Psychological Aspects of Religious Violence

Psychological factors are obviously important if only because they tend to get inflated into special approaches which detaches them from more common social issues, such as the mental difficulties faced by people who can no longer depend on the tried and tested ways of coping into which they have been socialised.

Individuals have a tendency to see the past as more anxiety free than the present and often relate this to patterns of religious belief and practice although there is never either adequate or socially available evidence that this was so. Since everyone experiences the present as full of change overriding any acceptance of the normal demographic processes of birth, morbidity and death which is usually seen and indeed experienced as mentally and socially disturbing, it is not difficult to anticipate widespread anxiety as lurking in every society.

Anxieties must have existed in the past when economics were just as unstable, the climate similarly unpredictable, politics just as intermittently violent and both mass and degenerative diseases much more lethal than in contemporary times when international aid and scientific medicine can at least modify the wholesale effects of some of these difficulties. Perhaps the veneer of science has suggested that these anxieties can be abolished; care is more in people's mind than coping. It is a contemporary world full of anxieties because the media have made it so.

Nevertheless in the past approved religious ways of coping were seen then and remembered in retrospect as effective, rain could be controlled, diseases put into remission if not cured, witchcraft was not a problem and self-sufficiency and its failures were shared by time tested methods.

The fact that this must have been largely illusionary does not alter the mentally accepted contrast between an imagined and satisfactory past and an unsatisfactory present for the majority who have not made a success of their contemporary lives in which consumer value tend to dominate.

In the past low key religious systems were both vague and comprehensive accounting equally well for success and failure. Now the Great Traditions with their abstractions and impersonality have nominally taken over from the Little Traditions and their social closeness. This has been combined with radical and rapid changes in almost everything they think about and do, combined with contrasts between the rich and the rest which were not so evident and widespread in the past. The controllers of misfortune are no longer controlled by the people for whom they act.

So the past is seen as having been better than the present and there is an emotional attractiveness in the impossible idea that it can be returned to. It is a contemporary life in which contrasts are forced into the consciousness of everyone by the mass media so that fear and anxiety has to be seen at least in part as the precursor of religious violence.

The Reactions to Loss of Identity

There is a divide rather than a gulf between those who kill in the name of religion and those who see this violence as something which at least in part as expressing their feelings without directly condoning it. This is the case in Northern Ireland where violence is not condoned but passively supported by the majority on both sides of the religious divide; which insures that the violence continues. Most Muslins would distinguish between the mass killings in the destruction of the World Trade Centre as both horrific and wrong, while perhaps approving this blow to American cultural dominance.

However, throughout the Muslim world and probably throughout the Third World generally, this has been combined with a far more general and indeed popular feeling that such acts fulfilled and indeed were appreciated as justified in supporting their feelings of anti-Americanism. The difference being that Muslims have a cohesive and ready made religious alternative rather than just a popular dislike for the magnitude of American material success.

The high standards of living depicted in what the African and Asian poor see as the generality of western living, is unquestionably accepted as the right way in which all should be able to live and have a chance to enjoy more or less immediately. Their animosity and their subliminal acceptance of this violence as it is paralleled by the self-sufficient religious thinking of the Muslims involved, is continually supported by the contrasts within their own societies; their humiliation in being governed by obviously corrupt rather than just undemocratic processes and receiving so little of the world's wealth. This is combined with a feeling that this poverty is to some considerable degree their own continuing fault and that of their parents. 'It is while living within this private sphere that most people in the world today are afflicted by spiritual misery. The feeling of impotence deriving from degradation, the failure to be understood and the inability of such people to make their voices heard. So it is neither Islam nor poverty that directly creates this widespread support for terrorists whose ferocity and ingenuity are unprecedented in human history; it is rather the crushing humiliation that has affected the Third World countries' (Pamuk, 2001).

Secularisation as the Framework of Political Thinking

We know that the newly independent India under the leadership of Nehru had a secular framework of political thinking in a country which the new leaders saw as deeply divided on religious grounds. This viewpoint was probably shared by the intellectual elite but not by the ordinary people who saw themselves primarily in terms of being Hindus or Muslims.

Many of the leaders of newly independent African states and certainly their senior civil servants, have been educated in secular European and American universities and their interventionist policies were less likely to see indigenous cultures with their specialised ideas and practices as something which should not be directly tampered with. They saw the traditional religious practices of their people not only as symptomatic of backwardness but also as a block to progress; an amalgam of nationalism, socialist ideas and a desire for modernisation.

During 1959-61 the Guinean authorities carried out an official demystification campaign; a state authorised and organised desecration of the secret religious artefacts of the Loma people. This campaign was carried out on a national scale and was aimed at destroying all local practices in contrast to Christianity and Islam which were subject to less oppression (Hojberg. 2002). It was part of a policy to breakdown the centrifugal forces countering the political hope for a national integration which included the official abolition of so-called traditional chieftaincy. This was also carried out in other countries after they had obtained political independence such as Myanmar, India and Tanzania.

According to people who were subject to this campaign, the masks which were central to their religious beliefs were burnt after a government official had explained that they did not give men any superior powers. Those who were forced to participate in these destructions were made to break customary religious taboos; the masks were unveiled in the presence of the uninitiated, ritual secrets were disclosed and in some cases ritual specialists were prosecuted. The authorities used theatre plays ridiculing these traditional specialists with press and radio campaigns explaining the futility of traditional religious practices and the utility of socialism and modern science. These effects of this campaign was to turn the public expression of traditional religious ideas into private ones which were just as useful and in demand as the abolished ones but for different social reasons; the traditional and largely undefined beliefs proved adaptable to persecution.

The Indonesian authorities considered traditional beliefs and practices to be not only a block to progress but an important part of the schismatic tendencies in a state which had nominal political unity but disparate cultures spread over different islands and peoples who had little in common. It was, therefore, decided that everyone must belong to one of the Great Tradition religions and that their religious affiliation would be recorded on their identity cards which enabled them to vote.

This led to mass conversions to Christianity, Islam and Hinduism in which islands and their inhabitants switched from one religion to another and in some cases moving through all three local options until at least for the time being settling on one (Spyer, 1996). This again will have destroyed the open aspects of each community's Little Traditions and created parallel secret practices to the official faiths to which they belonged.

These campaigns against the public aspects of the Little Traditions of these cultures will have had little effect on the underlying beliefs and practices in the minds of individuals and left them to be sustained in secret, diminishing their abilities to help them through their personal and communal difficulties.

Unitary Religious States and the Creation of Psychological Uncertainty

Little Traditions balance the wholesale nature of the Great Traditions and allow individuals to cope with their own problems in ways which in their own minds do not clash with their primary religious affiliations. Whenever religious practices and their structures are violently tampered with rather than altered by the slow processes of social and economic change, individuals are left without the means of easing their tensions within a loose framework of quasi-accepted religious practicalities; and this created uncertainty built on to the uncertainties which are already being experienced.

While a unitary hostility to all religion has been a feature of most Communist states, such a unitary approach making Islam the only recognised and indeed recognisable religion is a feature of Saudi Arabia which allows no specifically Christian presence or its rituals within the state. This means that all their immigrant workers whether from India, the Philippines or the western cannot practice their faiths except by subterfuge.

Official State Religion and Independent Churches

If we can assume that even in religious affiliations which are based on birth or parental beliefs that there is some feeling that the connection between believers and their God is one that is freely chosen, then the creation of state churches in Communist countries, is going to provide believers with anxieties as to whether their practises are authentic.

The Problem of Multiple Religious Allegiances

It is a commonplace aspect of modern life that from time to time individuals are asked to state their religious affiliation; in Britain it is recorded on anyone's admission form for hospital treatment, on the identity discs of military personnel and probably on the admission forms for children to enter particular schools or in relation to particular diets based on religious beliefs. This is apart from the possible recognition of religious affiliation from costume or appearance.

At other times membership is an entirely personal matter and the extent to which individuals actually practise the rituals of their recorded faiths is entirely unknown unless they wish to declare their commitment to outsiders and to the supervisors of their religions.

Of course, there may be some individuals who live their lives strict in accordance to their faiths and at some social and economic disadvantage to themselves but they must be few indeed. Even the Amish who live strictly religious lives based on their interpretations of the Bible, often have plaques against the Evil Eye on the ends of their houses. Life in association with strangers is always tied into religious anxieties as we have seen with caste pollution in India and everywhere that food requires special religious preparations, eaters have to take on trust that it has been done in the required way. The taking of interest in business transactions which was prohibited by the Prophet Mohammed requires some casuistry as does the prohibition of work on the Sabbath for practising Jews. But believers have always found away round these inconvenient prohibitions or just ignored them as too difficult to follow under the conditions of modern life.

So it would seem that most believers may well be in various degrees of lapsing from the requirements of their faiths or more specifically find that their faiths do not provide the metaphysical support which they need and so work out for themselves alternative aids which they believe in and practice. Indeed lapsing may be a feature of commitment to any of the Great Traditions with their widespread and popular Little Traditions. In tribal religions particularly there cannot be any significant idea of lapsing since most practises are synchronised into the social aspects of communal life and are carried out by social demands.

However the more integrated the individual and community may be into global interrelationships and this is to all intents and purposes unavoidable, the more likely that they are to be faced with some understandings of their own faith and its listed requirements, which cannot happen with non-literate beliefs and any awareness of the diversity of faiths.

They cannot avoid knowing that the modern world is an open market for various faiths and their various known requirements coming into the eyes and ears. This is combined with the unsettling reality of its inherent challenge to personal beliefs. It is not only that other faiths exist but that they claim to exclusive understanding of religious truth which is particularly worrying for those who have religious commitments closely linked to communal social practices.

It is a widespread feature of contemporary life that there is an almost universal faith in protective amulets as well as in mascots and to a lesser extent in tattooing common enough among western soldiers and sailors who are in dangerous occupations and now spreading more widely in Western societies. There are also the constant evocations to 'good luck' which is expected to upset statistical and practical realities. So it seems that even the monotheistic faiths have their Western believers running parallel religious practices based on beliefs which are usually specifically disallowed by the religious institutions to which they belong.

Many faiths are covertly polytheistic which can be seen in the Roman Catholic Church's cults of the saints. Many people are in practice polytheistic as in the Roman Catholic shrine in Colombo attended by petitioners from every faith on the island and in many Javanese religious ceremonies which invoke Hindu and Muslims saints as well as traditional spirits which have no theological part of the Muslim faith to which they belong. This is not a matter of public anxiety or discussion since individuals can combine diametrically opposed systems without feeling any need to disguise what they are doing.

Hinduism is overtly polythesistic and Ishwaran's study of Shivapur (Ishwaran, 1968: 76) found the Brahmans worshipping 9 gods, the Lingavats 30 and so on and even the Muslims were recorded as worshipping 8, while the community as a whole worshipped Hanuman, the monkey god, Basava the bull god and Banashankari the consort of Shiva.

It would seem that this almost universal polytheistic theme rather than just being a contemporary trend perhaps more obvious in the East then in the West, should be a powerful handicap against the development and need for religious violence since it is easier to become antagonist and protective to a narrowly defined faith than one which has so many themes as to almost defy analysis.

Thus the narrower the defined requirements of faith and its likelihood simplified applicability, the greater the likelihood of violence. The need to defend deeply held beliefs which are linked to social behaviour is perhaps a universal human attribute and this becomes easier when the requirements of a faith have been repetitively laid out and are universally known to believers as would be the case with the Five Pillars of Islam rather than the more obscure and less than universal Christian beliefs and requirements. It is easier to fight over what has been defined than what is inexact.

This often requires the restriction of the faith to particular needs which are amplified developments from factors which are not in the main related in any way to religion. It is rare indeed to have violence which can be analytically attributed to religion alone and even in some historical events we cannot be sure from the paucity of the evidence that religion was quite as dominant as we may have been led to believe.

If we look at Shivapur again, individuals were grouped according to streets, lineage, sub-caste, caste, religion and village but they were also divided by land-holding, the village council, the cooperative society, personal rivalries and conflicts of interests; should violence develop in such an environment it would be difficult to state with any force, the relative contribution of religion as opposed to any other individual or communal factors (Ishwaran, 1968: 38).

Nevertheless modernity with its uncontrollable spread of new ideas and practices available to individual minds and expressed in their material hopes, must be unsettling to those who want to believe in an incontrovertible religious truth in order to give meaning to their lives which appears to be more out of human control.

Violence and the Stimulus from Boundary Breaking

Most Great Tradition religious systems that have developed from the social practices of traditional societies were based on togetherness, and stress the desirability and moral correctness of close personal relationships between members of different groups. In most modern societies these benign or hostile attitudes to both religious and social matters show a high degree of stability over generations (Huesmann *et al.*, 1984). We have already suggested that there are ethological correlations to account for hostility to out-groups.

These attitudes are closely related with opportunities for inter-group contact particularly within the same language group and its dialects and with geographical closeness. Thus there is for individuals a personal as much as social cognitive map in which there are balances of negative and positive inter-group understandings. In this there are moral inconsistencies in which individuals may feel closer to a familiar enemy than to little known strangers.

There is usually psychological distancing from people with low socio-economic status such as Hindu Untouchables in India and Muslim Pakistanis as opposed to Sikhs in Britain. Towards high status groups such as the Brahmins there is an approach-avoidance conflict as they represent a desired status and there is considerable Sanskritisation of Hindu rituals lower down in the caste hierarchy.

They also provide visible targets for resentment and blame over their grasping behaviour in such matters at Banaras over the necessary prayers for the eleventh day after death.

There is always some degree of dissonance between long-term cultural stereotypes and specific ascriptions from personal experience. There is always the problem of the generality of stereotypes and the very limited range of interpersonal contacts in which people meet those from outside their immediate social circle such as Buddhist-Christian-Hindu-Muslim contacts in a single Indian village. A village environment may not mean social contacts and propinquity does not necessarily correlate to any social knowledge. Beyond this circle of partial social and economic acceptability, there are those whose beliefs and practices are way outside these personal understandings and acceptance. In contemporary towns and cities, the proportion of unknown stop-and-go interrelationships increases out of all proportion to the comfortable and partially understandable limitations of small group ones.

The Jews with their difficult requirements for the fulfilment of Orthodoxy have always felt a need for territorial identity; a landed exclusivity which was preferable because of the difficulty of following their religious prescriptions in non-Jewish environments. The Amish and the Hutterites have attempted to make their farming settlements as exclusive as possible which the latter found easier in the relative emptiness of the Canadian west. The Mormons move into the part of the western United States unwanted by both the Indians and the expansionist western movement of the new Americans. This need for territorial exclusiveness for a religion has some correlations to Robert Ardrey's territorial imperative (Ardrey, 1966).

While there are simple single dimensional attitudes to out-groups with whom individuals have little or no contact, there are 'boundary' distinctions which generate more polarized responses relating to trust-conflict, attraction-repulsion and admiration-disrespect (Brewer & Campbell, 1976: 144).

There are thus 'boundary' defining mechanisms which make for these distinctions because they clash in our case with the ascriptive religious ideas of particular communities as any personal religious assessment starts with the assumption of one's own group's correctness and the out-groups lack of this essential religious ingredient. Individuals if there are no other predisposing reasons for closeness, are more comfortable with people of the same faith and usually their degree of active religious commitment is not a factor.

In this the assessments are not based on any use or understanding of basic beliefs or their more easily observable practices associated with their faith; Jews wear their hats in their synagogues, Christians do not take off their shoes in church and Muslims use loud speakers to disturb the peace of others. These behaviours which may be quite understandable intellectually but they nevertheless produce firm and relatively unchangeable contributions to 'us' and 'them' attitudes correlating on occasions with inter-religious violence. Professor Evans-Pritchard in referring to the major inter-community quarrels amounting to civil war in the southern Sudan, once said that such violence often started with an inconsequential quarrel over a cow. It is a mistake to downplay what outsiders from another culture would describe as trivialities.

It seems likely that cultural and religious pluralism as a contemporary phenomenon is a creation of new methods of analysis and stems from assumptions that material and ethical standards are now more pluralistic than in the past. This is certainly materially correct if one sets aside the material differences in stock and grain holdings, but ethnically and religiously this may be something of a new creation created at least in part by literacy and bureaucratisation. It could be said that men and women in all cultures are inherently polytheistic.

It is more likely that moral-cum-religious behaviour has always been very diverse between what people state that they should do, what they say that they do and what they actually do. It is very doubtful if there ever has been in any community any socially uniform system of internal or external religious behaviour and even in inter-religious violence, there is always significant variations in individual participations.

Hinduism is very obviously pluralistic but ıhen so is both Christianity and Islam with their amulets and the worship of saints defined by creative cultural memories rather than history.

Without literacy and a religious establishment using literacy and some measures of enforcement, uniformity cannot even be attempted and when it is then the question of boundaries comes to the fore and 'us' and 'them' becomes part of peoples day to day patterns of thinking.

When there is no literacy, disagreements over what may or may not be religious 'truth' become negotiable since there cannot be any hard line digging in of positions supported by sacred books and definitions derived from them. There may be some broad agreement in quasi-traditional societies about the existence and behaviour of spirits but the form that this takes and the rituals needed to quieten the violence which they inflict on the living cannot be consistent. Amongst the five million Sukuma of Tanzania every ancestor propitiation ceremony is different within an assumption of similarity and their young have been acculturated to religious pluralism long before outsider religious faiths became available. The violence of the spirits in upsetting the lives of a particular family can only appear to be consistent and there can certainly never be any assumption of any such consistency between even neighbouring families; the workings of the minds of diagnosing diviners about varying situations would insure this. Religious violence in quasi-traditional social situations without the boundaries laid down by literacy would be difficult to correlate to any consistencies.

In fact many quasi-traditional people if asked for their religion would give their ethnicity as their religion. If we accept modern ethnic classifications and group people under these headings, we have a similar boundary creating situation, dual nationality can create divided loyalties. One cannot be an Indian and a Pakistani at the same time but then there are people in Rajputana who have both Hindu and Moslem names and use them as the occasion demands (Lokhandwala, 1985: 87-101), so it would seem that people can believe in two seemingly opposing ideas at the same time and use each when the occasion demands; people may rarely think lineally.

The five million tribal groups called the Sukuma is quite a modern creation since the word itself may mean the people living to the north of the main caravan route between the Indian Ocean and the Great Lakes. In the past individuals were constantly acculturating to their different matrilineal, and affinal configurations and the advantageous and disadvantageous balances at various social levels and situations. There were also the factors of whether or not they lived in some hypothetical core areas and the extent of their travelling for work as porters and of course, the wanderings of Buddhist and Hindu ascetics. What more modern peoples might classify as uncertainty may have been part of the lives of traditional peoples so that they would describe this uncertainty of kinship status as normality

It would seem likely that all individuals have always been faced with 'boundary' breaking events, perhaps made more salient by institutionalisation and literacy and that these provide reasons for religious tensions and violence when the interests of two groups are worked out in religious terms.

Increased travel, social, economic and television contacts with other groups means that individuals and groups will have an increasing number of ways in which to make differential ratings and their correlating irritations and these may not lead to or even require any process of acculturation. A study of Canadian Indians showed that those who make many differential distinctions between themselves and the surrounding Euro-Canadian society suffered less stress (Berry & Annis, 1974). While personal experience showed that differences between the two societies were one of degree rather than requiring from the Indians any degree of acculturation. The implications being that a sense of difference whether peacefully or violently religious, may be better psychologically for the individual than any sense of obligation for togetherness with people from whom they can expect no advantageous relationships.

It is boundary breaking events which may lead to religious violence when individuals or groups overstep the socially acceptable lines between faiths. Further that in the days when the mass media insures that outrageous behaviour which is possibly acceptable in certain societies, will engage a much wider audience as breaking acceptable boundaries. Examples would be the Nigerian woman condemned to death by stoning for adultery by a religious court and the burying of drugged children for a short periods to placate a Hindu Goddess in southern India which break boundaries in an international sense. At a lower level Hindu-Muslim violence is often initiated by the deliberate breaking of long accepted social and religious boundaries by members of one or the other community.

However, there are situations in which profound breaking of accepted behaviour are the principal part of conversion; the freeing from one form of the past to entering into a new life. Islamic suicide bombers would seem to have gone through such process and the core members of the Mau Mau in Kenya took oaths which involved breaking many of their social and natural taboos as a prerequisite for commitment to violence.

Religious Nationalism and the Fundamentalist Environment

While most societies have had pockets of religious exclusivity where groups have endeavoured to follow particular beliefs in an isolation which allows their practices to be as independent as possible from their surrounding societies whether it is in ashrams, monasteries or communes. This self-segregation has only appealed to small numbers of those who could be described as religious eccentrics perhaps being more the objects of hostility than creating violence themselves.

The ideology and the practices of the 'pure' albeit fundamentalist environment in contemporary terms has moved upwards from the community in religious nationalism. Although this is evident in Israel, it has not yet become a dominant factor in a state with secularised Judaism dominating over orthodoxy with its rather obvious difficulties for expansion in a modernised society.

For the Muslims and in particular the Arabs for whom there is a conflict between community and consumerism, there is a sense of loss building on the feeling of cultural decline. The glories of the Arab and the incompetence of the present as in the failures of the wars against Israel (Zurrayk, 1948) and that so much of their present social, economical and political lives have been derived from non-Islamic sources although the Prophet Mohammad had created a functionally complete Muslim state. For them there is the balancing push to individualised violent alternatives.

For many people in the Third World the secular future has failed to produce anything like what it set out to do in the political and economic programmes of their rulers; it has failed to create any rise in their standards of living. For Muslims with successful models available from the life of the Prophet and subsequently in successive Islamic empires stretching from southern Spain to Delhi and from the Sudan to the Caucasus, a wish to return to the successful past is understandable. In Muslim states this need tends to be confined to narrower objectives within the parameters of compulsion and the physical exclusion of alternatives. Saudi Arabia allows no specifically non-Islam presence much less their performing of public rituals within the state; customs officials confiscate bibles or crucifixes if they are found in baggage.

State Religions and Independent Religious Practices

While this appears to be now a feature only of Islamic states, it has been a feature of Communist ones. In Czechoslovakia in 1948 all the church property was nationalized and religious instruction made illegal and in the next year the state created a Catholic Action Organisation. Cardinal Beran in a pastoral letter declared this movement schismatic and was then placed under house arrest for fourteen years.

In March 1950 most heads of religious congregations were given long prison sentences for espionage and treason and in April all nuns and lay leaders were herded into a number of concentration camps. This was followed after the short Prague Spring of 1968 by a policy of blackmail, threats and intimidation against an ageing clergy, combined with a national Church which continued until the collapse of Communism in 1989.

Much the same occurred in all Communist states after 1945 which resulted in the taking out of commission of all the older clergy of all denominations. This resulted in the development of a more grassroots process of Christianisation without a reliance on clergy. So the persecution of the prominent Roman Catholic Church did not result in the extinction of religious practices but the alteration of their form. Christian denominations which relied on the Bible rather than an ordained priesthood, were better able to survive as small prayer groups centred on concerned believers.

A similar process occurred in the People's Republic of China where only the National Catholic Church was allowed to survive severing any ostensible links with Rome and under current relaxations of Communist domination there has been a resurgence of Christian practices with a more efficient system of personalised social support providing welfare for their members.

Current persecution has been centred on the Falun Gong, a system of meditation and social action which has incurred the hostility of the government through it ability to exhibit its presence and to protest at its treatment through the use of cellular phones. Most of this persecution seem to demonstrate that the persistent persecution of a belief system may have made some of those involved believe that they possessed something of particular value to have all this official attention paid to it.

Communal Cognitive Dissonance and Religious Violence

In some situations the hostility of two opposing religions has gone on so long and is focused on a particular issue that it erodes any possibility of solution. The hostility of Jews and Muslims in Palestine started over a century ago with its supporting socio-cultural clash fuelling economic disputes between the Arabic speaking Muslim majority and the newly arrived European Jewish Zionists.

This new Jewish community was then a highly politicised secular socialist and assertive if not aggressive one which was seen by the local Muslim Arabs as threatening their economic interests, social order and cultural norms. The Jews were well organised and created a network of national institutions while the Palestinian national movement as with Pan-Arabism always lagged substantially behind its Jewish opponents in cohesion, organisation, motivation and performance. Pan-Arab largely ineffectual belligerency based in the last definition by increasing religious fundamentalism, was never able to negotiate pragmatically (Ma'oz, 1992).

Neither side is likely to get what they want. Muslim fundamentalism based on the Koran is intractable and Jewish secular education and the way in which Jewish immigrants from Arab countries turned their back on their Arab background, led to similar Jewish intransigence; on both sides there is the brutalism that comes from exclusive power.

Anxiety is a feature of human thinking and for this if there are secular solutions, they are short term and soon replaced by other worries. Where secular governments have tried to abolish religion as obstructing progress, worries have still not been coped with. Public religious practices are made more difficult and the religious powers of the Great Traditions in this respect have been severely modified. This has led to a reliance on private practices independent of public activities. Anxieties are then coped with by recourse to private worship and the use of the Bible and the Koran as well as the continuation of the Little Traditions practised in private as they have always done.

Pushed too far into forms of uniformity which do not relate to personal anxieties and indeed which are inefficient or out of tune with what individuals see as their religious and indeed secular rights, there is likely to be a build-up of tensions leading to violence correlated to religious ideas and memories.

14

Environmental Issues and Religious Violence

Population pressure leads to pressure on resources but it seems doubtful whether this is seen by those involved as the primary cause of violence. Human societies quarrel over immediate issues which are popularly understandable and over which they find it easier to fight than to compromise. Their quarrels and difficulties are seen in terms of race (visibly different), ethnicity (tribally different), nationality (politically different) and religion (ideologically different).

These themes are easier to understand and are more satisfying tools for mobilising effort than the environment which is a complex of issues for which no word may exist in many languages. The environment often seems to be a matter of concern to those whose livelihoods are assured and who do not feel themselves threatened in any real pragmatic and personal way by their neighbours who are different in their ways of living. This is all the more inevitable as all humans are socialised from childhood to distrust, dislike and avoid outsiders.

The Environment and Metaphysical and Material Security

Very few people in the contemporary world have any sense of material security, certainly not in the sense of institutionalised supports which are perceived as guaranteed for a lifetime. Even in national states which can economically provide comprehensive welfare systems, it is doubtful whether more than a small minority see themselves as secure since the concept of security changes with economic and social development and involves more psycho-social factors for which there are no answers; death, disease and disasters occur all the time in all societies to all people. Comparative poverty is more widespread than real poverty in developed societies and both combine in the Third World to make it much more comprehensive.

Even the most comprehensive and effective welfare system does not eliminate threats from without and indeed such threats are inevitable for all human beings. Most people live under if not economic, then social threats from other people whom they assess as being different to themselves.

It is trite to state that security for individuals is for them to live out their lives without being faced with unsolvable difficulties; that is to say that outsiders are defining what is reasonable security. Most people are prisoners within a particular social system and outsiders tend to state that once a people are past Maslow's Stages 1 and 2 (Maslow, 1987), then they are materially secure and should thus be able to consider the environment.

Most people in developed societies would see environmental security as pleasant neighbours who are not socially rather than physically polluting and that they should be able to walk on occasions through well-maintained parks and an orderly countryside with not too much manure on the ground.

Many environmental concerns are facts because we are told that they are facts; we have no personal experience of them and they are beliefs which we have about AIDS, radiation sickness, BSE and soil exhaustion. In social terms they are presented as dogmas with the characteristics of religious ones which we are invited to believe because the scientific elite in our societies tells us that they should be believed.

Religious Systems Affecting the Use of Natural Resources

In theory secular rather than religious governments should be better able to restrict religious violence and to appreciate and promote the long-term value of a benign environment for their citizens. In practice there has been a growth in specifically religious nation states where once there were only the Vatican and Saudi Arabia; now there are several Islamic Republics and of course Israel.

While Western secular states have a reasonable record in withstanding the demands of Christian pressure groups or more specifically preventing fundamentalism from turning to persistent violence, states with Muslim populations have had a continuing problem with violent fundamentalists who would be almost by definition oblivious to environmental issues.

At levels below the nation state, religions are not structures administratively or theologically capable of taking action to improve or indeed prevent the decline of the environment; it is not their job and moreover there is no public demand for any such change of focus. All religions focus on the individual's behaviour in relation to God(s) and their fellows; these are primary considerations and the environment is at best a tertiary one.

The difficulty may be that the environment is an abstract idea in which there are no real people except perhaps visitors and without a focus on individuals rather than groups the environment has no link up with religion except in the destructive events already described. The concentrations are individually eschatological rather than related to this life collectively. One life religions have no interest in promoting the welfare of their descendents for the inconvenience of their current and only lives and Eastern religions with their multiplicity of rebirths have similarly little psychological need to focus on anything so immediately relevant as the environment. Where religions have been a benign influence on the environment, it seems to have been cultic and local rather than ethical and general.

Conflicts Over Resources Affecting Environmental Controls

It would seem that where there are physical conflicts, there is always territory at stake and that these territorial conflicts are given justifications which can be as easily religious as for any other reason. Whether religion initiates the push to dispute an environment or the need to occupy an environment initiates a religious justification, is probably answered by where in history the analyst starts looking for causes. An historically distant tertiary cause can be updated into violence as a contemporary primary cause as in Israel today.

The Religious Perception of Environmental Changes

Since religions are individually experienced but usually collectively expressed, Maslow's hierarchy of needs (Maslow, 1987) seems a reasonable way of assessing the individual's relationship to the environment and from these to see the possible links with religion.

Stage I. Physiological needs. At this level survival is the only issue, the need is for food and water and individuals in order to survive will ruthlessly destroy any environment in the face of starvation, cutting down trees to get the fruit and occupying water holes by force to keep others away. The flood of Ruanda refugees into the Ngara district of Tanzania striped the countryside of all wooded vegetation as effectively as a swarm of locusts. In these circumstances individuals are self-centred and aggressive. There is not likely to be any collective activity at this level and no religious considerations are involved in famine situations except that provided by outsiders.

In certain circumstances religion taboos will override the physiological need for food. Most societies and their religions are run by men and male-run power structures and the religions themselves except for Buddhism, are expansionist encouraging their members to breed and expand their socio-religious community. While overpopulation is not their aim, it would certainly be the consequences of following these injunctions. At this level the short-term environmental consequences are hostile to immediate human group survival but the long-term ones are likely to be beneficial since it reduces human population levels.

Stage 2. Safety and protection needs. These are predominantly short-term needs which are likely in some localities to be repeated year after year in contrast to Stage I physiological needs which are more likely to be occasional. Again they are likely to be destructive of the environment surrounding any group seeking security as in the use of scarce materials for defence and over-cultivating near to the safety of villages.

On the other hand safety and protection needs can lead to the dispersal of human populations away from their normal habitats which will be to the long-term advantage of particular environments. Wars in south-east Asia had this effect. Religions may increase the need for safety and protection from persecution which can lead to concentrations of devotees as with the Alice Lenshina villages in Zambia and the movement of Mormons westwards into a waterless area which they dominated through innovative farming and water control. In this we see the beginning of perceived as opposed to real needs beginning to coincide.

Stage 3. Belongingness and the need for affection. Once the earlier stage needs of the nuclear groups have been satisfied, the range of belongingness needs increases with the development of different larger groups, including religious ones, with which individuals and their families can become associated. It is possible that the greater the needs which have been shown to exist in their social and geographical environment, the greater the need for these memberships.

Such religious groups can occupy territory and keep others out by force or legal ownership and being so successful in doing this that ultimately they either overrun their environment causing its decline or the religious social system itself adapting or declining. In the short run the Amish system is environmentally beneficial (Seguy, 1973) but in the long-run less so with a growing shortage of land and the dispersal of possible communal help. Aggression is now beginning to have an ideological tinge rather than being based on ordinary and acceptable necessity.

Stage 4. The need for esteem, prestige and status. This stage is likely to have the greatest effect on the environment since the higher the religious commitment of any community when viewed hierarchically, the greater the need to protect it. The Iranian leaders invoked religion as a means of resisting Iraqi aggression over territory which had little value as real estate but their prestige was at stake. The environmental effects on both sides of the border were probably benign since the loss of so many breeding males will have relieved population pressure in both the short and long-term.

Stage 5. Self-actualisation needs and the removal of anomie. In this final stage religious leaders in relative security are in a position to attract followers and to initiate environmental change. We see this in Israel where Jewish aggressiveness in the planting of settlements in the occupied territories with high standards of living in such matters as the use of water alongside Palestinian Muslim villages with lower standards of living makes prolonged hostility inevitable from an increasing shortage of elbow room resulting from the higher Palestinian birth rates.

Religious leaders from a secure dogmatic base which is their interpretation of God's word as in the present instances of Islamic and Christian fundamentalism can whip-up hostility to outsiders which is extremely damaging in the short-term but much more benign in the long-term provided that the violent hostility is sufficiently intense and prolonged.

Conflicts Over Resources Affecting Governance Structures

It seems unlikely that except in situations where there is an already existing identifiable resource such as oil, that conflict in the popular mind will be directly related to resources. The successes of western scientific medicine in controlling mass diseases and the relentless work of Aid agencies has led to population pressures everywhere. In both the mountains of Myanmar and the cultivation steppe of Tanzania expanding human populations have eaten up the land and its resources with the persistence and competence of insects.

For most of the world's population half-empty stomachs will act to promote violence for which any number of emotional triggers will be adequate. Democracy or 'anything for a quiet life' systems of popular government are perhaps no better than fascist or oligarchic political systems in thwarting pressures for immediate improvements in standards of living; the popular framework of thinking or rather hoping is almost always short-term.

Certainly population pressure reduces elbow-room and few see the logic of depriving themselves of children now for highly speculative longer-term benefits of people yet to be born and to whom they are not likely to be related. If believers are rubbing up against those of a different religion demonstrated officiously by mosques, churches and synagogues, then the religious beliefs will dominate over wider ranging secular needs.

Scientific facts can be argued about and perhaps knitted together into semi-rational but useful compromises but ideological arguments based on the printed words of God do not have this plasticity. The Mediterranean single life religions have an in-built tendency to fight over territory which is seen as a spiritual rather than material resource whatever it contains.

The Perception of Environmental Change

Most people everywhere have a 'golden age' perception of the past and the oral memories of most of the people of Asia and Africa are of a past without guns, population pressures, desertification, famine, drought, mass diseases and in eastern Africa without the spread of the tsetse fly. It is a perception of the past which never existed, but is true in respect of population pressures.

For a short time during the decolonialisation era there was a widespread 'golden future' perception of what would happen from the end of direct European domination and the disappearance of white administrators and professional controllers. This has now largely disappeared in a plethora of corruption, civil disorders, AIDS and more observable widespread inequality.

The people are in the main subsistence farmers or hand-to-mouth unskilled workers for whom the immediate future will always be problematic so that their framework of thinking is short-term. As we have seen some languages have no indefinite future tense with which to think about long-term environmental issues but they also have no word for the environment beyond what might be called 'the neighbourhood', which in effect means 'out of sight, out of mind'.

Religious taboos may protect small spirit-filled localities but no religion has any enforceable moral ideas which relate to the environment since they are all here and now in this life people centred. Even the word 'environment' has a detached depersonalised tone to it. Perhaps one can conclude that land as property will be fought over for a variety of reasons including religion, but never in order to protect the environment.

In the developed world it has perhaps popular equivalents to something like aesthetic inconvenience. If any action is to be taken to protect the environment, it does not start with any self-abnegation by denying themselves an immediate higher standard of living as opposed to a lower one for the sake of their unborn grand children. Even for those directly involved the environment is a cause not a personal reality.

For most people the facts of science and the facts of religion are in practical terms both dogma; they are believed in rather than understood. Perhaps the only difference lies in the fact that the former are based on human calculation and thus have no emotional pull and some long-term validity if the history of science is anything to go by, while the dogmas of religion provide answers and emotions which science can neither create nor dispel.

There is little reason to suppose that the majority of the world's population grappling with persistent short-term insecurity will be any less likely than in the past to see their interests as best protected by violent confrontations based in many cases on religion by which the environment is destroyed in the short term for perhaps the longer term benefits of mankind.

15

Modernity Aiding Religious Violence

It is obvious that the last fifty years have seen profound changes in what men are able to achieve because of greater technical efficiency particularly in the field of electronics. This has resulted in a broad extension of utopian hopes to all corners of the world about the raising of their standards of living which have gone beyond any assessable possibilities for most of mankind. This is where religions have become a potent force since they retain utopias in the mind without much relationship to social and economic realities.

Of course, consumerism is a potent force as it is so visible in clothes and in shops and in virtually every form of mass media whether as news or advertising and above all it is sustained by envy and hope. However, there is perhaps a more influential and invisible homogenisation which enables religious ideas, practices and organisation to move more quickly than the pedestrian and paper-bound movements of previous centuries. Newspapers show Israeli tanks destroying Muslim houses and the Hindu millions who come to bathe in the Ganges at the Kumbh Mela. These events in the mind may be just as influential as actually witnessing the destruction of the World Trade Centre in September 2001. The effect of seeing a picture may be important for its cumulative effects on what overall images are retained in the mind.

Jet travel allows religious leaders to move at will over national borders which Muslim theologians suggest was always the intention of the Prophet Mohammad. Sayyid Qutb (Qutb, 1964) before his execution in 1966 wrote in his Sign Posts on the Road 'The Prophet Mohammad was no doubt capable of setting forth a movement for Pan-Arab nationalism in order to unite the strife riven tribes of Arabia…Yet Allah, the Omnipotent and Omniscient did not instruct His messenger to go in that direction. He only told him that there was no God but Allah'. Monotheism was seen to require domination beyond national and tribal boundaries.

Theologians of all religions have seen in quick travel an important and divinely acceptable way towards spreading their faiths and for others to experience the centralities of their faiths by seeing pictures of the multitudes circling the Kharba while on the Hajj which had in previous centuries been restricted to those with extreme religious needs and the well-to-do who could make such journeys. Much the same would apply to pictures of the pilgrimage crowds at Lourdes and Banaras.

E-mail and web sites give religious data an almost instantaneous global circulation and mobile phones enable religious organisations to produce crowds for demonstrations with little likelihood of the authorities being able to tap into their arrangements. This enabled the Falun Gong to demonstrate peacefully in Beijing, which was seen by the Chinese Government as a threat to the stability of the state and their monopoly of power.

Then there are tapes and videos of the lives and views of real and would-be charismatic leaders as well as their programmes which allow their influence to permeate far more widely than could ever have been the case through personal contacts and any inner circle of disciples (Al-Rasheed, 1999). This has been linked to inter-religious violence.

It is possible to overestimate the potential of electronics to promote violence in any general public since there are other factors which must predispose them to action or inaction for which electronics are no more than a channel. It may enable the committed to organise themselves more efficiently and remain hidden as there would be less personal contact and less committed to paper. Mobile phones would clearly enable the provokers of religious demonstration to control it more effectively and to mobilise their resources to achieve their objectives. In the destruction of the Ayodhya mosque the instigators were able to organise the presence there of many Hindus foreign to that area.

The fact that information and opinions are broadcast and that analyses of the contents often conclude that contents were inflammatory but to have such effects would depend very much on the framework of thinking of those who see or read about these events. A heated discussion between Greeks which appeared to be on the verge of blows was commented on by another Greek as a very well argued discussion.

In another context a tourist guide driving along and through the boundaries of Croatia and Bosnia described the line as the boundary between east and west, the Muslim and Christian worlds. Those having such thoughts in mind would see much which fitted in with this framework of thinking. It is salutary to remember that the Ottoman Turkish authorities found the repetitive quarrelling of denominational Christians over features of the Holy Sepulchre in Jerusalem so irritating, that they put the door key into the hands of a Muslim custodian (Armstrong, 1992: 534).

Broadcasts related to Israeli-Palestinian confrontations would certainly be classified as inflammatory if listened to with some degree of detachment and in distinct pieces. However, since virtually every adult in Israel, Palestine and the surrounding Arab countries has grown up in this environment of intermittent violence, it cannot be described as anything more than a regrettably normal use of wireless and television and at worst keeping mutual hate and distrust in front of the public mind.

While Christians in Asia Minor may well have welcomed Ottoman dominance after generations of Byzantine instability, the Christian Balkans were conquered by Muslim force and hostility to this is still in the forefront of Greek thinking; it is still unlucky to marry on the weekday when the Turks first occupied the Cathedral of St. Sophia in Constantinople now Istanbul. At that time there may not have been much difference between Muslim and Christian religious practices at the level of subsistence village farming communities.

The contemporary mass media in Greece (Tsagarousianou, 1999) mainly represent Islam as antagonistic to Christianity with the additional connotation of the 'barbaric Orient' as opposed to Christian values and civilisation. More importantly in the context of religious violence, the European credentials of Christian Greece and Greek values is linked to antagonism to Turkey. On occasions it suggests that the Bosnian government is associated with Saudi Arabia, evoking an alleged threat to Greek security and culture. Much the same could be said about the Indian popular press about Pakistan and their own Muslim minority.

It is certainly correct that electronics have a direct influence on sustaining and creating antagonisms through education and the mass media as well as in exclusive forms of worship. It is always the question of balancing the valuable returns from the inclusion of violence at that particular moment against the more distant considerations of excluding the satisfactions of violence.

While the greater issues may dominate the thinkers of policy makers, theologians and administrators, electronics in the cause of religion may have a needling effect in some social settings. The Muslim call to prayer was originally and for many centuries no more than the power of the human voice from a minaret; this could be heard, but it was not intrusive and by implication not too offensive to those of other faiths. 'When Israelis are awakened at dawn by the *muezzin*, have their conversations interrupted and are forced to suspend their activities until the sometimes deafening call to prayer is over, they are being regularly reminded of a fact which many would prefer to forget (Armstrong, 1992: 533).

Religious issues are always in competition with economic, social and political needs and, however, electronically enhanced their messages may be, it is probably only infrequently and in relation to special events that electronics have an influence. Of course, the messages carried by electronics is intrusive and influential when it is examined in isolation. In practice the mass media has overloaded the ability of the human mind to absorb all that is on offer, so humans pick and choose by accident and by choice what they want to see and hear; its availability does not necessarily correlate with it being influential.

The airways are overpopulated with the voices of those trying to influence others and conversion from one pattern of thought to another which might possibly lead to violence is not all that common. The Indian policeman who states that loud speakers frequently make Hindu-Muslim confrontations worse is certainly correct. This Indian violence is based on contemporary and historical themes which are not all that different to those of Croatia and Bosnia and in other places where religious differences are part of the overall tensions of their contemporary life.

Constitutionalism and the Growth of Religious Violence

Constitutions which involve abstract terms like 'equality' and provide no definitions allow for change to take place as legal decisions come to fit in with current affairs. Constitutions with fixed definitions of what the citizens in the state are entitled to get in their current lives, provide serious occasions for violence because they are often aims rather than possible realities and these realities changes almost from day-to-day. Such statements in a constitution become a provocation in the gulf between what is possible and what is really no more than political and social hope and human optimism.

The United States Constitution refers to equality and the exclusion of Afro-Americans from a large range of public facilities as well as opportunities to vote required a long campaign and widespread passive resistance to white aggression. This was headed by Martin Luther King, a Baptist pastor and progress was mainly obtained by recourse to the courts rather than by any changes in public opinion.

The Constitution of India abolished Untouchability and discrimination on the basis of caste and although some progress has been made, court rulings have not been followed. Substantial violence continues against Untouchables attempting to have their constitutional rights practised and to have those who resist this persisting erosion of their traditional status prosecuted. Article 15 of the 1950 Constitution under Fundamental Rights asserted that the State was not 'to discriminate against any citizen on grounds of religion, race, caste, place of birth' and the First Amendment in the following year allowed for positive discrimination. In effect this anticipated rather than paralleled the putting into practice of the United States constitutional provision for equality which had already been unimplemented on the statute books for a century and a half.

However, Article 17 went much further in abolishing Untouchability and its practice in any form was forbidden with possible penalties detailed under the Untouchability (Offences) Act, 1955. The punishable offences were for enforcing religious disabilities, denying access to public facilities or the performance of a social or religious custom, usage, or ceremony, goods and services, entry to educational establishments and finally, against anyone who by words or signs incites or encourages any person or class of person or the public generally to practice 'Untouchability' in any form whatsoever. This was subsequently amended and expanded by the Protection of Civil Rights Act, 1976.

Yet again the legislation was found to be inadequate and was followed by the Scheduled Castes and Scheduled Tribes (Prevention of Atrocities) Act, 1989. This Act specifically listed a depressing catalogue of the occasions in which the reassertion of ancient customs had been attempted and which were now criminal offences; the dumping of excreta, waste matter, carcasses or any other obnoxious substances in his premises or neighbourhoods, forcing people to eat or drink any inedible or obnoxious substances, forcibly removing clothes or parading them naked, exploiting women sexually, stealing land and forced or bonded labour. Penalties started from six months imprisonment up to life imprisonment as well as the confiscation of property.

The Government of India has certainly laid out the legal foundations for this wholesale change in the practices of Hinduism on which that society has been based for many centuries and so they were not attempting to change some reprehensible but seemingly fringe activity. Equally the pace of change cannot be enforced by a government, however, ideologically committed to such changes it may be. It requires substantial support from public opinion, the aggrieved to initiate the enforcement of changes affecting them rather than its enforcement by government orders for which it had neither the democratic will nor the personnel to oversee. What public support there was came from the middle classes who were little affected by these religious discriminations anyway.

There can be no question that global ideas of social justice requires such changes in any political system aiming at the social betterment of its peoples in this life. However, social justice in the abstract and its implementation operate on different levels and this is a fundamental religious issue which touches virtually every paradigm in the Hindu understanding of life.

Access to temples in urban areas was perhaps the easiest to implement as Untouchability is not recognisable by appearance. People entering temple compounds bring alms which would not be in anyone's interest to refuse, particularly as they were creating their own temples and local devotions. In villages devotion is segregated by caste and any Untouchables attempting to enter a temple inappropriate for their caste certainly knows that they are likely to initiate violence.

But other aspects were not so easily accommodated as getting entry into urban temples. Getting their rights at the village level rested on a combination of their voting power and their legally enforceable access to wells and common land for grazing. In all of these issues intricate local community balances were seriously altered from a slow rate of change to a precipitous one. The power-holders in terms of both religion and local economics had what they considered their historical rights challenged, overturned or at least drastically modified. The reaction to this has been a substantial and increasing amount of inter-caste violence directed specifically at Untouchables obtaining rights to which the local power-holders did not consider them to be entitled.

In the period 1960-80 caste Hindus have committed 37,000 known atrocities against Untouchables which included burning their houses and crops, killing their men and raping their women (Bayly, 1999: 345-57). This was occasioned by the Untouchables growing sense of their own voting power, the granting to them of new leases with legal land rights at a time of rising land values and the Green Revolution of improved grain yields making farming more profitable. These were all combined with the increased opportunities available to them in the towns, with the overall result that block voting became increasingly important.

Democratic Voting and Politicised Religion

Prior to democratic voting and universal suffrage, elites of various types worked out their differences in a variety of situations and through different materials; there were no particular regularities in this rivalry. In some countries with a long tradition of consultative government, constitutions came into existence, a form of self-regulatory control without the use of overt power, but this form of government has caught on in only a few western nations with high standards of living which were not in the first place obtained because of constitutional changes.

Into such countries as India with its well developed system of political rivalry, came the vote for every adult citizen. The western idea of a secular and diffuse public opinion in which individuals may be important and there is institutionalised concern for the views of minorities rather than their ongoing subordination, may not apply in India.

So politicians compete for the votes of numerically significant blocks of supporters whose religious-*cum*-caste affiliation is the easiest tool for them to use. But the winner does not represent the whole constituency. The winners may not have the power to rule by consent but through their control of the bureaucracy; they have the power to block and to promote in order to maintain the political support of those who voted for them. The structures of the state are not strong enough to enlarge the concept of consent over deeply engrained religious differences.

Prior to the arrival of democratic voting the dislike of those who had different beliefs certainly existed but perhaps was not a dominant interest. It was there sure enough and could be activated whenever the popular need arose but it had none of the hard edges of voting majorities with its characteristics of either/or alternatives.

Once voting became a statutory requirement, it is easier for an elite to appeal to what are now either/or voters and faith takes on hard edges and numerical success became the bases for exclusive demands. When we see how long it took for western countries to develop systems of universal but not overly popular or successful voting systems, it is not surprising that the often abrupt installation of such systems in economically less successful societies, has resulted in the development of new forms of political uncertainty and religious violence.

Periodic censuses essential for economic and social planning in India, Israel, Northern Ireland and the Lebanon have had the effect of making the birth rates of each religion and sub-caste matters of political significance. The first census in India in 1872 came after Hindu and Muslim laws of marriage and inheritance had become national statute law which initiated the process of religious and national separatism.

So with censuses came the recognition of numbers in adult voting and that babies were future voters particularly as mass immunisation extended the length of expected life making for general political anxieties. Lebanon has not had a recent census perhaps because it would unleash renewed inter-religious violence and Israel has looked on the immigration of Russian Jews as a useful balance to the higher birth rates of Muslims over Jews.

Long after the separation of Pakistan and Bangladesh from India on religious grounds, the 1981 Indian census disclosed that the birth rate for Muslims was 4.1 and for Hindus 3.6; a significant difference. So not only was India surrounded by Muslim states but it was faced with an enormous and expanding Muslim minority. Hindu politicians may have been slow to appreciate that Islam so far had been the only religion to control states and to be attracted to that idea. In all of these periodic censuses brought into immediate political being not only a heightened sense of religious identity, but an equally strong sense of religious separatism.

Democratic Voting and the Development of Overt Political Religion

While western political ideologies attempt to separate politics from religion, the effect of periodic censuses and universal adult suffrage has had the opposite effect in many countries. The 1872 Indian census recorded caste as the British administration considered it to be an important demographic characteristic, basing their ideas on the reading of classical Hindu texts. Although religion has not been included in recent censuses, it is easy enough to recognise religious affiliation from names, locations and occupations. Having to record ones caste in earlier censuses contributed to the hardening of hierarchical caste positions which hitherto may have been more socially negotiable. The British demographers saw the census in secular terms, but those who were counted usually saw enumeration in terms of religious power.

This gave sub-castes a formal and constitutional way of negotiating the use of power but doubled the number which they thought they had by the giving of voting rights to women. Further it was not only the counting of people which was an innovation to religiously divided politics, but it created leaders who had been put in place by a controllable bureaucratic process and their positions were inviolable until the next election.

In India it was not only the counting of people separated by religion and by caste but that their numbers were put into a national context. While still remaining important it was no longer just what the members of a sub-caste did in a certain location but how many and their understandings of what was happening in other communities nearby.

The basic divisions between religions shown by any census did not disclose the extent of their necessary economic and social interrelationships. Periodic outbreaks of violence, became much more difficult to control and negotiate as they were based on numbers outside the control of politicians except as they could be expressed in terms of active and passive violence encouraging and enforcing migration and segregation.

The Provocation of Secularist Policies and Influences

Secularism can be seen in two ways, the decline of religious practices and ideas which is difficult to define and enumerate. Much religious activity is within the boundaries of the Little Traditions and the invasion of social life by practices which have nothing to do with religion but which are seen by the religiously minded as the cutting down of the significance of religion overall.

Secularism as a cultural process in which not only do people become ostensibly less religious but more logical in the design and carrying out of their behaviour is a very doubtful conjunction of two possibly loosely correlated processes. The Western world may have changed its religious practices towards the magical end of any religious scale, but the degree that their decision making is individually or even communally logical is highly speculative.

The policies of a government in a country in which religion is considered to be of great importance has many of its policies evaluated in religious terms according to either the exactnesses of Islamic law or the vaguer necessities of Hinduism so well promoted by Mahatma Gandhi who never held political office and was perhaps of minimal influence in reducing the inter-religious violence which erupted after the decision to partition India.

As we have seen most modern politicians are secularist in what they try and do and Jawaharlal Nehru, the first Prime Minister of India, was no exception. He certainly saw the beliefs and practices of his fellow Indians to be governed by superstition and magic and he saw it as one of the tasks of any modern government not to underwrite these out-of-date considerations. Muslim politicians would take an opposing view seeing that any stable government depended on the inclusion of Islamic law becoming part of state law whether or not this would be either popular or economically or socially sensible in terms of global trends.

In cultures which do not have highly developed economic systems based in some ways on secular logic, secularism has had limited effects on government policies. Walking about the streets of Japanese, Thai and Philippine towns, villages and indeed their fields, it is impossible to avoid seeing the voluntary involvement of religion in their daily lives apart from feasts and holidays. This is apart from the religious police of Iran and Saudi Arabia enforcing public religiosity.

Thus the Indian government found itself caught between a Constitution outlawing discrimination based on caste when the superiority or inferiority of an individual's social position and caste related opportunities formed the basis of much of the social, economic and political life of India's Hindu majority. Much the same applied to the Muslims both independently and in reaction to the realities of Hindu dominance. Some commentators are quite explicit 'I submit that in the prevailing circumstances secularism in South Asia as a general shared credo is impossible, as a basis for state action impractical and as a blue print for the future because by its very nature, it is incapable of countering religious fundamentalism and fanaticism' (Madan, 1987).

So we must assume that even the most obviously necessary secularist policies such as women's education and opportunities for their advancement, birth-control and the control of disease and overall considerations of personal freedom are tied in with religion at every stage. Further as the majority of power holders are inevitably men which correlates to potentiality of violence occurring based on religious ideas and commitments.

The Failure of Secular Development and the Onset of Religious Violence

The post-war period with the decline of western colonial dominance and its increase in economic success and influence has had profound effects on the thinking of those who have not benefited from the progress which they had anticipated.

There can be little doubt that the removal of European sovereignty from African and Asian countries with its legalistic ideas and the structure of impersonal service to those involved, left these people with an almost magical concept of what could be achieved in a short space of time. The laudable hopes of the retiring colonial administrators of passing on constitutional government restrained by responsible universal suffrage and incorrupt civil servants and politicians has not been fulfilled.

The new governments were faced with problems which had only begun to be seen in the colonial era particular the success of mass preventative medicine leading to rapid population growth, the widespread possession of weapons and the expenses of running the apparatus of states for which there was not the necessary supporting economic base which did not have to be paid for during the colonial period.

Most of the new politicians and administrators were the products of Western education and European political thinking and if they had religious beliefs such as the Roman Catholicism of Július Nyerere of Tanzania, they were taken to be private and not to be extended into public influence. The exception to this were the Muslim politicians who had at least in the backs of their minds the ideal models of earlier and contemporary Muslim states.

In India on independence the incoming Congress Party government despite the influence of the fundamentally Hindu Mahatma Gandhi, tried to avoid the label of being a Hindu state. At that time it seems that even Jinnah, the founding father of Pakistan saw that state as one for Muslims but not one which was to be dominated by Islamic thinkers. The Indian leader Nehru despite being a Kashmiri Brahmin, thought in secular terms and wanted India to be a state without the dominance of the Hindu majority whose ideas he probably thought were outdated from the framework of European thinking into which he had been educated. He also recognised that India would still have within its borders many millions of Muslims and lesser numbers of Buddhists and Christians.

So it would seem that these new states just as much as China with its Communist ideology and the taking over of a state in chaos, had a few decades in which they would have to deliver noticeable rises in their standards of living to their peoples. Popular memories of what went before such as the indignities of colonialism and the universal unrest in China, could only influence the thinking of those who had lived in those times and they had progressively died out or lost interest and influence. The impoverishment of new states in Africa and Asia could not be blamed indefinitely on colonialism and came to be seen more in terms of corruption and inefficiency and over-dependency on Western aid.

It was not surprising, therefore, that so-called secular development failed to have much effect except among the professional classes who usually benefited from any form of secular changes in bureaucracy, industry and commerce, rather than among the poor who were now expectant voters; the social gap between the better off and the poor became more visibly obvious. The popularist leader Gamal Nasser díd his best in Egypt to keep Muslim influences as much as possible out of government power by acting vigorously against the Muslim Brotherhood. Population growth and the narrowness of the Nile valley in terms of development, had little relation to what the people expected to get in return for their allegiance to optimistic political programmes.

This led in turn to two diametrically oppose developments. In one form this led to military governments coming and going in Pakistan, Nigeria, Sudan and Myanmar. These had orderly conception of how governments should be run since armies were disciplined organisations with answers for the limited range of problems. They were not able to provide for development which required a different framework of thinking and certainly not one which relied fundamentally on weapons.

The other alternative was to return to religion since secular alternatives had failed to deliver but even here there were snags since Buddhism did not want to be involved in secular activities and when it was, then only at the level of social work. Much the same applied to Christianity which from its historical development should have learnt to avoid involvement in politics. When it had become involved as in Ruanda and Colombia and found itself backing the wrong side, if morally based politics could be seen in such terms.

Hinduism in the one country with an enormous following but no centralised or centralisable ideas from its sacred literature and organisation, has developed with the Hindutva political theme through the appeal of the vote and the manipulation of caste and anti-Muslim tensions. Certainly in Gujarat this has led to substantial violence and popular support for the continued Hindu control of Muslim dominated Kashmir.

This leaves only Islam as an alternative to secular controlled development and in this it has the model of the original Muslim state lead by the Prophet Mohammad who was a success in his life-time. He left in the Koran many administrative instructions for the running of this new state in which he was the sole key figure. But this was in the 7th century and these administrative ideals are not directly applicable to the contemporary needs of societies which can potentially control their own developments without the need for divine intervention.

Of course, for Christians there is the appeal of a return to the simplicities of early Christian life but not to its macro-application and there are plenty of attempts both monastically and communally to return to this. This austerity has rarely been seen as an answer to overall popular development at a national level. The Chinese do not particularly want to love their neighbours but want bicycles and colour television sets for which there is no religious answer in Taoism any more than there is in Christianity.

For Muslims there is the vivid dream of a past Islamic state which worked and with known values and a return to a seemingly pleasant and historically largely fictional past, which has a compelling and popular pull. It was this pull which has led in Egypt to the assassination of President Sadat by Muslim fundamentalists, the mullah led governments of Shia Iran and Taliban Afghanistan. It is also the undercurrent for reform in Saudi Arabia and Pakistan. In all of which cases there has been either substantial direct violence as in the Sudan in which the Muslim north continues to attack the Christian and animist south even initiating its broadcasts with a Muslim invocation and indirect violence in restricting the rights of women and minorities.

The overview must be that any return to the past as a template for the administration of a modern state cannot hope to succeed. It is now a matter of public comment that the Arab states following these Islamic ideals are not developing as fast as the states which are not so ideologically confined. These states are losing large numbers of educated men and women by emigration who do not see any useful future for themselves in their own societies (United Nations Development Report, 2002). The answer to developmental needs and the gaining of contemporary popular support does not lie in administrative systems which have religious police. Let us now look at the extent to which contemporary religions have restricted the global opportunities of women.

Gender and Religious Violence

This is a much discussed and modern aspect of religious violence which is perhaps overburdened with modern ethical polemics without examining the data which relates to the social secular and biological differentials involved. It is correct that most historical and contemporary religions are governed by men under what they interpret as a divine mandate and if there is an analogy so are the majority of occupations and professions. If there is oppression of women it would appear to have become an issue in modern Islam and in the developed nations as a consequence of legislation to protect their economic equality in which women have become subordinated to the interests of men.

There are well documented cases in which religions and their sub-divisions have been and are led by women in which either the social situation allowed their pre-eminence or their personal charisma developed into leadership. Mother Teresa started her own religious order for the help of the destitute and dying in India and there were numbers of such forceful women in recent religious history such as the flounders of the Shakers and the Chrístian Science Church as well as in the Kenyan Legio Maria the Roman Catholic breakaway sect.

The ancestor propitiating Sukuma have women diviners and in their Buchwezi cult women hold equal rank with their leaders. There are 'nat' priestesses in Myanmar connected with snakes on Mount Popa and in addition Sande secret societies led by women in West Africa, women shamans in Korea and Okinawa, the matrilineal spirit religions of northern Thailand, the Garifuna ancestor religion of Belize and the Candomble and Macumba sects in Brazil (Stone, 1997). There is certainly no global case for assuming that there is any overall religious justification for the enforced subordination of women.

It is easy to assume that women only rise to pre-eminence in cults and sects which have little relevance beyond particular social circumstances such as in the zar cults of Muslim women in the Sudan and Somalia which are free from orthodox thinking about the divinely ordained inferiority of women. Even their ordination as priestesses in some Protestant Churches has caused tension and the movement of some priests into other Churches.

We have also seen that in immigrant communities there is a steady potential for change when both men and women are isolated from the restricting influences of their natal religious environments and surrounded by new social ones in which restrictions on the public religious behaviour of women begin to appear slightly ridiculous.

In orthodoxy there may be little point in taking the issue of male-female discrimination head-on as an immoral form of right deprivation. Iran which has a reputation of violence against their interpretation of orthodox behaviour, has seen women working round these discriminations for their own religious and secular benefit. While men have retained their control over public worship in mosques, women have come to prominence in worship at the shrines of saints, in organising increases in women's religious education and particularly through the increased use of electronics, so that they may be getting a new form of equality through the back-door (Kamalkani, 1991). Islamic states, two of which have had women prime ministers, may well be coming to recognise that violating what are now considered to be the global rights of women, is an international embarrassment and depriving them of an important national resource.

The Widening of Cognition and its Correlation to Religious Violence

How people think about their lives has always been a contemporary combination of fantasy, reality and unrealistic hopes. The current mixtures in any mind is a constantly changing one as it must have been in the past. Individuals react imaginatively to the social world in which they live and except for the sudden eruptions of originality in the minds of a few original thinkers and charismatics, these would tend to reflect some aspects of what they already know.

Certainly the devout and the hopeful have always gone on pilgrimages but now many more are travelling physically and mentally because of oil, electronics and literacy. Many more are now travelling for every conceivable purpose including religion since it is no longer based on walking. The Indian village of Shivapur with its 4000 population in 630 households had in one year 542 people travelling to religious fairs within 60 miles and 167 travelling over 200 miles (Ishwaran, 1968: 76-77). At the same time these people have increasingly heard news through transistor radios and seen it all on television apart from pictures and headlines rather than the texts of newspapers.

It is virtually impossible to think that there are Muslims anywhere who have not been repeatedly aware of Israeli/Jewish violence in what they consider to be the immorally occupied Palestine. Much the same would apply to the results of Tamil Tiger activities in Sri Lanka, Muslim Chechnya and so-called Bin Laden violence in Moscow and New York and in Christian-Hindu-Muslim violence in India and Pakistan. People are no longer made suddenly aware of violence, whether it is related to religion or not, it is part of the cognitive world into which they are socialised.

Now virtually everyone has become aware of social, economic, political and religious worlds far outside the social environments in which they will spend most of their lives. Uncertainties have always existed and now they have been enlarged by their publicity and thus appear less controllable and in their seemingly uncontrollable nature have become a predisposing factor in reactive religious violence.

The cognitive processes of most contemporary people certainly recognise the widespread existence of religiously motivated violence and that in its impersonality almost anyone can be a victim; tourists in Luxor, Egypt, theatre-goers in Moscow, commuters in Tokyo and Colombo and those who are mutilated by the land-mines left-over from the religious civil wars in Croatia and Sudan.

It is not only that most people are now aware of religiously motivated violence outside their own communal experience but that their cognitive awareness which might be expanded in the first instance from the pictures in a school book. This has widened even more through the mass media so that there is always a balancing act going on in their minds between the innumerable predisposing distant factors to religious violence and those within their primary social contacts Let us now look at the influence of the mass media.

The Mass Media and the Maintenance of Religious Violence

A Shinto priest may paint a religious phrase for the personal use of a petitioner and in Second World War large numbers of Japanese servicemen went into battle and their deaths wearing religious inscriptions. Large numbers of British and American soldiers wore protective amulets. Although this was almost universally found to be of personal support in times of danger, these were often mass produced.

The mass media in print, television and wireless are not in general produced for keeping; they are usually daily productions and almost as soon as they have been printed or sent out on the air, they are replaced by new words, print and pictures. So there are three parts to the influence of the mass media on religious violence, the producer, the medium used and those who read, see or listen to what has been produced and all three are perhaps acting to a large degree independent of each other.

The producer of what is shown, read or heard is inevitably a biased person, no matter how dedicated they are to the obligation to produce something which as far as possible is in their opinion related to impersonal truth, they provide a particular view point if only by excluding certain information. Of course, there are rational reasons for this such as the time required to produce, the cost and the market but for most of these mass media items and the influence they have on their consumers it is head-line stuff in large print aided by pictures. Muslims kill Pakistani Christians in their church, Tamil-Hindu terrorists blow up Buddhist civilians and Hindu-Buddhist civilians burn a mosque in Nepal and so on.

While the *New York Times*, the *London Times* and the *Times of India of India* may be considered responsible papers, the mass media includes popular local papers producing for a much more limited public. In addition there are the whole range of politically and religiously committed producers of hand-outs which have no obligation at all to send out balanced views. Leaving aside the producers who may have a deliberate policy of provocation, the writers in a Christian or Muslim paper are not thinking of Hindu readers just as Hindu ones have no interest in the reactions of Muslims; neither group has any interest in spending money on buying a paper which they know will be biased against their own views.

This type of data is probably correct in its substance that people were killed in the circumstances listed but it will be soon forgotten if printed as a story and told as a news item because each will be superseded by the next day's horrors. In this sense it is not particularly provocative unless repeated time and time again and this is certainly the case with reports of Indian communal tensions, Kashmir, Afghanistan. American influence which is not seen as quasi-Christian reactions to such atrocities as the destruction of the World Trade Centre but as anti-Muslim in general and in particular over its support for Israel against the Palestinian Muslims.

So it is this repetitiveness linking everyday biased understandings which is likely to be influencing behaviour but the words themselves, however, they are combined, are ephemeral. It seems likely that pictures remain in the memory longer than words and that even in moving sequences, it is particularly static pictures that are kept in the mind. Few ever balance this with any recognition that the camera only records what it sees that in this sense it is even more biased than what the reporter writes. No reporter is going to write about the usual or photographers record the placid events of everyday life.

Religious writings or writings about religious events can be stuffed away and forgotten or used for fire lighting or wrapping goods sold in the market place, but religious iconography is altogether different. Almost all religions except the traditional ones in less developed societies have produced enormous and increasing quantities of religious pictures to be seen on many walls whether in the house of an Egyptian farmer or in the apartment of a Puerto-Rican family in a New York slum. In India this is considered to be a largely new form of religious popularism.

It is these pictures which keep religious identities in mind almost as much as attendances at mosques, churches or temples; Christians in their kitchens are reminded of Christ and the Virgin Mary just as the Hindu in Southall, a suburb of London, is reminded of their devotion to Krishna, even if the same wall has pictures of Miss India produced by the same publisher.

In addition to this it is the newspaper picture of the aftermath of an atrocity committed in the name of a religion which catches the eye and is retained in the memory. If for example, ten people are killed in a suicide bomb attack in Israel, there is a picture on the front page as there was yesterday and probably tomorrow as well. Comparable numbers killed everyday on the roads through alcohol related driving get no mention at all. Religious killing is news particularly in the Western world and to their way of thinking this is neither an acceptable nor rational way to behave.

For those who belong to the religion of those killed or those killing, the pictures are not representations of immoral horrors but support their public opinions that they are the victims of religious persecution. Alternatively their attacks in the name of religion are successful as they are being publicly displayed and are having just the influence which they wanted as showing that some people whether Hindu or Muslim take their religion sufficiently seriously to die in its cause.

Much information which is passed on through the mass media is either rumours since it may not have been checked either deliberately for political or religious reasons or because there is no time or interest to do so. Such items become part of the circulation of rumours. In situations of communal religious tension rumours may start with a fact, but as it passes from mind to mind it becomes part of an accumulation of rumours to form public and in our case religious opinion which may end up with very little relationship to what may in fact have actually happened.

Incidents which might become inflated into predominantly religious confrontations are commonplace whether or not they have been reported in the mass media and it is another process which turns them into this. An analysis of mass media references to religious incidents would seem to be taking them out of context (Brass, 1997).

We have seen in the rumours related to the 1968 Uganda coup d'etat that beyond acknowledging that something out of the ordinary had happened, they were to a large extent unreal and even at the magical end of religious understandings. Rumour also had its consequences of the mass production of the thoughts of Mao Tse-Tung, his little red book originally produced for the Chinese army and the repetitive singing of 'the east is red' as a Communist song which soon became something in the nature of a hymn. Rumour soon produced evidence in the letters to the press of the miraculous consequences of using and holding the book and singing the 'hymn', which cannot have been the promotional intentions of its editors.

All forms of mass media whatever the correctness of their origins or intentions of their producers have a cognitive permanency independent of its origins and originators. An inflammatory speech however loud the amplifiers may have made the words, is lost with the evaporation of its sound but record it on tape and video and it has unlimited longevity. In video form is likely to have entertainment as well as religious importance as well as a popularity which will only be restricted by the reliability of the electricity supply, the availability of screens to show it and the time to watch which is likely to be particularly high among the unemployed who are readily available for participation in public protests.

On the other hand in a picture of a burning mosque or church in Indonesia the message is clear for its architecture tells the viewer what is being burnt. But the picture of a burnt-out Indian railway carriage in which some fifty Hindus were burnt to death, regardless of the circumstances in which this horrible event occurred, the headlines beneath in the vernacular press can be a permanent incitement to retaliatory violence. Rumour propagated by word of mouth may not be as influential as the background of repetitive ideas promulgated in the media as a background to religious hostility.

The modern world has provided societies with far greater possibilities of violence based on religious ideas because the idea of the democratic vote has created the means of protest and the concept of numerically based legitimacy. This combined with mass communication of events and ideas which are largely independent of literacy have made societies much more malleable to mass ideas which are not always based on the rationalities of social and economic development.

16

Conclusions

Religion includes both the Great Traditions of Buddhism, Christianity, Hinduism, Islam, Judaism and Taoism and the Little Traditions within and outside these faiths which have often been defined as magic, are part of the social practices and thinking patterns of all societies and everyone in them. A varying quality of whatever social life in which various aspects of violence occur.

Any tentative conclusions correlating religion and violence is handicapped by the absence of precision about what is being connected. To correlate violence with religion cannot just be a breakdown of the forms and extent of the violence involved as it requires a dominating religious intention. This involves both violence between and within religions but also secular violence against religion and religious violence against secularism.

We have taken violence to include not only its physical aspects in the destruction of people and property but the more elusive restrictions on people's wishes by the violence of fear and the social and political dominance of religious regimes. There are rarely forms of violence which can be accepted as almost exclusively religious such as the occasional crucifixions of Christians and forced circumcision in Islam. Communal violence for what can be accepted analytically as an exclusively religious purpose may not have occurred after the Middle Ages.

Violence may seem easy to define if always inaccurately when it relates to material damages to people or property but violence in the religious context must be considered in a much broader context. It involves eschatological issues of the next life in an unending series of rebirths or the single heavenly life following a single earthly life, as well as the realities of everyday fear. At one end of the scale there is religiously motivated genocide and at the other the pathologies of individual religious anxieties and extreme behaviour.

Religion is equally imprecise and there are perhaps as many definitions as there are social scientists making them. Definitions do exist and have a practical as much as theoretical existence, but they are not for religions in any general sense but are for a religion. This is particularly characteristic of Christian denominations and to a lesser extent Islam with its Five Pillars of Faith of which four require no more than physical performance for their fulfilment. Definitions of what is required of believers in a religion is a feature of a minority of the Great Traditions and does not exist at all in the Little Traditions in which belief is more implicit than an explicit requirement. Indeed most theologians would exclude the Little Traditions from their religious definitions as being magical or at best on the fringes of true faith partially acceptable as intellectualised charity or as traditional social necessities in certain environments.

The practices and ideologies of religions have always been changing irrespective of what those involved consider to be divine intervention. The forms of the Great Traditions have a certain longevity but the Little Traditions embodied as they are in religious behaviour which is not much related to literacy, vary between individuals and families as well as generations. It is never a constant and is thus is an elusive theme to link to violence.

Since we use the term religion to cover all activities which relate to non-pragmatic beliefs and practices connecting social hopes and anxieties with god(s), spirits, ancestors and impersonal evil involving individuals, communities, societies and nations, it is obvious that violence can be correlated to a much wider range of activities than the theologically defined ones related to the Great Traditions or indeed excluded on similar grounds.

It is a reasonable conclusion that every religious category of behaviour is correlated somewhere in living memory with violence. It is the commonplaceness of violence and religious activities which defeat attempts at finite categorizations on which social welfare, religious and governmental agencies can plan.

Of course, there are certain wide ranging occasions of violence such as the suppression of women's rights in Islamic countries and the frightening initiation rites in some traditional societies which either deprive people of status or enable them to gain it which are so common as to be the subjects of international comment and agitation. Such occasions of violence may not be explicitly supported by a religion but are certainly correlated to it.

Other events such as processions connected with particular faiths certainly seem to be the occasions of repetitive violence in numerous riots in India, Northern Ireland and elsewhere or at least the mass media promote this connection. Analysts work backwards from these riots, but in terms of the number of religious processions for funerals, weddings, saints days and other cyclical religious celebrations, occasions of religious violence became statistically uncommon even in religiously mixed societies. So we must conclude that definitions are of little value in considering either religion or violence as discrete entities and also that the data on which attempts are made to define is generally unreliable in both quality and quantity.

There is certainly nothing of definitional value in attempting to analyse religious violence comparing Eastern and Western cultures. Apart from the intermingling of religious cultures in the Mediterranean basin, all religions are to some extent syncretic either in what contributed to their originating ideas or in how these religions are practised within their Little Traditions. Boxing off a religion has never been an analytical possibility when one remembers the medieval monk Fa-Hsien carrying Buddhist scriptures from India to China, early Christian presences in both China and India and Islam travelling along the veins of trade to East Africa and Indonesia apart from the Greek Gandaran influence on Buddhism in ancient Afghanistan. Religious ideas and their subtended practices have never had any restrictions on their movement.

So violence which can be attributed to religion cannot be divided along any East-West cultural and geographical divide. Islam which predominates in contemporary violence occurring mainly outside its core areas in the Middle East and Christianity is predominantly non-Western but is currently involved in persistent violence in Northern Ireland. Similarly there is no case for an ethnic division over who are the victims or perpetrators of violence except for Judaism which appears now in the context of violence to be both politically and geographically ethnic and in a Western form.

Biology and psychology may also be of little use in connecting religion to violence and *vice versa* except perhaps in the area of individual psycho-pathology. Human beings are capable of thinking about violence or being violent for any number of correlating factors and should be set aside as having any dominating influence on this issue. The ability to be violent or to think about violence is not the same thing as having a predisposition or compulsion to be violent, much less one in relation to religion.

Any analysis of violence correlated to religion tends to be dominated by primary factors laid down after the events, but secondary initiating factors are more important and indeed an enormous number of these which push and pull Muslims, Christians and other believers into violence. In this it is never possible to isolate these or reduced their number to something approaching scientific cohesion. In individuals and societies there will always be something approaching Parallel Distributive Processing (McClelland, 1986), a psychological theory that while there is a sequence of processes in the mind, they are virtually instantaneous and involve an almost unlimited number of factors, operating on the patterning of a complex computer.

This would mean that there may be persistent factors correlating to violence but that they fluctuate in importance as influences on individuals, groups and societies. Moreover that they fluctuate very rapidly in both space and time and the religious and secular rationalities involving an individual or indeed a thousand people in the same society, may disappear in an instant and reappear an instant latter. The stability of a factor may be correlated to a range of people and it may be that only the visible grossness of the violence that creates the illusions of similarities.

So in the use of violence for a purpose connected or correlated to religion individuals, groups and societies may be moved by a large number of coinciding factors. Indeed an American writer of violent fiction (King, 2001) wrote in connection with the September 11 World Trade Centre atrocities, that he did not believe that his writings or any isolated factors could drive an individual to violence but that they could act as accelerants. Thus there are accelerants acting on precipitating factors such as the destruction of the Ayodhya mosque and there are many other contemporary examples acting on a range of factors going back several centuries.

There is a parallel here with fire for which almost every material has a point in which it will ignite. We have in the situations of religious violence the presence of social, economic, political and environmental accelerants which have turned a social event into a violent one and in a specialised sense connecting it with religion.

Perhaps the most easily understood of such contemporary correlations has been the creation of the state of Israel precipitated by centuries of western anti-Semitism and this itself creating the existing intermittent and persistent bilateral religious terrorism by and against Israeli and America on a global scale. At the other end of the scale petty local insults over caste privileges have precipitated and will continue to precipitate thousands of violent acts in India (Kambie, 1981).

We see that it is not possible to isolate either religion or violence except by restricting the terms of reference and confining certain events to their primary correlations. In the first place it is not possible to define religion except in cases where the religion defines itself and by such definitions usually excluding other Great Traditions apart from the difficulties with Buddhism whose thinkers would not describe their understandings as religious.

Violence which is correlated in some ways to religious beliefs has no overall regular appearance but it does appear to correlate much more specifically to some types of societies more than others. The dominance of Christianity more than Islam in gross historical violence is obvious even though today this correlation is being reversed. The violence related to Hinduism is much less and is mainly a reaction to Islam and that of Buddhism and Taoism it is negligible.

In the four types of societies which have been examined (Hsu, 1972), it appears that the social system of the West based on independent nuclear families correlates to repeated instances of religious violence, but this is certainly not enough to establish a closer connection.

Possible additional clues are firstly the growth of philosophical logic in the West which in the religious sphere has led to concepts of all-embracing rightness separated from wrongness; the early appearance of definitions and dogma used and developed by an elite who did not have to worry about their own livelihoods.

Wholesale literacy may not be a factor as this is a modern and not a particularly relevant issue in religion where most of its popular forms are mnemonic. Indeed the Eastern religions and their thinkers have been highly literate for millennia and recording their thoughts far longer than Western theologians without coming to a stage of definition and attempted exactitude.

It is not so much that literacy is a factor which correlates to both religion and violence but the form which literacy takes. Alphabetical languages may be easier to learn, use and change than the non-alphabetical ones which are both rigid and require much greater intellectual effort to learn and specialise in. In English the same letters are used for theology and market trading whereas in Mandarin the dictionary may contain over forty thousand different ideograms in which there is no sharing between the language used in philosophy and in bicycle repairing. Modern Chinese intellectuals have no particular difficulty over the ideograms which are a thousand years old and which have remained the same, but this does not apply to alphabetical languages which require experts to read medieval documents.

The simplicity and adaptability of alphabetical languages has not only allowed a wider spread of literacy which may not have been all that important for the average commonplace practice of religion at both the levels of the Great and Little Traditions, but has allowed the development of definitions for a wide range of affairs including religion.

This in turn has correlated to other factors. The European Enlightenment as opposed to the Buddhist one which has stressed the need for detachment from each and every social involvement, has promoted the understanding that anything of importance need to be and could be defined accurately for the understanding if necessary of many who are not directly involved in the subject matter.

So Christian theologians as specialists in religious thought with the example of Thomas Aquinas before them, felt the need to follow the principles of scientific logic in matters which are basically beyond human comprehension except in terms of faith. From this came the monotheistically defined categories of those 'inside' and those who were 'outside' this faith.

The second factor must be the extension or parallel development of definitions to administration in which every citizen is confined within a range of defined categories in the creation and administration of which they had little say. While it is reasonable to conclude that religious definitions for those who are 'saved' or 'not saved' has often contributed to religious violence, it should also be remembered that administrative definitions and their legal backups have contributed to far more violence. These administrative rulings have defined citizenship, age, education and indeed it is hard to think of any modern social activity which has not involved definitions. The German bureaucracy between 1933 and 1945 defined who was a Jew or Jewess and killed millions of those so defined.

Non-literate societies or parts of other societies which avoid documentary literacy in their disputes, treat each issue as negotiable. It is accepted as a social fact that those involved know that the circumstances of all disputes and differences of opinion and that these will always vary from any ideal but undefined root which provides moral paradigms for that society. This would account for the fact that traditional societies may have fought on and off for a number of secular and objective reasons relating to prestige, property and food but not over religious issues. It would seem likely therefore that a major contribution to religious violence must be a combination of alphabetical literacy, the spreading nature of the European Enlightenment and the inevitability of bureaucratic definitions as part of administration. The main key to religious violence would seem to be dogma which has been extensively institutionalised in both Christianity and Islam which laid down specific and required sectarian beliefs and practices.

The religions of the other three types of social systems either never recorded their beliefs or made them exclusive because they were non-literate or formulated their ideas in forms which never developed into definitions. This developed from their fundamental understanding of the impermanence of all social activities or of the undesirable nature of such attachments. There was nothing in their beliefs which were sufficiently exact about which it was possible to quarrel violently despite their complex literacy. Indeed the Lord Buddha advised monasteries in which disputes arose on religious questions to split rather than continue to argue.

Contemporary violence correlated to religious beliefs and practices is common enough but its profile has changed. Historically Christians either actively or passively have predominated in this, although they may not have been acting as Christians as was the case with the Crusades. Today Christians have been actively violent in the Balkans and reactively so in the Sudan and northern Nigeria and in any case Christians are so divided denominationally that any lumping them together as a single religion does not make for any confining conclusions.

Buddhism has become nationalistically violent in Sri Lanka and Hinduism is perennially linked nationally with reciprocal violence with their fellow Muslim Indians (Engineer, 1983, 1988). Traditional religions and Christo-centric spirit possession cults have erupted violently in Uganda with the end of the Amin regime from which came some anti-Muslim violence (Khiddu-Makubuya, 1994)

It seems clear that Islam now dominates occurrences of violence connected with religion with such a wide range of correlations to make it distinct from outbreaks of violence related to other religions with its numerous suicide bombings, anti-American terrorism, and protests in reaction to what are locally interpreted rightly or wrongly as insults to Islam as in the November 2002 riots in Nigeria over the Miss World contest.

Islam is based on the belief that God revealed to the Prophet Mohammad His message which were recorded in the Koran in Arabic which is regarded as holy in its entirety in both its specific instructions and its ambiguities. Other religions have holy books which do not have this direct element of revelation and which are available in translations or in languages not in common use.

Islam in comparison to Christianity is a unified faith in which the majority are Sunni and a minority of the more emotional Shia concentrated in Iran between which there has been periodic violence (Hussain, 1990) but nothing on the scale of the medieval Thirty years War in Europe between Christians.

It would be easy to correlate outbreaks of religious correlated violence to social, economic, political and environmental changes. However the whole world and not just the Third World societies has been subjected to radical, accelerated and continuing changes. In the latter societies these have destroyed many traditional practices rather than the ideas behind them and has left them emotionally as well as materially dependent on Western consumerism and its higher standards of living and more importantly its overbearing sense of social, bureaucratic and technical superiority.

In this respect Muslim societies in the Third World are not definably different to other countries there which have Buddhist, Christian, Hindu and Taoist majorities. Yet only the Islamic ones have seen violence to be part of their required religious practices and as a solution to what their religious elite interpret to be their own failure to follow the details of the Prophet Mohammad's divinely provided message and to the encroaching immoralities of the Western rather than specifically Christian way of living.

All religions other than Islam do not have this observable unity and moreover do not have its precision of definition and a body of scholars who have no sacramental role and are devoted to the interpretation of fixed texts which then become part of divinely ordained law. So there is in Islam a unified message and moreover this faith is based on the well authenticated life of the Prophet Mohammad. In this there is an important connection between what he said and what he did. Very little of Christ's message can be authenticated in this way and not only did he reject a political role and his inspired programme of behaviour for believers is very far from aggressive. No modern Christian theologian has to rearrange any ancient specific instructions to fit in with contemporary life.

Almost nothing is known of the Lord Buddha and his sayings are reconstructions on a pattern of thinking which are complex and unworldly. There are few social roles open to Buddhists since they are required to detach themselves from worldly commitment. Hinduism and Taoism have commentators but no founding figures as models. The models for behaviour in all religions other than Islam and perhaps Sikhism have no founding theological precedents for violence against members of other faiths or against defaulting members of their own beliefs.

So we are left with Islam in which the Word of God is written in the Koran. So it is a matter of faith for Muslims to follow the requirements of the Koran and to model themselves on the life of the Prophet Mohammad and in this they are no different to those wanting to copy the lived of Buddha or Christ and indeed any other charismatic religious leader.

In this the most important points must be that the Prophet Mohammad not only created a new religion in place of outdated traditionalism but that it was established by a combination of personal charisma and force of arms. At the end of his life he was the Messenger of God for this new religion and as head of state in negotiation with other rulers.

The model here is as much social and political as religious. No other religious leader who has become the undisputed creator of an international religion has a personal record of having fought in nine battles and led many raids. No other religious leader of such undoubted eminence has ordered the killings of others for what can be argued as circumstantial necessity. The model here is a justification for violence against unbelievers and for behaviour which is the reverse of pacific.

A feature of all theological thinking is the updating of the original message to make it appropriate for use in societies of great variability and in situations which have virtually nothing in common with the social environments in which the original message was made. This is a perennial problem and most religions have institutionalised processes for authenticating necessary changes. Sunni Islam does not have any such process and it is stuck with the original model in an increasingly urbanised, electronic and internationalised world.

The conclusion must be that believing Muslims have in their faith ample divinely ordained reasons and justifications for violence against non-believers and defaulters based on the original situations in which the Messenger of God found himself. But there is a reverse approach for those who seek an alternative approach from the Koran as promoting peace. So there would appear to be a choice for Muslims between violence and peace and a choice moreover which is no part of the doctrines of other religions which are dominating by peaceful requirements.

Religious violence has no identifiable and universal profile. It is clear that it is rarely if ever the sole and primary element in contemporary violence and the religious component will vary in intensity at the various levels at which it is studied. It is certainly primary in the minds of Islamic suicide bombers or martyrs but even that may depend on who is reaching that conclusion; loaded phrases get loaded answers. But at whatever possible level violence is examined as having religious correlations, there are numerous other possible factors beyond the conscious control of individuals or communities, but certainly both covertly and overtly influential over their behaviour. Their interpretation of this violence as related to their religion may be no more than a personally convenient one, while others would attribute it to jealousy or some other more commonplace factor.

It would also be unwise to see contemporary religious violence as a general response to uncertainties and misfortunes or that there has been any increase in these in the absence of comparable data. Most individuals and communities has always come to terms with the commonplaceness of misery and disaster. Natural disasters come and go and may last only in folk memories; the 1884 rinder pest epidemic in East Africa caused widespread lethal misery and the cholera epidemics in India along the lines of pilgrimages only stopped in 1948, and they have been replaced by earthquakes and drought in Gujarat and AIDS in Uganda and elsewhere. The achieved dominance of the Han and Islam in China and northern India and elsewhere remain for one side or the other a cause of shame or pleasure. Past imagined glories and present miseries make an unstable mix.

The final conclusions must be that there are no clear correlations between a specific religion and violence except for Islam; it is both too common and too varied for any such identification. But there are three paradigmatic levels that can be identified.

Firstly, violence is no part of human genetic make-up and there is no violent activity which is sufficiently exact to be correlated to any social or indeed religious activity. However, human groups rather than societies as the basic form of social life do have common characteristics. There is a combination of small group bonding and a dislike and avoidance of outsiders; the greater the social distance separating them, the greater the distaste and tension. While this may be obvious enough for clearly defined and observable social and economic differences, the tensions over religious issues may be rougher because they are often not definable and therefore more useful for expressing tensions. It is the dislike of outsiders which provides accelerants.

Secondly, violence is nearer to the surface in societies such as the Mayan Indians of Mexico whose dissatisfaction with modernity could be fitted into the ideas remaining of their medieval civilisation with its spectacular buildings and specialised writing system, and provide a justification and an accelerant for violence. This writing may have provided them with long lasting patterns of thinking such as their concepts of cyclical time and spiritual essence (Justeson and Kaufman, 1993) which have not been displaced by conversion to Roman Catholicism and the political dominance of semi-Spanish outsiders.

Whereas the Russian Christians after decades of Soviet persecution emerged liturgically and hierarchically modified if not damaged, the Muslims with their liturgical simplicity and absence of any necessary hierarchy with an unmodified and essential liturgical language, retained their rites of passage and personal rituals emerging from the Communist era without any modified system or need to create any new religious approaches for new social realities. A second level ancient paradigm providing a background to self-legitimating violence in Chechnya and elsewhere.

The third or proximate paradigm for religious violence provides the immediate solutions for difficulties which may require public rather than private expression. How does a society cope with matters which go beyond the more or less face to face solutions which work with small groups. For matters which involve people at the outer limits of social distance acceptability such as the inter-clan negotiations of the Leopard skin 'chiefs' of the Nuer (Evans-Pritchard, 1940) and the private and informal heading off of trouble by the Hindu and Muslim leaders in Hyderabad (Naidu, 1990). The complexity of the issues involved and the length of time in negotiating possible solutions makes violence capable of acceleration by innumerable religious and secular factors.

In conclusion we can summarise religious violence in the ways that it seems to correlate to the four general socio-religious systems. African traditional societies had no specifically religious violence until Islam in West Africa and Christianity in East Africa introduced monotheism and its current violent derivatives. Polytheistic and ancestor worshipping oriental religions had no conception of a single true God and again had little religious violence except for reformist Buddhist movements and the Christo-centric Taiping rebellion in China. The Indian social system seems to have had little religious violence until Islamic monotheism became widespread causing reactions by and to Hindus. All three have not totalled anything like the widespread and persistent violence correlated to the monotheistic religions coming out of the Middle-East firstly dominated by Christianity and then supplanted by Islam, the religion of dogma and absolute faith.

The future for violence correlated to religion is likely to be both persistent and sporadic particularly around two foci which are neither likely to diminish or indeed to be soluble. Firstly, contemporary Islamic violence is likely to continue its current prominence focusing on hostility to Jewish expansionism and its American support. The spin-offs in global Islamic reactive violence is likely to continue for generations.

Secondly, at a more national level caste in India in which the social structure of Hinduism has existed for so long as to be impervious to global socio-political ideologies when it became linked to democratic voting procedures and bureaucratic legalism. In this matter it is inevitable that violence will continue between the locally interpreted 'have not' castes and Untouchables and the 'have' castes.

In the well developed West there is an absence of cohesive religious beliefs and minimal religious violence. It seems unlikely that the lack of economic progress rather than political failures can account for violence connected with religion, or it would be more widespread. In the Third World with its failure to develop or create sound political systems insuring stability, violence that can be correlated to religion is sporadic and politically motivated civil wars are widespread.

The history of Islamic states with their still conspicuous architecture and exceptional art may remain in the minds of contemporary Muslim leaders and laity as a might-have-been model for its recreation in the present. In comparison to this past glory current Islamic states with their corruption and administrative shortcomings as well as their inability to present a common policy against what they assess as their current enemies without and within, has made the past a seductive model for the future regardless of its inappropriateness to a contemporary global unity centring on scientific advances.

The unconsciously created overbearing nature of Western progress and material power and its insidious and destructive advances into traditional understandings against which Islamic fundamentalists see violence authorised by the Koran to be the only virtuous response. There is little reason to anticipate any reduction in Islamic violence

Overall there will always be the occasions for religious violence either definitely provoked by those whose religious and secular interests are served by this and in reactions to secular events which are interpreted as antagonistic to a particular faith.

Bibliography

The Numbers in boldface in brackets following each reference give the text page on which the article or book is cited.

Abbink, J. (2000). '*Violence and the Crisis of Conciliation*' Africa. 70(4): 527-550. **[59]**

Abu-Lughod, L. (1993). 'Finding a Place for Islam. Egyptian television serials and national interest'. *Public Culture*. 5: 493-513 . **[107]**

Abu-Lughod, J.L. (1996). 'Palestinians; Exiles at Home and Abroad'. In R. Cohen.(ed). *The sociology of migration.* Elgar, Cheltenham. **[177]**

Adler, E.N. (1908). *Auto de Fe and Jew*. Oxford University Press, Oxford.

Aiyappan, A. (1958). 'Theories of Culture Change and Culture Contact' in J.P. Mills.(ed). *Essays in anthropology presented to Rai Bahadur Sarat.* Chandra Roy, Lucknow. **[11]**

Alba, V. (1950). *Histoire des Republique Espagnoles*. Vincennes. **[201]**

Allport, G.W. & L. Postman. (1947). *The Psychology of Rumour*. Holt, Rinehart & Winston, New York. **[263]**

Al-Rasheed, M. (1999). 'Evading State Control. Political Protest and Technology in Saudi-Arabia'. In A. Chester.(ed). *The anthropology of power. Empowerment and disempowerment in changing structure.* Routledge, London. 149-162. **[290]**

Altekar, A.S. (1950). *The Position of Women in Hindu Civilisation.* Benarsidas, Benares.

Alther, L. (1975). 'The Snake Handlers'. *New Society*. 34: 532-5. **[201]**

Al-Waqidi. (1882). *Kitab al-maghazi*. J. Wellausen. (trans). Berlin. **[70]**

Anderson, J. (1994). *Religion, State and Politics in the Soviet Union and Successor States*. Cambridge University Press, Cambridge. 38-67. **[193, 207]**

Andreski, S. (1964). *Elements of Comparative Sociology*. Weidenfeld and Nicolson, London. **[23]**

Anonymous. (1943). 'The Chaplain's Duty in Battle'. *The Chaplains Magazine*. Middle East. 12. Army Headquarters, Cairo. **[51]**

Ardry, R. (1966). *The Territorial Imperative*. Blond, London. **[275]**

Arendt, H. (1964). *Eichmann in Jerusalem*. Viking, New York.

Armstrong, K. (1992). *Holy War. The crusades and their impact on today's world.* Macmillan, London. **[7, 65, 89, 291-2]**

Aronson, E. (1996). 'The Return of the Repressed. Dissonance Theory Makes a Comeback'. *Psychological Enquiry*. 3: 303-352.

Aurobindo, Sri (1922). *Essays on the Gita*. Arya Publishing House, Calcutta. **[105]**

Averill, J. (1982). *Anger and Aggression: An essay on emotion.* Springer-Verlag, New York.

Bakker, H.T. (1986). *Ayodhya*. Forsten, Groningen. **[64]**

Balda, J.L. (1993), 'The Role of kiSwahili in East African Islam'. In L. Brennen.(ed). *Muslim identity and social change in sub-Saharan Africa.* Hurst, London. **[50]**

Bandura, A. (1973). *Aggression, A Social Learning Analysis.* Prentice-Hall, New Jersey. **[76]**

Bannerjea, A.C. (1951). 'A note on cholera in the United Provinces'. *Indian J. Medical Research.* 39: 17-40. **[236]**

Barkindo, B.M. (1993). 'Growing Islamism in Kano City since 1970. Causes, Forms and Implications'. In L. Brenner.(ed). *Muslim identity and social change in sub-Saharan Africa*. Hurt, London. 91-195. **[155]**

Barrett, D.B. (1968). *Schism and Renewal in Africa*. Oxford University Press, Nairobi. **[50, 128]**

Bauer, W. (1976). *China and the Search for Happiness: Recurring themes in four thousand years.* Seabury, New York. **[19]**

Bax, M. (1995). *Medjugorje, Religion, Politics and Violence in Rural Bosnia*. Vrije Universiteit Vitgeverij, Amsterdam.**[4]**

Baxi, U. (1990). 'Reflections on the Reservations Crisis in Gujarat' in V. Das.(ed). *Mirrors of violence, communities, riots and survivors*. Oxford University Press, New Delhi. 216-39. **[144]**

Bayly, S. (1999). *Caste, Society and Politics from 18th Century to the Modern Age*. Cambridge University Press, Cambridge. **[295]**

Becker, E. (1993). *When the War Was Over: The voices of Cambodia's revolution and its people.* Touchstone, New York. **[202]**

Behrend, H. (1991). 'Is Alice Lakwena a Witch? The Holy Spirit Movement in its Fight against Evil in the North'. In H.B. Hansen and M. Twaddle.(eds). *Changing Uganda.* Currey, Oxford. **[80, 128]**

(1997). 'The Power to Heal, Power to Kill. Spirit Possession and War in Northern Uganda. 1986-94'. In H. Behrend and U. Luig. (eds). *Spirit possession: Modernity and power in Africa.* Currey, Oxford. **[80, 121, 132]**

Bekaert, S. (1997). *System and Repertoire in Sakata Medicine.* Catholic University Press, Louvain. **[35-6]**

Bel-Ami, I. (1984). *Saint Veneration among the Jews of Morocco.* (in Hebrew). Magnes Press, Jerusalem.

Benedict, P. (1991). *The Huguenot Population of France.* 1600-85. American Philosophical Society, Philadelphia. **[216]**

Berkowitz, L. (1962). *Aggression; A Social Psychological Analysis.* McGraw-Hill, New York.

Bernard, Saint. (1919). 'Sermon in Praise of the Templers' in A. Vanderpool.(ed). *La doctrine scholastique du droit de guerre.* Paris. **[102]**

Berndt, R. (1962). *Excess and restraint.* Chicago University Press, Chicago. **[183]**

Bernstein. B. (1975). *Class, Codes and Control.* Routledge and Kegan Paul, London. **[7]**

Berry, J.W. and Annis, R.C. (1974). 'Acculturative Stress: The Role of Ecology, Culture and Differentiation'. *J. Cross-cultural Psychology.* 5: 382-405. **[278]**

Bhardwaj, S.M. (1973). *Hindu Places of Pilgrimage in India.* University of California Press, Berkeley. **[237]**

Black-Michaud, J. (1975). *Cohesive Force.* St Martin's Press, New York.

Blais, Y.M. (1985). 500 Messages a Vivre. *SUN*, Nijmegen.

Blank, J. (2001). *Mullahs on the Main Frame: Islam and modernity among the Daudi Bohras.* University of Chicago Press, Chicago. **[182]**

Blickle, C.P. (1981). '*The Revolution of 1525. The German Peasants*' war from a New Perspective. Johns Hopkins University Press, Baltimore. **[41]**

Bleich, A.R. (1950). 'Prophylaxis of Penile Carcinoma'. *J. American Medical Association.* 143: 1054-7. **[162]**

Block, R. (1993). '*Killers*'. New York Review of Books. 18 November. 9-10.

Boal, F.W. (1982). 'Segregation and Mixing: Space and Residence in Belfast' in F.W. Boal and J.N.H. Douglas.(eds). *Integration and division: geographical perspectives on the Northern Ireland problem.* Academic Press, London. **[89]**

Boardman, E.P. (1952). *Christian Influence upon the Ideology of the Taiping Rebellion.* University of Wisconsin Press, Madison. **[216]**

Boddy, J. (1989). *Wombs and Alien Spirits: Women, Men and the Zar Cult.* Wisconsin University Press, Milwaukee. **[130]**

Bogoras, W. (1904-9). *The Chuckjee: Jessup North Pacific Expedition.* 7: 372-3. Brill, Leiden. **[209]**

Boehm, C. (1984). *Blood Revenge: The Anthropology of Feuding in Montenegro and other Tribal Societies.* University of Kansas Press, Lawrence.

Bolton, J.M. (1972). 'Food Taboos among the Orang Asli in west Malaysia'. *American J. Clinical Nutrition.* 25: 789-99. **[247]**

Borhek, J.J. and Curtis, R.F. (1975). *A Sociology of Belief.* New York. **[67]**

Bourdeaux, M.A. (1970). *Patriarch and Prophets.* MacMillan, London. 96-115. **[193]**

Bourdieu, P. (1990). *The Invention of Culture,* Chicago University Press, Chicago. **[29]**

Bourdieu, P. (1991). Language and symbolic power. Polity Press, Cambridge. **[102]**

Boyajian, D.H. (1972). *The Case for a Forgotten Genocide.* New York. **[216]**

Brailsford, H.M. (1906). *Macedonia: Its Races and Their Future.* London. **[188]**

Bramwell, P.M. (1943). *The Army Chaplain: Duties.* Royal Army Chaplains Department, London. **[51]**

Brandon, S.G.F. (1970). *Dictionary of Comparative Religion.* Weidenfeld and Nicolson, London. **[247]**

Brass, P.R. (1997). *The Theft of an Idol. Text and Context in the Representation of Collective Violence.* Princeton University Press, New Jersey. **[307]**

Breil, J. (1959). *La population en Algerie.* Imprimarie National, Paris. **[228]**

Brett, A. (1996). 'Testimonies of War Trauma in Uganda' in T. Allen.(ed). *In Search of Cool Ground.* UN Research Institute for Social Development, Geneva. **[80]**

Brewer, N.B. and Campbell, D.T. (1976). *Ethnocentrism and Intergroup Attitudes. East African evidence.* Wiley, New York. **[275]**

Brhat Tantrasara. Krsnananda Agamavagisa. (1934). *Basvimati Sahitiya Mandir*, Calcutta. **[105]**

Bringa, T. (1995). *Being Muslim the Bosnian Way. Identity and Community in a Central Bosnian Village.* Princeton University Press, New Jersey. **[188]**

Broom, L & P. Selznick. (1977). *Sociology: Harper & Row*, New York. **[17]**

Brown, C.H. (1984). 'Tourism and Ethnic Competition in a Ritual Form: The Fire-walkers of Fiji'. *Oceania.* 54: 229-44. **[29]**

Brownmiller, S. (1975). *Against our Will: Men, Women and Rape.* Simon and Schuster, New York.

Bruce, S. and Wallis, R. (1985). *Sociological Theory, Religion and Collective Action.* Queens University Press, Belfast.

Buddha, the Dialogues of (1921). T.W. and C.A.F. Rhys Davids (trans). Oxford University Press, London.

Buijtenhuijs, R. (1971). *Le movement Mau Mau.* Mouton, The Hague. **[186]**

Burke, J. (2000). *An Intimate History of Killing.* Granta, London. **[52]**

Burridge, K. (1969). *New Heaven, New Earth.* Schocken, New York. **[186]**

Burton, R. (1963). *The Perfumed Garden of Shaykh Nefzawi.* Spearman, London. **[73]**

Burton, R. and Arbuthnot, F.F. (1963). *The Kamasutra of Vatsyayana.* Allen and Unwin, London. **[73]**

Buruma, I. (2002). '*The Blood Lust of Identity*' New York Review of Books. 11 April: 12-4. **[175]**

Butallia, U. (1993). 'Community, State and Gender: On Woman's Agency During Partition'. Economic and Political Weekly. 28(17): WS 12-24. April 24. **[88]**

Callan, H. (1970). *Ethology and Society. Towards an Anthropological View.* Clarendon Press, Oxford. **[20, 23]**

Callicott, J.B. (1994). *Earth's Insights. A survey of ecological ethics from the Mediterranean basin to the Australian outback.* University of California Press, Berkeley.

Carstairs, G.M. (1983). *Death of a witch. A village in north India.* Hutchinson, London. **[148, 150]**

Casanova, J.(1994). *Public Religions in the Modern World.* Chicago University Press, Chicago. **[167-8]**

Chadwick, O. (2002). '*Bad for the Jews*'. New York Review of Books. 28 March: 14-6. **[53]**

Chagnon, N.A. (1977). *Yanomamo–the Fierce People*. Holt Rinehart and Winston, New York. **[56, 228]**

Chambers, I. (1994). *Migrancy, Culture, Identity*. Routledge, London. **[119]**

Chandler, D.P. (1991). *The Tragedy of Cambodian History*. Yale University Press, New Haven. **[202]**

Chandrasekhar, S. (1959). *Infant Mortality in India*. 1901-55. Allen and Unwin, London. **[228]**

Chao Chien-Min. (1958). *People's Daily*. Beijing. 17 June. **[205]**

Chapple, C. (1986). 'Non-injury to Animals: Jain and Buddhist Perspectives'. In T. Regan.(ed). *Animal sacrifice. Religious Perspectives on the Use of Animals in Science*. Temple University Press, Philadelphia.

Chelkowski, P.J. (1980). 'Mourning becomes Revolution'. *Asia*. 3: 30-7. 44-5.

Chevers, N. (1870). *A Manual of Medical Jurisprudence*. Thacker Spink, Calcutta. **[228]**

Chuang-Tzu. (1964). *Writings*. B. Watson (trans). Columbia University Press, New York. **[47]**

Chubin, S. & C. Tripp. (1988). *Iran and Iraq at War*. Tauris, London. **[154]**

Cloudsley, A. (1983). Women of Omdurman: Life, Love and the Cult of Virginity. *Ethnographica*, London. **[163]**

Cohen, D. et al. (1998). 'The Sacred and the Social. Cultures of Honor and Violence'. in P. Gilbert and B. Andrews.(eds). *Shame: Interpersonal behaviour in Psychopathology and Culture*. Oxford University Press, New York. **[77]**

Collins, E.F. (1997). *Pierced by Murugan's Lance, Ritual, Power and Moral Redemption among Malaysian Hindus*. Chicago University Press, Chicago. **[29]**

Comaroff, J.L. and D.C. Stern. (1995). *Perspectives on Nationalism and War*. Gordon and Breach, Amsterdam.

Commission for Scheduled Castes and Scheduled Tribes. Annual Report.(1981). Government Press, New Delhi. **[156]**

Conklin, B.A. (1995). 'Thus our Bodies, thus Was Our Custom; Mortuary Cannibalism in an Amazonian Society'. *American Ethnologist*. 22(1): 75-101. **[166]**

Contursi, J.A. (1989). 'Militant Hindus and Buddhist Dalits; Hegemony and Resistance in an Urban Slum'. *American Ethnologist.* 16(3): 441-57. **[81]**

Cooper, B.M. (1998). 'Gender and Religion in Hausaland. Variations in Islamic Practice in Niger and Nigeria.' In H.L. Bodmin & N. Tohidi.(eds). *Women in Moslem Societies.* Rienner, Boulder. **[115]**

Cormack, R.J. and R.D. Osborne. (1983). *Religion, Education and Employment.* Appletree Press, Belfast.

Cribb, R. (1991). 'Problems in the Historiography of the Killings in Indonesia'. In R. Cribb.(ed). *The Indonesian killings 1965-66.* Monash University Press, Victoria. **[201]**

Cribb, R.(ed). (1991). *The Indonesian killings. 1965-66.* Monash University Press, Victoria. **[201]**

Cribb, R. *et al.* (1991). 'The Mass Killings in Bali'. In R. Cribb.(ed). *The Indonesian killings. 1965-66.* Monash University Press, Victoria. **[201]**

Dandekar, K. (1959). *Demographic Survey of Six Communities.* Asia Publishing House, Bombay. **[245]**

D'Andrade, R. (1992). 'Schemas and Motivation' in D'Andrade, R. and C. Strauss.(eds). *Human motives and cultural models.* Cambridge University Press, New York. **[55]**

Daniel, C. (1966). *The Story of the Eyam Plague.* Privately Printed, Eyam.

Daniel, E.V. (1987). *Fluid Signs; Being a Person the Tamil Way.* University of California Press, Berkeley. **[161]**

Das, V. (1990). 'Our Work to Cry, Your Work to Listen'. In V. Das.(ed). *Mirrors of violence. Communities, riots and survivors in South Asia.* Oxford University Press, Delhi.

Deedat, A.H. (1990). '*Crucifixion or Crucifiction*' Mizani, 8. I June. MHK Publications, London.

De Groot, J.J.M. (1903-4). *Sectarianism and Religious; Persecution in China: A Page in the History of Religion.* Amsterdam. **[194]**

Deshpande, S. (2000). 'Hegemonic Spatial Strategies. The Nation's Space and Hindu Communalism in 20th century India'. In P. Chatterjee & P. Jegernathan.(eds). *Community, gender and violence.* Hurst, London.

Diehl, C.G. (1956). *Instrument and Purpose. Studies on Rites and Ritual in South India.* Gleerups, Lund. **[31]**

Dillon, M. (1999). *China's Muslim Hui Community: Migration, Settlement and Sects.* Curzon, Richmond. **[195]**

Dirie, M.A. (1985). '*Female Circumcision in Somalia: Medical and Social Implications*'. SOMAC/SAREC. Mogadishu, Somalia. **[165]**

Dirie, M.A. and Landmark, G. (1991). 'Female Circumcision in Somalia and Women's Motives'. *Acta Obstetrica Gynaecologica.* 70: 50-7.

Dobson, R.B. (1974). *The Jews of Mediaeval York and the Massacre of March.* 1190. Borthwick Papers. 45.York.

Dodge, O.G. *et al.* (1963). 'Circumcision and the Incidence of Carcinoma of the Penis and Cervix; A Study in Kenya and Uganda'. *East African Medical J.* 40: 440-4. **[162]**

Dubois, J.A. (1972). *Hindu Manners, Customs and Ceremonies.* Oxford University Press, Oxford. **[227]**

Dumont, L (1970a). *Religion, Politics and History in India.* Mouton, Dumont, L. Paris. (1970b). Homo hierarchicus; the caste system and its implications. Weidenfeld and Nicolson, London. **[147, 170, 233]**

Dundas, P. (1992). *The Jains*, *Routledge*, London. **[215]**

Durkheim, E.(1968). *The Elementary Forms of Religious Life.* Free Press, New York. **[160]**

Dwivedi, O.P. (1990). 'Satyagraha for Conservation: Awakening the Spirit of Hinduism'. In J.R. Engel and J.C. Engel.(eds). *The ethics of environment and development. Global challenge and international response.* Arizona University Press, Tucson. **[250]**

Ehrlich, P.R. and Ehrlich, A.H. (1972). Population, Resources, Environment. Issues in *Human Biology.* Freeman, San Francisco. **[232]**

Eibl-Eibesfeldt, I. (1975). *Ethology, The Biology of Behaviour.* Holt, Rinehart and Winston, New York. **[19, 20]**

Ekvall, R.B. (1964). *Religious Observances in Tibet.* Chicago University Press, Chicago. **[44, 247]**

Elba, I. (1995). *Examination of the Rulings about the Killing of Gentiles.* Memorial Book for Dr Baruch Goldstein, the Saint. Special Publication, Jerusalem. **[176]**

El Dareer, A. (1982). *Women, Why do You Weep?* Zed, London. **[163-4]**

Eliot, G. (1859). *Adam Bede.* London.

Ellis, J. (1986). *The Russian Orthodox Church.* London. 139-41. **[192]**

Elshtain, J.B. (1987). *Women and War.* Basic Books, New York.

El Tayeb, E.M. (1976). '*Health Problems in the Sudan Associated with the Mecca Pilgrimage*'. Dissertation. Ross Institute, London. **[237]**

Encyclopedia Judaica, (1971). Keter, Jerusalem. **[216]**

Encyclopedia Judaica Yearbook (1974). Keter, Jerusalem. **[191, 230]**

Engineer, A.A. (1983). '*Developing a Theory of Communal Riot*'. Mainstream. 21August: 14-8. 34-6. **[315]**

Engineer, A.A. (1988). *Delhi-Meerut Riots. Analysis, Compilation and Documentation.* Ajanta Publications, Delhi. **[315]**

Erlanger, P. (1962). *St. Bartholomew's Night.* Weidenfeld and Nicolson, London. **[216]**

Evans-Pritchard, E.E. (1940). *The Nuer.* Oxford University Press, Oxford. **[208, 319]**

Evans-Pritchard, E.E. (1965). '*Zande Cannibalism*' in The position of women in primitive society and other essays in social anthropology. London. **[165]**

Ewing, K.P. (1990). 'The Illusion of Wholeness. Culture, Self and the Problem of Inconsistency'. *Ethos.* 18: 251-279.

Farooq, M. and Malla, M.B. (1966). 'Behavioural pattern of social and religious water–contact activities in Egypt-49 Bilharzia Project Area. *Bulletin World Health Organisation.* 35: 377-87.

Fernandez, J.W. (1978). 'African Religious Movements'. *Annual Review of Anthropology.* 7: 195-234.

Feshback, S. (1970). 'Aggression' in Mussen, P.H.(ed). *Carmichael's Manual of Child Psychology.* Vol. 2. Wiley, New York. **[22, 254]**

Festinger, L. (1957). *A Theory of Cognitive Dissonance.* Row Petersen, Evanston. **[111, 150]**

Fortier, B. de la. (1963). 'Les Infants Troves a Hospital General de Montreal. 1754-1804'. *Laval Medical.* 34: 442-53. 35, 335-47. 36, 351-97. **[233]**

Foucault, M. (1986). *Of Other Spaces.* J. Miskowiec (trans). Essential Works. Allen Lane, London. **[265]**

Francaviglia, R.V. (1978). *The Mormon Landscape. Existence, Creation and Perception of a Unique Image in the American West.* A.M.S. Press, New York. **[214]**

Fraser, M. (1973). *Children in Conflict.* Secker and Warburg, London. **[152]**

Freed, S.A. and Freed, R.S. (1964). 'Spirit Possession as Illness in a North Indian Village' *Ethnology.* 3: 152-171. **[182]**

Freed, S.A. and Freed, R.S. (1972). 'Cattle in a North Indian Village'. *Ethnology*. 11: 399-408. **[244]**

Fried, M.H. (1987). 'Reflections on Christianity in China'. *American Ethnologist*. 74(1): 94-106. **[195]**

Friedland, R. and Hecht, R.D. (1991). 'The Politics of Sacred Place. Jerusalem's Temple Mount'. In J. Scott and P. Simpson-Housley (eds). *Sacred places and profane spaces. Essays in the geographics of Judaism, Christianity and Islam.* Greenwood Press, New York. 21-61. **[82]**

Fry, D.B. (1992). 'Respect for the Rights of Others is Peace. Learning Aggression versus Non-aggression among the Zapotec'. *American Anthropologist.* 04: 621-39.

Fu Tie-Tzu. (1989). *Peasant Daily*. 2 May. **[206]**

Gadgil, M. and Vartak, V.D. (1975). 'The Sacred Groves of India–a Plea for Continued Conservation'. *J. Bombay Natural History Society.* 72(2): 314-29. **[251]**

Gaffney, P.D. (1994). *The Prophet's Pulpit. Islamic Preaching in Contemporary Egypt.* University of California Press, Berkeley.

Gajdusek, D.C. (1973). 'Kuru in the New Guinea Highlands'. In J.D. Spillane. (ed). *Tropical neurology.* Oxford University Press, London. **[166]**

Gandhi, M.K. (1954). *How to Serve the Cow*. Navajivan Publishing House, Ahmedabad. **[243]**

Gardner, R. & Heider, K.G. (1969). *The Gardens of War. Life and Death in the New Guinea Stone Age.* Random Harvest, New York. **[71]**

Geertz, C. (2000). *Available Light. Anthropological Reflections on Philosophical Topics.* Princeton University Press, New Jersey. **[125]**

General Cause, The. (1953). Mass Lawsuit Brought by the Spanish Nationalist Government. Madrid. **[201]**

Ghosh, S.K. (1971). *Riots. Prevention and Control*. Eastern Law House, Calcutta.

Gibson. T. (1986). *Sacrifice and Sharing in the Philippine Highlands. Religion and Society among the Bulo of Mindoro.* Athlone Press, London. **[262]**

Giddens, A. (1985). *The Nation-state and Violence*. Polity Press, Cambridge. **[10]**

Giddens, A. (1991). *Modernity and Self-identity. Self and Society in the Late Modern Age.* Polity Press, Cambridge.

Gieling, S. (1999). *Religion and War in Revolutionary Iran.* Tauris, London. **[171]**

Gilsenan, M. (1982). *Recognizing Islam.* Croom Helm, London. **[57]**

Ginsberg, Y. (1995). Quoted Comments in Elba, I. Examination of the rulings about the killing of Gentiles in M. Ben Horin.(ed).*Baruch Hagever. Memorial book for Dr Baruch Goldstein, the saint.* Special Publication, Jerusalem. **[84]**

Gladney, D.C. (1996). *Muslim Chinese. Ethnic nationalism in the Peoples Republic.* Harvard University Press, Cambridge, Mass. **[196]**

Glucklich, A. (2001). *Sacred Pain. Hurting the Body for the Sake of the Soul.* Oxford University Press, New York. **[160]**

Gobind, Guru. (1909). *Collected Works.* Clarendon Press, Oxford. **[169, 170]**

Goldhagen, D.J. (1996). *Hitler's Willing Executioners. Ordinary Germans and the Holocaust.* Little Brown, London. **[64, 111]**

Goodall, J. (1986). *The chimpanzees of Gombe.* Harvard University Press, Cambridge, Mass. **[22]**

Gordon, D. (1991). 'Female Circumcision and Genital Operations in Egypt and the Sudan a Dilemma for Medical Anthropology'. *Medical Anthropology.* 5(1): 302-6. **[163-4]**

Gosden, M. (1935).; '*Tetanus Deaths from Ccircumcision*'. Transactions Royal Society Tropical Medicine and Hygiene. 28: 645-48. **[162]**

Gourou, P. (1963). 'Civilisation et Economic Pastorale'. *L' Homme.* 123-39. **[246]**

Grader, C.J. (1969). 'Pura Heduwe Karang at Kubitambahan'. In J. van Baal *et al.* (eds). *Bali. Further Studies in Life, thought and Ritual.* Hoeve, The Hague. **[249]**

Green, M. (1991). '*Witchcraft Suppression Practices and Movements. Public Politics and the Logic of Purification*'. Comparative Studies in Society and History. 37: 319-345.

Greenoak, F. (1985). *God's Acre; The Flowers and Animals of the Parish Churchyard.* Orbis, London. **[241]**

Grieg, A. (1999). *Kingdoms of Experience: Everest, the Unclimbed Ridge.* Cannongate, London.

Gross, J.T. (2001). '*Neighbours*'. New Yorker. 12 March, 64-77.

Groussert, R. (1970). *The Empire of the Steppes.* University of New Brunswick Press, New Jersey. **[216]**

Guha, R. (1990). *The Unquiet Woods. Ecological Change and Peasant Resistance in the Himalayas*. University of California Press, Berkeley. **[250]**

Gvitz, Y. (1996). 'Death's Perverted Servant'. *Yediot Aharonot Magazine.* 29 March. **[176]**

Haimendorf, C. von. (1967). *Morals and Merit.* Weidenfeld and Nicolson, London. **[21, 24]**

Hallie, P.P. (1979). *Lest Innocent Blood be Shed.* Harper and Row, New York. **[9]**

Hanks, J.R. (1968). *Maternity and Its Rituals in Bang Chan.* Cornell University Press, Ithaca. **[231]**

Hardin, R. (1995). 'Self Interest, Group Identification'. In J.L. Comaroff and P.C. Stern.(eds). *Perspectives on Nationalism and War.* Gordon and Breach, Amsterdam. 15-45.

Harris, M. (1966). 'The Cultural Ecology of India's Sacred Cattle' *Current Anthropology.* 7(1): 51-65. **[244]**

Harris, R. (1999). *Lourdes. Body and Spirit in the Secular Age.* Allen Lane, London. **[4]**

Hartington, S. (1996). *The Clash of Civilisations and the Remaking of World Order.* Simon and Schuster, New York.

Hartley, L.P. (1953). *The go-between.* Hamish Hamilton, London. **[85]**

Hasan, M. (1996). 'The Changing Position of the Muslims and the Political Future of Secularism in India'. In T.V. Sathyamurthy. (ed). *Region, Religion, Caste, Gender and Culture in Contemporary India.* Oxford University Press, London.

Hassan, N. (2001). 'An Arsenal of Believers' *Sunday Times.* 9 December. **[158]**

Hassan, R. (1985). *A Way of Dying. Suicide in Singapore.* Oxford University Press, Kuala Lumpur.

Hathout, H. (1972). 'Abortion and Islam' *J. Medical Lebanais.* 25: 237-9. **[232]**

Hathout, H.M. (1963). 'Some Aspects of Female Circumcision'. *J. Obstetrics and Gynaecology British Commonwealth.* 70: 50-7. **[164]**

Hawley, J.S. (1994). 'Hinduism. Sati and its Defenders' in J.S. Hawley.(ed). *Fundamentalism and Gender.* Oxford University Press, New York. **[159]**

Hayden, R.M. (2000). 'Rape and Rape Avoidance in Ethno-national Conflicts: Sexual Violence in Liminalized States'. *American*

Anthropologist. 102(1): 27-41.

Hechter, M. (1975). *Internal Colonialism; The Celtic Fringe in British National Development.* Routledge and Kegan Paul, London.

Herodotus. (1952). *History.* Heinemann, London. **[163]**

Herskovits, M.J. (1926) 'The Cattle Complex in East Africa'. *American Anthropologist.* 230-72; 361-88; 494-528; 633-64. **[246]**

Hickey, J. (1984). *Religion and the Northern Ireland Problem.* Barnes and Noble, Totowa, New Jersey. **[67, 220]**

Hinde, R.A. (1987a). 'Can Non-human Primates help us Understand Human Behaviour' in Smuts, B.B. *et al.* (eds). *Primate society.* Chicago University Press, Chicago. **[19]**

Hinde, R.A. (1987b). *Individuals, Relationships and Culture. Links between ethnology and the social sciences.* Cambridge University Press, Cambridge. **[19]**

Hinton, A.L. (1996). 'Agents of Death. Explaining the Cambodian Genocide in Terms of Psychosocial Dissonance'. *American Anthropologist.* 98: 818-31. **[42]**

Hiro, D. (1989). *Holy Wars. The Rise of Islamic Fundamentalism.* Routledge, London. **[155]**

Hisham, ibn. (1859-60). *Kitab Sirat Rasul Allah.* F. Wustenfeld.(ed). Gottingen. **[70]**

Hoban, B. (1994). *Quoted in Tanner,* M. (2001). **[151]**

Hojberg, C.K. (2002). 'Inner Iconoclasm. Forms of Reflexivity in Loma Rituals of Sacrifice'. *Social Anthropology.* 10(1): 57-75. **[270]**

Holland, D. and Quinn, N. (eds). (1987). *Cultural Models in Language and Thought.* Cambridge University Press, New York. **[56]**

Holt, S. (1964). *Terror in the Name of God: The Story of the Sons of Freedom*; The Doukhobors. McClelland & Stewart, Toronto. **[85]**

Hooft, U.A. Visser't. (1973). *Memoirs.* SCM Press, London. **[54]**

Hookham, H. (1962). *Tamburlane the Conqueror.* London. **[216]**

Hopkins, E. (1970). 'The Nyabingi Cult in South-western Uganda'. In Rotberg, R.I. and Mazrui, A.A. (eds). *Protest and Power in Black Africa.* Oxford University Press, New York. 258-336. **[126]**

Hoskins, J. (1982). 'The Etiquette of Spirit Communication among the Kodi'. In R.S. Kipp and S. Rodgers.(eds). *Indonesian religion in transition.* University of Arizona, Tucson.

Hostetler, J.A. (1993). *Amish Society.* Johns Hopkins University Press, Baltimore. **[214]**

Hostetler, J.A. and Huntington, G.E. (1974). *The Hutterites in North America*. Rinehart and Winston, New York. **[214]**

Hsu, F.L.K. (1972). 'Kinship and Ways of Life; an Exploration'. In F.L.K. Hsu.(ed). *Psychological Anthropology.* Schenkman, Cambridge, Mass. **[11, 313]**

Huber, J. (1960). 'Uterus Carcinoma and Circumcision: Studies in Ethiopia'. *Wiener Medizinische Wochenschrift.* 110: 571-4. **[162]**

Hubert, H. and M. Mauss. (1964). *Sacrifice; its Nature and Function.* Cohen & West, London.

Huesmann, L.R. et al. (1984). 'Stability of Aggression Over Time and Generation'. *Developmental Psychology.* 20: 1120-1134. **[274]**

Hulka, B.J. (1982). 'Risk Factors for Cervical Cancer'. *J. Chronic Diseases*. 35: 3-11. **[162]**

Hunt, J.H. (1934). 'Indian fakirs'. *St Batholomew's Hospital J*: 1-17. **[160]**

Huntington, S.P. (1993). 'The Clash of Civilisations'. *Foreign Affairs.* 72(3): 22-49. **[2]**

Hussain, A. (1990). 'The Karachi Riots of December 1986. Crisis of State and Civil Society in Pakistan'. In V. Das.(ed). *Mirrors of Violence. Communities, Riots and Survivors in South Asia*. Oxford University Press, Delhi. 185-193. **[316]**

Iliffe, J. (1975). 'The Creation of Group Consciousness among the Dock Workers of Dar es Salaam.1929-56' in R. Sandbrook and R. Cohen.(eds). *The Development of the African Working Class; Studies in Class Formation and Action.* University of Toronto Press, Toronto. **[122]**

Iliffe, J. (1979). *A Modern History of Tanganyika.* Cambridge University Press, Cambridge. Chapter 6. **[126]**

Inoguchi, R. and Nakajima, T. (1960). *The Divine Wind. Japan's Kamikazi Force in World War Two*. Bantam, New York. **[157]**

International Criminal Tribunal. (1996). Prosecutor v Radovan Karadzic and Ratko Mladic. 11 July.

International Criminal Tribunal for Yugoslavia (1996). Review of the Indictments Pursuant to Rule 61 of the Rules of Procedure and Evidence. 11 July. **[64]**

Irwin, Z.T. (1984). 'The Islamic Revival and the Muslims of Bosnia-Herzegovina'. *East European Q.* 17(4): 437-58. **[188]**

Ishwaran, K.(1968). *Shivapur. A South Indian Village*. Routledge & Kegan Paul, London. **[273-4, 304]**

Israeli, R. (1979). 'Islamization and Sinicization in Chinese Islam'. In N. Leutzion.(ed). *Conversion to Islam*. Holmes and Meier, New York.159-176. **[195]**

Izzedine, C.(nd). *Le cholera et l'hygiene a la Mecque.* **[215]**

Jackson, K.D. (1989). *Cambodia: 1975-78, Rendezvous with Death.* Princeton University Press, New Jersey. **[202]**

Jaiminiya (Talavakara) Brahmana of the Samaveda (1954). R. Vira and L. Chandra.(eds). Saraswati Vihara Series Vol. 31, Nagpur. **[105]**

Jakobovits, I. (1961). 'Medical Aspects of Circumcision in Jewish Law'. *Hebrew Medical J.* 1: 258-70. **[162]**

Jing, J. (1999). *'Villages Damned, Villages Repossessed; A Memorial Movement in North-west China'. American Ethnologist.* 26(2): 324-343.

Johnson, D.H. (1994). *Nuer Prophets.* Clarendon Press, Oxford.

Johnson, D.H. (2002). *The Root Causes of Sudan's Civil Wars.* Currey, Oxford.

Johnson, F. (1950). *English-Swahili-English Dictionary.* Oxford University Press, London. **[38]**

Johnson, P. (1987). *A History of the Jews.* Weidenfeld and Nicolson, London.

Josephson, W.L. (1995). *Television and Violence. A Review of the Effects on Children of Different Ages.* Department of Canadian Heritage, Ottawa. **[94]**

Josephus, F. (1890). *Antiquity of the Jews.* W. Whiston.(trans). Nimmo, Hay and Mitchell, Edinburgh. **[106]**

Josephus, F. (1981). *The Jewish War.* G.A. Williamson.(trans). Penguin, London. **[70]**

Juergensmeyer, M. (1988). '*The Logic of Religious Violence. The Case of the: Punjab*'. Contributions to Indian Sociology(ns). 22(1): 65-88. **[168-9]**

Juergensmeyer, M. (1993). *The New Cold War. Religious Nationalism Confronts the Secular State.* University of California Press, Berkeley. **[218]**

Junod, M. (1951). *Warrior without Weapons.* London. **[201]**

Justeson, J. and T. Kaufman. (1993). 'A Decipherment of Epi-Olmec Hieroglyphic Writing'. *Science.* 293: 1703-11. **[319]**

Kakar, S. (1995). *The Colours of Violence.* Viking, Delhi. **[61]**

Kaku, K. (1975). 'Increased Induced Abortion Rate in 1966. An Aspect of Japanese Folk Superstition'. *Annals Human Biology.* 2: 111-15. **[231]**

Kamalkani, Z. (1991). *Women's Islam. Religious Practice Among Women in Today's Iran*. Kegan Paul, London. **[116, 303]**

Kambie, N.D. (1981). *Atrocities on Scheduled Castes in Post-Independence India*. Ashish Publishing House, New Delhi. **[155, 313]**

Kamusi ya Kiswahili Sanifu. (1981). Oxford University Press, Dar es Salaam. **[38]**

Kan, S. (1999). *Memory Eternal*. Tlingit Culture and Russian Orthodox Christianity through two Centuries. University of Washington Press, Seattle. **[184, 204, 206]**

Kapferer, B. (1994). 'Remythologisations of Power and Identity; Nationalism and Violence in Sri Lanka'. In K. Rupesinghe and M. Rubio.(eds). *The Culture of Violence*. United Nations University Press, Tokyo.14-41.

Kapoor, C. (2002). 'Children Buried Alive to Appease Goddesses'. Report from Delhi. *The Times*. 23 August. **[152]**

Katz, Y. (1991). '*The Jewish religion and spatial and communal organization; the implementation of Jewish religious law in the building of urban neighbourhoods and Jewish agricultural settlements in Palestine at the close of the 19th century*'. In J. Scott and P. Simpson-Housley.(eds). Sacred places and profane spaces. Essays in the geographics of Judaism, Christianity and Islam. Greenwood Press, New York. 1-19.

Kav-venaki, S. et al. (1976). 'The Effect of Russian versus Hebrew Instruction in the Reactions to Social Pressures of Russian born Children'. *J. Experimental Social Psychology.* 12: 70-86. **[152]**

Keiser, R.L. (1986). 'Death Enmity in Thull. Organized Vengeance and Social Change in a Kohistan Community'. *American Ethnologist*. 13(3): 489-505.

Kelman, H.C. and V.L. Hamilton. (1989). *Crimes of Obedience. Toward a Social Psychology of Authority and Responsibility.* Yale University Press, New Haven. **[9]**

Kemelman, H. (1979). *Tuesday the Rabbi Saw Red.* Hutchinson, London. **[103]**

Kennan, G. (2000). The provocateur. Interview with N. Lehmann. *New Yorker Magazine.* 13 November. **[11]**

Kenyon, S.M. (1999). 'The Case of the Butcher's wife. Illness, Possession and Power in Central Sudan' in H. Behrend and U. Luig.(eds). *Spirit Possession. Modernity and Power in Africa.* Currey, Oxford. **[114, 130]**

Kertzer, D. (2002). *The Unholy War. The Vatican's Role in the Rise of Modern Anti-Semitism.* Macmillan, Basingstoke. **[53]**

Khiddu-Makubuya, E. (1994). 'Violence and Conflict Resolution in Uganda'. In K. Rupesinghe and M. Rubio.(eds). United Nations University Press, Tokyo. 144-177. **[315]**

Kiernan, B. (1996). *The Pol Pot Regime. Race, power and genocide in Cambodia under the Khmer Rouge.1975-9.* Yale University Press, New Haven. **[202]**

Kimambo, I.N. and Omari, C.K. (1972). 'The Development of Religious Thought and Centres among the Pare'. In T.O. Ranger and I.N. Kimambo.(eds). *The Historical Study of African Religion.* Heinnman, London. 111-21. **[251]**

King, S. (2001). Interview with BBC Quoted in a Review Article on his Books. J. Leonard. King of High and Low. *New York Review of Books.* 14 February. **[132, 312]**

Knight, H. (1954). *Food Administration in India.* 1939-47. Stanford University Press, Stanford. **[245]**

Knutsson, K.E. and Selinus, R. (1970). 'Fasting in Ethiopia. An Anthropological and Nutritional Study'. *American J. Clinical Nutrition.* 23: 956-9. **[161]**

Koran, The. (2000). A.Y. Ali.(trans). Wordsworth, Ware.

Krings, M. (1999). 'On History and Language of the European 'Bori' Spirits'. In Behrend, H & Luig, U. (eds). *Spirit Possession. Modernity and Power.* Currey, Oxford. **[132]**

Krzywicki, L. (1934). *Primitive Society and Its Vital Statistics.* Macmillan, London. **[160]**

Kuhn, T.S. (1982). *The Structure of Scientific Revolutions.* Chicago University Press, Chicago. **[27]**

Kwaak, A van der. (1992). 'Female Circumcision and Gender Identity, a Questionable Alliance'. *Social Science and Medicine.* 35(6): 771-87. **[164]**

Ladd, J. (1957). *The Structure of a Moral Code.* Harvard University Press. **[30]**

Laden, Osama Bin. (1998). Interview for Al Jazeera Television and the Febuary Fatwa Quoted in K. Makiya and H. Mneimneh. Manual for a Raid. *New York Review of Books.* 17 January. 2002: 18-21. **[63]**

La Fontaine, J. (1985). *Initiation.* Penguin, Harmondsworth. **[145]**

Lal, B.K. (1986). 'Hindu Perspectives on the Use of Animals in Science'. In T. Regan.(ed). *Animal Sacrifice. Religious*

Perspectives on the Use of Animals in Science. Temple University Press, Philadelphia.

Lamb, T. (1932). *Tamerlane the Earth Shaker*. New York. **[216]**

Lambek, M. (1989). 'Certain Knowledge, Contestable Authority; Power and Practice on the Islamic Periphery'. *American Ethnologist.* 17(1): 23-44. **[103]**

Landland, D.K. and Moyer. R.S. (1978). *Psychology. The experimental approach.* McGraw-Hill, New York.

Langer, S.K. (1951). *Philosophy in a New Key*. Menton, New York. **[37]**

Lansing, J.S. (1991). *Priests and Programmes. Technologies of Power in the Engineered Landscape of Bali.* Princeton University Press, New Jersey. **[250]**

Lao-Tzu. (1934). *Tao-te-ching.* A. Waley. (trans). The Way and Its Power. Allen and Unwin, London. **[46]**

Lasaga, J.I. (1980). 'Death in Jonestown. Techniques of Political Control by a Paranoid Leader'. *Suicide Life-Threatening Behaviour.* 10: 210-3. **[8]**

Leach, E. (1977). *Custom, Law and Terrorist Violence*. Edinburgh University Press, Edinburgh.

Leaf, M.J. (1985). *The Punjab Crisis*. Asian Survey. 25(5). **[170]**

Le Bon, G. (1895/1960). *The Crowd.* Viking. New York. **[59]**

Legrain, J.F. (1994). 'Palestinian Islamisms. Patriotism as a Condition of Their Expansion'. In M.E. Marty and R.S. Appleby (eds). *Accounting for fundamentalism. The dynamic character of movements.* Chicago University Press, Chicago. **[178]**

Lehmann, D. (1961). 'Alice Lenshina Mulenga and the Lumpa Church' in Taylor, J.V. and Lehmann, D. (eds). *Christians of the Copper Belt.* London. 248-68. **[128]**

Levine, D.H. (1981). *Religion and Politics in Latin America.* The Catholic Church in Venezuela and Colombia. Princeton University Press, New Jersey. **[23, 24, 79]**

Levy, G. (1974). *Religion and Revolution.* Oxford University Press, Oxford.

Levy, R. (1969). *The Social Structure of Islam*. Cambridge University Press, Cambridge. **[77, 234]**

Lewis, B. (1982). *The Jews of Islam*. Princeton University Press, New Jersey. **[191]**

Lewis, I.M. (1986). *Religion in Context; Cults and Charisma.* Cambridge University Press, Cambridge. **[166]**

Lewontin, R. (1982). *Human Diversity*. W.H. Freeman, London.

Lifton, R.J. (1974). *Home from the War. Vietnam Veterans; Neither Victims nor Executioners*. London. **[51]**

Lincoln, B. (1985). 'Revolutionary Exhumation in Spain'. *Comparative Studies in Society and History*. 27: 241-60. **[197]**

Llorente, D.S.A. (1827). *History of the Inquisition in Spain*. G.B. Whittaker, London.

Lodrick, D.O. (1981). *Sacred Cows, Sacred Places. Origins and Survival of Animal Homes in India*. University of California Press, Berkeley. **[180, 244-5]**

Lokhandwala, S.T. (1985). Indian Islam; Composite Culture and Integration. *New Quest*. March-April: 87-101. **[277]**

Long, D.E. (1979). *The Hajj Today. A Survey of the Contemporary Makkkah Pilgrimage*. State University of New York, New York. **[34]**

Lorenz, K.S. (1966). *On Aggression*. Harcourt. Methuen, London. **[20]**

Luukkanen, A. (1997). *The Religious Policy of the Stalinist State*. Finnish Historical Society, Helsinki.

Maalouf, A. (2002). *In the Name of Identity. Violence and the need to belong*. Trans B. Bray. Arcade, London. **[177]**

Mac Farlane, A. (1970). *Witchcraft in Tudor and Stuart England: A Regional and Comparative Study*. Routledge and Kegan Paul, London. **[150]**

MacInnis, D.E. (1972). *Religious Policy and Practice in Communist China*. Macmillan, New York. **[194]**

Madan, T.N. (1987). 'Secularism in Its Place'. *J. Asian Studies*. 46(4): 747-59. **[298]**

Madan, T.N. (1991). 'The Double-edged Sword. Fundamentalism and the Sikh Religious Tradition'. In M.E. Marty and R.S. Appleby.(eds). *Fundamentalism Observed*. Chicago University Press, Chicago. 531-593. **[170]**

Maier, W. (1964). 'Die Sauglingssterblichtkeit Chelich and Unchelich Lebendgeborener: Todessursachen, Lebensdauer' *Archiv fur Gynakologie*. 199: 468-74. **[235]**

Makiya, K. and Mneimneh, H. (2002). 'Manual for a Raid'. *New York Review of Books*. 17 January, 18-21.

Malinowski, B. (1926). *Crime and Custom in Savage Society*. Routledge, London. **[25]**

Malinowski, B. (1929). *The Sexual Life of Savages*. Routledge, London. **[166]**

Mandelbaum, D.G. (1938). 'Polyandry in Kota Society'. *American Anthropologist.* 40(4): 574-583.

Mandelbaum, D.G. (1941). 'Cultural Changes among the Nilgiri Tribes'. *American Anthropologist.* 43: 19-26. **[246]**

Mani, L. (1992). 'Cultural Theory, Colonial Texts; Reading Eye-witness Accounts of widow burning'. In L. Grossberg *et al.* (eds). *Cultural Studies. Routledge,* New York. 96-116. **[8]**

Manley, G.T. and Neech, A.S. (1950). 'Hinduism' in J.N.D. Anderson.(ed). *The World's Religions.* Inter-Varsity Fellowship, London. 99-117. **[243]**

Manor, J. (1994). 'Organisation Weakness and the Rise of Sinhalese Buddhist Extremism'. In M.E. Marty and R.S. Appleby.(eds). *Fundamentalism Observed.* Chicago University Press, Chicago. 770-84. **[170]**

Ma'oz, M. (1992). 'The Jewish-Zionist and Arab-Palestinian National Communities. The Transposition Effect of a Century of Confrontation'. In J.P. Spagnolo.(ed). *Problems of the Modern. Middle East in Historical Perspective.* Ithaca, Reading. **[281]**

Manu, Laws of. (1969). *Buhler*, G. (trans). Dover, New York.

Marnham, P. (1980). *Lourdes. A Modern Pilgrimage*. Heinemann, London.

Marquelier, A. (1999). 'The Invention of Anti-tradition. Dodo Spirits in Southern Niger'. In H. Behrend & Luig, U.(eds). *Spirit Possession. Modernity and Power in Africa.* Currey, Oxford. **[132]**

Marshall, J. (1994). 'The Mosque in Erb Street. A Study in Sacred and Profane Space'. *Environments.* 22(2): 55-66. **[115]**

Maslow, A.H. (1987). *Motivation and Personality*. Harper and Row, New York. **[283-6]**

Matthiessen, P. (1962). *Under the Mountain Wall*. Viking, New York.

Mayadas, C. (1954). *Between us and Hunger*. Oxford University Press, London. **[244]**

Maycock, A.L. (1927). *The Inquisition*. Constable, London.

Mazumbar, S. & Mazumbar, S. (2002). 'In Mosque and Shrine. Women's Agency in Public Sacred Space'. *J. Ritual Studies.* 16(2): 165-78. **[116]**

Mbiti, J.S. (1969). *African Religions and Philosophy*. Heinemann, London. **[108]**

Mboria, L. (1938). *La Population de l'Egypte. Pro Caccia,* Cairo. **[228]**

McClelland, J.L. et al. (1986). 'The Appeal of Parallel Distributive Processing'. In D.E. Rumelhart *et al.*(eds). *Parallel Distributive Processing. Explorations in the Microstructure of Cognition.* MIT Press, Cambridge, Mass. 3-44. **[312]**

McKay, S. (1995). *Northern Protestants. An Unsettled People.* Blackstaff, Belfast. **[99]**

McWilliam, A. (2001). 'Prospects for the Sacred Grove: Valuing Lulic Forests in Timor' *Asia Pacific J. Anthropology.* 2(2): 89-113. **[251]**

Meerloo, J.A. (1950). *Patterns of Panic.* International Universities Press, New York. **[263]**

Meier, Z. (1984). 'Violent Effects on Children and Teenagers through Television and Movies' in Meier, Z.(ed). *Violence in the Media.* Ottawa. **[106]**

Meller, H. (1999). *London Cemeteries.* Ashgate, Aldershot. **[251]**

Melzack, R. (1975). 'The McGill Questionnaire: Major Properties and Scoring Methods'. *Pain.* 1: 277-95. **[160]**

Menendez, A.J. (1973). *The Bitter Harvest. Church and State in Northern Ireland.* Robert. B. Luce, Washington, DC.

Merton, R.K. (1957). *Social Theory and Social Structure.* Free Press, Glencoe. **[30]**

Mesaki, S. (1992). 'The Preponderance of Women as Victims in Sukuma Witch Killings'. In Foster, P.G. and S. Maghimbi.(eds). *The Tanzanian Peasantry; Economy in Crisis.* Avebury, Aldershot. **[123, 149]**

Messing, S.D. (1958). 'Group therapy and Social Status in the Zar Cult of Ethiopia'. *American Anthropologist* 60: 1120-5. **[130]**

Michall, F. (1966). *The Taiping Rebellion.* University of Washington, Seattle. **[216]**

Midgely, M. (1992). 'Towards a More Humane View of the Beasts'. In D.E. Cooper and J.A. Palmer.(eds). *The Environment in Question.* Routledge, London. 28-36. **[242]**

Momboise, R.M. (1969). *Confrontations, Riots, Urban Warfare.* MSM Enterprises, Sacramento. **[259]**

Money, J. and Emrhardt, A.A. (1972). *Man and Woman/Boy and Girl.* Johns Hopkins University Press, Baltimore.

Moore, B. (1965). *The Emperor of Ice-cream.* Penguin, Harmondsworth. **[100]**

Moore, B. (2000). *Moral Purity and Persecution in History*. Princeton University Press, New Jersey. **[144]**

Moorkerjee, A. and Khanna, M. (1977). *The Tantric Way*. Thames and Hudson, London. **[75]**

Morris, I. (1975). *The Nobility of Failure*. Secker and Warburg, London.

Morris, J. (1973). *Heaven's Command. An Imperial Progress*. London. **[33]**

Moskowitz, M.L. (2001). *The Haunting Fetus*. Abortion, Sexuality and the Spirit World in Taiwan. University of Hawaii Press, Honolulu. **[231]**

Moyer, K.E. (1968). 'Kinds of Aggression and their Physiological Basis'. *Communications in Behavioural Biology.* 2: 65-87. **[22]**

Moyer, K.E. (1969). 'Internal Impulses to Aggression'. *Transactions New York Academy of Sciences.* 31(2): 104-114. **[22]**

Moyer, N. (1991). *Escape from the Killing Fields*. Zonervan Publishing House, Grand Rapids. **[202]**

Muller, F.M. (1860). *A History of Ancient Sanskrit Literature*. London. **[104]**

Murra, J.V. (1965). 'Herds and herdsmen in the Inca State'. In A. Leeds & A.P. Vayda.(eds). *Man, Culture and Animals.* American Association for the Advancement of Science, Washington, DC. **[209]**

Mustafa, A. (1966). 'Female Circumcision and Infibulation in the Sudan'. *J. Obstetrics and Gynaecology British Commonwealth.* 73: 302-6. **[164]**

Nagengast, C. (1994). 'Violence, terror and the Crisis of the State'. *Annual Review of Anthropology.* 23: 109-36.

Nandra, P.N. *et al.* (1955). *Report of the Expert Committee on the Prevention of Slaughter of Cattle in India.* Government of India Press, Delhi. **[244]**

Naidu, R. (1990). 'The Impact of Processions in the City of Hyderabad'. In P. Chatterjee & P. Jegernathan.(eds). *Community, Gender and Violence.* Hurst, London. **[319]**

Nehru, J. (1991). *The Discovery of India*. Oxford University Press, New Delhi. **[260]**

Nelson, S. (1984). *Ulster's Uncertain Defenders; Loyalists and the Northern Ireland Conflict.* Appletree Press, Belfast.

Newsome, A.E. (1980). 'The Ecomythology of the Red Kangaroo in Central Australia'. *Mankind.* 12: 327-33. **[248]**

Nicoloson, N. (1975). *Wednesday Early Closing*. Faber and Faber, London.

Nida, E.A. and W.D. Reyburn. (1981). *Meaning Across Cultures*. Orbis, New York. **[40]**

Nida, E.A. and C.R. Tabor. (1974). *The Theory and Practice of Translation.* Brill, Leiden.**[40]**

Nodari, R. and Piruvane, G. (1970). 'Sulla mortalita infantile: Raffronte dei dati statistici referiti ai bambini nati nel matrimonio e fuori delo matrimonio'. *Minerva Pediatricaa.* 22: 1254-6, 1449-51. **[233]**

Nolan, M.L. (1991). *The European Roots of Latin-American Pilgrimage*. Greenwood Press, New York. **[237]**

Nolan, M.L. and Nolan, S. (1989). *Christian Pilgrimage in Modern Western Europe*. University of North Carolina Press, Chapel Hill. **[237]**

Nordenstam, T. (1968). *Sudanese Ethics*. Scandinavian Institute for African Studies, Uppsala. **[164]**

Nottingham, J. and Rosberg, C.C. (1966). *The Myth of the Mau Mau. Nationalism in Kenya.* Praeger, New York. **[126]**

O'Dowd, L. *et al.* (1980). *Northern Ireland; between Civil Rights and Civil War*. C.S.E. Books, London.

O'Flaherty, W. (1976). *The Origins of Evil in Hindu Mythology*. University of California Press, Berkeley.

O'Flaherty, W.D. (1985). *Tales of Sex and Violence. Folklore, Sacrifice and Danger in the Jaiminya Brahama.* Chicago University Press, Chicago. **[105]**

Okumiya, M. (1980). *Kamikazi and the Japanese*. New York. **[157]**

Oliver, S. (1894). *Historia Damiatana.* Bibliothek Der litterarischen Vereins in Stuttgart. Tubingen. **[6, 216]**

O'Malley. L.S.S. (1935). *Popular Hinduism. The Religion of the Masses.* Cambridge University Press, Cambridge. **[45, 234]**

O'Malley, P. (1983). *The Uncivil War: Ireland Today.* Houghton Mifflin, Boston. **[220]**

Ong, A. (1989). 'State versus Islam; Malay Families, Women's Bodies and the Body Politic in Malaysia'. *American Ethnologist.* 17(1): 258-276. **[117, 164]**

O'Toole, F. (2002). '*Guns in the family*' Review of J.O' Neill. Blood Dark Track. A Family History. Granta. *New York Review of Books.* 11 April, 30-2. **[151]**

Paidar, P. (1995). *Women and the Political Process in Twentieth Century Iran*. Cambridge University Press, Cambridge. **[141]**

Pakrasi, K.B. (1970). Female Infanticide in India. Editions Indian, Calcutta. **[228]**

Pakter, J. (1961). 'Out of Wedlock Births in New York City. II. Medical Aspects' *American J. Public Health.* 51: 846-55. **[235]**

Pamuk, O. (2001). 'The Anger of the Damned'. *New York Review of Books*. 15 November, 12. **[269]**

Pandey, G. (1990). *The Construction of Communalism in Colonial North India.* Oxford University Press, Delhi. **[257-8]**

Parker, C. (1997). *The Thirty Years War*. Routledge, London. **[153]**

Parrack, D.W. (1969). 'An Appraisal of the Biogenetics of Rural West Bengal'. In P.A. Vayda. (ed). *Environment and Cultural behaviour.* Natural History Press, Garden City, New Jersey. **[245]**

Parry, J.P. (1994). *Death in Banaras.* Cambridge University Press, Cambridge. **[147, 236]**

Patterson, H. (1980). *Class Conflict and Sectarianism; the Protestant Working Class and the Belfast Labour Movement,1868-1920.* Appletree Press, Belfast.

Payne, J. (1997). 'The Roots of Violence and Symbolism in Childhood and Adolescence'. In I. Lewis.(ed). *Symbols and Sentiments. Cross-cultural studies in symbolism.* Academic Press, London.

Peires, J.B. (1989). *The Dead will Arise. Nongqawuse and the Great Xhosa Cattle Killing Movement of 1856-7*. Raven Press, Johannesburg. **[211]**

Peletz, M.G. (1997). "Ordinary Muslims' and Muslim Resurgent in Contemporary Malaysia" in R.W. Hefner & P. Horvatch.(eds). *Islam in an era of nation states.* University of Hawaii Press, Honolulu. **[114]**

Pillsbury, B.L.K. (1978). 'Being Female in a Muslim Minority in China' in Beck, L & Keddie, N.(eds). *Women in the Muslim World.* Harvard University press, Cambridge, Mass. **[116]**

Platvoet, A.G. (1993). 'African Traditional Religions in the Religious History of Mankind'. *J. Study of Religions.* 6(2): 29-48. **[121]**

Pollock, J.H.H. (1950). *Memorandum to Foreign Office*, London. PRO. FO371/82233. Public Record Office, Kew, London. **[82]**

Power, S. (2002). Genocide and America. *New York Review of Books.* 15-18. 14 March. **[54]**

Prunier, G. (1995). *The Rwanda Crisis*: *1959-94. History of a Genocide*. Hurst, London. **[238-9]**

Qurantelli, E.L. and Dynes, R.R. (1970). 'Property Norms and Looting: Their Patterns in Community Crises'. *Phylon.* 31. Summer: 168-82. **[259]**

Qutb, Sayyid. (1964). 'Signposts on the Road' Quoted in E. Swan. (1995). *Radical Islam.* Yale University Press, New Haven. 30. **[289]**

Radcliffe-Brown, A. (1970). Preface in M. Fortes and E.E. Evans-Pritchard.(eds). *African Political Systems.* Oxford University Press, Oxford.

Raheja, G. (1990). 'Centrality, Mutuality and Hierarchy; Shifting Aspects of Inter-caste Relationships in North India' in M. Marriott.(ed). *India through Hindu categories.* Sage, New Delhi. 79-101. **[147]**

Ranger, T.O. (1967). *Revolt in Southern Rhodesia.* Heinemann, London. **[126]**

Rapoport, D.C. (1982). 'Terror and the Messiah. An Ancient Experience and Some Modern Parallels' in D.C. Rapoport and Y. Alexander. (eds). *The Morality of Terrorism. Religion and Secular Justification.* Pergamon Press, New York. **[220]**

Rappaport, R.A. (1967). *Pigs for Ancestors. Ritual in the Ecology of a New Guinea People.* Yale University Press, New Haven. **[208]**

Rashid, A. (2000). *Taliban. Islam, oil and the New Great Game in Central Asia.* Tauris, London. **[138]**

Rasmussen, K. (1931). *The Netsilik Eskimos.* Report of the Fifth Thule Expedition. 1921-4. Gyldendalske Boghandel, Copenhagen. **[228]**

Read, P. (1993). *Alive.* Arrow, New York. **[165]**

Redfield, R. (1956). *Peasant Society and Culture; An Anthropological Approach to Civilisation.* Chicago University Press, Chicago. **[3]**

Reynolds, V. (1986). 'Primate Social Thinking' in Gelse, J. and Lee, P.C.(eds). *Primate Ontogeny, Cognition and Social behaviour.* Cambridge University Press, Cambridge. 53-60. **[19]**

Reynolds, V. and Tanner, R. (1983). *The Biology of Religion.* Longmans, London. **[222, 241]**

Reynolds, V. and Tanner, R. (1995). *The Social Ecology of Religion.* Oxford University Press, New York. **[215]**

Rheubottom, D. (1993). 'The Seeds of Evil Within'. In D. Parkin.(ed). *The Anthropology of Evil.* Blackwell, Oxford. 77-91.

Richards, A.I. (1935). 'A Modern Movement of Witch Finders'. *Africa*. 8(4): 448-61. **[148]**

Richardson, L.F. (1960). *Statistics of Deadly Quarrels*. Boxwood, Pittsburgh. **[217]**

Riches, D. (1986). 'The Phenomenon of Violence'. In D. Riches.(ed). *The Anthropology of Violence.* Blackwell, Oxford.

Riddle, D.W. (1931). *The Martyrs*. Chicago University Press, Chicago. **[158]**

Roberts, A.D. (1970). 'The Lumpa Church of Alice Lenshina'. In Rotberg, R.I. and Mazrui, A.A. (eds). *Protest and Power on Black Africa.* Oxford University Press, New York. 513-568. **[128]**

Rogers, L. (1926). '*The Conditions Influencing the Incidence and Spread of Cholera in India*'. Proceedings Royal Society of Medicine. Epidemic Section. 19: 59-91. **[236]**

Roseman, M. (2002). *The villa, the lake, the meeting. Wannsee and the Final Solution.* Penguin, London. **[53]**

Rosenblatt, P.C. *et al.* (1976). *Grief and Mourning in Cross-cultural Perspective.* Hraf Press, New York. **[160]**

Rowland, B. (1954). *The Art and Architecture of India*. Penguin, London. **[73]**

Roy, P. (1955). 'The Sacred Cow in India'. *Rural Sociology.*20: 8-15 **[245]**

Runciman, S. (1957). *The History of the Crusades*. 1. *The First Crusade*. Cambridge University Press, Cambridge. **[96, 98]**

Rupesinghe, K. (1994). 'Forms of Violence and Its Transformations'. In K. Rupesinghe and M. Rubio.(eds). *The culture of violence.* United Nations University Press, Tokyo. 14-41.

Rutter, M. and Giller, H. (1983). *Juvenile Delinquency. Trends and Perspectives.* Penguin, Harmondsworth.

Ryan, B. (1953). *Hinayana Buddhism and Family Planning in Ceylon*. Milbank Memorial Fund Conference Paper, New York. **[231]**

Said, E.W. (1985). *Orientalism; Western Conceptions of the Orient*. New York.

Salomon, G. (1987). *Statement to Los Angeles Times*. 12 October.

Sanchez, J.M. (2001). *Pius XII and the Holocaust*. Catholic University of America Press, Washington, DC. **[53]**

Saraswati, B. (1975). *Kasli. Myth and Reality of a Classical Cultural Tradition.* Indian Institute of Advanced Studies, Simla. **[235-6]**

Savarkar, V.D. (1964). *Samagra Savarkar Wangmaya*. Maharashtra Pramtik Hindu Sabha, Poona. Volume 1. **[45]**

Schafer, E.H. (1962). 'Conservation of Nature under the Tang Dynasty'. *J. Economic and Social History of the Orient.* 5: 280-1. **[241]**

Schull, W.J. et al. (1953). 'Kuroshima: The Impact of Religion On An Island's Genetic Heritage'. *Human Biology.* 34: 271-98. **[86]**

Schutz, A. (1962). *Collected Papers. 1. The Problem of Social Reality.* Nijhoff. The Hague. **[36]**

Scúrletis, T.D. *et al.* (1969). 'Trends in Illegitimacy and Associated Mortality in North Carolina: 1957-66'. *North Carolina Medical J.* 10: 214-21. **[233]**

Seguy, J. (1973). 'Religion and Agricultural Success. The Vocational Life of the French Anabaptists from 17th to 19th Centuries'. M. Shank.(trans). *Mennonite Quarterly Review.* 47, July. **[286]**

Sells, M.A. (1996). *The Bridge Betrayed. Religion and Genocide in Bosnia.* California University Press, Berkeley. **[171, 188]**

Sen, A. (1956). *Asoka's Edicts*. Institute of Ideology, Calcutta. **[45]**

Sered, S. (1999). *Women of the Sacred Groves: Divine Priestesses of Okinawa*. Oxford University Press, New York. **[115]**

Shaheed, F. (1990). 'The Pathan-Muhajir Conflicts 1985-6. A National Perspective'. In V. Das.(ed). *Mirrors of Violence; Communities, Riots and Survivors in South Asia.* Oxford University Press, Delhi. **[182]**

Shastri, C.P. (1960). 'Bullock Utilisation in Agriculture'. *Economic Weekly.* 12: 1585-92. **[244]**

Sherrard, P. (1973). 'The Desanctification of Nature'. In D. Baker.(ed). *Sanctity and Secularity: The Church and the World.* Blackwell, Oxford.

Sherring, M.A. (1872). *Hindu Tribes and Castes*. Thacker Spink, Calcutta. **[160]**

Shibutani, T. (1966). *Improvised News*. Bobbs-Merrill, Indianopolis. **[263]**

Shi-Meifen. (1989). *Peasant Daily*. 1 February. **[205]**

Shipley, D. (1982). Report on Jerusalem Events. *New York Times.* 12 April.

Shore, B. (1996). *Culture in Mind. Cognition, Culture and the Problem of Meaning*. Oxford University Press, New York. **[54]**

Shulman, J. (1964). 'Surgical Complications of Circumcision'. *American J. Diseases of Childhood.* 107: 149-54. **[162]**

Shweder, R.A. (1991). *Thinking Through Culture. Expeditions in Cultural Psychology.* Harvard University Press, Cambridge, Mass. **[54]**

Simoons, F.J. (1968). *A Ceremonial ox of India; The Mithan in Nature. Culture and History.* University Wisconsin Press, Madison. **[247]**

Singer, D.G. & Singer, J.L. (1984). 'Television Violence'. *Television and Children.* Spring: 30-41. **[78, 106]**

Singh, Y. (1995). 'Traditional Culture Patterns of India and Industrial Change'. In A.B. Shah and C.R.M. Rao.(eds). *Tradition and Modernity in India.* Manaktalas, Mumbai. **[260]**

Sluglett, P & M. Farouk-Sluglett. (1992). 'Sunnis and Shias Revisited: Sectarianism and Ethnicity in Authoritarian Iraq'. In J.P. Spagnolo.(ed). *Problems of the Modern Middle-East in Historical Perspective.* Ithaca, Reading. **[154]**

Smith, J. (nd). The Black Dragon. 'Australian War Memorial.' Quoted in J. Burke. (2000). *An Intimate History of Killing.* Granta, London. 286. **[51]**

Smith, W.C. (1957). *Islam in Modern Society.* Princeton University Press, New Jersey.

Snodgrass, J.G. (2001). 'Beware of Charitable Souls; Contagion, Roguish Ghosts and the Poison(s) of Hindu Alms'. *J. Royal Anthropological Institute.* 7(4): 687-703. **[147]**

Soga, T. (1857). *Comment on the Xhosa Cattle Killing Movement.* UPC Mission Record. **[211]**

Spence, J. (1996). *God's Chinese Son. The Taiping Heavenly Kingdom of Hong Xiuquan.* Harper Collins, London. **[216]**

Spiro, M.E. (1971). *Buddhism and Society. A Great Tradition and its Burmese Vicissitudes.* Allen and Unwin, London. **[45, 74]**

Spyer, P. (1996). 'Serial Conversion/conversion to Seriality: Religion, State and Number in Aru, Eastern Indonesia' in P. van der Veer.(ed). *Conversion to Modernity; the Globalisation of Christianity.* Routledge, London. 171-198. **[132, 270]**

Srinivas, M.N. (1958). 'India's Cultural; Values and Economic Development'. *Economic Development and Cultural Change.* 7: 3-6. **[244]**

Stevenson, H.N.C, (1943). The Economics of the Central Chin tribes. *Times of India* Press, Bombay. **[246]**

Stone, M. (1997). *When God Was a Woman.* Harvest, New York. **[303]**

Storr, A. (1970). *Human Aggression.* Penguin, Harmondsworth.

Strabo. (1950). *Geography*. Heinemann, London. **[163]**

Strathern, A. (1982). 'Witchcraft, Greed Cannibalism and Death: Some Related Themes from the New Guinea Highlands' in Block, R and Parry, J.(eds). *Death and Regeneration of Life*. Cambridge University Press, Cambridge. **[166]**

Suriyabongse, L. (1954). 'Human Nature in the Light of the Buddha's Teachings' *J. Siam Society*. 42: 11-22. **[231]**

Swantz, L. (1974). The Role of the Medical Man among the Zaramo of Dar Es Salaam. Dphil mss. University of Dar Es Salaam, Tanzania. **[123]**

Swearer, D.K. (1991). 'Fundamentalist Movements in Theravada Buddhism'. In M.E. Marty and R.S. Appleby.(eds). *Fundamentalism Observed*. Chicago University Press, Chicago. 531-593. **[173]**

Tak, J. van der. (1974). Abortion, Fertility and Changing Legislation. An International Review. Lexington Books, Lexington, Mass. **[231]**

Takahashi, Y. (1989). 'Mass Suicide by Members of the Japanese Friend of the Truth Church'. *Suicide Life Threatening Behaviour*. 19(2): 289-96.

Tambiah, S.J. (1992). *Buddhism Betrayed? Religion, Politics and Violence in Sri Lanka*. Chicago University Press, Chicago. **[173]**

Tannenbaum, N. (2000). 'Protest, Tree Ordination and the Changing Context of Political Ritual'. *Ethnology*. 39(2): 109-27. **[250]**

Tanner, M. (2001). *Ireland's Holy Wars. The Struggle for a Nation's Soul 1500-2000*. Yale University Press, New Haven. **[156]**

Tanner, R.E.S. (1955). 'Law Enforcement by Communal Action in Sukumaland'. *J. African Administration*. 7(4): 159-165. **[149]**

Tanner, R.E.S. (1956). 'Introduction to the Northern Sukuma's Idea of the Supreme Being'. *Anthropological Quarterly*. 29(2): 45-56. **[132]**

Tanner, R.E.S. (1969a). 'Reasons for Entering the Christian Community'. The Christian who Does Not Practice'. *African Ecclesiastical Revue*. 11(2). April. **[130, 149]**

Tanner, R.E.S. (1969b). '*The Christian Who Does Not Practice in Usukuma*'. African Ecclesiastical Revue. 11(3). July. **[132]**

Tanner, R.E.S. (1970). *The Witch Murders in Sukumaland*. Scandinavian Institute of African Studies, Uppsala. **[130, 148]**

Tanner, R.E.S. (1974). '*Sociologist at Heathrow*' Clergy Review. September, 596-605.

Tanner, R.E.S. (1975). '*A Note on Christian and Traditional Religious Practices in Ngara*'. J. Religion in Africa. 6(3): 161-166. **[120]**

Tanner, R.E.S. (1978). '*Rumour and the Buganda Emergency: 1966*'. J. Modern African Studies. 16(2): 329-338. **[263]**

Tanner, R.E.S. (1979). '*Word and Spirit in Contemporary African Religious Practice and Thought.*' J. Religion in Africa. 9(2): 123-135.

Tanner, R.E.S. (1992). '*The Impact of Christianity and Islam on Two East African Societies*'. Missionalia. 20(3): 201-15. **[129]**

Tanner, R.E.S. (1993a). '*African Traditional Religions and their Reactions to Other Faiths*'. Studia Missionalia. 42: 371-94.

Tanner, R.E.S. (1993b). '*East African Ethical Ideas and Translation: Some Possible Consequences of a Bilateral Process*'. Anthropos. 88: 29-37. **[131]**

Tanner, R.E.S. (1997). '*Cognitive Development, Socialisation and Cognitive Mutations. A Critique and Elaboration of Boyer's Naturalness of Religion. A Case Study of the Sukuma of Tanzania*'. J. Social Sciences. 1(2): 91-98. **[32, 122]**

Tanner, R.E.S. (2001). '*Intra-faith and Inter-religious Tensions in East African Tribal Environments*' in G. Pfeffer & D.K. Behera.(eds). Contemporary Society: Tribal Studies. 5; 323-340. Concept, New Delhi. **[118]**

Tanner, R.E.S. and Wijsen, F. (1993). 'Christianity in Usukuma a Working Misunderstanding'. *Nouvelle Revue de Science Missionnaire.* 49: 177-194. **[130]**

Teltsch, K. (1990). 'Scholars and Descendents Uncover Legacy of Jews in South West'. *New York Times.* 11 November. **[179]**

Thion, S. (1993). 'Genocide as a Political Commodity'. In B. Kiernan.(ed). *Genocide and democracy in Cambodia.* The Khymer Rouge, the United Nations and the international community. Yale University Southeast Asia Monograph Series No.41: 163-190. **[202]**

Thomas, H. (1961). *The Spanish Civil War.* Eyre and Spottiswoode, London. **[148, 196-7]**

Thomas, W.I. & Thomas, D.S. (1928). *The Child in America.* Knopf, New York. **[262]**

Tierney, P. (2000). 'The Fierce Anthropologist'. *The New Yorker.* 9 October, 50-61. **[56]**.

Tinbergen, N. (1951). *A Study of Instincts.* Oxford University Press, London.

Tinklenberg, J.R. & Ochberg, F.M. (1981). 'Patterns of Adolescent Aggression'. In Hamburg, D.A. & Trudeau, M.B.(eds). *Bio-behavioural Aspects of Aggression.* Liss, New York. **[22, 254]**

Tohidi, N. (1983). 'Gender and Islamic Fundamentalism: Feminist Politics in Iran'. In C.T. Mohanty *et al.* (eds). *Third World women and the politics of feminism.* Indiana University Press, Bloomington. 251-267. **[42, 234]**

Toland, J. (1971). *The Rising Sun. The Decline and Fall of the Japanese Empire. 1936-45*, Cassel. London. **[65]**

Trimingham, J.S. (1949). *Islam in the Sudan.* Oxford University Press, Oxford. **[163]**

Tsagarousianou, R. (1999). 'Nationalism, Ethnic Antagonism and Mass Communication in Greece'. In T. Alleen and J. Seaton. (eds). *The Media of Conflict.* Zed, London. 175-191. **[291]**

Turner, R.H. and Killian, L.M. (1972). *Collective Behaviour.* Prentice-Hall, New Jersey. **[260]**

Turner, V. (1967). *The Forest of Symbols.* Cornell University Press, Ithaca. **[30, 36, 56]**

Tyan, E. (1965). Djihad. *Encyclopaedia of Islam.* 11: 538-40. **[171]**

Uden, M.H.F van and Pieper, J.Z.T. (1990). *Christian Pilgrimages. Current Studies on Rituals. Perspectives for the Psychology of Religion.* **[237]**

Underwood, P and Underwood, Z. (1980). 'New Spells for Old; Expectation and Realities of Western Medicine in a Remote Tribal Society in Yemen, Arabia' in Stanley, N.F. and Joshe, R.A. (eds). *Changing Disease Patterns and Human Behaviour.* Academic Press, New York. **[58]**

United Nations Development Programme. Arab Development Report. (2002). United Nations, New York. **[302]**

Vauchez, A. (1977). *Sainthood in the Later Middle Ages.* I. Birrell.(trans). Cambridge University Press, Cambridge. **[160]**

Vincentnathan, S.G. (1996). 'Caste Politics, Violence and the Panchayats in a South Indian Community'. *Comparative Studies of Society and History.* 42: 484-509.

Veer, P. Van Der. (1994). *Religious Nationalism. Hindus and Muslims in India.* California University Press, Berkeley. **[90]**

Victoria, F de. (1934). *De jure belli.* J.P. Batec.(trans). Clarendon Press, Oxford. **[41]**

Vukovic, Z. (1993). *Bijanae Sarajeva. Kron, Podgorica.* Quoted by Hayden. (2000). 31-2. **[219]**

Wakeman, F. (1966). *Strangers at the Gate. Social disorders in South China. 1839-61.* University of California Press, Berkeley. **[216]**

Waters, T. (1999). 'Assessing the Impact of the Rwandan Refugee Crisis on Development Planning in Rural Tanzania: 1994-96'. *Human Organisation.* 58(2). **[214]**

Watt, W.M. (1953). *Muhammad at Mecca.* Oxford University Press, Oxford. **[100]**

Watt, W.M. (1956). *Muhammad at Medina.* Oxford University Press. Oxford. **[71, 100]**

Watt, W.M. (1970). *The Faith and Practice of Al-Ghazali.* Allen and Unwin, London. **[162]**

Weber, M. (1958). *The Religions of India.* Free Press, New York. **[43, 66]**

Weber, M. (1965). 'The Social Psychology of the World Religions'. In N. Gerth and C.W. Mills.(eds). *From Max Weber.* Oxford University Press, New York.

Weber, M. (1978). *Economy and Society. An Outline of Interpretive Sociology.* University of California Press, Berkeley.

Weiss, C. (1962). 'Ritual Circumcision: Comments on Current Practices in American Hospitals'. *Clinical Pediatrics* (Philadelphia). 1: 65-72. **[162]**

Weiss, N. (1888). 'La Seine et le nombre des victimes pariisiisiennes de la Saint Barthelemy'. *Bulletin de la Societie de l'histoire du Protestantisme Francais.* 36: 341-74.

Welbourn, F.B. (1961). *East African Rebels.* SCM Press, London. **[127]**

Welbourn, F.B. & Ogot, B.A. (1966). *A Place to Feel at Home.* Oxford University Press, London. **[128]**

Werbner, R.P. (1977). 'Introduction'. in Werbner, R.P.(ed). *Regional Cults.* Academic Press, London. **[128]**

Weyl, N. (1968). 'Some Possible Genetic Implications of Carthaginian Child Sacrifice'. *Perspective Biological Medicine.* 12: 69-78. **[65, 160]**

Whyte, S.R. (1997). *Questioning Misfortune. The Pragmatics of Uncertainty in Eastern Uganda.* Cambridge University Press, Cambridge. **[121, 124]**

Wijsen, F. & Tanner, R. (2001). *I am just a Sukuma. Globalisation and Identity Construction in Northwest Tanzania.* Rodopi, Amsterdam.

Wilkie, J.W. (1966). 'The Meaning of the Cristero War Against the Mexican Revolution'. *J. Church and State.* 8. **[198]**

Wilkinson, D. (1980). *Deadly Quarrels. Lewis. F. Richardson and the Statistical Study of War.* University of California Press, Berkeley. **[217]**

Willis, R.G. (1968). 'Kamcape: An Anti-sorcery Movement in South-west Tanzania'. *Africa.* 38(1): 1-15. **[148]**

Wilson, E.O. (1975). *Sociobiology: The New Synthesis.* Harvard University Press, Cambridge, Mass. **[16]**

Winnington, A. (1957). *Tibet: International Publisher*, New York. **[44]**

Wipper, A. (1970). 'The Gusii Rebels'. In Rotberg, R.I. and Mazrui, A.A.(eds). *Protest and Power in Black Africa.* Oxford University Press, New York. **[126]**

Wolfe, M. (1994). *The Hadj. A Pilgrimage to Mecca.* Secker and Warburg, London. **[34]**

Worger, W.H. (2001). 'Parsing God; Conversations about the Meaning of Words and Metaphors in Nineteenth Century Southern Africa'. *J. African History.* 42: 417-47. **[39]**

Worsley, A. (1938). 'Infibulation and Female Circumcision.' *J. Obstetrics and Gynaecology British Commonwealth.* 45: 686-691. **[164]**

Worsley, P. (1968). *The Trumpet Shall Sound. A Study of Cargo Cults in Melanesia.* Schocken Books, New York. **[203, 263]**

Wright, Q. (1964). *A Study of War.* University of Chicago Press, Chicago. **[217]**

Yadin, Y. (1970). *Masada: Herod's Fortress and the Zealot's Last Stand.* Weidenfeld and Nicolson, London. **[6]**

Yaukey, D. (1961). *Fertility Differences in a Modernizing Country.* Princeton University Press, New Jersey. **[232]**

Yediot Ashardnot. (1995). 'Statement by Fifteen Rabbis' Published in Daily Papers. Jerusalem. **[84]**

Young, E.P. (1996). 'The Politics of Evangelism at the End of the Qing: Nanchang: 1906' in D.H. Bays.(ed). *Christianity in China from the 18th Century to the Present.* Stanford University Press, Stanford. **[195]**

Yu-wen, J. (1973). *The Taiping Revolutionary Movement.* Yale University Press, New Haven. **[216]**

Zaehner, R.C. (1970). *Concordant Discord. The Interdependence of Faiths.* Clarendon Press, Oxford. **[42, 46, 48, 69]**

Zaman, M.Q. (2002). *The Ulama in Contemporary Islam.* Princeton University Press, New Jersey.

Zuccotti, S. (2002). *Under His Very Window. The Vatican and the Holocaust in Italy.* Yale University Press, New Haven. **[53]**

Zuk, G.H. *et al.* (1961). 'Maternal Acceptance of Retarded Children. A Questionnaire Study of Attitudes and Religious Background'. *Child Development.* 32, 525-40. **[230]**

Zurrayk, C. (1948). *Maana al Nakba (the lesson of disaster).* **[279]**

Index